Maurice

Maurice Blanchot

The Refusal of Philosophy

Gerald L. Bruns

THE JOHNS HOPKINS UNIVERSITY PRESS

Baltimore & London

© 1997 The Johns Hopkins University Press
All rights reserved. Published 1997
Printed in the United States of America on acid-free paper

Johns Hopkins Paperbacks edition, 2005
2 4 6 8 9 7 5 3 1

The Johns Hopkins University Press
2715 North Charles Street
Baltimore, Maryland 21218-4363
www.press.jhu.edu

Library of Congress Cataloging-in-Publication Data will be found
at the end of this book.

ISBN 0-8018-8199-4 (pbk.)
A catalog record for the book is available from the British Library.

For Don Marshall

Contents

Contents

Contents

Preface

Maurice Blanchot (b. 1907) belongs to the generation of French intellectuals who came of age during the 1930s, survived or flourished during the Occupation, and dominated Parisian intellectual life for a quarter century or so after the Liberation. We know less about him than we would like. During the crisis years of French politics (1933–39) Blanchot was a journalist who moved among various groups of young intellectuals who were strongly antidemocratic, anticapitalist, anti-Marxist, anti–Popular Front, and therefore (in the nature of the case) both profascist and, in varying degrees, anti-Semitic. His writings during this period are typical of what came to be called a young "dissident." During the Occupation Blanchot served briefly as a director of a young person's literary association sponsored by the Vichy government and contributed essays on literary matters to the pro-Vichy *Journal des débats*, but otherwise he seems to have kept himself at a distance from Collaborationist circles.

In 1941 Blanchot published his most famous narrative, *Thomas l'obscur* (available now only in a much reduced version that appeared in 1950). In 1943 he published his first collection of critical essays, *Faux pas*. After the Liberation he began contributing critical essays to *La nouvelle française* and *Critique* on a regular basis. In 1949 he published a second collection of essays, *La part du feu*, which contains his most important theoretical essay, "Littérature et la droit à la mort," in which literature is defined against Hegel as the interruption of the dialectical movement of negation that produces concepts, works, cultures, and the end of history. A number of collections followed over the next twenty years. Blanchot became a premier example, perhaps the last example, of the intellectual whose mode of existence was the literary journal rather than the academic appointment. Meanwhile he continued as a writer of narratives—*L'arrêt de mort* (1948), *Le très-haut* (1948), *Au moment voulu* (1951), *Celui qui ne m'accompagnait pas* (1953), *Le dernier homme* (1957).

During the Algerian crisis in the 1950s Blanchot emerged as an adversary of De Gaulle and is usually credited with the authorship of the "Manifeste des 121" (1960), a declaration of "the right to insubordination" signed by 121 intellectuals of various political sorts (Jean-Paul Sartre, no friend of Blanchot's, was among the signators). Sometimes this is taken as evidence that Blanchot had shifted politically from right to left, but this seems to me a ready-to-wear judgment that a closer look might not support. In 1962 Blanchot published *L'attente l'oubli*, a work in dialogue or, more accurately, fragments of dialogue, and before long the fragment would become his characteristic form of writing, especially in *Le pas au-delà* (1973) and *L'écriture du désastre* (1980). Most recently Blanchot has published *La communauté inavouable* (1983), the first part of which concerns, among other things, Georges Bataille's experiments in secret societies and underground communities during the late 1930s, and "Les intellectuels en question" (1984), an essay that, among other things, contains what Blanchot calls his "personal confession [*mon aveu personnel*]."

My purpose in this book is to work through a substantial portion of Maurice Blanchot's writings, and to do so in some detail. It seems to me we are very far from understanding what his writings are about, nor do we know what sort of a reading these texts can sustain. My ambition was to do a comprehensive close reading of Blanchot's work, with particular attention to those more recent texts that so far have received only modest commentary, but clearly not every question can be asked at once. A comprehensive reading could never mean adopting a single comprehensive point of view from which everything could be seen at once and understood as a whole. And no one is without confusion or the capacity for blunder, garble, and pointless digression. Nor is there a method of criticism that one could bring to bear upon these texts that would lay bare anything like an underlying logic. My method, just to call it that, is philological. Philology works from the bottom up. Since ancient times it has meant a concentration on bits and pieces of texts, moving from one fragment to another as best one can, taking guidance from the light texts shed on one another and also from whatever commentary is at hand.

Fortunately in this last respect much of what has been written on Blanchot is excellent, and, as my citations show, I rely a good deal on what others have taught me. One must mention in particular studies by Françoise Collin, Roger Laporte, and Joseph Libertson, as well as the historical research of Jeffrey Mehlman, Steve Ungar, and Michael Holland. I have found studies by Simon Critchley, Paul Davies, Donald Marshall, Allan Stoekl, and John Gregg to be especially helpful. An early essay by Geoffrey

Hartman has always been important to me. There are fiction writers whom I admire, like Lydia Davis, who are among Blanchot's best readers (and translators). Perhaps most illuminating are the uses that many philosophers have made of Blanchot's ideas, especially Emmanuel Levinas, Jacques Derrida, Gilles Deleuze, and Jean-Luc Nancy. I've tried in particular to consider in detail the relationship between Levinas's thinking and Blanchot's. It also seems to me that there is an internal coherence between Blanchot and the poet Paul Celan that is worth close study.

I first began reading Blanchot more than thirty years ago as part of an effort to understand the difference between Mallarmé's poetics and Martin Heidegger's conception of poetry, both of which emphasize language in radical but apparently antithetical ways. Blanchot was the only writer I knew about who had studied both Mallarmé and Heidegger. Moreover, his thinking brought them together in a form that seemed to me to capture something essential about poetry. Naturally I now use the word essential with some self-doubt. As my friend Marjorie Perloff has cautioned me more than once, the extension of the concept of poetry cannot be closed by a frontier. Neither Hölderlin nor Paul Celan can be made stand-ins for poetry as such. There is no poetry as such. What counts as poetry is internal to the heterogeneous social spaces in which it is composed; it can only be approached historically, that is, locally and with close attention to the facts. Poetry is, much like any form of life, untheorizable. I always end up having to agree with her about these things, but not without wondering how it might be otherwise.

So I try to negotiate the matter by saying that poetry belongs to multiple histories, with someone like Blanchot assigning it a critical place in the history of philosophy, where poetry first emerges as a limit-concept that gives philosophy what might be the only definition it could ever have. In part this book is an attempt to understand Blanchot's poetics as a renewal of the ancient quarrel between philosophy and poetry, a quarrel that Aristotle tried to resolve by rationalizing poetry, fitting it into his organon or rule of discourse, making it, for all practical purposes, a species of philosophy and a branch of rhetoric. Meanwhile within ancient and medieval rhetorical culture the quarrel continued to play itself out in interesting and even foundational ways. For Cicero, for example, philosophy and poetry define two opposed forms of eloquence, the adorned and the unadorned. Poetry is a versified, ornamental or figurative version of what philosophy (subsequently theology) expresses plainly and without amplification.

Dante and Milton could still recognize themselves in Cicero's theory.

Rhetorically, poetry is richly embellished, highly visible language: it is language that obtrudes into speech as an inversion of words and things. Poetics (a special kind of rhetoric) is basically the art of setting poetry straight, that is, keeping it under control in a just balance of words and things. In a word, art means control: it means mastery, technique, reproducibility, that is, subordination to norms and the recognizability of results. Poetry's rule of identity lies in its system of genres, which of course eventually went to pieces.

Modernity is the name of the conceptual revolution in which the culture of rhetoric is superseded by what is sometimes called "the rationalization of the world," that is, the project of scientific enlightenment and the reduction of the lifeworld to the norms of representational-calculative reason and instrumental control.[1] Here poetry is once more situated in opposition to philosophy—not, however, as its adversary, but as its preliminary. Poetry is primitive, mythico-magical reason, reason in its prelogical, undissociated form. Poetry is synthetic rather than analytic, imaginative rather than conceptual, intuitive rather than inferential, original rather than mimetic, subjective rather than objective, creative rather than critical, expressive rather than descriptive, sensuous rather than spiritual, concrete rather than abstract, but also, at the same time, visionary rather than empirical, transcendental rather than historical, universal rather than particular—however one separates it out, poetry, as Wordsworth said, is different not from prose but from matters of fact or science.

Much of romantic and postromantic poetics is tangled in irresolvable disputes as to whether poetry is cognitive or not—whether it is connected to reality actively in the way of knowledge or only passively in the way of feeling or emotion; or whether, failing of cognition, poetry has at least got some laws or lawlike deep structures that make it, at day's end, rational and coherent after all. Arguably poetry is what knowledge looks like in the form of unmediated experience; or, alternatively, it is one of those things that look like knowledge but are only pseudostatements underwritten by desire. Or let us say, speaking as humanists, that instead of knowledge poetry aims at the animation of values and beliefs that are dreary in themselves; it is secularized religion, the consolation of our naturalisms, and can therefore hold us together when knowledge tears us apart. Especially if its deep logic is the logic of unified or at least self-regulating systems.

Postmodernism is a crisis of enlightened rationality in the sense that now every discourse, whether of fact or of value, whether literary or scientific, empirical or imaginative, is taken to be internal to culture and history, a product of social forces, each one therefore no more than a genre difference within the total cultural fabric, able (perhaps) to trace its own thread but as a cultural product not constituted differently from any other. There is no rationality (or poetry) as such. What is poetic in this milieu is just self-consciously innovative discourse, the reweaving of the cultural fabric for the hell of it, antifoundationalism without apocalypse, as if every discourse (physics, philosophy, social theory, economics) were poetic in the sense of searching for conceptual breakthroughs that will enable it to supersede its own history or obsolescence. Make it new and newer still— and so we go from Aristotle's poetics to rhetorical poetics to romantic poetics to structuralist poetics to cultural poetics to poetized culture. "Cyberpoetics" is perhaps only the newest item on our menu.

Is Maurice Blanchot a character in this story? If so, he is one of the last romantics, where romanticism is a name for the persistence of whatever is irreducible or excessive with respect to the Enlightenment's unfinished project of housing everything in its condominium. By Enlightenment I mean whatever Jürgen Habermas means when he says that philosophy is "the guardian of rationality."[2] Poetry is the Enlightenment's "other night," not the dark age that it supersedes but that which accompanies it and keeps it awake. Poetry is a limit of reason that philosophy finds unthinkable. Thinking this way about poetry, Blanchot stirs to life the ancient quarrel of philosophy and poetry. He believes that poetry is responsible for philosophy—that which makes the discourse of philosophy possible or necessary precisely by withdrawing from it. A bit of what I have written over the years has been an attempt to make sense of this relation of poetry and philosophy. Poetry is a refusal of philosophy, not a movement beyond it, not an alternative. The whole idea of moving beyond or overcoming (the driving metaphor of each of our intellectual disciplines) is for Blanchot a highly dubious concept.

So as a last romantic Blanchot is not simply a repetition of the romantic repudiation of anteriority in behalf of the future. On the contrary, he is, in a way that students of Walter Benjamin will appreciate, radically antimessianic: the end of history, possibly even the future, is what he thinks will never arrive, which is perhaps why he is sometimes taken for a reactionary. Maybe he is someone who has just never been modern. In an essay from 1962 he writes: "The 'modern era' presupposes relations that have been maintained between the present, the past, and the future, be these relations of opposition or of contrast. But let us imagine changes such that these relations would no longer have a directing force. We will now no longer be conscious of belonging to modern times, nor of opposing ourselves to an age that is past; the modern will in its turn be outmoded as a mode of becoming. When history turns, this movement of turning that implies even the suspension of history (in the name of a utopian truth) also revokes 'the tradition of the new' " (*EI*584/*IC*398). In contrast to "the new," the chief event in Blanchot is that of growing old to the point of agelessness; in Blanchot's temporality nothing is ever *vergangen*. It is, unfortunately, impossible to die.

At the end of history, poetry remains unfinished, and so perhaps it keeps history open. Poetry is, Blanchot would say, neither matter nor spirit. It is writing on that side of language which belongs to flesh and breath (very different things from matter and spirit); it is the unconstructed voice of the singular and irreducible, that which cannot be assimilated into a system or a theory of constituted subjects, objects, and relations. Very roughly, the idea is that poetry is external to the world, not just in its usual "poetic" place outside of philosophy, knowledge, and the good, nor even just outside of human culture and its languages, but in an ontological condition of displacement or errancy. The poem, however, is not a sealed-off artifact (not the hermetic work of aesthetic legend); rather, it is porous, exposed to the world, subjected to it, and vice versa: poetry is an event in which the world and its discourses are themselves exposed to the nonidentical, or in which they experience a failure of self-identity. So things are open-ended after all. This notion of poetry isn't meant to prejudice traditional materialist-formalist debates concerning aesthetic differentiation. In these debates the poem is either a social fact or an autonomous object—or, as Adorno says, both (*AT*334–38/*AeT*320–21). But Blanchot's poetics asks us to understand the sense in which poetry lies on the hither side of both immanence and transcendence, or the hither side of the world and whatever lies beyond it.

Poetry in this sense is a limit-concept rather than a genre-distinction. Blanchot seems to think of it as a limit-experience as such (if we can think of a limit not only spatially as a wall that stops us cold but also temporally as an event to be lived through without passage). This is perhaps where Blanchot is most difficult and unsettling. In one of his first essays on poetry (which is also his first essay on Heidegger), "La parole 'sacrée' de Hölderlin" (1946), he writes:

How can the Sacred, which is "unexpressed," "unknown," which is what opens provided only that it is not discovered, which reveals because unrevealed—how can it fall into speech, let itself be alienated into becoming, itself pure interiority, the exteriority of song? In truth, that cannot really be, that is the impossible. And the poet is nothing but the existence of this impossibility, just as the language of the poem is nothing but the retention, the transmission, of its own impossibility. It is the reminder that all worldly language, this speech that takes place and goes on in the domain of radical ease, has as its origin an event that cannot take place; it is linked to an "I speak, but speaking is not possible," from which nevertheless emerges the little sense that remains to words. (PF128/WF126)

One could say that Blanchot's poetics remains "mystical," even religious, just in the sense that its aim is to experience the sacred, perhaps not so much in the way Hölderlin's poetry bears witness to the sacred as in Georges Bataille's sense of the term, where the sacred is whatever is excluded from the rationalization of the world, that is, from a cultural homogeneity in which all human relations are reduced to the rule of identity and the principle of efficiency. Bataille's list of heterogeneous elements is worth citing: "Included are the waste products of the human body and certain analogous matter (trash, vermin, etc.); the parts of the body; persons, words, or acts having a suggestive erotic value; the various unconscious processes such as dreams or neuroses; the numerous elements or social forms that homogeneous society is powerless to assimilate: mobs, the warrior, aristocratic and impoverished classes, different types of violent individuals or at least those who refuse the rule (madmen, leaders, poets, etc.)" (OC1.346/VE142). Blanchot, we might say, is one who adds the man of reason to this list.

However, it is not an accident that Bataille's list of heterogeneous elements is taken from an essay called "The Psychological Structure of Fascism" (1936), and that among the "madmen, leaders, and poets" who "refuse the rule" of homogeneity are Mussolini and Hitler. The "fascist leaders," Bataille writes, "are incontestably part of heterogeneous existence. Opposed to democratic politicians, who represent in different countries the platitude inherent to *homogeneous* society, Mussolini and Hitler immediately stand out as something *other* [*tout autres*]. Whatever emotions their actual existence as political agents of evolution provokes, it is impossible to ignore the *force* that situates them above men, parties, and even laws: a *force* that disrupts the regular course of things, the peaceful but fastidious homogeneity powerless to maintain itself (the fact that laws are broken is only the most obvious sign of the transcendent, *heterogeneous* nature of fascist action)" (OC1.348/VE143). In France during the 1930s, it looked very much like fascism could be enlisted against the rationalization of the world. Certainly this was the source of fascism's appeal to someone like Blanchot.

The account of Blanchot's thinking that I try to give in this book is not meant to override the question of his early fascism (or his quasi- or proto-fascism), which Jeffrey Mehlman and Steven Ungar have tried to document. On the contrary, this question is one that should be kept open, if only because of the way Blanchot's case (among others of a similar sort) exposes the limits or narrow focus of our received or conventional interpretations of fascism, which emphasize social and economic conditions and underestimate or ignore the enormous appeal of fascism among European intellectuals between the wars. Basically one can distinguish three principal categories of fascist-interpretation, each of them still authoritative and widely circulated. One takes fascism to be a mass reaction of the lower middle classes against the intellectual elite of the European cultural order. This was the view of Karl Mannheim and the Frankfurt School generally, and it still underlies much of the recent research that invokes Walter Benjamin's famous motto about fascism as the introduction of aesthetics into politics. This first view is continuous with a second, which is that fascism was the political reaction of monopoly capitalism against socialism and the threat of the proletariat to the bourgeois order of things. Meanwhile (and third) the cold-war theory locates fascism and Stalinist communism along a single plane as principal species of twentieth-century totalitarianism. This is the position associated almost canonically with Hannah Arendt.

These interpretations are not wrong, but they are pitched at a level that makes it difficult to see what was happening in France during the 1930s, where fascism was neither a regime nor a party nor, arguably, a movement or mass politics of any substantial or coherent sort. So in my first chapter I emphasize Zeev Sternhell's research, which takes fascism to be, from its basic inception in the late nineteenth century and continuing through the 1930s, an ideological revolt against modernity that had substantial appeal among the European intellectual elite—an appeal that we are perhaps only now coming to understand in trying to assess Heidegger's fascism and Paul de Man's. Indeed, Sternhell's conception of fascism—as, on the one hand, an antimaterialist revision of Marxism, and, on the other, a moral and intellectual revolt against rationalism, individualism, parliamentary democracy, and bourgeois capitalism—is troubling for the way it demystifies fascism, replacing the demonic, pathological, and aesthetic aspects that we have always used to identify it with a conceptual content and a logical coherence that bring it into the mainstream of European intellectual history. Much of our political self-understanding presupposes, Sternhell says, an opportunistic fascism that can be dismissed "either as entirely lacking a system of ideas or as having rigged itself out, for partisan purposes, in the semblance of doctrine that could not be taken seriously and that did not deserve even the minimum of consideration given to the ideas of any other political movement." But perhaps we have constructed our definitions of fascism in order to distance ourselves from it:

> To admit that fascism was anything other than a simple aberration, an accident, an outburst of collective folly, or a phenomenon that could be explained simply by the economic crisis, to observe that in nearly all the European countries there existed homespun fascist movements that were not simply imitations or caricatures of the Italian movement, to concede that the armed bands of Rome and Bucharest, Paris and London, Berlin and Vienna were backed by a body of doctrine no less logically defensible than that of the democratic or liberal parties, and to recognize, finally, that the ideas put forward did not belong only to the rejects of society—the dregs of the European capitals—manipulated by international high finance—would [require] the revision of a whole scale of values, a whole chain of reasonings.[3]

We want to say: no rational person could be a fascist. But the fact is that many rational persons saw it differently.

It is certainly the case that the concept of an "intellectual fascism," or fascism of the intellectuals, has proved hard to swallow. Sternhell's book, *Ni droite, ni gauche,* caused a furor in France when it was published in 1983. His principal provocation was that during the 1930s, and across the whole political spectrum, French intellectual culture was "impregnated" with fascist concepts, beliefs, and desires, and he supported this claim by close and comprehensive scrutiny of what was actually published, and by whom, in the French periodicals of the time. The effect of this research was to widen the net of what counts as fascism, catching many who had seemed to have got free. Sternhell was sued by the distinguished economist Bertrand de Jouvenel, whose pro-Nazi writings Sternhell had uncovered and which he did not hesitate to quote. The court basically shrugged its shoulders. It found against Sternhell, but fined him only one franc and did not require him to alter his text.[4]

Interestingly, the reaction of academic historians has been to marginalize Sternhell by reaffirming a longstanding consensus that real history is social and economic, and that the study of material events must take precedence over the study of discourse and meanings.[5] Even if one grants this distinction, one has a right to suspect that there are aspects of fascism that are invisible to social and economic categories. Anyhow, it is only through the mediation of Sternhell's kind of historical inquiry (which literary critics like Jeffrey Mehlman and, more extensively, Steven Ungar and David Carroll have pursued) that the question of Blanchot's fascism comes up at all. Sternhell aside, professional historians take little interest in fascism and the intellectuals.

Was Blanchot a fascist? Both Mehlman and Ungar stop short of calling him one, and Michael Holland thinks that "his honour, despite being jeopardized at the time by the logic according to which it sought to act, and however open to question it therefore is in certain quarters today, remains fundamentally intact."[6] My thought at this stage of the research is that Blanchot was ideologically attracted to fascism because it was, whatever else it was, an ideology of rejection. Obviously there is much about fascism that has little application in Blanchot's case—for example, its cult of physical action and heroic conquest. He seems to have held National Socialism, and Nazi sympathizers like Robert Brasillach, in contempt. I don't share Mehlman's view that the young Blanchot was anti-Semitic, but Blanchot's recourse to anti-Semitic rhetoric in attacking Léon Blum and the Popular Front makes it hard to defend him. If, as Sternhell says, "totalitarianism is the very essence of fascism, and fascism is without question the purest example of a totalitarian ideology," then Blanchot, who seems to have rejected totalism and authoritarianism from the start, was an eccentric fascist. But then perhaps fascism in France was eccentric by comparison with Italy and Germany, if only in the sense that it was not a reactionary mass-politics articulated through triumphant national liturgies, but rather found its major voice among newspapers and reviews staffed by young nationalists contemptuous of the whole cultural and political establishment. In this respect Blanchot may or may not have been much of a fascist, but fascist ideology offered a ready form of dissent. And what seems unmistakable is that the posture of dissidence formed in Blanchot's early years has remained constant over the long term.

Indeed, I think Blanchot's "dissidence," if that is the word, has to be taken in the strongest sense possible, because it expresses itself throughout his career in all the forms in which he wrote (including that of the political manifesto). The idea here, at any rate, is to construe his dissidence as a philosophical anarchism that embraces both poetry and politics. The burden of this book will be to explain what this means. This task is not an easy one, not the least because a philosophical anarchism is in certain respects a contradiction in terms, possibly for the same reason that anarchism as a social philosophy could never really be put into practice except in the form of radical or unsatisfiable resistance to any centralized or self-regulating order of things. Anarchism seems more dystopian than utopian (certainly this is true in Blanchot's case). An anarchic society would be much like the one Blanchot alludes to in *La communauté unavouable*—"It must not last, it must have no part in any kind of duration" (CI56/UC32). Hence his antimessianism, that is, his skepticism against hope. His refusal of philosophy is, in a certain sense, the refusal of redemption. Blanchot's later preoccupation with the Holocaust is perhaps consistent with this movement of thought.

It is plausible to think of anarchism as the natural companion of modernity. Anarchism presupposes (and refuses) the ideal of a social and cultural order administered from the top down, or according to a model of rational procedures and smooth functioning as a good in itself. Anarchism rejects the idea of an ordered world, but not by offering itself as a substitute or alternative order (a world of misrule, for example). It is perhaps more intelligible and defensible as an ethics or micropolitics than it is as a political philosophy writ large, unless it were as a philosophy of freedom of a kind that we don't know how to develop.[7] Blanchot's anarchism, moreover, specifically presupposes a Hegelian concept of spirit in which everything coincides with itself in a total system. His is a philosophical anarchism in the paradoxical sense that it is a refusal of philosophy understood in terms of the rule of concepts and principles, of representational and calculative thinking, of strategic, problem-solving, instrumental rationality. The later Heidegger, who speaks of the self-refusal of philosophy and of thinking as wandering, is an anarchist in something like this sense.[8] In Deleuze's language, Blanchot's thinking is *rhizomatic*, whereas philosophy is, in the nature of the case, *arboreal* (MP9–37/TP3–25).

One might make this somewhat clearer by noticing the interesting conceptual agreement, evidently traceable to Heidegger, between Blanchot and Theodor Adorno on the relationship between art and modern Western culture. There is no doubt that Adorno's aesthetics is, at least up to a point, anarchic in Blanchot's sense. In the *Ästhetische Theorie* (1971), Adorno's theme is the constitutive resistance of art to the rationalization of society. Adorno's idea is that the social nature of art consists in its remaining external to society, that is, in some sense, free of it—free in the sense of negative and critical. To be sure, the work of art is a social product, a piece of social furniture—it is an artifact of someone's labor and a sign of the times that historians and anthropologists might one day come along to study—but it "is social primarily because it stands opposed to society. Now this opposition art can mount only when it has become autonomous [in the Kantian sense of differentiated or belonging to its own region]. By congealing into an entity unto itself—rather than obeying existing social norms and thus proving itself to be 'socially useful'—art criticizes society just by being there" (*AT335/AeT321*).

The assumption common to Adorno and Blanchot is that culture or society is (if not an explicitly totalitarian regime) at least a regulated system, as in analytic philosophy's theory of the conceptual scheme in which the world hangs together according to some principle of identity, or law of noncontradiction, or logic of integration. What Adorno calls self-identical art—art that corresponds to nothing outside of itself, summarized in "Schönberg's statement that the painter paints a picture rather than what it represents"—contests such a theory in behalf of what the system excludes; art is, as Adorno says, "meant to assist the non-identical [the singular and refractory] in its struggle against the repressive identification compulsion that rules the outside world" (*AT14/AeT6*). Again: "Art negates the conceptualization foisted on the real world" (*AT15/AeT7*)—which is not to say that art has some foundation in a pure, unconceptualized reality, but rather that it is excessive and satirical with respect to the whole idea of subsumptive reasoning or the idea of rationality as a totalizing conceptual dominion where the nonidentical is excluded as a mere contradiction. The validity of art, says Adorno, "lies in the critique it levels by its sheer existence against the hypostatization of rationality" (*AT93/AeT86*). And the goal of critique, of course, is freedom—freedom, here, not just for human beings, but for the world of things as well, which are allowed once more their singularity and self-possession (their an-archy). "The formative categories of art," Adorno says, "are not simply different in kind from those outside. They actively seek to impart what is peculiar to themselves to the outside world. In the latter the prevailing forms are those that characterize the domination of nature, whereas in art, forms are being controlled and regimented out of a sense of freedom. By repressing the agent of repression, art undoes some of the domination inflicted on nature" (AT207/AeT199–200).

In a totalist scheme a thing is intelligible (it means) if it fits, causing no friction, whereas the task of art is to produce a crisis of intelligibility through its resistance to interpretation or allegorical integration into a scheme. "Aesthetics," says Adorno, "cannot hope to grasp works of art if it treats them as hermeneutical objects. What at present needs to be grasped is their unintelligibility" (AT179/AeT173)—that is, their materiality, density, or enigmatic darkness. This darkness is the refuge of the self-identity of the work of art; resistance to appropriation is what makes art what it is: "art in general is like a handwriting. Its works are hieroglyphs for which the code has been lost, and this loss is not accidental but constitutive of their essence as works of art" (AT189/AeT182). "Actually," says Adorno—in what could be allowed to stand as the motto of philosophical anarchism—"only what does not fit into this world is true" (AT93/AeT86).

All of this resonates powerfully with Blanchot's writing, except that Blanchot never speaks of the autonomy of art. His anarchism extends (both in theory and in practice) to the work of art itself, which is not a thing that ever comes into existence as such. The work is always a *désœuvrement*, an unworking of the productive logic of labor and discourse. Writing is always a fragmentary event. But we must wait to take up this matter in its proper place.

I don't pursue the symmetry between Blanchot and Adorno in this book, but it is worth some thought, and it helps to forestall a possible misunderstanding. Blanchot's refusal of philosophy is not a withdrawal into a primitive world of images and feeling. On the contrary, his thinking is deeply, even coldly, analytical. There is a sense in which only a rationalist could understand rationality so thoroughly as he does. The only emotion that registers in Blanchot's work is that of sadness. (It is true that he speaks of fear, but only as a way of characterizing a certain kind of philosophical experience.)

Some parts of this book have appeared elsewhere. Chapter 5, "Blanchot/Levinas: Interruption (On the Conflict of Alterities)," was published in *Research in Phenomenology*, 26 (1996). Some paragraphs from chapter 4, "Blanchot/Celan: *Unterwegssein* (On Poetry and Freedom)," in a form now revised, appear in my introduction to Hans-Georg Gadamer's commentary on Paul Celan, *Who Am I, and Who Are You?*, trans. Bruce Krajewski (Albany: SUNY Press, 1997).

A portion of chapter 7 was presented at the October 1995 meeting of the Society for Phenomenology and Existential Philosophy under the title "Blanchot, Char, and the Theory of the Fragment." In replying to my paper Herman Rapaport made two points, both of them well-taken. The first warned me (not for the first time) against trying to extract theories, concepts, or positions of any sort from Blanchot's writings. In response I stammered something about trying to clarify texts, not concepts. The second point (following from the first) was that readings (such as mine appear to be) that "disincorporate" Blanchot's language by reducing his texts to their ideas are all very well, but what is the result if these ideas turn out to be someone else's? In Rapaport's words, "Blanchot is not a very original thinker." If his ideas interest me so much, why don't I address them in those primary versions in which they are logically developed and conceptually coherent?

I take the point that Blanchot thinks by thinking through what others have thought, which he then turns to his own account, as in his early appropriations of Heidegger (but it must be added that Blanchot has taken Heidegger's thought where it could not have gone of itself). Blanchot's mode of discourse was not the course lecture or seminar paper but the critical review and the avant-garde text. In both cases he seems to take on the substance and identity of whatever happens to have engaged him. On occasion he will describe himself as, basically, a writer of marginalia—perhaps the quintessential form of fragmentary and anonymous inscription (*EI*255/*IC*452). But then those who engage Blanchot often become a forceful medium of his thinking—Joseph Libertson, as I indicate below, has noted how it is often impossible to distinguish among texts by Bataille, Blanchot, and Levinas written in the 1940s. I think that Blanchot's influence on Levinas was massive and profound, a thought that certain Levinasians with a congenital suspicion of poetry find deeply offensive (something to do with self-sufficiency as a necessary condition of philosophy). It will take years to sort out the relationship between Derrida and Blanchot.[9] Sometimes when I read Foucault or Lyotard I have the conviction that Blanchot's timepiece has been lifted, but Foucauldians like William Connolly think it is the other way around, and the philosopher Jack Caputo thinks Lyotard either comes from the future or falls from the sky, I forget which. Part of the problem here may lie in the closely interanimated character of French intellectual culture, in which writers borrow freely from one another according to extremely subtle rules of reference. In his essay on Blanchot and Jean-Luc Nancy cited in chapter 10 below, for example, Robert Bernasconi has a very perceptive comment on "the somewhat discreet forms of criticism that often operate between French thinkers, in marked contrast to the rather more direct approach that is customary in Britain and the United States."[10] What looks like a secret citation or theft is sometimes a pretext, parody, or counterstatement serving as a window onto something else; but often it is just the silent invocation of a precedent or authority which no one can be expected to miss.

My readings of Blanchot have tried to take into account the dialogical or, better, the contextual character of his thinking. Much of what follows is in fact not just a reading of Blanchot but an inquiry into his engagements and kinships, and in particular I try to be fairly precise about where he and his friend Emmanuel Levinas reached an impasse in their long debate (if "debate" is the word). It is perhaps in his engagement with Levinas that Blanchot's refusal of philosophy is most clearly articulated—just as the overcoming of poetry, as Levinas explicitly shows, is foundational for ethics as first philosophy. I try to say a little bit about Blanchot and Bataille. And it seems to me that Blanchot and Paul Celan are moving along parallel lines—perhaps (again) owing to the common background of Heidegger.

All but the final two chapters of this book were written during the 1993–94 academic year while I was a Fellow at the Center for Advanced Study in the Behaviorial Sciences at Stanford, California. What an extraordinary place this is, and what an extraordinary year I had there. I'm deeply indebted to the Center and its staff, particularly then director Phil Converse and associate director Bob Scott, whose warmth and great good humor capture the spirit of the place. The people I met at the Center will always remain with me, particularly John Gillis, Bill Connolly, and Arthur and Joan Kleinman, whose conversations were filled with wisdom and mischief in exuberantly equal parts.

It will be thought that the support of an institution called the Center for Advanced Study in the Behaviorial Sciences, with its deep commitment to the rationalization of the world, is being poorly repaid by a book on a doubtful character like Maurice Blanchot. I've thought this very thing myself, the more so since I took enormous inspiration from what I learned at the Center about quantitative methodology and, in particular, about the "game-theoretic" or strategic mode of thinking, which has application, believe it or not, to biology as well as to economics and political science. Indeed, the pleasures of rational choice theory are without number, and not the least of these is the meaning that attaches to the word *hyperrationality* (which is, as we shall see, Blanchot's definition of madness).[11] At the Center I learned, with relief, that randomness and contingency don't sneak up on you but can be factored in or out as desired. I did not realize that there were Chomskyan musicologists, not to say Chomskyan linguists who could sound, for all the world, like Walter Benjamin. I found out (obviously, at my age, too late) that anthropologists are more real, and psychiatrists more anarchic, than English professors. I discovered that if one spends an evening reading poetry to a group of social scientists one is likely to be asked how a species of autism can exercise such captivation, and can it be maximized? Mostly I learned that a world without positivists would be sober and dull.

Thirty years ago Jim Kincaid read the first thing I ever wrote on Blanchot and remarked, connoisseur of the dubious that he is, that there seemed to be all round a serious want of comedy. That's what I call understanding Blanchot in a twinkling. Recently Kincaid read much of what follows and, as I thought, passed his hand gently across his eyes before declining comment.

A final word of thanks to my colleagues at Notre Dame, Joseph Buttigieg, Steve Fredman, Jay Walton, Steve Watson, and Ewa and Krys Ziarek, sources of clarity in a world of contradiction.

Abbreviations

Theodor Adorno

AeT *Aesthetic Theory*. Trans. C. Lenhardt. London: Routledge & Kegan Paul, 1984.
AT *Ästhetische Theorie*. Heraus. Gretel Adorno and Rolf Tiedemann. Frankfurt: Suhrkamp, 1970.

Georges Bataille

AM *The Absence of Myth: Writings on Surrealism*. Trans. Michael Richardson. London: Verso, 1994.
AS *The Accursed Share*. 2 vols. Trans. Robert Hurley. New York: Zone Books, 1993.
ExI *L'expérience interieure*. Paris: Éditions Gallimard, 1954.
G *Guilty*. Trans. Bruce Boone. Venice, Calif.: The Lapis Press, 1988.
I *The Impossible*. Trans. Robert Hurley. San Francisco: City Lights Books, 1991.
IE *Inner Experience*. Trans. Leslie Anne Boldt. Albany, N.Y.: SUNY Press, 1988.
OC *Œuvres complètes*. Paris: Éditions Gallimard, 1970–86.
VE *Visions of Excess: Selected Writings, 1927–39*. Trans. Allan Stoekl. Minneapolis: University of Minnesota Press, 1985.

Maurice Blanchot

A *L'amitié*. Paris: Éditions Gallimard, 1971.
AC *Après-coup, précédé par le ressassement éternel*. Paris: Éditions de minuit, 1983.
AO *L'attente, l'oubli*. Paris: Éditions Gallimard, 1962.
AM *L'arrêt de mort*. Paris: Éditions Gallimard, 1948.
AMV *Au moment voulu*. Paris: Éditions Gallimard, 1951.
BR *The Blanchot Reader*. Ed. Michael Holland. London: Basil Blackwell, 1995.
CAP *Celui qui ne m'accompagnait pas*. Paris: Éditions Gallimard, 1953.

Abbreviations

CI   *La communauté inavouable.* Paris: Éditions de minuit, 1983.

DH   *Le dernier homme.* Paris: Éditions Gallimard, 1953.

DM   *Le dernier mot.* Paris: Editions de la revue Fontaine, 1948.

DS   *Death Sentence.* Trans. Lydia Davis. Barrytown, N.Y.: Station Hill Press, 1978.

ED   *L'écriture du désastre.* Paris: Éditions Gallimard, 1980.

EI   *L'entretien infini.* Paris: Éditions Gallimard, 1969.

EL   *L'espace littéraire.* Paris: Éditions Gallimard, 1955.

FJ   *La folie du jour.* Montpelier: Fata Morgana, 1973.

FP   *Faux pas.* Paris: Éditions Gallimard, 1943.

GO   *The Gaze of Orpheus and Other Literary Essays.* Trans. Lydia Davis. Barrytown, N.Y.: Station Hill Press, 1981.

IC   *The Infinite Conversation.* Trans. Susan Hanson. Minneapolis: University of Minnesota Press, 1992.

IQ   "Les intellectuels en question: Ébauche d'un réflexion," *Le débat,* 29 (Mars 1984), 3–28.

LM   *The Last Man.* Trans. Lydia Davis. New York: Columbia University Press, 1987.

LS   *Lautréamont et Sade.* Paris: Éditions de minuit, 1963.

LV   *Le livre à venir.* Paris: Éditions de minuit, 1959.

MD   *The Madness of the Day.* Trans. Lydia Davis. Barrytown, N.Y.: Station Hill Press, 1985.

NCC "Notre compagne clandestine." *Textes pour Emmanuel Levinas,* ed. François Laruelle. Paris: Jean-Michel Place, 1980.

OCC "Our Clandestine Companion." *Face to Face with Levinas,* ed. Richard Cohen. Albany: SUNY Press, 1986.

OW   *The One Who Was Standing apart from Me.* Trans. Lydia Davis. Barrytown, N.Y.: Station Hill Press, 1993.

PD   *Le pas au-delà.* Paris: Éditions Gallimard, 1971.

PF   *La part du feu.* Paris: Éditions Gallimard, 1949.

SL   *The Space of Literature.* Trans. Ann Smock. Lincoln: University of Nebraska Press, 1982.

SS   *The Sirens' Song.* Trans. Gabriel Josipovici. Bloomington: Indiana University Press, 1982.

SNB *The Step Not Beyond.* Trans. Lycette Nelson. Albany, N.Y.: SUNY Press, 1992.

TH   *Le très-haut.* Paris: Éditions Gallimard, 1948.

TO   *Thomas l'obscur* (new edition). Paris: Éditions Gallimard, 1950.

TTO *Thomas the Obscure.* Trans. Robert Lamberton. Barrytown, N.Y.: Station Hill Press, 1973).

Abbreviations

UC   *The Unavowable Community.* Trans. Pierre Joris. Barrytown, N.Y.: Station Hill Press, 1988.

VC   *Vicious Circles: Two Fictions and "After the Fact."* Trans. Paul Auster. Barrytown, N.Y.: Station Hill Press, 1985.

WD   *The Writing of the Disaster.* Trans. Ann Smock. Lincoln: University of Nebraska Press, 1986.

WF   *The Work of Fire.* Trans. Charlotte Mandell. Stanford: Stanford University Press, 1995.

WTC   *When the Time Comes.* Trans. Lydia Davis. Barrytown, N.Y.: Station Hill Press, 1977.

Paul Celan

CP   *Collected Prose.* Trans. Rosemarie Waldrop. New York: Sheep Meadow Press, 1986.

GW   *Gesammelte Werke.* Frankfurt: Suhrkamp, 1983.

LP   *Paul Celan: Last Poems.* Trans. Katharine Washburn and Margret Guillemin. San Francisco: North Point Press, 1986.

PPC   *Poems of Paul Celan.* Trans. Michael Hamburger. New York: Persea Books, 1983.

René Char

OE   *Œuvres complètes.* Paris: Gallimard, 1983.

PRC   *Poems of René Char.* Trans. Mary Ann Caws and Jonathan Griffin. Princeton, N.J.: Princeton University Press, 1976.

Gilles Deleuze

DeR   *Différence et repetition.* Paris: Presses Universitaires, 1968.

DR   *Difference and Repetition* Trans. Paul Patton. New York: Columbia University Press, 1994.

K   *Kafka: Pour une littéraire mineure.* Avec Félix Guattari. Paris: Éditions de minuit, 1975.

KFM   *Kafka: For a Minor Literature.* With Félix Guattari. Trans. Dana Polan. Minneapolis: University of Minnesota Press, 1986.

LdS   *Logique du sens.* Paris: Éditions de minuit, 1969.

LS   *The Logic of Sense.* Trans. Mark Lester. New York: Columbia University Press, 1990.

Abbreviations

MP   *Mille plateaux: Capitalisme et schizophréne.* Avec Félix Guattari. Paris: Éditions de minuit, 1980.
QP   *Qu'est-ce que la philosophie?* Paris: Éditions de minuit, 1991.
TP   *A Thousand Plateaus: Capitalism and Schizophrenia.* With Félix Guattari. Trans. Brian Massumi. Minneapolis: University of Minnesota Press, 1987.
WP   *What Is Philosophy?* With Félix Guattari. Trans. Hugh Tomlinson and Graham Burchell. New York: Columbia University Press, 1994.

Jacques Derrida

AL   *Acts of Literature.* Ed. Derek Attridge. London: Routledge, 1992.
EeD   *L'écriture et la différence.* Éditions du Seuil, 1967.
DE   *De l'esprit: Heidegger et le question.* Paris: Éditions Galilée, 1987.
OS   *Of Spirit: Heidegger and the Question.* Trans. Geoff Bennington and Rachel Bowlby. Chicago: University of Chicago Press, 1989.
P   *Parages.* Paris: Éditions Galilée, 1986.
S   *Schibboleth pour Paul Celan.* Paris: Éditions Galilée, 1986.
SH   "Shibboleth." Trans. Joshua Wilner. *Midrash and Literature.* Ed. Geoffrey Hartman and Sanford Budick. New Haven: Yale University Press, 1986, pp. 307–47.
WaD   *Writing and Difference.* Trans. Alan Bass. Chicago: University of Chicago Press, 1978.

Martin Heidegger

BT   *Being and Time.* Trans. John Macquarrie and Edward Robinson. New York: Harper & Row, 1962.
BW   *Martin Heidegger: Basic Writings.* Ed. David Michael Krell. New York: Harper & Row, 1977.
EB   *Existence and Being.* Trans. Douglas Scott. Chicago: Henry Regnery, 1949.
EGT   *Early Greek Thinking.* Trans. David Farrell and Frank A. Capuzzi. New York: Harper & Row, 1975.
G   *Gelassenheit.* Pfullingen: Günther Neske, 1959.
GA   *Gesamtausgabe.* Frankfurt: Vittorio Klosterman, 1977.
OWL   *On the Way to Language.* Trans. Peter Hertz. New York: Harper & Row, 1971.
PLT   *Poetry, Language, Thought.* Trans. Albert Hofstadter. New York: Harper & Row, 1971.
SZ   *Sein und Zeit.* 15th ed. Tübingen: Max Niemeyer, 1984.
US   *Unterwegs zur Sprache.* Pfullingen: Günther Neske, 1959.

Abbreviations

W   *Wegmarken.* Frankfurt: Vittorio Klostermann, 1967.
VA   *Vorträge und Aufsätze.* Pfullingen: Günther Neske, 1954.
WhD *Was heißt Denken?* Tübingen: Max Niemeyer, 1984.
WT   *What Is Called Thinking?* Trans. J. Glenn Gray. New York: Harper & Row, 1968.

Emmanuel Levinas

AE   *Autrement qu'être; ou, Au-delà de l'essence.* 2nd ed. The Hague: Martinus Nijhoff, 1978.
BC   "Bad Conscience and the Inexorable." Trans. Richard A. Cohen. *Face to Face with Levinas.* Ed. Richard A. Cohen. Albany, N.Y.: SUNY Press, 1986.
CPP *Collected Philosophical Papers.* Trans. Alphonso Lingis. The Hague: Martinus Nijhoff, 1987.
DEE *De l'existence à l'existant.* Paris: Éditions de la revue fontaine, 1947.
DHH *En découvrant l'existence avec Husserl et Heidegger.* 2nd ed. Paris: Librarie Philosophique, 1967.
EE   *Existence and Existents.* Trans. Alfonso Lingis. The Hague: Martinus Nijhoff, 1978.
HAH *Humanisme de l'autre homme.* Paris: Fata Morgana, 1972.
HS   *Hors sujet.* Cognac: Fata Morgana, 1987.
IH   *Les imprévus de l'histoire.* Cognac: Fata Morgana, 1994.
LR   *The Levinas Reader.* Ed. Sean Hand. Oxford: Basil Blackwell, 1989.
MC   "La mauvaise conscience et l'inexorable," *Exercises de la patience,* 2 (Winter 1981), 109–13.
NP   *Noms propres.* Montpellier: Fata Morgana, 1976.
OTB *Otherwise than Being: or, Beyond Essence.* Trans. Alphonso Lingis. The Hague: Martinus Nijhoff, 1981.
SMB *Sur Maurice Blanchot.* Cognac: Fata Morgana, 1975.
TeI   *Totalité et infini; essai sur l'extériorité.* The Hague: Martinus Nijhoff, 1961.
TI   *Totality and Infinity: An Essay on Exteriority.* Trans. Alphonso Lingis. Pittsburgh: Duquesne University Press, 1969.

Stéphane Mallarmé

C   *Correspondance de Mallarmé, 1862–1871.* 2nd ed. Ed. Henri Mondor. Paris: Éditions Gallimard, 1959.
OC   *Œuvres complètes.* Paris: Éditions Gallimard, 1945.
SP   *Mallarmé: Selected Prose Poems, Essays, Letters.* Trans. Bradford Cook. Baltimore: Johns Hopkins Press, 1956.

Abbreviations

Jean-Luc Nancy

CD   *La communauté désœuvrée.* Paris: Christian Bourgois, 1986.
EF   *The Experience of Freedom.* Trans. Bridget McDonald. Stanford: Stanford University Press, 1993.
EL   *L'expérience de la liberté.* Paris: Éditions Galilée, 1988.
IC   *The Inoperative Community.* Trans. Peter Connor, Lisa Garbus, Michael Holland, and Simona Sawhney. Minneapolis: University of Minnesota Press, 1991.
PFi   *Une pensée finie.* Paris: Éditions Galilée, 1990.

Jean-Paul Sartre

QL   *Qu'est-ce que la littérature.* Paris: Éditions Gallimard, 1948.
WL   *"What is Literature?" and Other Essays.* Ed. Steven Ungar. Cambridge, Mass.: Harvard University Press, 1988.

PART I

Poetics of the Outside

CHAPTER 1

This Way Out

An Introduction to Poetry and Anarchy

> Let us note well that all the contradictions in which we exist—
> the misfortune of a thought that has nothing with which to
> begin and dissipates from one infinite to the other; the am-
> biguity by which we are scattered, not dwelling, incessantly
> coming and going, always here and there and yet nowhere,
> curious with regard to everything in order not to stop any-
> where; a world in which nothing is either present or absent,
> where there is neither proximity nor distance, where every-
> thing escapes, leaving us the illusion of having everything—
> all this is the consequence of a dispersing, pervasive, and er-
> rant obscurity that we have not had the force to fix in place.
> — Blanchot, "La pensée tragique"

What Is Poetics?

In his last major text, *L'écriture du désastre* (1980), Maurice Blanchot writes: "A philosopher who would write as a poet would be aiming for his own destruction. And even so, he could not reach it. Poetry is a question for philosophy which claims to provide it with an answer, and thus to comprehend it (know it). Philosophy, which puts everything into question, is tripped up by poetry, which is the question that eludes it" (*ED*104/*WD*63).

Eludes philosophy, that is, eludes poetics, where *poetics* is Aristotle's word, one of the premier concepts of philosophy, the word for keeping poetry in its place. Poetics is the site or place of poetry within the organon of discourse, where *organon* means the rule, logic, or system of categories

3

and conventions that defines the rationality of our speech. Poetics—Aristotle's poetics, but of course not just Aristotle's—refers to what is rational or what passes for rational in poetry, namely that it is a sort of cognition after all and it has a sort of logical coherence about it. The task of the concepts of mimesis and plot is to justify poetry as a subspecies of knowledge and reasoning. It's not clear that we could know what poetry could be outside of poetics. Just to this extent we might have to say that poetry is Greek.

Basically what Aristotle did was to conceptualize poetry so that it could be made to fit inside Plato's Republic; that is, he described it so as to make it consistent with the demands of a just and rational state, the state as rule-governed, founded upon knowledge and the control of the unruly—a state governed by the rule of necessity as against the interventions of randomness and contingency. Rules can indeed produce the effects of order and justice. Near the end of *L'écriture du désastre* Blanchot says of rules that in place of the reign of the powerful they "establish the reign of pure procedure—a manifestation of technical competence, of sheer knowledge—[which] invests everything, submits every gesture to its administration, so that there is no longer any possibility of liberation, for one can no longer speak of oppression" (*ED218/WD144*). One could take this as a gloss on Habermas's utopia of procedural rationality.

It would not be too much to think of rule-governed as synonymous with philosophy ("Philosophy," says Lyotard, "is a discourse that has as its rule the search for its rule [and that of other discourses]").[1] So poetics conceived on the model of the rule is not a theory of poetry come what may; it is meant to mediate the conflict between philosophy and poetry. That is, the task of poetics is to describe the inner logic or deep structure of poetry—together with its point. After all, why is there such a thing as poetry? What calls for poetry? Nothing is without reason, without a place in the scheme of things or of discourse, not even poetry, unless poetry were in some sense a limit of this scheme, part of the scheme but not quite internal to it. Possibly only in a culture already philosophical in its deep structure—already, for example, deeply committed to the law of noncontradiction and the grasping of things by means of concepts—could the subject or practice of poetry arise, for example as a possibility of transgression, or (as in this book) as the language of the singular or nonidentical. "Only within metaphysics is there the metaphorical," says Heidegger, meaning that the very distinction between the literal and the figurative, as between the poetic and the nonpoetic, or between poetry and philosophy, presup-

4

poses the institution of philosophy as, in some sense, a theory or practice of the rationality, the ruliness, of discourse (SG89).

What happens if one refuses or defies this presupposition and the discursive region it sustains? In an early essay, "Comment littérature est-elle possible?" (1942)—as if parodying the figure of Socrates, whose daimon restrained him from speech and action in the world—Blanchot says that there is in the heart of every writer a "demon" who causes him, if him is the word, to break with the organon that makes discourse, and therefore poetry or literature (not to say philosophy), possible (FP97/BR56). The task of this study of Blanchot's thought is to clarify the work of this demon of impossibility, this figure of worklessness, interruption, uneventfulness (désœuvrement). The task is to make sense of poetry or writing as a radical exteriority, or what Blanchot calls "a writing that could be said to be outside discourse, outside language," where language is to be understood in its strong foundational sense of conceptual mediation or, in Hegelian terms, as the dialectic of negation and signification that organizes everything into a totality (EIvii/ICxii). This means writing outside the world, outside all possible worlds, outside possibility as a logical category (anarchic with respect to conditions that have to be in place before discourse can begin). Therefore, in the bargain, it means writing outside art, outside the text, outside culture, where "the ideal of culture," Blanchot says, "is to bring off pictures of the whole, panoramic reconstitutions that situate in the same view Schönberg, Einstein, Picasso, Joyce—throwing Marx into the bargain, if possible, or better yet, Marx and Heidegger. Then the man of culture is happy; he has lost nothing, he has gathered up all the crumbs of the feast" (EI588/IC400). Starting out in the 1930s, the whole thrust of Blanchot's intellectual career is, paradoxically (or, rather, impossibly) to free itself from "the whole," as if it were possible to "unwork" or disengage the machine of cultural production in order to prevent the proper name of Blanchot from being reconstituted—woven into the "total fabric"—as a Schönberg or Einstein, Picasso or Joyce, Marx or Heidegger. (Conceivably Blanchot's practice of invisibility, his refusal of any public image, serves not so much to resolve as to emphasize the contradiction inherent in this conception of writing as "unworking.")

In an essay from 1962, "Ars nova," Blanchot recalls Thomas Mann's *Doctor Faustus*, with its idea that the "new music" is "politically and socially tainted" (EI506–7/IC345). For Blanchot Mann is, preeminently, the "man of culture" who, in the name of politics, condemns what cannot be contained within the organon. "Let us say more precisely: what they [Mann, Lukács] deny and (rightly) dread in artistic experience is that which renders it foreign [*étrangère*] to all culture. There is an a-cultural part of literature and art to which one does not accommodate oneself easily, or happily" (*EI507/IC346*). What they fear is the anarchy of art, its irreducibility to principle and rule. Blanchot cites Adorno on Webern's anarchic aesthetics: " 'If atonality may well originate in the decision to rid music of every convention, it by the same token carries within itself something barbaric that is capable of perturbing always anew the artistically composed surface; dissonant harmony sounds as though it had not been entirely mastered by the civilizing principle of order: in its breaking up, the work of Webern remains almost entirely primitive' " (*EI508/IC346*). Anarchy here is, however, not chaos, nor is it a Dada-like desire for the destruction of cultural forms as such. Still appealing to Adorno on Webern, Blanchot writes: "If the musician renounces with austere rigor the continuity of a unified work . . . , he does so not in order to deny all coherence or the value of form, or even to oppose the musical work considered as an organized whole (as sometimes appears to be the case with Stravinsky); on the contrary, it is because he places himself beyond aesthetic totality [*au-delà de la totalité ésthétique*]" (*EI509/IC347*). Anarchy, in other words, is to be understood in its original sense of that which is outside, on the hither side, of the concept of principle: *an-arche*.[2] The anarchic is not opposed to order dialectically as a Dionysian project of overcoming or undoing; it is rather the refractory region excluded by an integral rationality that disposes everything according to the rule of unity and identity (*EI508/IC347*). The anarchic is outside the relation of identity and difference; it is the domain of the singular, the *aliquid*, the aleatory, and the neutral (that is, neither one nor the other, neither the other nor the same).

Mallarmé: "a perspective of parentheses"

Two figures, Mallarmé and Heidegger, are foundational for the reading of Blanchot; that is, they help to constitute the conceptual background—the basic theory of exteriority—against which Blanchot emerges (but which he will almost at once exceed).

Mallarmé was the first poet to conceptualize poetry strictly in terms of language. He was the first language-poet, that is, the first to take to its limit the idea that a poem is made of language and not of any of the uses of lan-

guage. Poetry is not made of ideas, images, feelings, expressions, or representations of any kind; poetry is made of words and not of what words are
used to produce. But perhaps even the concept of word, the word as sign,
has begun to lose its application. Better to say that poetry is made of language but is not a use of it; poetry is made of language but is not a product
of it. It is not a language game, not a form of life.

Mallarmé speaks famously of a "crise de vers"—a crisis or turn in the
history of verse—which occurs when poetry turns away from discourse,
taking language with it, turning language into something else, something
foreign to itself: "Out of a number of words, poetry fashions a single new
word which is total in itself and foreign to the language [*langue*] . . . . Thus
the desired isolation of language [*parole*] is achieved; and chance (which
might still have governed these elements, despite their artful and alternat-
ing renewal in meaning and sound) is thereby instantly and thoroughly
abolished. Then we realize, to our amazement, that we had never truly
heard this or that ordinary poetic fragment" (OC368/SP43; translation
amended slightly). This is a crisis provoked by writing (*l'écriture*), which
frees language from the control or interference of the speaking subject.
Imagine language not as a system for framing representations, nor as a native tongue, nor the expressiveness of a spirit—possibly it is not even a
vocabulary of any sort but is only something disclosed in writing: for example, the alphabet, but also the page on which letters appear. These letters of the alphabet are foundational: Mallarmé thinks of them as the origin of language. Language at all events is in some sense internal to the
space of writing itself.[3]

What appears on the page is not something that was merely invisible
otherwise and is now suddenly summoned to show itself; that is, there is no
sense to be made of a language existing independently of the alphabet. In
fact concepts of the visible and the invisible have only an uncertain application here, where writing is external to phenomena. In a certain sense
writing is outside the whole idea of something appearing. Writing is incommensurable with revelation of any sort; writing is on the side of disappearance. This is, so to speak, Mallarmé's Copernican revolution.

Mallarmé introduces the concept of *écriture* into poetics, without however quite making *l'écriture* the term of art it will later become. Poetry is
the site or space of *écriture*, where *écriture* is more event than mark. It is
the blank page on which nothing is to be seen, the white space that occurs
as such in the appearance of letters. Poetry is made of letters, but only in

virtue of the spaces between or around them. Mallarmé came to think of poetry as typographical composition, a total book, a book which is not anything except itself: paper, ink, leaves folded and bound together, letters of the alphabet sounding and resounding musically or of themselves according to every possible combination and permutation of relations.[4] The space of poetry is outside anything we would recognize as semantic space. It is not so much a space that contains as one that disperses, the way *Un coup de dés* disperses its letters. It is surface rather than volume. This does not mean that poetry is meaningless, only that meaning, for example naming something, is no longer anything productive.

Quite the contrary. Perhaps the most famous of all Mallarmé's texts is the following:

> I say: "a flower!" and, outside the forgetfulness to which my voice consigns all floral form, something different from the usual calyces arises, something all music, essence [aroma], and softness: the flower which is absent from all bouquets

> [Je dis: une fleur! et, hors de l'oubli où ma voix relègue aucun contour, en tant que quelque chose d'autre que les calices sus, musicalement se lève, idée même et suave, l'absente de tous bouquets.] (OC368/SP42)

Blanchot's poetics—or perhaps we should say, the whole career of his thinking—is in certain respects an extended, open-ended commentary on this passage. In poetry language is not the medium of anything, unless it is of disappearance itself (PF38–39/WF30–31). "All Mallarmé's researches," Blanchot writes in 1946, "tend to find a boundary where, by means of terms nonetheless fixed and directed at facts and things, a perspective of parentheses might be sketched out, each opening out into each other and into infinity and endlessly escaping themselves" (PF40/WF33). If one could assign a characteristic figure of speech to Blanchot's thinking, it would be the parentheses: a figure of interruption.

We can try to clarify this perspective by saying that poetry as *l'écriture* is an event that goes on outside the poet's subjectivity. So poetry can never be expression. It is nonsubjective, outside the realm or reach of the subject, which means outside its objects as well: outside consciousness and its representations. What is nonsubjective cannot have objectivity as an alternative. This nonsubjectivity of poetry has to be taken in absolutely the strongest sense possible: poetry as *écriture* is outside of *all* subjectivity, and this means outside of all knowing and practice, outside of all individual or

8

cultural production and experience, external to discourse and its many signifying systems (that is, it is not another system or field or genre). Poetry as *écriture* is neither true nor false but outside the alternatives of truth and falsity; it is neither transcendent nor immanent but outside all transcendence and immanence. The poet, at work at writing, suddenly or inevitably discovers him or herself outside of all places and relations, outside all identities and differences (in the event that Gilles Deleuze will later call "difference in itself" [*DR*74–82/*DeR*52–55]). Mallarmé tried to characterize the event of writing, of entering into the space of the page, by appealing to death and nothingness (the suicide of the poet and the hierophany of *le Néant*). "My work was created only by elimination," he says. "Destruction has been my Beatrice."[5] *L'écriture* is not an inscription of something other than itself; what is inscribed disappears.[6] Mallarmé says that "everything, the world, was made to exist in a book": but we must imagine things emptying through the book as if it were "a hole in Being."[7] Annihilation is poetry's condition of possibility, its *reason:* but now the concept of "conditions of possibility," or of reason, no longer has any coherent application. One could just as well say that poetry is impossible, or outside the alternatives of possible-impossible. Poetry is now a question of a writing that remains open, unjustified, without place or reason: "Très avant, au moins, quant au point, je le formule:—A savoir s'il y a lieu d'écrire" (*OC*645/ *SP*45).

Mallarmé can be thought of as a limit-figure: someone who constitutes an absolute boundary for poetry or writing. He is the dark side of Aristotle: poetics without light. At the Mallarméan limit, poetry is outside our discursive possibilities, outside our power, outside mastery. It is, in ways Maurice Blanchot will try to explain, impossible.[8]

Having established the originary position of Mallarmé, however, it is important to note that Blanchot's first full account of the exteriority of language occurs in his essay "Quelque refléxions sur surréalisme" (1945), in which he remarks that the surrealists appear, at first glance, to be "destroyers" who "loose their fury on discourse; they take away from it any right usefully to mean something; fiercely they break discourse as a means for social relationships, for precise designation. Language seems not only sacrificed, but humiliated" (*PF*93/*WF*88). However, surrealist anarchism— automatic writing, for example—is neither destructive nor negative, at least not with respect to language. To be sure, "language disappears," but only as an instrument. "That rational constructions are rejected, that universal significations vanish, is to say that language does not have to be *used*, that it does not have to serve to express something, that it is free, freedom itself. When surrealists speak of 'freeing' words, of treating them other than as little servants [*petits auxiliaires*], it is a veritable social revindication they have in view" (PF93/WF88).

And the term "social revindication" means just what it says. The surrealist releasement of language is not just another chapter in the story that characterizes aesthetic modernity in terms of the foregrounding of language at the expense of social and political reality. Blanchot's construction of surrealist poetics is, on the contrary, entirely political (assuming we think of freedom as a political concept). "There are men and a class of men," Blanchot says, "that others think of as instruments and elements of exchange: in both cases, freedom, the possibility for man to be the subject, is called directly into question." But the "emancipation of words" is not just an emancipation of subjectivity. Of course, "in automatic writing, it is not, strictly speaking, the word that becomes free; rather, the word and my freedom are now no more than one. I slide into the word, it keeps my imprint, and it is my imprinted reality; it adheres to my non-adherence." But there is more, namely that freedom is not merely a subjectivist concept, that is, a negative freedom. "[This] freedom of words means that words become free for themselves: they no longer depend exclusively on things that they express, they act on their own account, they play, and, as [André] Breton says, 'they make love'" (PF93/WF88).

The surrealists were perhaps even more forceful than Mallarmé in proposing to think of language noninstrumentally, or expressly as a limit or critique of subject-centered rationality. This at all events is the construction that Blanchot places upon the surrealists. "The surrealists became well aware—they made use of it admirably—of the bizarre character of words: they saw that words have their own spontaneity. For a long time, language had laid claim to a kind of particular existence: it refused simple transparency, it was not just a gaze, an empty means of seeing; it existed, it was a concrete thing and even a colored thing. The surrealists understand, moreover, language is not an inert thing; it has a life of its own, and a latent power that escapes us" (PF93/WF88–89). Words are things, but they are not objects, that is, they are not under our conceptual or manipulative control: "they move, they have their demand [*exigence*], they dominate us." Or, as Breton says, language is only part "'of this uncompromising little world over which we can sustain only a very insufficient surveillance'"

(*PF*93/*WF*88–89). So the issue here is not just aesthetic; or the aesthetic is not just nonpolitical.

The An-arche of the Work of Art

The essay on the surrealists shows that already in 1945 Blanchot was a close reader of Martin Heidegger's texts (his first essay on Heidegger, "La parole 'sacrée' de Hölderlin," dates from 1946). To be sure, at first glance it appears that Heidegger is a counterpoint to Mallarméan or surrealist conceptions of language. In "Hölderlin und das Wesen der Dichtung," Heidegger says that the task of language is to make manifest the world, that is, the human world of time and history, the world of constructions and projections onto the future, the world of struggle and destiny, of *Bildung* and work. Language is not a system for describing a world already there; rather, it is only in language that the world comes to be as something describable or inhabitable, that is, as a world around us and for us. Language gives us the horizon against which we appear for the first time as beings-in-the-world.

Poetry (*Dichtung*) is Heidegger's word for this event of disclosure in which the world is established for the first time and in which we are thereby introduced into time and history. He says: "Poetry is the establishment of being by means of the word [*Dichtung ist worthafte Stiftung des Seins*]" (*GA*4:41/*EB*282). Poetry is an originary event in which the world is there for us and around us as beings. It opens up — it lightens or illuminates this space in which beings are in being. Poetry discloses this space between Being and beings; it speaks the difference of Being and beings.

So whereas Mallarmé thinks of poetry as the elimination of things, Heidegger thinks of it as the event of disclosure in which things enter into the openness of being. Hence the temptation to situate Heidegger and Mallarmé along a plane between two evidently different poetic theories. In the one (call it *Orphic*), the poet calls the world into being; in the other (*hermetic*), the poet produces the pure work of language from which every trace of the world (including the poet as a subject who objectifies or gives voice to the world) has disappeared. Taken together the Orphic and the hermetic appear to define the topology of poetry. They are not alternative genres or traditions but limits.

However, the Orphic and hermetic are not opposites; they are perhaps simply different interpretations of poetry's outsidedness. It is important to notice that the disclosure of the world is not Heidegger's whole story about poetry.[9] It remains true that poetry as *Dichtung*—literally, poetizing—is the opening up of the world; poetry is the situating of the world and of ourselves as beings in the world, where situating means historicizing in the sense of exposing us to time and history. Poetry is a name for beginning.

The question is: What happens to poetry in this event? What is the history of poetry once the opening up or beginning of the world is under way? Suppose there were no end to beginnings? What would a world be like with too many beginnings?

Just so. The poet, Heidegger says, lightens up a world, lightens up the place of being; however, in the event, "the overpowering brightness has driven the poet into the dark [*Die übergroße Helle hat den Dichter in das Dunkel gestoßen*]" (*GA4:44/EB285*). This line is Heidegger's way of accounting for Hölderlin's madness (which is part of a constellation of legendary poetic curses: silence, blindness, exile, suicide). It is perhaps also Heidegger's way of keeping faith with Plato and Hegel: poetry discloses— it is the origination of—the world, but it always remains itself on the hither side of the world. If it exposes us to the future, it remains for us, as Hegel said, a thing of the past, but as something *anarchic* rather than archaic or merely *vergangen* or obsolete.

As Heidegger pictures it in "Der Ursprung des Kunstwerkes," the work of art—a Greek temple—is, to be sure, a ruin, a fragment from a lost civilization. And what Heidegger gives us is an account of the original and originary work or truth of this work, as if it were long ago: "The temple-work, standing there, opens up a world" (*GA5:28/PLT42*). But there is no mistaking the extraneous position of the temple. It is not too much to say that this exteriority is the main point of Heidegger's aesthetics. This in fact is Blanchot's argument in his earliest writings on Heidegger. The deep reserve or irony of the poet's speech is that its work is originary but that it provides no place for itself in the world, no place in the world's time or space or history (there is no "moment" of poetic existence [*PF125/WF123*]). The work of art remains on the hither side of the origin that it brings about: it is an-archic or sacred in Hölderlin's sense of the sacred as that which is "absolutely anterior" to the world and which can never be brought into it, certainly not by speaking (*PF130/WF129*). But this unspeakability is precisely the contradiction at the heart of Hölderlin's sacred speech. Putting matters into Kant's language: the poem is the condition of the world's possibility, but this condition remains itself outside the world—outside possibility (outside language). Blanchot figures this as the "foundational" contradiction of poetry, "the heart of poetic existence . . . its essence and its law" (*PF*121/*WF*117). The poem "makes the future possible, and firmly maintains history in the perspective of 'tomorrow' that is richer with meaning" (*PF*121/*WF*118); but the poem remains outside the world in the "not yet" of anarchic temporality. If you ask what makes the poem possible, the answer is that there is no answer: the poem is, like the sacred, impossible. Neither the sacred nor the poem can be put into words. Much of Blanchot's work—his conception of worklessness or fragmentary writing (*désœuvrement*)—is a lifelong attempt to understand and even rationalize this impossibility.

To be sure, as Heidegger describes it in "Der Ursprung des Kunstwerkes," the work belongs to the realm that it originates, but only in the sense that this realm is earthly as well as worldly. That is, there is more to the work of the work of art than the opening of the world; there is also the setting forth of the earth. The work is in the world but it is of the earth. The work of art is not a being-in-the-world. As an event, its work is originary, but as a created work it is made of earth, where the earth is that which closes itself up as the limit or finitude of the world.[10] The work is thinglike in its self-refusal or reserve with respect to the world; it is self-standing, strange, and uncommunicative.[11] It is not the medium of anything; it *is* (*es gibt*). Its createdness exposes us to the density and imperturbability of this fact. Here the work shows itself as poetry (*Dichtung*: literally, thick, dense, impermeable). As poetry, the earthly character of the work emerges as that which withdraws from the world that it opens up.

This means first of all that the work of art is not an object for us; its truth is always outside the realm of experience. Still, it bears upon us (as we are, in the world) in a critical way. It is this bearing that Heidegger tries to elicit in his remarks on the createdness [*Geschaffensein*] of the work. The work of art is not expended or exhausted by its work. The work is an event, but it is also an implacable thinglike thing (an *aliquid*) that cannot be done away with or made transparent by figuring it as this or that sort of object in an ensemble of identities. This implacability is its createdness, and in addition to our understanding of the truth of the work "we must," Heidegger says, "also be able to experience the createdness explicitly in the work [*müssen wir auch das Geschaffensein eigens am Werk erfahren können*]" (*GA*5:52/*PLT*65).

"The emergence of createdness from the work does not mean that the work is to give the impression of having been made by a great artist"

(GA5:52/PLT65). Createdness has nothing to do with spiritual or cultural production; it is simply the "factum est" of the work: it *is*. Talk of the artist or of modes of production obscure the createdness of the work, which Heidegger thinks of in terms of the self-containment of the work, its self-subsistence [*Insichruhen*], thrusting itself into the Open of the world.

Heidegger says that of course it is obvious that everything around us *is*; what could be more ordinary [*gewöhnlicher*] than everything that is? But the mode of being of the work, its createdness, is out of the ordinary; it is uncanny and strange:

> In a work, by contrast, this fact, that it *is* as a work, is just what is unusual [*Ungewöhnliche*]. The event of its being created does not simply reverberate through the work; rather, the work casts before itself the eventful fact that the work is as this work, and it has constantly this fact about itself. The more essentially the work opens itself, the more luminous becomes the uniqueness of the fact that it is rather than is not. The more essentially this thrust comes into the Open, the stranger [*befremdlicher*]and more solitary the work becomes. . . . [12]
>
> The more solitarily the work . . . stands on its own and the more cleanly it seems to cut all ties to human beings, the more simply does the thrust come into the Open that such a work *is*, and the more essentially is the extraordinary [*Ungeheure*] thrust to the surface and the long familiar thrust down. (GA5:53–54/PLT65–66)

To experience the createdness in (not of) the work is to experience this turning upside down of things. To experience here is *erfahren*, which should be taken in the strong sense of undergoing a reversal (*Umkehrung*), of being turned inside out and exposed. For Heidegger, however, experience cannot adequately be conceived as a purely subjective event, a mere reversal of consciousness. For what happens in the work is not an event for spectators. We ought rather to imagine the experience of a world so turned round as to be no longer recognizable to itself: a world upside down. Our relation to the world in this event can no longer be thought of as subjective; that is, the place we occupy is no longer the site of action and cognition: "To submit to this displacement [of the ordinary] means: to transform our accustomed ties to world and to earth and henceforth to restrain all usual doing and prizing, knowing and looking, in order to stay within the truth that is happening in the work. Only the restraint of this staying lets what is created be the work that it is" (GA5:54/PLT66). As if what the work called for were the renunciation of subjectivity: a *Sichversagen*. Thus Heidegger does not hesitate to speak of *Bewahrung* as "an opening up of human being, out of its captivity in that which is, to the openness of Being" (GA5:55/ PLT67). Here the Open turns out to be much more a place of exposure than a dwelling place or homeland: in the Open it is the earth that shelters, not the world; and this shelter is a limit of what the world can reach.

Just so, the Heideggerian work, like the Mallarméan poem, is irreducible to the condition of a cultural object; or, rather, as a cultural object its outsidedness, its exteriority, is captured or controlled, no longer at work but brought within the orderly confinement of the museum, the gallery, the library, the archaeological slide show, the church or concert hall, the seminar room (the condominium of structuralist and cultural poetics). And we imagine that now we can regard the apartness of the work from within the haven of subjectivity at an aesthetic rather than ontological distance. By contrast the renunciation of subjectivity is the renunciation of the aesthetic and its distances; it is a renunciation of disengagement. The consequences of this renunciation are not clear.

In the museum the createdness of the work, its thingli- or earthliness, is repressed or invisible. The work becomes a transparent mediation of something other than itself, something worldly. The task of poetics is to lay bare the rule or logic of this mediation. For Heidegger, however, as for Mallarmé, the truth of the work is outside all mediation. It is not a truth that we can see or grasp by way of the work; it is rather an event that takes us out of the logic of mediation—takes us out of ourselves, turns us inside out. But again it must be stressed that this is not an event of subjectivity, something that simply alters our outlook or the look of the world. It is the world itself that is turned inside out. Hence the anarchy of the work of art.

Heidegger's poetics is topological. When he comes to speak of poetry (*Dichtung*) in "Der Ursprung des Kunstwerkes," he uses the term to characterize what the work of art does to a world already in place: "It is due to art's poetic nature that, in the midst of what is, art breaks open an open place, in whose openness everything is other than usual [*Aus dem dichtenden Wesen der Kunst geschieht es, daß sie inmitten des Seienden eine offene Stelle aufschlägt, in deren Offenheit alles anders ist als sonst]*" (GA5:59/ PLT72). One can take this event (as Paul Ricoeur does, for example) in a utopian spirit that sees the work of art projecting onto the future a possible world different from our own and which we can try to bring about by intervening in our world and altering its direction.[13] But this is still to see poetry as imaginative projection, that is, the work of subjects—poets and visionaries—who can imagine things differently. Heidegger, however, says rather more darkly that by virtue of this throwing-open (*Entwurf*), "everything ordinary and hitherto existing becomes an unbeing" (GA5:60/PLT72). Poetry throws open the world in the sense of exposing it to what is not itself. In poetry the world loses its self-identity, is turned out of itself; in poetry the world is elsewhere, not in place, on the way. Perhaps this only refers to the historicity of the world, where the historicity of anything means simply that it cannot be objectified. Poetry in this event cannot be a species of objectification. For example, it "cannot adequately be thought of in terms of imagination and the power of image-making [*Einbildungskraft*]" (GA5:60/PLT72–73). In fact, we don't really know how to think of poetry as anarchic, neither subjective nor objective, outside of projects and products. Poetry here is irreducible to a work of art that one can identify according to its formal features. Or say that *Poesie* is always in excess of its form, because it is made of words, and words can never be kept in place; they are unprincipled, an-archic, always getting away, unruly. A just and rational *Poesie* is poetry under confinement, no longer loose in the opening of *Dichtung*.

As *Dichtung*, poetry is not the work of imagination but of language, which "alone brings what is, as something that is, into the Open for the first time" (GA5:61/PLT73). However, a work of language is not the same as a use of it. Poetry is not the medium of anything. It is the work of language understood as the disclosure of the realm where earth and world enter into their originary conflict. So there is no differentiation of poetry from language; it is not a species of discourse. "Language itself is poetry in the essential sense" (GA5:62/PLT74). But we don't really know how to think of language in this sense. For this would be to think of language as earthly as well as worldly, that is, language as that which withdraws from the world that it works to open up. One could say (as Blanchot does most fully) that poetry is this withdrawal of language from the world, that is, from the uses of language that the world puts into play. Poetry is the resistance of language vis-à-vis our projects and systems. It is, as Plato knew, the refusal of philosophy. It is the density (*Dichtung*) of language, its reserve or self-refusal with respect to our efforts as logical subjects. Like the thing, language remains strange and uncommunicative, outside subjects and objects, outside the world. Language in this strange and uncommunicative sense is poetry.

Disengagement

Let us situate these topics historically. In Paris after World War II two philosophers—Jean-Paul Sartre and Emmanuel Levinas—confronted the Mallarméan/Heideggerian exteriority of language, or poetry, in ways that perhaps helped to shape (or possibly were themselves already shaped by) Blanchot's early thinking.

In *Qu'est-ce que la littérature* (1948) Sartre, evidently alluding to Mallarmé, speaks of the "crisis of language" that occurred at the beginning of this century and that "showed itself in an attack of depersonalization when the writer was confronted by words" (*QL*22/*WL*32). You and I when we speak do so from within language as from inside our bodies and therefore from inside the outside world. "The poet," by contrast, "is outside language [*hors du langage*]" (*QL*19/*WL*30), and therefore outside the world. The poet has become someone who no longer uses language. For the poet words have become things rather than signs. Even meaning in poetry is thinglike—"Having flowed into the word, having been absorbed by its sonority or visual aspect, having been thickened and defaced [*épaissie, dégradée*], it too is a thing, uncreated and eternal" (*QL*29/*WL*30).[14]

The poet works on the reverse side of language, the side which faces away from the world that it encloses like flesh: the side which leaves things unnamed. ("Deeper than any ground," says Deleuze, "is the surface and the skin" [*LdS*166/*LS*141].) Names are internal to language; they constitute the spirit of the world, its sense and meaning—and not just its sense and meaning but its action and its history. In contrast to the poet the prose writer is on the "right side" of language (*QL*26/*WL*35) where the word is "a certain particular moment of action and has no meaning outside it" (*QL*27/*WL*35). Prose is always an intervention in the world; it makes a claim upon the action and conduct of its readers to alter the world in order to bring it into synchrony with—or to remove it from of horror of— what is written. "To write," says Sartre, is "both to disclose the world and to offer it as a task to the generosity of the reader. It is to have recourse to the consciousness of others in order to make one's self be recognized as essential to the totality of being" (*QL*76/*WL*65). It's time to get on the right side; the side of prose and engagement with the world. Otherwise, why write?

In "La réalité et son ombre" (1948), Emmanuel Levinas is thought to have disagreed with Sartre, or to have missed his point. "We are not always attentive to the transformation that speech undergoes in literature"

(*IH*125/*CPP*2), says Levinas. For whatever reason one writes, there always remains a dark side that speech turns toward the world. It is true that we cannot help thinking of the work of art as a species of cognition and expression; yet, for itself, the work remains "essentially disengaged" (*IH*125/ *CPP*2). This is true even of the most mundane ("commercial and diplomatic") forms of art. However adaptable to our prose purposes, "it bears witness to an accord with some destiny extrinsic to the course of things, which situates it outside the world, like the forever bygone past of ruins, like the elusive strangeness of the exotic" (*IH*125/*CPP*2).

What is the meaning of this disengagement? It is not that the work is a product of aesthetic differentiation whereby it transcends the world; rather, the work is an interference with the functions of the world. It is not otherworldly; it is "an interruption of time by a movement going on on the hither side [*en deçà*] of time, in its 'interstices'" (*IH*126/*CPP*3). It is a mistake to try to understand the work of art by comparison with the truth of things. The work is outside the light of this truth. "It is the very event of obscuring, a descent of the night, an invasion of shadow [*Il est l'événement même de l'obscurcissement, une tombée de la nuit, un envahissement de l'ombre*]" (*IH*126/*CPP*3).

A concept coincides with what it represents, covering it over with itself. In a true concept there is no longer anything to choose between a thing and its meaning; it is the thing in the grasp of meaning. The concept is the meaning of the thing shining out; it is the voice of the thing, the announcement of its availability to the world of action and responsibility. ("What is today called being-in-the-world is an existence with concepts"— Levinas [*IH*130/*CPP*5].) An image by contrast is not a concept. It does not make anything available to us; rather it takes hold of us, grips us, makes us passive. "This is the captivation of poetry and music. It is a mode of being to which applies neither the form of consciousness, since the I is there stripped of its prerogative of assumption, of its power, nor the form of the unconscious, since the whole situation and all its articulations are in a dark light, *present*" (*IH*128/*CPP*4).

In other words: ecstasy. Whoever is confronted by an image is no longer a being-in-the-world. Likewise the thing of which it is an image is no longer an object in the world but a thing doubled, shadowed, followed by a semblance of its former self. And a semblance is opaque, not the sign of the thing but a non-thing with a density and exigency of its own. Even the thing itself can exhibit qualities of an image—for example, color, form, a certain way of occupying the light. We can look at a thing and be overcome by its exhibition of itself. Whence there is a sense in which the thing is and is not itself (nonidentical). "It is what it is and it is a stranger to itself" (*IH*133/*CPP*6): outside of itself.

The image does not go beyond the thing as its excess; it is on this side of the thing, the hither side of what it is in truth. The question is "*where* this hither side [*l'en-deçà*] . . . is situated" (*IH*137/*CPP*8). It is the place of the almost, the not quite; Levinas speaks of "the meanwhile" (*l'entre-temps*), which is the interval between neither and nor (neither one nor the other)—not a present, not a moment or an instant, but a pause, a setting of time to one side, a spacing of time, as when the work of art exhibits the world at length while time passes. Art disengages time from its passing. Art is not eternal, not outside of time; it endures on the hither side of time, in the meanwhile. "The eternal duration of the interval in which a statue is immobilized differs radically from the eternity of a concept; it is the meanwhile, never finished, still enduring—something inhuman and monstrous" (*IH*143/*CPP*11). It is in this interval, this incessant and interminable *entre-temps*, the time of the impossible, outside possibility, that Blanchot is to be found.

Indeed, in "La réalité et son ombre" Levinas sounds for all the world like Blanchot and can be taken, without much qualification, as speaking for Blanchot—until the very end when he retracts everything and, philosopher that he is, throws in with Sartre.[15] Levinas says, without equivocation: "art, essentially disengaged, constitutes, in a world of initiative and responsibility, a dimension of evasion" (*IH*145/*CPP*12). So it is necessary, if art is to have a reason, to reconceptualize it as engaged. This is Sartre's project, basically a resumption of Aristotle's.

Likewise with "La réalité et son ombre" Levinas, Hegel-like, tries to put the domain of art, if not his friend Blanchot, behind him as that which ethics as a first philosophy must overcome (we will examine later how far he succeeds). Philosophy of course—including Levinasian ethics—is also disengaged, but differently and justifiably. Recall Kant's "What Is Enlightenment?," with its figure of the philosopher as a transcendental spectator presiding over the human world, adjudicating the truth claims of such things as religion and politics. (But what's it like to be presided over, supervised, in this way?) The work of art, by contrast, is inobservant. As Levinas says, its detachment "is not the disinterestedness of contemplation but of irresponsibility. The poet exiles himself from the city. From this point of view, the value of the beautiful is relative. There is something wicked and egoist and cowardly in artistic enjoyment. There are times when one can be ashamed of it, as of feasting during a plague" (*IH*146/*CPP*12). This sounds severe, but the fear and loathing of art have always been essential to philosophical experience.

Levinas, to be sure, is more Aristotelian than Platonist. The idea is not to forbid the writing of poetry outright. Rather, the task of philosophy, or of criticism, Levinas says, is to do what Sartre tries to do for writing: to integrate "the inhuman work of the artist into the human world" (*IH*146/*CPP*12). One might compare here Jürgen Habermas's characterization of the project of modernity or enlightenment with respect to art—namely, "to bring the experiential content of the work of art into normal language." The function of art and poetry is to enrich our "life worlds and life histories . . . in a renovation of value orientations and need interpretations, which alters the color of modes of life by way of altering modes of perception."[16]

Poetry, however, is a refusal of philosophy and its regimes of normalcy. It is a refusal of the world or at least of a poetics of integration, of a politico-cultural or communicative poetics that puts poetry at the instrumental disposal of the world. Blanchot calls it "le grand refus" (*EI*46/*IC*33). It is, we shall see, a refusal, not of life, but of death.

In 1949 Samuel Beckett complained famously about painters who "never stirred from the field of the possible, however much they enlarged it. The only thing disturbed by the revolutionaries Matisse and Tal Coat is a certain order on the plane of the feasible."

> D.—What other plane can there be for the maker?
> B.— Logically, none. Yet I speak of an art turning from it in disgust, weary of its puny exploits, weary of pretending to be able, of being able, of doing a little better the same old thing, of going a little further along a dreary road.
> D.—And preferring what?
> B.— The expression that there is nothing to express, nothing with which to express, no desire to express, together with the obligation to express.[17]

One might mistake this for shameless pilfering. In "De angoisse au langage," the introduction to his first collection of essays, *Faux pas* (1943), Blanchot had written that "the writer finds himself in this more and more comical condition—of having nothing to write, of having no means of writing it, and of being forced by an extreme necessity to keep writing it" (*FP*11/*GO*5). According to Kierkegaard, *angoisse* is inspired by possibility, that is, by the infinity of possibilities and by the impossibility of choosing when confronted by the totality of everything. Following a well-plotted course, let us say that Blanchot—as, after him, Beckett—situates writing outside this totality, as if in a region of aesthetic (but also perhaps political) disenchantment.

In "De angoisse au langage" Blanchot writes: "The world, things, knowledge, are for [the writer] only reference points across the void" (*FP*11/*GO*5). It is no trouble to read this void directly back into the precedent of Flaubert's beautiful dream of "a book about nothing, a book dependent on nothing external, which would be held together by the strength of its style, just as the earth, suspended in the void, depends on nothing external for its support; a book which would have almost no subject, or at least in which the subject would be almost invisible."[18] But Blanchot's disengagement is more radical still. Any writer, he says, might well imagine "a book in which the operation of all his forces of meaning will be reabsorbed into the meaningless. (Is the meaningless that which escapes objective intelligibility? These pages composed of a discontinuous series of words, these words that do not presume any language, can always, in the absence of assignable meaning, and through the harmony or discordance of sounds, produce an effect that represents their justification . . .)" (*FP*16/*GO*11). For Blanchot, however, the event of writing is outside justification; not even aesthetics can save it. It is external to what is possible, as if its task were to inscribe the limit that possibility cannot overcome and that being cannot eliminate (not even hypothetically) since it is already the line that being draws to protect itself.

Blanchot's statement in *Faux pas*—"Nothing is [the writer's] material [*Le rien est sa matière*]" (*FP*11/*GO*5)—is not (as it would be in Flaubert's case or even in Mallarmé's) a statement of principle.[19] The writer, Blanchot says, "rejects the forms in which it [*le rien*] offers itself to him as being something [that is, as a possibility]. He wants to grasp it not in an allusion but in its own truth. He seeks it as the no that is not no to this, to that, to everything, but the pure and simple no. What is more, he does not seek it; it stands apart from all investigation; it cannot be taken as an end; one cannot propose to the will that it adopt as its end something that takes possession of the will by annihilating it: it is not, that is all there is to it; the writer's 'I have nothing to say,' like that of the accused, contains the whole secret of his solitary condition" (*FP*11/*GO*5). A pure refusal. Writing belongs to the space (or say the *entre-temps*) of the neither/nor (what Blanchot will later call *le Neutre*—neither this nor that, "the pure and simple no" or difference in itself, unopposed by identity). Granted that, at the end of history, speech or discourse surrounds the moment of writing completely or absolutely, surrounds it with all that is already said and all that can be said in all of its infinite possibility. Think of this, Hegel-like, as the totality of the spirit, or of "the world completely known and totally transformed, in the unity of knowledge [*Savoir*] which knows itself" (*ED*118/*WD*73). What interests (or obsesses) Blanchot is what is outside this whole, as if uncontainable. To write is not to belong to this totality but to experience what it excludes—a terrible alterity, which Blanchot sometimes figures, almost euphemistically, as "the unknown [*l'inconnu*]," as if the unknown were not something negative, not merely the absence of knowledge but its impossibility. There is no short way to make sense of this impossibility, unless it were to say that impossibility is an anarchic concept rather than simply a negative one.[20]

Anarchy, however, is a political as well as philosophical concept. For example, the figure of the writer as someone who responds to accusations with "I have nothing to say" is decisive, not because it might be Blanchot's self-portrait but because it registers, not for the first time, Blanchot's lifelong fascination with the complicity (if not identity) of speech and violence. *Faux pas* was published during the Occupation; presumably it was not extracted from him. But it is not difficult to see that all that Blanchot henceforth has to say about language and writing presupposes the structure of Occupation—including the dialectical opposition of Collaboration and Resistance—from which discourse (any discourse) is able to free itself only at the cost of what would justify it, as if there were ways, against all contradiction, that it could release itself from its conditions of possibility.[21]

In "Comment découvrir l'obscur" (1959), Blanchot writes: "When I speak I always exercise a relation of force [*puissance*]. I belong, whether or not I know it, to a network of powers of which I make use, struggling against the force that asserts itself against me. All speech is violence"—and perhaps the more so for not being brutal or bloody but covert and, one might say, rational and just: "Language is the undertaking through which violence agrees not to be open, but secret, agrees to forgo spending itself in a brutal action in order to reserve itself for a more powerful mastery"—say the sovereignty of the possible: of knowledge, reason, and truth. The refusal of complicity is, therefore, almost utopian in its difficulty—a thought that inspires Blanchot as follows:

> This is why (I say this in passing, and these things can only be said in passing) we are so profoundly offended by the use of force that we call torture. Torture is the recourse to violence—always in the form of a technique—with a view to making speak. This violence, perfected or camouflaged by technique, wants one to speak, wants speech. Which speech? Not the speech of violence—unspeaking, false through and through, logically the only one it can hope to obtain—but a true speech, free and pure of all violence. This contradiction offends us, and in the contact it reestablishes between violence and speech, it revives and provokes the terrible violence that is the silent intimacy of all speaking words; and thus it calls again into question the truth of our language understood as dialogue, and of dialogue understood as a space of force exercised without violence and struggling against force. (The expression "We will make him see reason" that is found in the mouth of every master of violence makes clear the complicity that torture affirms, as its ideal, between itself and reason.) (EI60–61/IC42–43)

One could say (loosely) that the refusal to speak is the starting point of Blanchot's poetics (or of his refusal of philosophy); that is, his *arche* is not resistance to forces that repress speech in the traditional manner (as in the endless historical transaction of our tyrannies—as in Leo Strauss's analysis or, for that matter, in Derrida's) but rather resistance to the extracted confession as a kind of transcendental event: resistance to the power that "wants one to speak, wants speech," that compels us to speak *its* truth under the auspices of a freedom bestowed on us—a sovereignty, according to our only philosophical definition of sovereignty, that is given first of all in the logic of language and culture, or in the total fabric that constitutes the conditions of possibility of speech as such. Blanchot's "refusal" is a refusal of these conditions, that is, a refusal to speak.[22]

The "Spiritual Fascist"

Surprisingly little has been written about the political involvement of intellectuals in France during the 1930s.[23] For a long time the standard (and still very useful) work was Jean-Louis Loubet de Bayle's study, *Les non-conformistes des années 30*, whose first chapter gives an account of La Jeune Droite, a group of anticapitalist, antidemocratic dissidents among whom he identifies Blanchot, chiefly as a contributor to *Combat*, a journal founded in 1935 by Jean de Fabrègues and Thierry Maulnier.[24] Bayle provides a brief biographical note on Blanchot, mentioning, for example, that during the Occupation Blanchot served as "Directeur littéraire de Jeune France, association culturelle subventionée par le Secrétariat général à la Jeunesse de Vichy" (p. 458). Bayle adds that after the liberation Blanchot began a second career as a novelist and critic distinguished by "his refusal of political engagement" (p. 459).

Bayle downplays the fascist character of La Jeune Droite and in general regards it as rather admirable by comparison with more extreme factions— he notes (p. 76) that in 1937 the group condemned "l'antisémitisme hitlérian," causing a rupture with self-declared fascists like Robert Brasillach, editor of *Je suis partout*, an enthusiastically pro-Nazi and violently anti-Semitic publication.[25] A very different picture of La Jeune Droite and the *Combat* group emerges from the research of Zeev Sternhell, whose studies of fascist ideology are really the first to explain convincingly and in detail why fascism had such an enormous following among European intellectuals between the wars.[26] Sternhell rejects the still widely prevailing view of fascism, that it was simply a reactionary convulsion of capitalism and imperialism and that it is completely lacking in a theoretical content of its own; on the contrary, fascism was revolutionary rather than reactionary, and more intrinsically opposed to bourgeois liberalism than to Marxism (indeed, in France during the 1930s as many fascists were from the left as from the right [*Neither Right nor Left*, p. 14]). Fascism was, in a sense, one of the first major "postmodernisms." Its ideological formation took place at the end of the nineteenth century as part of a crisis within the intellectual and political traditions of the European Enlightenment. As Sternhell characterizes it, fascism is "a new and original political culture" born of "a synthesis of organic nationalism with the antimaterialist revision of Marxism":

> This political culture, communal, anti-individualistic, and antirationalistic, represented at first a rejection of the heritage of the Enlightenment and the French Revolution, and later the creation of a comprehensive alternative, an intellectual, moral and political framework that alone could ensure the perpetuity of a human collectivity in which all strata and all classes of society would be perfectly integrated. Fascism wished to rectify the most disastrous consequences of the modernization of the European continent and to provide a solution to the atomization of society, its fragmentation into antagonistic groups, and the alienation of the individual in a free market econ-

omy. Fascism rebelled against the dehumanization that modernization had introduced into human relationships, but it was very eager to retain the benefits of progress and never advocated a return to a hypothetical golden age. Fascism rebelled against modernity inasmuch as modernity was identified with the rationalism, optimism, and humanism of the eighteenth century, but it was not a reactionary or an antirevolutionary movement in the Maurrassian sense of the term. (*The Birth of Fascist Ideology*, pp. 6–7)

Fascism, Sternhell says, was "an independent cultural and political phenomenon that was not less intellectually self-sufficient than socialism and liberalism" (*The Birth of Fascist Ideology*, p. 4), and this was so, he says, especially in France during the 1930s, where for many fascism was the only morally and intellectually coherent alternative to Marxism and liberal individualism, which had not only proved unable to respond to the crisis of capitalism that had produced a politically and economically disintegrating cultural system, but had by 1936, when the Popular Front came to power, come to constitute the established order and therefore became exactly the problem to be solved.[27] Especially among the young, but equally for "all the dissident elements in revolt against the established order, adherence to fascist ideology represented the wish to break with a particular society, with a particular way of life, with ideologies that every day demonstrated their incapacity to change the world. Fascism satisfied both a longing for revolution and a desire to preserve the past, the national history, and the cultural paraphernalia of society. Fascism wanted to do away with democracy, liberalism, and Marxism; it wanted to end the immobility and materialism of bourgeois society, yet without endangering the national collectivity" (*Neither Right nor Left*, pp. 228–29).

In France, in other words, fascism was neither a regime nor a party but an intellectual and even spiritual movement—"Spiritual Fascism" is Sternhell's term for it.[28] This description applies especially to Thierry Maulnier's *Combat* group to which Blanchot belonged, and which Sternhell describes as follows:

> At the end of the thirties, *Combat* constituted a laboratory of ideas of great influence, for though the review could lay claim to only a thousand subscribers in November 1936, ideas developed in small reviews of limited circulation soon found their way into the national press and became common currency. *Combat* developed a subtler political ideology than that of the self-declared fascists, but it is hard to see any real basic difference between them. Certainly, in its expression the ideology of *Combat* was less blatant,

less vulgar perhaps than *Je suis partout*, but one finds in *Combat* the same vehemence, the same intensity, and above all, the same intellectual content. The invectives also have a similar intention, but the campaigns of defamation and cries for murder of the Brasillach group are generally toned down and appear in a more refined fashion. To the young who were, in Brasillach's words, "caught between social conservatism and the Marxist rabble," *Combat* offered a relatively attractive alternative. The review combined the "antidemocratic and the anticonservative spirit," and, thanks to the place its contributors held in the world of letters, it exerted an influence that went far beyond the restricted circle of its readers. (*Neither Right nor Left*, p. 229)[29]

For Sternhell Maulnier is a representative case of the intellectual for whom fascism became a way of negotiating the ideological alternatives of "left" and "right," communism and capitalism, socialism and democratic individualism. We can take him as a mirror in which the young Blanchot can be glimpsed in the background, particularly in view of Maulnier's "refusal to take part in active politics" (p. 244). "Maulnier belonged," Sternhell says, "to that group of fascistically inclined intellectuals who played a major role in undermining democracy in prewar France without assuming any direct responsibility for membership in a fascist party or organization. . . . Unlike Drieu and Jouvenel, Maulnier assumed the role of a theoretician who, without indulging in party politics, nevertheless regarded himself as engaged in revolutionary political activity. In transcending 'abstract ideologies,' he felt that he was 'defining a truly realistic political action.' During the Occupation, Maulnier continued his educative task, taking care, however, never to participate in active collaboration" (p. 244).[30]

Interestingly, in passing Sternhell cites one of Blanchot's *Combat* essays, "On demand des dissidents" (1934)—Blanchot's first "manifesto" of insubordination—which contains, Sternhell says, "a perfect definition of the fascist spirit in claiming that it is a synthesis between a left that forsakes its original beliefs not to draw closer to capitalist beliefs but to define the true conditions of struggle against capitalism and a right that neglects the traditional forms of nationalism not to draw closer to internationalism but to combat internationalism in all its forms" (p. 223). This nonaligned fascism meant "the rejection not only of liberalism and socialism but also of ideological struggle, of war against dictatorial regimes," whether National Socialist or Stalinist (p. 223). "The Action Française and the Communist party, the people of the right and of the left were all held to be equally attached to the system—to the democratic parliamentary regime, to freedom of the press and of opinion—which meant that, in defending democracy, they were also defending capitalism" (p. 224). In effect, the words *neither right nor left* describe something like a "fascist refusal," namely the effort of intellectuals to stand outside the local power struggles that had characterized French politics since the beginning of the decade and therefore to define a fascism irreducible to the stereotype of street thugs financed by conservative industrialists. "Maulnier's journal," Sternhell says, "attacked democracy and materialism while taking up the defense of the spirit. . . . On this point, the fascists, quasi-fascists, and other 'nonconformists' were in complete agreement because they all had the same goal—to save the spirit and to regenerate the body of modern society" (p. 229).

One might just as well call it a fascism of the cafés and reviews—a "fascism beyond fascism," in David Carroll's perceptive phrase.[31] "This form of fascism," Sternhell says (pointedly), "was infinitely more subtle, more cultured, more sophisticated than the simplistic approach of Gustave Hervé in *La Victoire* and the brutality of *Je suis partout*. It was a fascism of people who do not die the violent death of agitators and rabble-rousers but end their days as members of the Académie Française. It is precisely this ordered, elegant, intellectual quality that has caused some authorities to doubt if this particular school of thought was authentically fascist" (p. 8).[32] But in concept and outlook, "there was no difference between Brasillach and Drieu on the one hand and Maulnier, Frabrègues, Massis, and René Benjamin on the other. We must see this clearly if we are to understand the fascist impregnation of France in the interwar period: its instruments were not only the men and movements stigmatized by collaboration with the Germans but also some of the most eminent French intellectuals of the second half of the twentieth century" (p. 247).

This helps to adjust and clarify Allan Stoekl's suggestion that Blanchot's political position, "far from being an echo of a right-wing ideology, is in fact much closer to a simple bourgeois liberalism that sees fascism and Stalinism as identical totalitarian evils" (*Politics, Writing, Mutilation,* p. 30).[33] This statement perhaps applies more completely to someone like Raymond Aron than to Blanchot, but it nevertheless captures something important. For another of the ambiguous features of the fascism of the *Combat* group was its rejection of collectivism and totalitarianism—collectivism, Maulnier wrote, "is a barbarous name for a barbarous thing."[34] Against the idea of a totalist regime exercising control from the top down by means of mass politics and technological power, Maulnier proposed something closer to Gramsci's notion of a hegemonic order whose unity emerges from the inside out, or to Yeats's vision of a culture totally integrated as a work of art.[35] In *Au-delà du nationalisme* ("Maulnier's main contribution to political thought," according to Sternhell [*Neither Right nor Left*, p. 235]), Maulnier sounds more like an antiliberal communitarian than a Mussolini touting "a state which controls all forces in nature."[36] What the *Combat* group admired in Italy or Germany was not so much the absolute power of the state as its success in achieving an antidemocratic, anticapitalist, anti-Marxist revolution that overcame the futility of class struggle (pp. 236–40).[37]

In an influential essay, Jeffrey Mehlman says that Blanchot during his association with *Combat* was an intense "propagandist for terrorism" (*Legacies of Anti-Semitism*, p. 13). The question is whether for Blanchot, as for the *Combat* group generally, violence and terror are not in some sense transcendental.[38] What stands out in Blanchot's writings from this period, as well as later, is an anarchism that desires revolution no matter what, as if (as Sternhell says in another context), "the nature of the regime that succeeded liberal democracy mattered less than ending liberal democracy" (*Neither Right nor Left*, p. 15). This comes out in what is perhaps Blanchot's most notorious essay from this period, "Le terrorisme, méthode de salut public" (*Combat* 1, no. 7 [1936]), from which the following is often cited as an example of "the verbal violence of the first Blanchot":

> It is necessary that there be a revolution because one does not modify a regime which controls everything, which has its roots everywhere. One removes it, one strikes it down. It is necessary that revolution be violent because one does not tap a people as enervated [*aveuli*] as our own for the strength and passions appropriate to a regeneration through measures of decency, but through a series of bloody shocks, a storm that will overwhelm — and thus awaken — it. This is not a totally secure undertaking [*cela n'est pas de tout repos*], but precisely what is needed is a failure of security. That is why terrorism at present appears to us as a method of public salvation [*comme une méthode de salut public*].[39]

One might compare Maulnier: "A revolutionary attitude in the most complete sense, the most demanding and the most brutal which the word can have, has become the only possible attitude for nationalism."[40]

Mehlman says that by 1942, in "Comment la littérature est-elle possible?" a Blanchot emerges who seems to have renounced not only violence and terrorism but politics, action, and discourse as well. In Mehlman's view, " 'Comment la littérature est-elle possible?' may . . . be read simultaneously as a discreet inauguration of French literary modernity and a coded farewell to plans for a French fascism in the 1930s" (p. 13). In other words, Blanchot's is a classic case of withdrawal of modernism from the conflicts of historical reality into the silence and serenity of art.[41] This is not wrong—in fact it is no trouble to read Blanchot's poetics as appropriation of the "fascist style" that simply turns upside down "the cult of energy, of dynamism and power, of the machine and speed, of instinct and intuition, of movement, willpower, and youth."[42] There is no doubt that Blanchot's poetics is antifuturist, irreducible even to the avant-garde (imagine a cult of fatigue, of weakness, of interminable processes of aging!). But having said this, it is nevertheless important to see the extent to which the gap between the "first Blanchot" of *Combat* and the disengaged, supposedly invisible post-Liberation literary man, whatever conversion or inversion may have occurred, is mediated by an anarchism in which the traditional oppositions between affirmation and negation, politics and aesthetics, engagement and disengagement, violence and nonviolence, mastery and submission, discourse and silence, metaphysics and critique, reason and madness, law and chance, philosophy and poetry, past and future, Marxism and capitalism, Action Française and the Popular Front, 1936 and 1968 (Blum and De Gaulle), are not so much resolved or overcome as, basically, *refused* as dialectical alternatives. Anarchism here is not reducible to the stereotype of the bomb-throwing nihilist; it is rather "the *generic* social and political idea that expresses negation of *all* power, sovereignty, domination, and hierarchical division, and a will to their dissolution; [it rejects] all dichotomizing concepts that on the grounds of nature, reason, history, God divide people into those dominant and those justly subordinated."[43] It is the refusal of the principle of subordination as such.[44] It is a break in the order of things.

What sort of break? What Blanchot's thought is about, what it returns to obsessively and as if from every conceivable angle, might be described as an encounter between adversaries liberated or separated from the struggle for dominance in which they are otherwise traditionally related and from which, moreover, each draws its historical self-understanding and philosophical justification. The encounter has the structure of a stop, a suspension, an interruption in the movement of forces that integrates the strong and the weak into their world-historical narrative. This liberation, however, is neither liberal nor utopian. On the contrary, it seems (as anarchism must necessarily seem) entirely dystopian. Instead of the dialectical relation of opposition that constructs the world there occurs a relation of radical alterity that Blanchot sometimes calls a nonrelation or a relation of the third kind, a relation of absolute foreignness in which adversaries, call them the one and the other, withdraw into a temporality that makes them inaccessible to any recognizable cultural form of order and signification. Here time is no longer the time of narrative. As Blanchot puts it in "Le grand refus": "we are delivered over to another time—to time as other, as absence and neutrality; precisely to a time that can no longer redeem us. . . . A time without event, without project, without possibility, an unstable perpetuity . . . in which we are arrested and incapable of permanence, a time neither abiding nor granting the simplicity of a dwelling-place" (*EI63/IC44*). Time of the exile.

My sense is that a close study of Blanchot's entire intellectual career will show that his "disengagement"—his politics of "refusal"—involves less a renunciation of violence than a relocation of it within the ongoing currents of his thinking. The "regime that controls everything, which has its roots everywhere" that Blanchot attacks in "Le terrorisme, méthode de salut public" is a constant presence in Blanchot's writings from the 1930s to *L'écriture du désastre* (1980) and *La communauté inavouable* (1983), and the idea is always to oppose or confound the regime, even if—especially if—there is no possibility of overcoming it dialectically. Notions of terror, violence, disarticulation, and fragmentation, not to mention a powerful antirationalism (of a very rational kind), remain basic features of Blanchot's poetics, where they never lose their political meaning: they are never simply aestheticized.[45] A fragment from *L'écriture du désastre*, on the anarchic power of the word cancer as a "political phenomenon," is worth citing here as a preliminary example:

> Of mythical or hyperbolic "cancer": why does it frighten us with its name, as if thereby the unnamable were designated? It claims to defeat the coded system under whose auspices, living and accepting to live, we abide in the security of a purely formal existence, obeying a model signal according to a program whose process is apparently perfectly normative. "Cancer" would seem to symbolize (and "realize") the refusal to respond: here is a cell that doesn't hear the command, that develops lawlessly, in a way that could be called anarchic. It does still more: it destroys the very idea of a program,

blurring the exchange and the message: it wrecks the possibility of reducing everything to the equivalent of signs. Cancer, from this perspective, is a political phenomenon, one of the rare ways to dislocate the system, to disarticulate, through proliferation and disorder, the universal programming and signifying power. (*ED*137/*WD*86–87)

A politics of cancer? This sounds very strange, but Blanchot does not hesitate to press the thought to its limit. Refusal is not an act, but neither is it merely a passive standing to one side. Perhaps it is something like an affliction (*l'malheur*)—one of Blanchot's most obsessive and difficult concepts—which is a condition that, "pretending to escape any cause (social, historical, or ethical) or at least always to surpass it . . . affirms itself in its dark sovereignty, in ruins" (*PD*171/*SNB*125). Refusal is not an act: like the "community of lovers" that Blanchot imagines in a late text on Marguerite Duras, refusal is a mode of alterity that the standing order cannot withstand, an exteriority where the order of things is inoperative. In *La communauté inavouable*, Blanchot writes: "The community of lovers—no matter if the lovers want it or not, enjoy it or not, be they linked by chance, by '*l'amour fou*,' by the passion of death (Kleist)—has as its ultimate goal the destruction of society" (*CI*80/*UC*48). (Interestingly, friendship for Blanchot seems symmetrical with love, and possibly more radical: it is an anarchic, non-dialectical relation, Jewish rather than Greek, that is, nomadic or unsettling rather than foundational in the sense in which Aristotle, and philosophy generally, pictures friendship.)

In any event, what seems always to have preoccupied Blanchot is the complication—derived perhaps from the experience of the Occupation—that resistance can never be straightforward nor is it perhaps even possible. In *La communauté inavouable*, Blanchot says (apropos of Bataille): "To write under the pressure of war is not to write about the war but to write inside its horizon and as if it were the companion with whom one shares one's bed (assuming that it leaves us room, a margin of freedom)" (*CI*14/*UC*4). Nice image, that. In Paris in 1943 one is, of course, free to write and to publish (who didn't? Jacques Lacan, for one), but Blanchot understands that one does so (that is, *he* did so) within and by means of the sovereignty identified euphemistically as "the pressure of war." One is (whatever one says, whatever one writes about: philosophy, art, politics, war) an operation of this sovereignty of Occupation. What is no doubt controversial is that, for Blanchot, it is not enough (retrospectively, it was not enough: this is what he comes to argue) to oppose the Occupation dialectically in the form of an active resistance, or even in the form of a passivity of subjective refusal (for example, plain silence), as if such resistance, active or passive, could never remove the subordination or reciprocity that establishes the system—as if rather it could only confirm and, in a sense, justify it.[46] This is a double bind familiar enough to us as a problem (or logic) of discourse, but Blanchot's generation was perhaps the first to get caught up in it in a concrete way.

Blanchot's anarchism is a critique of sovereignty, that is, a critique of Hegelian rationality in which the negation of the singular is the first principle of every systematic construction of the spirit. Blanchot speaks of an affirmation outside negation, outside the spirit (outside the law of non-contradiction), where anarchy is to be understood in its original sense of that which is on the hither side of principle and rule: not chaos, but that which is older than the distinction between chaos and order. As Blanchot already suggests in "De angoisse au langage," his way of thinking does not oppose the lawless to the rule-governed according to a simple dialectical equation (FP21–22/GO17–19). He does not propose an Artaud-like project of disruption or misrule which would, like the resistance of one will against another, simply duplicate the ongoing operations in which the self-same things are endlessly disseminated (oddly it is as much the madness of Artaud's undertaking as the undertaking itself that fascinates Blanchot). He comes to speak instead of *désœuvrement*, where the work of the work of writing (but not just of writing) is an unworking—a dispersal—of the forms of social, aesthetic, and political practice by which we reproduce and universalize our scheme of things.

In *L'écriture du désastre*, Blanchot recurs to one of his favorite figures, perhaps (for him) the figure of the writer as such: Melville's Bartleby the Scrivener, whose *I would prefer not to* expresses an insubordination or refusal that is prior to negation, that is, outside the dialectical struggle of Collaboration and Resistance—"an abstention which has never had to be decided upon, which precedes all decisions and which is not so much a denial as, more than that, an abdication. [Recall "De angoisse au langage": "I have nothing to say."] Bartleby gives up (not that he ever pronounces, or clarifies this renunciation) ever saying anything; he gives up the authority to speak. This is abnegation understood as the abandonment of the self, a relinquishment of identity, refusal which does not cleave to refusal but opens to failure, to the loss of being, to thought. 'I will not do it' would still have signified an energetic determination, calling forth an equally energetic contradiction" (ED33/WD17).[47] The emphatic statement "I will not do it" would still have continued the complicity, the internal kinship, between speech and violence; it would have preserved the structure of Occupation, that is, the dialectic of negation that makes domination and subordination possible (and indeed makes any other condition unimaginable). We should not, on reflection, think of Bartleby as therefore an alternative to terrorism; he could be simply an application of terrorism that cannot be contradicted, that is, defeated by the exercise of superior forces. Blanchot, at all events, thinks of him (together with the Marquis de Sade) as a figure of the revolutionary, where revolution is not so much a dialectical event of history (a reversal in the movement of forces) as a moment of insubordination that interrupts the dialectic: "At that moment there is a stop, a suspension. In that suspension, society falls apart completely. The law collapses: for an instant there is innocence; history is interrupted" (BR205).

It appears that this is the impossible moment that Blanchot lives for.

CHAPTER 2

Poetry after Hegel
A Politics of the Impossible

Sovereignty with no hold on ANYTHING, or poetry.
—Georges Bataille

What Is Poetry?

Traditional poetics, or the history of poetics, wants to know: What is poetry (or literature)?[1] The project of such a poetics would be to bring poetry under the rule or sovereignty of the concept—the rule of representational thinking or conceptual determination: in short, the rule of philosophy. Poetics describes a jurisdiction for poetry where poetry answers to the law of the concept. This is the inaugural moment for poetry. The question "What is poetry?" means: What justifies it? What gives it the right to exist?

This is the question that philosophy puts to poetry. Even Heidegger asks it ("Wozu Dichter?"—What are poets for? Where do they take us?). The end of poetry is sometimes said to occur when poetry is confronted by this question—and, as Hegel would say, subsumed by it, as if poetry were no longer an art but now only a question that its subsequent history must struggle to answer; or as if poetry were now simply a branch of philosophy, one of the things of which there could be a philosophy, something unthinkable or unintelligible apart from the philosophy that conceptualizes it.

Blanchot's first major theoretical essay, "Littérature et la droit à la mort" (1947–48), begins with a sort of parody of this Hegelian turn: "Let us suppose that literature begins at the moment when literature becomes a question" (PF293/GO21/WF300)—that is, not a question that anyone might pose, a writer or reader for example, but its own question.[2] Pointedly, Blanchot calls it "this question addressed to language . . . by language which has become literature" (PF293/GO21/WF301). As if the answer to our question (What is poetry?) might be this: it is the self-questioning of language.

But what could this mean, this (so-called) self-questioning of language? The temptation is to try to clarify this formulation in the shortest possible time. For example, we might imagine a sort of Copernican revolution where language is no longer conceptually reducible, that is, where it can no longer be objectified as a possession of the subject—a form of mediation, an expressive power, an extension of instrumental reason, a theme of linguistic or philosophical research. Language no longer belongs to the subject; instead it has come to occupy the place of the subject, as if language and subjectivity had suddenly undergone a dialectical reversal. In *Les mots et les choses* (1966), for example, Foucault speaks of the various ways in which language compensates for its objectification at the hands of a modernity that allows nothing to escape its theoretical scrutiny. One of these forms of compensation is called "literature," where language turns back on itself in "a radical intransitivity" and "addresses itself as a writing subjectivity." But for Foucault this reversal culminates in a kind of monumental serenity or Mallarméan aesthetic repose: "At the moment when language, as spoken and scattered words [*comme parole répandue*], becomes an object of knowledge, we see it reappearing in a strictly opposite modality: a silent cautious disposition of the word upon the whiteness of a piece of paper, where it can possess neither sound nor interlocutor, where it has nothing to say but itself, nothing to do but to shine in the brightness of its being."[3]

By contrast, for Blanchot language is not obviously something that takes the form of ideality, as if it were a vast self-contained superstructure of relations. Its irreducibility is of a different order and is perhaps not altogether intelligible in terms normally reserved for language. For Blanchot language is not so much an ensemble as an excess of words. Something of what this might mean comes out in the way Blanchot represents language (if that is what it is) in the fourth chapter of the revised *Thomas l'obscur* (1950), which we might figure as a sort of surrealist allegory of reading, or more exactly a surrealist allegory of poetic experience:

> Thomas stayed in his room to read. He was sitting with his hands joined over his brow, his thumbs pressing against his hairline, so deep in concentration that he did not make a move when anyone opened the door. Those

who came in thought he was pretending to read, seeing that the book was always open to the same page. He was reading . . . with unsurpassable meticulousness and attention. In relation to every symbol [*signe*], he was in the position of the male praying mantis about to be devoured by the female. They looked at each other. (*TO27/TTO25*)

The allegory (just to speculate) is of reading at the limits of reason, where consciousness begins to lose its capacity for presiding safely over its acts (imagine the text as a female predator), as if reading were no longer reducible to consciousness but were a traversal or violation of consciousness by language:

He perceived all the strangeness there was in being observed by a word as if by a living being, and not simply by one word, but by all the words that were in that word, by all those that went with it and in turn contained other words, like a procession of angels opening out into the infinite to the very eye of the absolute. Rather than withdraw from a text whose defenses were so strong, he pitted all his strength in the will to seize it, obstinately refusing to withdraw his glance and still thinking himself a profound reader, even when the words were already taking hold of him and beginning to read him. (*TO28/TTO25–26*)

Thinking of psychoanalysis, Stanley Cavell imagines "being read by a text" as a way of shaking the self loose from its isolation as an *ego cogito*.[4] Reading is to be thought of as a "reading cure" that frees the subject from its narcissism. In Blanchot's version, by contrast, reading becomes a transport or obsession, call it madness for short:

He was seized, kneaded by intelligible hands, bitten by a vital tooth [*une dent pleine de sève*]; he entered with his living body into the anonymous shapes of words, giving his substance to them, establishing their relationships, offering his being to the word "be." For hours he remained motionless, with, from time to time, the word "eyes" in place of his eyes: he was inert, captivated and unveiled. (*TO28–29/TTO26*)

"Obsession," writes Levinas, "traverses consciousness countercurrentwise [*à contrecourant*], is inscribed in consciousness as something foreign, a disequilibrium, a delirium. It undoes thematization and escapes any *principle*, origin, will, or *arché*, which are put forth in every ray of consciousness.

This movement is, in the original sense of the term, an-archical" (AE159/ OTB101). Obsession is a kind of madness, but not going to pieces or madness in the sense of Dionysian frenzy; rather, madness as a form of anarchy. Thomas is not deranged or disordered; he is astonishingly lucid. It is just that he is no longer a logical subject, self-identical, exercising rational control.

> And even later when, having abandoned himself and, contemplating his book, he recognized himself with disgust in the form of the text he was reading, he retained the thought that (while, perched on his shoulders, the word *He* and the word *I* were beginning their carnage) there remained within his person which was already deprived of its senses obscure words, disembodied souls and angels of words, which were exploring him deeply. (*TO*29/*TTO*26)

As if language were outside our concepts, inaccessible to subjectivity as an instrument of mediation, but not outside our passive, porous corporeality.

Imagine reading as an experience of this corporeality, not so much an out-of-body experience as a permeation of our body by words.[5] Of course one could take this as a form of inspiration—"disembodied souls and angels of words" reincarnating themselves in an abandoned subject, or in a body dispossessed of its inhabitant. But it is not as if these disembodiments were emissaries from a transcendental spirit. Thomas experiences them as a presence without substance or identity that engages him in a dialectical struggle in which he is himself turned into something strange (without substance or identity—this transformation occurs repeatedly in Blanchot's fiction): "He was locked in combat with something inaccessible, foreign [*d'étranger*], something of which he could say: That doesn't exist . . . and which nevertheless filled him with terror as he sensed it wandering about in the region of his solitude" (*TO*30/*TTO*27). If we ask what this terrifying, nonexisting being is (what obsesses Thomas?), the answer is that it is neither something nor nothing—a sort of fantastic, nonobjective alterity, a pure exteriority that Thomas experiences as a radical dislocation:

> He saw it, a horrifying being which was already pressing against him in space and, existing outside time, remained infinitely distant. Such unbearable waiting and anguish that they separated him from himself. A sort of Thomas left his body and went before the lurking threat. His eyes tried to look not in space but in duration, and in a point of time which did not yet exist. His hands sought to touch an impalpable and unreal body. It was such

POETICS OF THE OUTSIDE

a painful effort that this thing that was moving away from him and trying to draw him along seemed the same to him as that which was approaching unspeakably. (TO31/TTO27–28])

Like a frightened animal, Thomas retreats under his bed—"a place where he felt he belonged more properly than in himself" (TO32/TTO28): "It was in this state that he felt himself bitten or struck, he could not tell which, by what seemed to him to be a word, but resembled rather a gigantic rat, an all-powerful beast with piercing eyes and pure teeth" (TO32/ TTO28).

An allegory of poetic experience? It is not difficult or unusual to think of poetry in terms of the transformation of words into things. This is a basic romantic trope and mainstay of modernist aesthetics. But for Blanchot this transformation is not a formal process that a logic, rhetoric, or poetics might describe or produce. Poetics for Blanchot is not a theory of how poetry is possible—of how it might get made or how it might be differentiated as a genre (say from philosophy). His interest is not in the technology of linguistic performance; it is in the experience of language, where language is irreducible to the discursiveness of subjectivity, and where experience is no longer subjectivist, much less aesthetic, but is rather an experience of (or, more accurately, with) alterity or exteriority of which *Thomas l'obscur* gives us a sensational—but perhaps not all that extravagant—account.

The Aristotelian Argument

Now "Littérature et la droit à la mort" is Blanchot's first attempt to examine this experience theoretically and systematically—but first there is much to be cleared away. In an early paragraph, for example, Blanchot says that the question "What is literature?"—the philosopher's question: Aristotle's, Sartre's—"has received only meaningless answers" (PF294/ GO22/WF302). Not perhaps because we lack the wit to answer, but because of the way literature acts on the very form of the question. (In a surprising metaphor, Blanchot likens literature to a corrosive element, a *force caustique* capable of destroying the power of reflection [PF295/GO23/ WF302].) Out of courtesy to tradition one is prepared to say that writing is a productive activity, an action, an act of the mind, an exercise of power or agency, a *poiesis*, a mastery of the imaginary, creation *ex nihilo*, a breakthrough in which something new is made, a projection onto the future, an opening through which readers pass shouting in triumph. Or is it true that in consequence of writing nothing happens?

Perhaps (says Blanchot, citing Hegel's thought) nothing objective comes of writing—except the writer (PF296/GO24/WF303). Writing brings a writer into being. The appearance of the work serves mainly to underwrite this production, to justify it, but only when the work is relinquished to the world, most likely in the form of a book. A book to be sure is not a thing like a stove or some other product of labor (PF304/GO33/WF313). But at the same time it is not just nothing.

> The writer . . . produces something—a work in the highest sense of the word. He produces this work by transforming natural and human realities. When he writes, his starting point is a certain state of language, a certain form of culture, certain books, and also certain objective elements—ink, paper, printing presses. In order to write he must destroy language in its present form and create it in another form, denying books as he forms a book out of what other books are not. This new book is certainly a reality: it can be seen, touched, even read. In any case it is not nothing. (PF305/GO34/WF314)

Not nothing, but other than something: through the book, if the book is anything, something other is turned loose in the world of the same—and perhaps "I" am that other, a foreign body bumping into furniture. Blanchot says that writing is "an experiment whose effects I cannot grasp, no matter how consciously they were produced, and in the face of which I shall be unable to remain the same, for this reason: in the presence of something other, I become other. But there is an even more decisive reason: this other thing—the book—of which I had only an idea and which I could not possibly have known in advance, is precisely myself become other" (PF305/GO34/WF314).

> The book, the written thing, enters the world and carries out its work of transformation and negation. It, too, is the future of many other things, and not only books: by the projects which it can give rise to, by the undertakings it encourages, by the totality of the world of which it is a modified reflection, it is an infinite source of new realities, and because of these new realities existence will be something it was not before. (PF305/GO34/WF314)

"An infinite source of new realities": Take this as Blanchot's version of what philosophy (Aristotle, Hegel, Heidegger, Sartre, Ricoeur, Habermas) would make of poetry. The work of writing does not mirror a world already in place; it is a manifestation, a projection, a looking-glass through which time and history might pass, a species of hypothetical reflection, a speculum of world-disclosure or world-making.

Poetry makes the possible possible—this is the grand theory of mimesis. Nothing in itself, but nevertheless loose in the world, the poetic work acts on the world through the "transformation and negation" of what is actual. This is what it means to intervene between history and philosophy, between what has happened once for all and what cannot happen otherwise: a poetics of the possible. The work is a work of mediation: only through what is possible could the world make its appearance. In his first essay on René Char (1946) Blanchot had already said: "It is . . . because the poem exists that the future is possible" (PF108/WF103). The appearance of the world is what gives the work its meaning; it justifies the work, and also supersedes it, leaves it behind. The appearance of the world takes place through the transparency of the work, which is what it is only in virtue of its passing away. It is nothing until its work is completed; but at the same time it is not nothing unless over and done with, a "thing of the past," as Hegel called it. As if the work were the nothing out of which everything could be created. The work in this respect might be thought of as "a refusal to take part in the world" (PF314/GO35/WF315). As a work of mediation, it always remains outside the world that it makes possible, as if it were itself impossible.

The Mirror of Sade

So the argument is that the work of writing makes the possible possible through the negation of the actual. The work has done its work when what is possible makes its appearance. The work has no reality apart from this mediation; its task is to disappear into the appearance of the possible.

What Blanchot extracts from this argument is the idea of possibility as negation. What are the limits (or extremes) of this idea? Hegel-like, on a certain view of Hegel, we may think of writing as a movement whose most coherent or readily identifiable figure of speech is the question. The work of writing is perhaps structured as a question, or as a movement of questioning in the strong sense of a negative questioning that can only now and again be brought under control. Perhaps the task of philosophy is to achieve and maintain this control of the question in order to bring it to an end (that is, conduct it toward some conceptual purpose: "What is—?" is the teleological, that is, philosophical form of the question.

Whereas poetry implies the loss of this control. Imagine poetry as the mobility or anarchy of uncontrolled questioning, without beginning or end, questioning that cannot be brought to a stop: questioning as an endless "detour of speech" (EI28/IC21). Perhaps the difference between philosophy and poetry is this: Philosophy seeks to give reasons why (to establish that) a thing is so and not otherwise. It wants to fix things as what they are. Whereas poetry asks: Why this? Why not otherwise? (Why not nothing?) It wants to unfix things, turn them into something else, turn them loose. Philosophy settles, poetry unsettles. This seems at all events to have been Plato's thought. Blanchot in this respect represents something (perhaps everything) that Plato warned us against. For Blanchot—as in the essay "La question la plus profonde" (1960–61)—the question is no longer (or not yet) the *elenchus* of philosophy but is related to rumor, flight, detour, turning and overturning, disarrangement and dispersal. It is (like history, or anarchy) a "movement of turning and slipping away" (EI28/IC21).

During one of its principal moments "Littérature et la droit à la mort" tries to clarify this anarchic movement. It appears first of all as a movement of negation, perhaps a movement of radical negation—a negation that has run its course and no longer finds anything standing in its way, a total negation of the sort we can experience only in moments of revolution when everything is overturned, when everything is in question, that is, when everything is open and nothing is forbidden. Here revolution is not an event of mediation that brings about the millennium; it is a Bataille-like moment of nonproductive expenditure in which the revolution exhausts itself in an ecstasy of insubordination.[6] This is the classic Hegelian moment of absolute freedom (and terror) when everything, every rule of faith, every power of law and the state, is swept away and suddenly everything is free of every constraint, free of every sovereignty but that of freedom itself—a pure, unmixed, absolutely negative freedom where anything goes and nothing follows, that is, nothing is produced in the form of work or action (PF309/GO38/WF318).[7]

"Thus," says Blanchot, recurring to an old obsession, "the reign of Terror comes into being. People cease to be individuals working at specific tasks, acting here and only now: each person is universal freedom, and universal freedom knows nothing about elsewhere or tomorrow. At such times there is nothing left for anyone to do, because everything has been done"

(PF309/GO38/WF319). So the moment of revolution cannot be thought of as a moment (that is, an integer) of history. It is, on the contrary, an interruption or caesura of history—much like death or tragedy or (as Bataille would say) a moment of laughter or eroticism entirely outside the domain of knowledge or work.[8] Think of it as a disengagement of history or of the gears of history by which everything is driven into the future. Likewise it is a disengagement of the subject. "No one," Blanchot continues, "has a right to a private life any longer, everything is public"—as if turned inside out, or dispossessed of subjectivity (PF309/GO38–39/WF319). Blanchot presses this dispossession to its limit: "in the end no one has a right to his life any longer, to his actually separate and physically distinct existence. This is the meaning of the Terror. Every citizen has a right to death, so to speak: death is not a sentence [*condamnation*] passed on him, it is his most essential right so that he can proclaim himself a citizen and it is in the disappearance of death that freedom causes him to be born. Where this is concerned, the French Revolution has a meaning clearer than any other revolution. Death in the Terror is not simply a way of punishing seditionaries; rather, since it becomes the unavoidable, in some sense the desired lot of everyone, it appears as the very operation [*le travail*] of freedom in free men" (PF309–10/GO38–39/WF319).[9]

"Revolutionary action," Blanchot says, "is in every respect analogous to action as embodied in literature [notice the direction of this analogy]: the passage from nothing to everything, the affirmation of the absolute as event and of every event as absolute" (PF309/GO38/WF319).[10] Here is the Aristotelian argument at its limit (at the limit of the possible). Revolutionary action is literature as everything possible or everything otherwise turned loose in the world, where loose means sovereign in Bataille's sense of sovereignty as absolute freedom from containment within a totality ("Let us say that the sovereign or the sovereign life begins when . . . the possibility of life opens up without limit" [OC8:248/AS2:198], and where even "the limit of death is done away with"—an event symbolized by regicide [OC8:270/AS2:222]). Crucially, Blanchot thinks of the Marquis de Sade as "the writer *par excellence*" who most fully embodies this analogy of literature and revolutionary action. Never mind that Sade is isolated in the Bastille, part of the great confinement, because his madness is absolutely rational ("His writing is clear, his style natural, his language without detour. . . . He aspires to reason, and reason engrosses him" [EI323/IC217]), and so he takes rationality as far as it will go—"pushes further [than any mere rationalist] the movement that inhabits it" (*EI*325/*IC*219). This movement of rationality is the dialectical movement of the negative, which Sade inscribes in all its purity: "He is, finally, negation itself: his *œuvre* is nothing but the work of negation, his experience the act of a furious negation, driven to blood, denying other people, denying God, denying nature and, within this circle in which it runs endlessly, reveling in itself as absolute sovereignty" (*PF*311/*GO*41/*WF*321).

Sade is a special figure for Blanchot—we might think of him as a threshold figure: a window or perhaps a magic looking-glass onto the nature of things. He embodies what Blanchot calls "the madness of writing [*la folie d'écrire*]" (*EI*323/*IC*217). This is not madness as opposed to reason but madness as the excess of reason—reason, one might say, that doesn't know how to stop, a movement that cannot be brought under control and therefore brought to term. Blanchot thinks of it as an impossible exigency, a demand that cannot be satisfied. It is an "irrepressible necessity: a terrifying force of speech that [can] never be calmed. Everything must be said" (*EI*327/*IC*220). Everything must be said. This does not mean transgressing some interdiction—against, say, sodomy or blasphemy. No doubt Sade experiences pleasure "in the forceful scenes he imagines, in which all the truths of his time are flouted, where he says all that is not to be said and recommends the unspeakable." But obscene imagination or forbidden desire is not madness. "Something more violent comes to light in this frenzy of writing, a violence that cannot be either exhausted or appeased by the excesses of a superb and ferocious imagination, but that is nonetheless always inferior to the transports of a language that will not tolerate stopping any more than it can conceive of a term" (*EI*328/*IC*220–21).

"Everything must be said." In his early essay on René Char (1946), Blanchot says that for Char "poetry is revealed to itself, not only when it reflects itself but also when it decides itself and can thus speak of everything, exactly because it is itself in everything, the presence of everything, the search for totality, that it alone has the ability and right to speak of everything, to say everything" (*PF*111/*WF*106). The right to say everything. How is this possible, that is, on what is this right based? This, Blanchot says, "is the 'question' that seeks to pose itself in literature, the 'question' that is its essence" (*PF*311/*GO*41/*WF*322). The question exposes literature to its own duplicity or self-contradiction (or, as Blanchot likes to say) to its own impossibility—its hither or anarchic side.

From Violence to Anarchy

Blanchot says: "Sade is negation itself" (PF311/GO41/WF321). It is important to understand that negation here is a dialectical concept, and that Sade is Blanchot's stand-in for Hegel. Blanchot concedes that, to be sure, "Sade is not Hegel. . . . Nonetheless, I see no anachronism in calling dialectical, in the modern sense of this term, the essentially sadistic pretension to found the reasonable sovereignty of man upon a transcendent power of negation" (EI327/IC220). This was indeed Sade's deepest philosophical insight: "man's sovereignty is based on a transcendental power of negation" (LS36/BR89).[11] The power to say everything is just this transcendental power of negation. For Blanchot, this power is nothing other than language (on a certain view of language).

What happens when we speak? Speaking a language in the sense of predication, saying something about something, identifying this as that, propositional or representational thinking, conceptualization or concept formation, squaring things with their concepts: in other words, naming, signifying, asserting, describing, discursive reasoning—whatever you call the work of language, it is (Hegel-like, on Alexandre Kojève's reading of Hegel) a dialectical activity or movement of negation in which things are annihilated and replaced with their meanings.[12] In "Le grand refus" (1959), Blanchot describes the work of language as "the speech of death": "Language is of a divine nature," Blanchot writes, "not because it renders eternal by naming, but because, says Hegel, 'it immediately overturns what it names in order to transform it into something else,' saying of course only what is not, but speaking precisely in the name of this nothingness [néant] that dissolves all things, it being the becoming speech of death itself and yet interiorizing this death, purifying it, perhaps, in order to reduce it to the unyielding work of the negative through which, in an increasing combat, meaning comes toward us, and we toward it" (EI49/IC35).

In other words, things pay a high price for their intelligibility. Blanchot calls this "speech of death" the "beginning of the life of the mind [le commencement de la vie de l'esprit]" (EI49/IC35). In "Littérature et la droit à la mort," Blanchot (still thinking of Sade) calls it murder:

> I say, "This woman." Hölderlin, Mallarmé, and all poets whose theme is the essence of poetry have felt that the act of naming is disquieting. A word may give me its meaning, but first it suppresses it. For me to be able to say,

44

'This woman' I must somehow take her flesh and blood reality away from her, cause her to be absent, annihilate her. The word gives me the being, but it gives it to me deprived of being. The word is the absence of that being, its nothingness, what is left of it when it has lost being—the very fact that it does not exist. Considered in this light, speaking is a curious right. (*PF*312/*GO*41–42/*WF*322)

Considered in this light, as a movement of negation, speaking is indeed a curious right: a right to death, that is, not just a license to kill as if some law, some right to life, were being suspended for special reasons; rather the right to death is foundational, the first principle (*arche*), the law of laws, the meaning of law, the law that underwrites the just and rational order of things, the condition of every possibility, that which makes all things lucid and plain, transparent to consciousness, intelligible and therefore speakable, the origin of philosophy and science, of politics and culture, of art and beauty—and of literature: "Literature contemplates itself in revolution, it finds its justification in revolution, and if it has been called the Reign of Terror, this is because its ideal is indeed that moment in history, that moment when [quoting Hegel] 'life endures death and maintains itself in it' in order to gain from death the possibility of speaking and the truth of speech" (*PF*311/*GO*41/*WF*321–22).[13]

Imagine Nietzsche turned inside out: it is not so much that God is dead as that death is God.[14] (In *L'écriture du désastre* we read: "From the death of God it follows that death is of God" [*ED*143/*WD*91].) Language is of a divine nature, Blanchot says, not because it brings things into being in the act of naming them, but because the act of naming annihilates the being of things by transforming them into concepts (where the word concept [*Begriff*], entails the idea of grasping [*greifen*], as if comprehension were something like killing a thing with our bare hands).[15] (Compare Bataille: "Negativity is action, and action consists in taking possession of things" [*OC*:385/*G*136].)

The speech of death: "death speaks in me" (*PF*313/*GO*43/*WF*323). This is the language of command, of conceptual mastery, the subjection of persons and things, their confinement within the realm of consciousness: "My speech is a warning that at this very moment death is loose in the world, that it has suddenly appeared between me, as I speak, and the being I address: it is there between us as the distance that separates us, but this distance is also what prevents us from being separated, because it contains the condition for all understanding. Death alone allows me to grasp what I want to attain; it exists in words as the only way they can have meaning. Without death, everything would sink into absurdity and nothingness" (*PF*313/*GO*43/*WF*323–24). As if consciousness were a vast crypt (Blanchot in fact calls it "an immense hecatomb" [*PF*313/*GO*42/*WF*323]): but it is a crypt from which darkness has been eliminated, not the crypt in which Lazarus is wrapped in his burial clothes; rather a crypt in which everything is transparent and luminous, a place where spirits walk, conversing lucidly and without effort in the propositional style of philosophical discourse.

It is possible to read this part of "Littérature et la droit à la mort" as a gloss on the first section of Heidegger's "The Origin of the Work of Art," called "Thing and Work," in which philosophy's history-long attempt to clarify *das Ding* conceptually is understood as "an assault upon the thing [*ein Überfall das Ding heraus*]" (*GA*5:15/*PLT*30).[16] The thing, however, resists clarification: it withholds itself from its concepts. The self-refusal of the thing is, for Heidegger, part of its nature. In the nature of things *das Ding* is "strange and uncommunicative" (*GA*5:17/*PLT*32), outside the grasp of the speakable: outside language.

Heidegger has poetry taking the side of things. And also Blanchot: What is it *not* to call a cat a cat? What is it to refuse the power of the negative, to refuse language? To refuse the light? This is *le grand refus* [*EI*46/*IC*33]: "the refusal of death"—of work, of art, of philosophy, of the world. "This formulation," says Blanchot, "explains why literature's ideal has been the following: to say nothing, to speak in order to say nothing" (*PF*314/*GO*43/*WF*324).[17] Say nothing, speak and say nothing, not so much perhaps in the manner of Flaubert, dreaming of his ideal book, or even of Mallarmé, disappearing into *le Néant*, as of Georges Bataille: "Poetry was simply a detour: through it I escaped the world of discourse, which had become the natural world for me; with poetry I entered a kind of grave where the infinity of possibility was born from the death of the logical world" (*OC*3:222/*I*163).[18]

Language belongs to the day ("its kingdom is day and not the intimacy of the unrevealed" [*PF*316/*GO*45/*WF*326]); but literature is of the night. Language is the speech of death ("In speech what dies is what gives life to speech; speech is the life of that death. . . . What wonderful power" [*PF*314/*GO*46/*WF*327]); but literature is the refusal of power. It is the not-saying of language. "Language perceives that its meaning derives not from what exists but from its own retreat before existence, and it is tempted to proceed no further than this retreat, to try to attain negation in itself and to make everything of nothing. If one is not to talk about things except to say what makes them nothing, then to say nothing is really the only hope of saying everything about them" (PF314/GO44/WF324–25). Everything must be said—but how is this possible? The answer is: only through impossibility: "Say nothing, speak and say nothing."

Almost all of the essays gathered into *La part du feu* are obsessed (tortuously) with the manifold contradictions that constitute this poetic exigency ("Language is possible only because it strives for the impossible" [PF30/WF22]; "language is haunted by its own impossibility" [PF77/WF72]; "the poem claims to include its impossibility and its non-realization in its very existence" [PF108/WF204]; "the language of the poem is nothing but the retention, the transmission, of its own impossibility" [PF128/WF126]). The question is, how to make poetry out of the instrument of death? "How can I recover it, how can I turn around and look at what exists *before*, if all my power consists of making it into what exists *after*?" For Blanchot, the task of poetry is, in so many words, to preserve the world of things from the very stuff that it (poetry) is made of. Here is how Blanchot thinks of it: "The language of literature is a search for this moment which precedes literature. Literature usually calls it existence: it wants the cat as it exists, the pebble *taking the side of things*, not man, but the pebble, and in this pebble what man rejects by saying it, what is the foundation of speech and what speech excludes in speaking, the abyss, Lazarus in the tomb and not Lazarus brought back into the daylight, the one who already smells bad, who is Evil, Lazarus lost and not Lazarus saved and brought back to life" (PF316/GO46/WF327). As if the question of poetry were: *Comment ne pas parler?* How not to speak? (As if the poet were a negative theologian with respect to things rather than to God.)

Interestingly, Blanchot rewrites the parable of Lazarus as a story of Orpheus and Eurydice, where Orpheus renounces the power that would restore Eurydice to the day when he turns round to look at her as she is in the night. Poetry is this renunciation. Borrowing from Jean-Michel Besnier, we can call it a "politics of the impossible"—an anarchism—in which the refusal of negation is a refusal of the rule of subjectivity, a renunciation of possession and ownership of the world.[19] It is a renunciation of the sovereignty of the self in favor of the sovereignty or freedom of the other, that is, a renunciation of a Kantian freedom of the subject in favor of an ontological freedom in which things are allowed to exist without ref-

47

erence to consciousness and its cognitive or conceptual totalities.

Or, following Reiner Schürmann, we can think of poetry as "a passage from violence to anarchy."[20] Schürmann asks: "What is to be done at the end of metaphysics?" And the answer is, not nothing—it is not that action must be abandoned in behalf of disengaged reflection or indifference to the world; rather, action must now take the form of a renunciation of the violence of conceptual thinking (and of all that follows from it in the form of strategic and instrumental reasoning exercising control of the unruly). "By vocation and design, conceptual language places itself in a position of attack" (p. 275). Poetry, however, is not a species of conceptualization; on the contrary, poetry constitutes what Schürmann calls "the practical a priori capable of subverting systematic violence," precisely because in its refusal of discursive sovereignty it consists "in letting things enter their world in constellations essentially rebellious to ordering" (p. 279).

It bears repeating that renunciation is not the renunciation of action; rather, action now means the refusal of subordination, including the subordination of passivity to the assertiveness of the subject. Later Blanchot will try to clarify the concept of a passivity that is outside the dialectical alternatives of action and passion—a passivity that is not the mere negation of action. For him, insubordination cannot be located within the framework of a competition of forces that the movement of negation constructs; it is, in a way that his poetics was designed explain, a refusal of philosophy.[21]

Existence without Being

Poetry (or literature) is on the hither (anarchic) side of negativity, that is, outside of language and subjective sovereignty.

Or rather it is and it isn't. Blanchot can only speak of the "two slopes" of literature (PF318/GO48/WF330). He might have thought of literature as breaking in two. He recognizes at all events that much of literature is composed in Aristotle's name. Much of literature in fact appropriates "the movement of negation by which things are separated from themselves and destroyed in order to be known, subjugated, communicated" (PF319/GO48/WF330). This is literature housed within the organon; it is a species of rationality which brings the constructive or conceptualizing power of language under control. Here is literature as "meaningful prose. Its goal is to express things in a language that designates things according to what they mean. This is the way everyone speaks; and many people write the way we speak" (*PF*321/GO51/WF332). Here is literature that philosophy can live with. But poetry is this literature in crisis. Poetry is the withdrawal of literature from language; or rather it is the withdrawal of language from the organon: language outside of language—which is what Blanchot, after Mallarmé, calls *l'écriture*.

Mallarmé's poetics is the first to register this crisis; his poetry is the first to inscribe the movement of the negative as it reverses or interrupts itself in a double negative: chance abolishing chance, language abolishing discourse. Blanchot, speaking as if in Mallarmé's voice, writes: "My hope lies in the materiality of language, in the fact that words are things too, are a kind of nature. . . . A name ceases to be the ephemeral passing of nonexistence and becomes a concrete ball, a solid mass of existence; language, abandoning the sense, the meaning which was all it wanted to be, tries to become senseless. Everything physical takes precedence: rhythm, weight, mass, shape, and then the paper on which one writes, the trail of ink, the book" (*PF*316–17/GO46/WF327).[22] As if there were more to language than language, something irreducible, nonconvertible, nonproductive. In poetry, everything that negation excludes—the outside of language—returns to the surface.[23]

What is this outside? "By turning itself into an inability to reveal anything," Blanchot says, "literature is attempting to become the revelation of what revelation destroys" (*PF*317/GO47/WF328). Literature is a "refusal to mean anything" in behalf of what signification otherwise feeds on (*PF*317/ GO47/WF328):

> Literature is a concern for the reality of things, for their unknown, free, and silent existence; literature is their innocence and their forbidden presence, it is the being which protests against revelation, it is the defiance of what does not want to take place outside [that is, in the daylight]. In this way, it sympathizes with darkness, with aimless passion, with lawless violence, with everything in the world that seems to perpetuate the refusal to come into the world. In this way too, it allies itself with the reality of language, it makes language into matter without contour, content without form, a force that is capricious and impersonal and says nothing, reveals nothing, simply announces—through its refusal to say anything—that it comes from night and will return to night. (*PF*319/GO49/WF330)

If, therefore, on the one side, the work of writing makes the possible possible by negating what is actual, it also, on the other side, "through its refusal to say anything," withdraws from the possible as from light into darkness, day into night, law into anarchy: into impossibility. All the people we call poets respond to this impossibility: "they are interested in the reality of language, because they are not interested in the world, *but in what things and beings would be if there were no world*" (PF321/GO51/WF333; italics added). Poetry is not part of the work of the spirit; it is anarchic with respect to this work, siding with things in their materiality and opacity. "If this is what poetry is like," Blanchot adds, "at least we will know why it must be withdrawn from history, where it produces a strange insectlike buzzing in the margins" (PF321/GO51–52/ WF333).

Imagine poetry not as song but as the murmur of insects, an anonymous and incessant rustling of discourse just this side of earshot. It is not easy to say what sort of work results from the abandonment of what is possible. Samuel Beckett's *L'innomable*, one imagines, where the consciousness that ordinarily inhabits language as a speaking subject, a site of linguistic competence, loses its subjectivity, but not its consciousness. Wonderfully before the fact, Blanchot produces a poetics of the Unnamable when he calls literature "that experience through which the consciousness discovers its being in its inability to lose consciousness, in the movement whereby, as it disappears, as it tears itself away from the meticulousness of an I, it is recreated beyond unconsciousness as an impersonal spontaneity" (PF320/GO50/WF331). In *L'innomable* language occupies the site of the subject, dispersing consciousness along its endless recirculation of words—"this endless resifting of words without content, this continuousness of speech through an immense pillage of words, is precisely the profound nature of a silence that talks" (PF320/GO50/WF332). As day passes into night we lose ourselves and the world, but not consciousness. The Unnamable is outside this movement of the day. He can neither sleep nor die, nor can he ever stop talking. ("One can," Blanchot says, "accuse language of having become an interminable resifting of words, instead of the silence it wanted to achieve" [PF320/GO50].)

We should not prematurely think that the two sides of literature constitute separate genres of writing; possibly there is something in all writing that is in excess of every form, not a power that form cannot bring under control but rather a weakness, an impotence, that form cannot overcome, or perhaps something that form cannot protect itself from by rounding itself off, as though writing were not the unfolding or mediation of form but a weakness invading it—an ontological weakness, an impotence of being rather than of consciousness or the logos.

The novel shows the power of literature to represent the world in all of its intimate detail; but the novel's form cannot seal itself off from what is anarchic with respect to the world. "A novelist [*romancier*] writes in the most transparent prose, he describes men we could have met ourselves and actions we could have performed; he says his aim is to express the reality of the human world the way Flaubert did" (PF322/GO52/WF333–34). But there is always something outside the novelist's grasp, something unkillable. Blanchot calls it *existence without being*. "In the end," says Blanchot, "[the novelist] has only one subject. . . . The horror of existence deprived of the world, the process through which whatever ceases to be continues to be . . . whatever dies encounters the impossibility of dying. This *process* is day which has become fatality, consciousness whose light is no longer the lucidity of the vigil but the stupor of lack of sleep, it is existence without being, as poetry tries to recapture it behind the meaning of words, which reject it" (PF322/GO52/WF334).[24]

It is this last line that we need to try to understand: "existence without being, *as poetry tries to recapture it behind the meaning of words.*" In "Littérature et la droit à la mort" the notion of existence without being is still largely figured by turning Hegel (or Kojève) upside down, or inside out. If language is the language of "death, the amazing power of the negative, or (again) freedom [*liberté*]," there is for Blanchot "nothing to prevent this power—at the very moment it is trying to understand things and, in language, to specify words—nothing can prevent it from continuing to assert itself as continually differing possibility, and nothing can stop it from perpetuating an irreducible *double meaning,* a choice whose terms are covered over with an ambiguity that makes them identical to one another even as it makes them opposite" (PF330/GO61/WF343–44).

This is Blanchot crossing what will later become the orbit of a certain kind of deconstruction (deconstruction as a kind of logic of plural or hypersignification, speaking many languages at once). But it is important to see that Blanchot is not a poststructuralist before the fact. His concerns are more ontological than logical or linguistic, and so over and against the conceptual background of a language or speech of death he wants to clarify the impossibility of poetry as an "impossibility of dying [*l'impossibilité de mourir*]" (PF325/GO55/WF337)—or, as Blanchot will more accurately express it in *L'espace littéraire*, the *interminability* of dying, which onto-logically is a condition of absolute powerlessness, of consciousness de-prived of subjectivity, of a patience more passive than all passivity: an ec-stasy of waiting as within an interruption that cannot be overcome.[25]

Heidegger thought of the poet as an outcast in the Between (*Zwischen*) between Being and beings, gods and mortals (GA4:46/EB288), but he did not think very much about what this might mean. Blanchot in effect tries to think what Heidegger left unthought, namely that "literature seems to be allied with the strangeness of that existence which being has rejected and which does not fit into any category" (PF327/GO58/WF340). Exis-tence without being: existence refractory to any category of being: the *il y a*. This is, if anything is, the key to Blanchot's entire *œuvre*, from the *récits* of the 1930s and the various versions of *Thomas l'obscur* to *L'écriture du désastre* (1980).[26]

The *il y a*: there is. Blanchot will later call it: the Outside, the Neutral. Blanchot's first theoretical articulation of this condition occurs in an early essay, "La lecture de Kafka" (1945):

> If night suddenly is cast in doubt, then there is no longer either day nor night, there is only a vague, twilight glow, which is sometimes a memory of day, sometimes a longing for night, end of the sun and sun of the end. Exis-tence is interminable, it is nothing but an indeterminacy; we do not know if we are excluded from it (which is why we search vainly in it for something solid to hold on to) or whether we are forever imprisoned in it (and so we turn desperately toward the outside). This existence is an exile in the fullest sense: we are not there, we are elsewhere, and we will never stop being there. (PF17/WF9)

Interminable existence; existence as an exile, always elsewhere, never ar-riving. This is not a utopian existence; on the contrary, it is existence at the limit of the human. This passage certainly registers Blanchot's encounter with Bataille in the early 1940s. In *L'expérience intérieure* (1943) Bataille speaks of ecstasy as a condition achieved by the renunciation (or contesta-tion) of knowledge, action, work, or the whole idea of *project* whereby the subject constructs its experiences out of the future. Ecstasy is a condition of being at the extreme limit of the possible where nothing further can be projected—and this, as Bataille acknowledges in *L'expérience interieure*, is Blanchot's territory, or rather the space he traverses nomadlike (OC5:18–21/IE6–9). Inner experience does not occur in introspection but rather in the exposure or expenditure of the subject in communication, where communication is a species of contagion—"contagions of energy, of movement, of warmth, or transfers of elements, which constitute inevitably the life of your organized being. Life is never situated at a particular point: it passes rapidly from one point to another (or from multiple points to multiple points), like a current or like a sort of streaming of electricity. Thus, there where you would like to grasp your timeless substance, you encounter only a slipping" (OC5:111/IE94). However, for Bataille ecstasy is still linked to struggle (a Sadean *contra-attaque* against Hegel, but of course not just against Hegel: it is a dialectical struggle of base matter against the spiritual homogeneity or repose of the world).[27] For Blanchot, however, ecstasy is neutral, that is, it is *not* a form of counter-aggression or violence against violence but a refusal of the dialectic. Closer to Blanchot would be Levinas's Blanchot-like account of *fatigue*, which is a condition that opens an interval in time—a "time-lag," Levinas calls it, in which nothing is possible and which can only (and, for Levinas, *must*) be overcome by rest (DEE51/EE35–36). Rest is the foundation of activity, of *hypostasis* or the upsurge of existence (DEE52/EE35–36). For Blanchot, however, fatigue is *restless*; it is a mode of existence without repose, that is, without being—anarchic existence, existence without why, irreducible to the principial progress of founding and building a world (in a word: it is *exile*).

Existence without repose (without being): but whose existence? Poets, Blanchot has said, "are interested in the reality of language, because they are not interested in the world, but in what things and beings would be if there were no world" (PF321/GO52/WF333). How to characterize the nature of this interest? Aesthetic? ethical? political? philosophical? Each of these concepts has its application in this context. Joseph Libertson, discussing "Littérature et la droit à la mort," writes: "Literature does not change the world, as does an action rooted in the negative. Instead, it reveals the paradoxical and contaminated subsistence of a world underneath negation." Blanchot, Libertson says, "accepts the notion of literature as an anomalous, inauthentic instance on the margins of the 'real' world of totalization and negation" (*Proximity*, pp. 70–71). This is not wrong. But the point of view here is still that of a subjectivity vis-à-vis the world, a subjectivity deprived, to be sure, of its sovereignty over the world; and there is more to existence than the world. Poetry is not a species of worldly action, but only in the sense that it is outside the alternatives of center and margin, action and contemplation, engagement and disengagement, work and speech. Poetry for Blanchot is outside subjectivity and therefore outside the world that the subject creates for itself; but it is not therefore an autonomous entity floating in Flaubert's or Mallarmé's void. On the hither side of language conceived as an instrument of mediation or world-making, poetry, Blanchot says, "dispenses with the writer: it is no longer this inspiration at work, this negation asserting itself, this idea inscribed in the world as though it were the absolute perspective of the world in its totality. It is not beyond the world, but neither is it the world itself: it is the presence of things before the *world* exists, their perseverance after the world has disappeared, the stubbornness of what remains when everything vanishes and the dumbfoundedness of what appears when nothing exists" (PF317/GO47/WF328).

So in Blanchot's poetics poetry is anarchic rather than linguistic: it is a condition rather than a kind of work, namely, the presence of things before the world exists.

Still, poetry is not beyond (*pas au-delà*) the world. It is, for example, still made of words. However, it makes sense to say that poetry is made of words *but is not a use of them*. Poetry is not a species of mediation; it is anterior to the system of discourse and labor that constructs a world. Of course, it happens (it has already come to pass) that the world exists. Since death has done its work, the sovereign order, totality in all its forms, is complete. How does poetry stand with respect to this totality? From the standpoint of the whole, as Hegel thought, poetry is *vergangen* or obsolete. But, against Hegel, Blanchot's thought is that poetry survives the world, that is, it belongs to a different temporality from that which brings the world to completion—a temporality, Blanchot wants to say, in which death (like the messiah) never arrives.

"Littérature et la droit à mort" concludes with a discussion of ambiguity—"Literature," Blanchot says, "is language turning into ambiguity" (PF328/GO59/WF341). However, this is not just the ambiguity of a discourse in which something means too much, or in which the meaning of something is undecidable. It is not just a logical impasse. Indeed, one could as well say: Literature is language turning into something that is no longer language, that is, no longer a productive system. Ambiguity here means: a temporality that is irreducible to every narrative, whether a narrative of things coming into being or coming to pass, one thing following another, or a narrative that shows the structure, the beginning and end, of history. Imagine a temporality that interrupts the end-of-history narrative—call it (for now) a temporality of the impossible.

"Littérature et la droit à la mort" is a subversive gloss on Hegel's conception of the life of the spirit, which "supports death and maintains itself in it." Death is "the amazing power of the negative . . . through which existence is detached from itself and made significant" (PF330/GO59/WF343). Or, as Blanchot amplifies it, "If we call this power negation or unreality or death, then presently death, negation, and unreality, at work in the depths of language, will signify the advent of truth in the world, the construction of intelligible being, the formation of meaning" (PF330–31/GO61/WF344). But for Blanchot, "a death that results in being represents an absurd madness, a malediction of existence" [PF331/GO62/WF344]. Against Hegel, Blanchot imagines existence that occurs on the hither side of death: death never quite arrives to put an end to life as Blanchot imagines it. The nonarrival of death: the impossibility of dying.

The task now will be to understand the link between poetry and this impossibility.

CHAPTER 3

Il y a, il meurt

The Theory of Writing

> When we look at the sculptures of Giacometti, there is a
> vantage point where they are no longer subject to the fluc-
> tuations of appearance or to the movement of perspective.
> One sees them absolutely: no longer reduced, but with-
> drawn from reduction, irreducible, and, in space, masters of
> space through their power to substitute for space the unmal-
> leable, lifeless profundity of the imaginary. This point,
> whence we see them irreducible, puts us at the vanishing
> point [à l'infini] ourselves; it is the point at which here co-
> incides with nowhere. To write is to find this point. No one
> writes who has not enabled language to maintain or provoke
> contact with this point.
>
> —L'espace littéraire

The Essential Solitude

The novelist, Blanchot says, turns aside in horror of an existence outside of
being, an existence without objects: existence that cannot be objectified by
a subject but which invades the subject, turning it inside out, depriving it
of refuge. Whereas poetry sides with this existence: with the *il y a*. Poetry
is without refuge.

In his writings from the early 1950s, collected in *L'espace littéraire*
(1955), Blanchot tries to clarify a claim of radical exteriority—the claim
that "to write . . . is to withdraw language from the world, to detach it from
what makes it a power to which, when I speak, it is the world that declares
itself, the clear light of day that develops through tasks undertaken, through

action and time" (*EL*21/*SL*26). Withdraw where? Not into any Kantian privacy; not into any interiority. The withdrawal from the world, from the politics of power and action (work and fighting), is a departure into an exile in which inwardness itself is unhoused.[1]

L'espace littéraire begins with an account of "the essential solitude" (*EL*13–14/*SL*21). This is not the romantic condition of the solitary singer; it is rather very much a derivation of Heidegger's notion of the work of art as alien and uncommunicative, external to the world, all ties to human beings severed as if from the start. The solitude of the work is more essential than the solitude of the artist. Paraphrasing Heidegger, Blanchot says that the work of art is not any sort of thing at all; it is external to all categories. "What it says exclusively is this: it is [*elle est*]—and nothing more. Beyond that it is nothing. Whoever wants to make it express more finds nothing, finds that it expresses nothing" (*EL*14–15/*SL*22).[2] The work is not a work of mediation. In Heidegger's idiom, its work is an event: *es gibt*. The work itself as remainder remains on the hither side of this event, outside the reach of the world. It exists, but not as what is given exists: call it existence that cannot be objectified.

L'espace littéraire wants to know what happens when we enter into the essential solitude—the space: the *it is*—of the literary work. What is it to write or even to read within this space? Blanchot answers without waiting, as if it were already obvious: "The writer belongs to a language which no one speaks, which is addressed to no one, which has no center, and which reveals nothing. He may believe that he affirms himself in this language, but what he affirms is altogether deprived of self. To the extent that, being a writer, he does justice to what requires writing, he can never again express himself, any more than he can appeal to you, or even introduce another's speech. Where he is, only being [*l'être*: existence] speaks—which means that language doesn't speak any more, but is. It devotes itself to the pure passivity of being" (*EL*21/*SL*26–27). One must be careful of words here. It needs to be stressed that "being" here is not Heidegger's Being of beings, but only the sheer fact or event of existing. In the essential solitude, all subjectivity and objectivity has drained away; only existence remains.

That is, only a "pure passivity" remains, a passivity whose purity consists in its exteriority, that is, in the fact that it is outside the alternatives of action and repose; it is not the passivity of a subject who simply refuses to act, but the "passivity of being" (or, more exactly, of existence without being).

Such a passivity has to be clarified topologically as being set apart or being elsewhere (as if unfixed or unsettled).[3]

In Heidegger's version, the solitude of the work occurs in the space between Being and beings; it is the space defined neither by Being as presence nor by the presence of beings. It is not a habitation, nor is it a wilderness. It is neither an inside nor an outside but is rather outside the many-sided categories and dimensions of in and out. In this region nothing is to be counted or measured. It is outside time but not eternal; it is a space but it cannot be placed. It is aboriginal but only in the sense of being on the hither side of whatever begins or takes place: the hither side of beings and of human dwelling-places: the *es gibt*. Better to speak of it therefore as an-archic, outside of all beginnings and endings (like writing in the form of the fragment).

Blanchot calls this space, for reasons that will need to be clarified, "the indeterminate milieu of fascination" (*EL29/SL32*). Thinking temporally, it is "the opaque, empty opening onto that which is when there is no more world, when there is no world yet," as if in an interval (*entre-temps*) or interruption of being (*EL31/SL33*).

Fascination of the Exotic

In "Littérature et la droit à la mort" Blanchot had cited chapter 4 of *De l'existence à l'existant*, titled "Existence without a World," in which Levinas cites Blanchot's *Thomas l'obscur* as a narrative of the *il y a*, of "the horror of being" that deprives consciousness of its subjectivity (*DEE103/EE63*).[4] In this text Levinas speaks very much in the voice of Blanchot. He begins with reference to "the exotic reality of art" (*DEE88/EE55*). Exotic here is an ontological rather than anthropological concept: it refers to what one might call the mode of existence of the work of art, but more accurately it has to do with the existence to which the work of art exposes us: what Levinas calls "existence without existents," and Blanchot "existence without being"—existence that is external to anything existing, but not as an outside is external to an inside, nor as a domain is to its occupants.

It happens that the materiality of art exposes us to this radical exteriority, which Levinas tries to capture by means of the idiomatic expression *il y a*: there is—"this impersonal, anonymous, yet inextinguishable 'consummation' of being, which murmurs in the depths of nothingness itself" (*DEE93–94/EE57*)."[5] The *il y a* is the surreal equivalent of Heidegger's cornucopian *es gibt* ("of which Being itself stands in need to come into its own [*in sein Eigenes*] as presence").[6] The *il y a* is not anything, but neither is it nothing: it is being from which everything has been withdrawn: being without substance and without light. The *il y a* is nocturnal: not a night that passes into day but night which excludes every passage, including the movement of day into the night that brings sleep. Sleep enables us to finesse the night. By contrast the *il y a* is the interminable, incessant night of insomnia, a night of pure vigilance without anticipation or release, a night that persists through the day. Insomnia is the experience of impossibility, not just the impossibility of sleep but the impossibility of the day. (René Char, interestingly, says: "Poetry lives on perpetual insomnia.")[7] Blanchot calls it "the *other* night," the night which is no longer an interval within the day-to-day; it is a "muffled whispering" that will not go away (*EL221/SL168*). In this other night, nothing occurs, nothing can be done. It is the time of pure passivity, of waiting without beginning or expectation.

It is not easy to think of the *il y a* as an event or condition that one lives through or experiences. It has no temporal modality (anyhow not one we know how to conceptualize); it is a space from which all tangible volume and surface have been evacuated, a "space without place" (place being a category of sleep and rest) (*PD94/SNB66*). Levinas speaks of the *il y a* as a presence that lurks, an undifferentiated menace, or again as an incessant murmur, a rustling without location which noise cannot suppress. "Before this obscure invasion it is impossible to take shelter in oneself, to withdraw into one's shell. One is exposed" (*DEE96/EE59*). The *il y a* deprives consciousness of its interiority and security (its subjectivity, its shelter); and of course there is no alternative of flight: no exit (*DEE97–98/EE60*).

Response to the *il y a*, says Levinas, is one of horror: "In horror a subject is stripped of its subjectivity, of its power to have a private existence . . . horror turns the subjectivity of the subject, its particularity *qua* entity, inside out. It is a participation in the *there is*, in the *there is* which returns in the heart of every negation, in the *there is* that has 'no exits.' It is, if we may say so, the impossibility of death, the universality of existence even in its annihilation" (*DEE100/EE61*).[8] Horror of the *il y a* is adumbrated, Levinas says, in Shakespearean tragedy. Macbeth in the extremity of his crime confronts neither God nor Satan but existence as a boundaryless confinement. Horror is not terror; it does not produce recoil or flight.[9] It is the highest form of fascination: ecstasy—in the sense of the evacuation of the subject. Blanchot asks (speaking of the image): "What happens when what is seen

59

imposes itself upon the gaze, as if the gaze were seized, put in touch with its appearance?" In fascination, the subject is reduced to a pure passivity where subjectivity suffers a reversal, a dispossession, as if stolen away: "What happens is not an active contact, not the initiative and action which there still is in real touching. Rather, the gaze gets taken in, absorbed by an immobile movement and a depthless deep" (*EL*28–29/*SL*32). In fascination, seeing no longer sees what it sees but is swallowed up by it.

In fascination everything is withdrawn from the world, including our gaze (and with it our power of language). "What fascinates us robs us of our power to give sense. It abandons its 'sensory' nature, abandons the world, draws back from the world, and draws us along. It no longer reveals itself to us, yet it affirms itself in a presence foreign to the temporal present and to presence in space" (*EL*29/*SL*32). Fascination is not a cognitive relation; it deprives us of our concepts and so leaves us powerless to grasp what we see. It is our seeing that is grasped and held: neutralized. Fascination induces an essential solitude; it is "solitude's gaze" (*EL*29/*SL*32). To enter into this gaze is to enter into the neutral, impersonal space of the *il y a*.[10]

This is aesthetic experience turned inside out. It occurs when the surface of the work is no longer distant and observable, certainly not transparent or receptive; rather, the work becomes an imposition, an implacable density— "the materiality of being," Levinas calls it—that bears down on us as if from all sides, preventing escape. Levinas gives the example of cubist art:

> The breakup of continuity even on the surface of things, the preference for broken lines, the scorning of perspective and of the "real" proportions between things, indicate a revolt against the continuity of curves. From a space without horizons, things break away and are cast toward us like chunks that have weight in themselves, blocks, cubes, planes, triangles without transitions between them. They are naked elements, simple and absolute, swellings or abscesses of being. In this falling of things down on us objects attest their power as material objects, even reach a paroxysm of materiality. Despite the rationality and luminosity of these forms when taken in themselves a painting makes them exist in themselves, brings about an absolute existence in the very fact there is something which is not in its turn an object or a name, which is unnameable and can only appear in poetry. (*DEE*91/*EE*56–57)

Here materiality is no longer the stuff of mediation, the shapes beings take. "The discovery of the materiality of being is not a discovery of a new quality, but of its formless proliferation. Behind the luminosity of forms, by which beings already relate to our 'inside,' matter is the very fact of the *il y a*" (DEE91/EE57).

It is important not to miss Levinas's passing remark: "there is something which is not . . . an object or a name, which is unnameable and can only appear in poetry." This "something" is Blanchot's obsession. Blanchot's question is what sort of thing poetry would have to be in order to be that (and only that) in which this materiality of being, this anonymous, oppressive, invasive paroxysm of existence, this implacable density of the *il y a*, can appear. Appear, that is, in the form (the fascination or horror) of language. "My hope," said Blanchot in "Littérature et la droit à la mort," "lies in the materiality of language, in the fact that words are things, too, are a kind of nature" (PF316/GO46/WF327). As in Heidegger's analysis, just insofar as words are things they are worldless, outside the world. Speaking a language is an appropriation of words as well as of things. In speaking we introduce words into the world along with the things that we designate or conceptualize. In speaking we thin them out, make them transparent, spiritual. Blanchot would say: we turn them into ghosts. Poetry, whatever else it is, is not (not always, not ever?) this sort of speaking. Blanchot calls it writing, which preserves the anonymity of words and things, which is to say their density or thickness within the *il y a.*

It happens (or appears) that Levinas and Blanchot divide precisely here, with Levinas attempting to escape the anonymity or non-sense (or poetry) of the *il y a* as by "a passage from *being* to *a something*" (or, alternatively and better: to *a someone*), while Blanchot remains behind, on the hither side of being. This breaking free from poetry is the first moment of philosophy. It is an anarchic beginning, that is, it is anterior to the breakup of essence or cognition that Levinas designates formally as the event that constitutes ethics as *first* philosophy (its *arche*).[11] The question is whether the break with poetry can ever be clean or complete. Or, speaking from Blanchot's side of the question, it is whether the passage into philosophy is ever possible. As if Blanchot were, whatever else he might be, a philosopher for whom philosophy is never a possibility; a philosopher who remains within the space of poetry or writing, as if refusing philosophy.

Kafka

"The writer," Blanchot says, "belongs to a language which no one speaks, which is addressed to no one, which has no center, and which reveals nothing" (EL21/SL26). What is it to *belong* to this language that is no longer a language, no longer an instrument of expression or a system for framing representations, no longer a movement of negation in which the world is constructed as a totality of self-identical objects? A language not for use: a language that can only be described by a kind of topology, not by grammar and rules.

To belong to this language, this space or region of language, means losing all subjectivity. It means entering into an indeterminate existence where one no longer occupies any site or position, no longer possesses a standpoint or perspective, no longer has any place among any relationships. As Blanchot says in his first essay on Kafka: "we do not know if we are excluded from it (which is why we search vainly in it for something solid to hold on to) or whether we are forever imprisoned in it (and so we turn desperately toward the outside). This existence is exile in its fullest sense: we are not there, we are elsewhere, and we will never stop being there" (PF17/WF9).[12] What is it to experience this condition?

In *L'espace littéraire* Blanchot calls this "the original experience," and he gives us three case histories, an allegory, and a theory in which the radical exteriority of this experience is clarified through the figure of exile. The case histories are those of Kafka, Mallarmé, and Rilke, and the allegory is Ovid's story of Orpheus and Eurydice. The theory is a rewriting of Heidegger's "Der Ursprung des Kunstwerkes."

With Kafka the experience is that of an absolute demand, an exigency of writing that leaves no space for anything else. The writer does not exist except within the space of this exigency. This exigency, this necessity of writing, becomes the writer's reality; everything else drains away.

In writing, says Blanchot, one "does not feel free of the world, but, rather, deprived of it" (EL57/SL53).

The concept of writing as exigency is, among other things, a way of relocating the origin of writing outside the writer. The writer remains of course responsible for the text, but not as an agent is responsible for an action or decision. Responsibility is no longer part of a logic of causation and explanation; it now means something like being under obligation or, better, an imposition. Responsibility imposes itself; it invades the space that surrounds and protects the subject. It is an intervention, an interruption, but not as if one were provoked by a sudden desire, compulsion, or inspiration. Exigency soaks up desire, including the desire to write. Given the exigency of writing, writing is an impossible task. Imagine writing as an in-

vasion of the writer by this impossibility. The event resembles the prophetic invasion of an alien divinity that breaks one off from the world. No
one asks to be a prophet, words stuffed in one's mouth, raving in the
desert. Responsibility takes the form of exposure, being exposed—not,
however, to others or to other people or another's gaze, as in Levinas, but
to something like an empty, abandoned space. In this space one is no
longer a cognitive subject that can take the measure of its surroundings.
Rather the subject has been turned out of its house, deprived of any
refuge; it is now a restless, itinerant ego, if "ego" is still the word.

Writing occupies the Levinasian site of the other in Blanchot's conception of responsibility—with roughly the same consequences for the
cognitive or expressive subject. Levinas writes: "There is a claim laid on
the same by the other in the core of myself, the extreme tension of the
command exercised by the other in me over me, a traumatic hold of the
other on the same. . . . It is an undoing of the substantial nucleus of
the ego that is formed in the same, a fission of the mysterious nucleus of
inwardness of the subject by this assignation to respond, which does not
leave any refuge, any chance to slip away." For both Blanchot and Levinas
the experience is comparable to prophecy, where the subject is no longer
self-possessed but, as Levinas says, "under assignation": "It is not an ego,
but me under assignation. There is an assignation to an identity for the response of responsibility, where one cannot have oneself be replaced without fault. To this command continually put forth only a 'here I am' (*me
voici*) can answer, where the pronoun 'I' is in the accusative, declined before any declension, possessed by the other, sick, identical. Here I am—is
saying with inspiration, which is not a gift for fine words or songs" (AE221–
22/OTB141–42). Imagine inspiration as taking one's breath away, depriving
one of speech.

Writing is forsakenness: being forsaken (not by others, says Kafka, but
by oneself): carried away by a worldless existence, inhabiting—no, not inhabiting, being lost, being at a loss, wandering in a place that is not a
world. Better to call it a space without a world: a placeless space, a surface
across which one is dispersed, no longer a resident of oneself but dispossessed, turned out of oneself, identifying oneself with errancy, separation,
drift. "Wandering in the Wilderness" becomes Kafka's watchword.[13] Blanchot refers to this as "the Abraham perspective" (EL82/SL70). In "How to
Read Abraham?"[14] Blanchot reads Kafka's *Diaries* (particularly the entries
from 1922) as a document of this perspective, summarized by Kafka's

remark: "I live elsewhere" (29 January 1922: *Diaries*, p. 409), where elsewhere is not a private, interior, subjective space: not an imaginary space, a dreamworld, nor is it a place set part on the model of aesthetic differentiation: a museumlike preserve free from the claims of knowledge. Rather it is a place where these claims have been superseded by the claim of writing itself.

This place is where art is. Art neither dreams nor creates, nor does it describe things either true or imaginary. What is true has no need for art; it is a plenum. The true exhausts everything that is. The same is true of the imaginary (in either its Aristotelian or Sartrean versions), which pours itself into every vacuum, exhausts every absence, consumes it with its power of possibility. But the world of art is the nonidentical; that is, in a world in which things are recognizable, identifiable, self-identical, part of language, "there is no place for art" (*EL89/SL75*).

> For art is linked, precisely as Kafka is, to what is "outside" the world [*"hors" du monde*], and it expresses the profundity of this outside [*dehors*] bereft of intimacy and repose—this outside which appears when even with ourselves, even with our death, we no longer have relations of possibility. Art is the consciousness of this "misfortune." It describes the situation of one who has lost himself, who can no longer say "me," who in the same movement has lost the world, the truth of the world, and belongs to exile, to the *time of distress* when, as Hölderlin says, the gods are no longer and are not yet. This does not mean that art affirms another world, at least not if it is true that art has its origin, not in another world, but in the other of all worlds. (*EL89–90/SL75*)

Art is a "movement outside the true" [*démarche hors du vrai*]" (*EL92/SL77*). It neither dreams nor creates—it demands. In this event the writer experiences art as an incapacitation, a pure passivity, insomnia, waiting, dying—"not death, alas, but the eternal torment of dying" (*Diaries*, p. 302). This is a demand which presupposes, not the possibility of action, but its impossibility: a demand that exacts a useless patience.[15] Kafka calls it, Beckett-like, the "old incapacity" (*Diaries*, p. 330).[16]

So Kafka remains on this side of possibility. Deleuze and Guattari give a nice turn to this idea when they explain that Kafka writes in a "deterritorialized" language: Prague German is a language outside of language, a "nomad" language, where words leave behind the space of their meanings. German is "reterritorialized" in Prague, where its sounds enter into a space that neutralizes their sense. Kafka intensifies the neutralization of German. He takes German into the space of Yiddish, where "he will make it cry with an extremely sober and rigorous cry. He will pull from it the barking of the dog, the cough of the ape, and the bustling of the beetle. He will turn syntax into a cry that will embrace the rigid syntax of this dried-up German. He will push it toward . . . an absolute deterritorialization, even if it is slow, sticky, coagulated. To bring language slowly and progressively to the desert. To use syntax in order to cry, to give a syntax to the cry" (K48/KFM26).

The cry (like the murmur) belongs to the neutral space of *écriture*, that is, of "writing outside of language" (EI389/IC260). Writing, says Blanchot, is "a rupture with language understood as that which *represents*, and with language understood as that which receives and gives meaning" (EI390/ IC261). It is symmetrical or coherent with the voice that is outside of speech:

The voice sets free from speech; it announces a possibility prior to all saying, and even to any possibility of saying. The voice frees not only from representation, but also, in advance, from meaning, without, however, succeeding in doing more than commiting itself to the ideal madness of delirium. The voice that speaks without a word, silently —in the silence of a cry—tends to be, no matter how interior, the voice of no one. What speaks when the voice speaks? It situates itself nowhere, neither in nature nor in culture, but manifests itself in a space of redoubling, of echo and resonance where it is not someone, but rather this *unknown* space—its discordant accord, its vibration— that speaks without speaking. (Hölderin, in his madness "declaiming" at the window, gives this voice an organ.) (EI386/IC258)

Silence is perhaps a word, a paradoxical word, the silence of the word *silence*, yet surely we feel that it is linked to the cry, the voiceless cry, which breaks all utterances, which is addressed to no one and which no one receives, the cry that lapses and decries. Like writing (and in the same way that the quick of life has always already exceeded life), the cry tends to exceed all language, even if it lends itself to recuperation as language effect. It is both sudden and patient; it has the suddenness of the interminable torment which is always over already. The patience of the cry: it does not simply come to a halt, reduced to nonsense, yet it does remain outside of sense—a meaning infinitely suspended, decried, decipherable-indecipherable. (ED86/WD51)

A cry, not a scream. A cry is not a spontaneous outburst, not an expression, not an emanation from an interior but the sound of an interior already emptied of occupation. Perhaps a cry is to screaming as affliction (*malheur*) is to suffering (*souffrance*): anonymous, impersonal, interminable and incessant like the *il y a* or the eternal return or dying.

Perhaps at some point it will be appropriate to contrast the cry and the yell. The cry is, in some sense, the language of the Holocaust, a cry from the outside that goes unheard, drowned out by the yell: "The howling voice of Fascist orators and camp commandants shows the other side of the same social condition. The yell is as cold as business. They both expropriate the sounds of natural complaint and make them elements of their technique. Their bellow has the same significance for the pogrom as the noise generator in the German flying bomb: the terrible cry which announces terror is simply turned on."[17] Probably one should add the bark of guard dogs.

The Impossibility of Dying

With Mallarmé and Rilke the "original experience" is understood by analogy with death; or, more accurately, the loss of subjectivity in writing is thought of as a kind of dying, as if death were the work of art that dying produces, or leaves behind, or as if death were merely the trace of dying, not the completion of this process but simply the presence of everything finished.[18] (In *Le pas au-delà* we read: "the book is to writing what death would be to the movement of dying" [PD143/SNB104].)

So a cadaver is for Blanchot the consummate form of the image, a self-resemblance, a shadow more real than the reality of which it is the remainder: not an addition or supplement to the original, but a depletion of it; that is, not a double or a mirror image, but the original itself, in the form death leaves it, where death does the work elsewhere attributed to imagination.[19] Death produces a form of the imaginary more fascinating than any original because it haunts the original, haunts the world of the original, which is the world left behind: what remains with the remains. (In other words your world and mine, in which we are living remains, restless images of ourselves.) We can't take our eyes off of a corpse, neither can we grasp it, because it is both there and not there in a neutral zone outside of being: existence without being. Blanchot writes: "Man is made in his own image: this is what we learn from the strangeness of cadavers. But this for-

66

mula should first of all be understood this way: *man is unmade according to his image.* The image has nothing to do with signification, meaning, as implied by the existence of the world, the effort of truth, the law and the brightness of the day" (*EL*350/*SL*260).

Writing is an act of dying, but not like suicide is an act, since suicide is still a subjective act of self-expression, an intention and a meaning, an assertion of the right to death, a will-to-power over death, a command or order issued to death, an impatience with death.[20] Think of Walter Benjamin's modernist hero: "Modernism must stand under the sign of suicide, an act which seals a heroic will that makes no concessions to a mentality inimical towards this will. This suicide is not resignation but a heroic passion. It is *the* achievement of modernism in the realm of passions [*Leidenschaften*]."[21] Whereas Blanchot makes us think of Samuel Beckett's Malone, who is the definition of patience, and of writing.

Heroic death is a death staged in the world, by and for the world, outside of death's space: it is a death for the world to see, not so much death as death's spectacle: death not as a work but as an object of art: death as the mother of beauty. Blanchot writes: "It is not enough . . . to approach the adversary with the strength of a combative mind that wants to conquer, but from afar and in such a way, apparently, as to prevent death's approach. A death that is free, useful, and conscious, that is agreeable to the living, in which the dying person remains true to himself, is a death which has not met death. It is death in which there is much talk of life, but in it is not heard the unheard language from which speech emerges like a new gift. Those who do not abandon themselves elude thus the absolute abandon. We are spared the worst, but the essential escapes us" (*EL*126/*SL*101). Essential death cannot be approached as a possibility. "It is what I cannot grasp, what is not linked to *me* by any relation of any sort. It is that which never comes and toward which I do not direct myself" (*EL*129–30/*SL*104). Death comes of waiting. In waiting we are already outside the world, in death's space. The suicide tries to take command of death's space as if it were part of the world, a territory like any other. The suicide wants to occupy the space of death in his or her own name; the suicide wants to stand in for death, as if to become death's philosopher. Socrates, for example, does not die; he stands in for death, gives an interpretation of it. By his example the suicide "mistakes one death for another" (*EL*130/*SL*104).

The suicide is like the artist as masterworker who projects an idea onto the future; but what the suicide and the artist seek to achieve is "a stranger to the world, it remains foreign to all achievements, and constantly ruins all deliberate action" (EL132/SL106). Both the suicide and the master-worker experience the future as "a radical reversal, through which the death [or the work of art] that was the extreme form of my power not only becomes what loosens my hold upon myself by casting me out of my power to begin and even to finish, but also becomes that which is without any relation to me, without power over me—that which is stripped of all possibility—the irreality of the indefinite [*l'irréalité de l'indéfini*]" (EL33/SL106).[22] What is true of death is at all events true of art: both inscribe a radical limit of reality, a limit that is experienced by our inability to grasp what is there, that is, our inability to act as cognitive subjects or as agents of any sort. Death and art exert a fascination because they inscribe the limits of being human, or rather they beckon or draw us to these limits and only by forsaking ourselves can we respond.

However, it would be better to speak of temporality rather than of reality, that is, of events that interrupt rather than substances that can be objectified. For example, Mallarmé's *Igitur* is an unfinished work or bundle of fragments about the elaborate staging of a suicide. However, the death that occurs, Igitur's death, if it occurs, is not a productive or destructive action; it is a moment at which, like midnight, the past passes without the completion of a present. The present does not flee into the past; it remains open, an unfinished present, as if not part of a sequence. It is, in Blanchot's idiom, "inattentive" to reduce the moment to an empirical concept—e.g., to the fleeting, ungraspable, unstoppable passing of instantaneous sensations. For Blanchot, Walter Pater is a pathology of inattention. The moment is not a dimension of subjective experience. It is purely passive and empty, outside the possibility of narrative, excessive or anarchic with respect to structure, a fragment of time that lies waiting, interminably, as if for a Messiah endlessly on the way. The Messiah is a pure imminence, a mystery of uneventfulness.

Dying means entering into this passivity of time, disappearing through the absence of mediation between past and future when time is prolonged, incomplete, and unceasing. This is the experience of Igitur; it is the experience of the passivity of dying, of waiting or attention in the anarchic sense that Blanchot will give it in *L'attente, l'oubli* (1962), namely, that of an afterlife lived in time: "At each step, one is here and yet beyond [*A chaque pas, on est ici, et pourtant au delà*] (AO56). The pun here, as in the title of *Le pas au-delà* (1971), can be traced to Blanchot's earliest texts on

Kafka—for example, "La lecture de Kafka" (1945), where the untheoriz-able condition of "impossibility of dying" is elucidated for the first time. Blanchot cites Kafka's "The Hunter Gracchus," where the hunter arrives heroically at the point of death only to have the accomplishment absurdly withheld from him—it matters that Kafka's narrator doesn't hesitate to call this nonevent a "disaster": "'Then,' he said, 'the disaster happened.' This disaster is the impossibility of death, it is the mockery thrown on all hu-mankind's great subterfuge, night, nothingness, silence. There is no end, there is no possibility of being done with the day, with the meaning of things, with hope: such is the truth that Western man has made a symbol of felicity, and has tried to make bearable by focusing on its positive side, that of immortality, of an afterlife that would compensate for life. But this afterlife is our actual life" (PF15/WF7–8). The incipient argument here is against Hegel, or rather against all end-of-history theories advanced in Hegel's name. Blanchot's principal idea is perhaps as follows: "Existence is interminable, it is nothing but an indeterminacy; we do not know if we are excluded from it (which is why we search vainly in it for something solid to hold on to) or whether we are forever imprisoned in it (and so we turn desperately toward the outside). This existence is an exile in the fullest sense: we are not there, we are elsewhere, and we never stop being there" (PF17/WF9).[23]

Levinas gives a theory of this experience of interminability when he says that death as something clear and distinct is always the death of other people; death itself, as such, is a survivor's concept. Dying meanwhile is intransitive and indeterminate, a translation of something intelligible into what is alien and unspeakable where the process is always incomplete, a movement incapable of transgression or transcendence because its law or limit is absent, is absence or impossibility as such. Levinas says: "The time of *dying* itself cannot give itself the other shore. In *dying*, the horizon of the future is given, but the future as a promise of a new present is refused; one is in the interval, forever an interval" (IH143/CPP11). This is Igitur's ex-perience (Levinas mentions Poe's characters and the horror or boredom of premature burial—but *Igitur* is in its way a rewriting of Poe): "It is as though death were never dead enough, as though parallel with the dura-tion of the living ran the eternal duration of the interval—the *meanwhile* [*entre-temps*]" (IH143/CPP11).[24] The meanwhile: Levinas refers to it as "something inhuman and monstrous" (IH143/CPP11)—and this certainly captures Blanchot's conception of it. Dying is not a relation between life and death but an event outside all relations ("as if we only died in the infinitive" [PD130/SNB94]). And that which is outside all relations is, by definition, monstrous.

Orpheus and His Companions

The *entre-temps* is the moment, the between-time, that occurs when Orpheus turns his forbidden look toward Eurydice. The task of Orpheus is to bring light out of darkness—*phainaesthetics*: it is to bring Eurydice into the daylight, to make the daylight more luminous through the visibility of Eurydice (think of Romeo, who figures Juliet as the sun). Passage into the day is the movement of the true, the movement of negation that brings life (of a certain sort) out of death. The task of Orpheus is to clarify this movement, to give it form, to bring out its beauty, its harmony and fullness, its intelligibility; it is to make truth radiant. This is the meaning of Eurydice or the work of art: the radiance of truth.

Orpheus, however, cannot bear *not* to see Eurydice in her concealment. It is not her beauty that he desires but Eurydice herself, Eurydice in darkness, *as* darkness, the essence of the night (the other night): Eurydice the foreign and inaccessible (*autrui*). It is as though Orpheus were responding to a deeper claim, an exigency more powerful than his essentially philosophical task of restoring Eurydice to the light of being. This would be the exigency of writing, or of a speech that "speaks outside all power to represent and to signify" (EI274/IC183). Sometimes Blanchot calls it an "exigency of strangeness" (EI189/IC129).

Of course everything is opaque when Orpheus turns to look behind him. Eurydice vanishes in that look, dying a death that reverses death because it is the death of possibility, of *aletheia* and therefore of art as the work of originary construction. So Eurydice—Eurydice's "naked visage"—becomes "the non-transparency that escapes being, escapes the power of being and the power of violence that forces and seizes" (EI275/IC184).

Blanchot says that "writing [*écrire*] begins with the gaze of Orpheus" (EL232/SL176), that is, with a gaze turned toward impossibility, a gaze dispossessed of its objects, a transformation that preserves invisibility from the dialectic of conceptual clarity. Dispossessed, Orpheus returns to the daylight and dismemberment. He becomes a poem. Perhaps this expresses matters too vividly. It is enough to say that writing for Blanchot is not a performative or even a textual concept. It is an event or a space in which one enters into the kind of relation that Blanchot, following Kafka, thinks of as a transformation of an "I" into a "he" (*il*).

In 1953 Blanchot published *Celui qui ne m'accompagnait pas*, which to all appearances is a narrative about a relationship between two men, the narrator and a companion, although "companion" is perhaps not the right word (it is at all events an empty word, but unfortunately there are no alternatives [CAP42/OW20–21]). Nor is "relationship" quite the right word either, although it seems right to say that whatever relation there is between these two, it is made of language; it consists, for example, of a conversation in which, however, words are often not so much exchanged as repeated. At one point someone says: "I, too, think we aren't really talking: one can't call this speech" (CAP71/OW36). No words in this *récit* seem right or just, which seems a point worth remarking since nearly all that we are told of the companion is that he desires exactness in speech (CAP8/OW1).

The two men seem to share or occupy a house, or some rooms in a house. At one point, as if repeating a famous scene from Henry James's "The Turn of the Screw," the narrator sees someone standing outside, looking in through the window.

"I think someone is there."
"Someone? Here?"
"Just now someone was looking through the window."
"Through the window?"
Words spoken in a tone of voice so uncommon, so quiet, that I in turn began to feel a kind of fear. What frightened me was that he seemed to repeat my words without altogether understanding them, and this thought occurred to me: Does he know what a window is?" (CAP34/OW16)

In this *récit* words repeatedly detach themselves from their use or insist on being set apart in quotation marks, which (like the parenthesis, or perhaps like the house or its rooms) describe a space where time circulates endlessly (CAP39/OW19), or, much to the same point, "a place where nothing happens" (CAP40/OW20). But of course something happens (it happens, or is recited, twice): someone who is neither the narrator nor the companion looks in from the outside. One might take this someone as a kind of stand-in for the relationship in question, which is not a community—the narrator and the companion do not constitute a "we" or an "us." Intersubjectivity is an empty concept; neither are they a self and an other. The relation between them is a relation of strangeness such that neither of them is one or the other; the relation itself is a relation of alterity into which both enter and which they traverse but not as terms of identity between which a connection (that is, a relation that might be named) might occur. It is a anarchic relation without the mediation of principle. Instead of two people one could as well imagine "two moments in time perhaps entirely foreign to each other and coming together within their shared foreignness" (CAP66/OW33–34): in short, they inscribe an interval.

It is altogether possible—in fact, it turns out exactly that the companion is simply the narrator who has entered into this distance or space of separation, so that he no longer coincides with himself just at the point where there is no one else. At all events, from the start his relation to the companion is linked with writing, and the space of which he begins to speak is thought of as a reserve, a space within a place (and, more oddly, a not-here within a here) where the narrator, as he says, "has the right to speak of myself in the third person" (CAP49/OW25). This space, possibly a room in the house (possibly also a table on which someone is writing), is "the site of an encounter in which there was no one and in which I was not myself" (CAP53/OW27). It is, not surprisingly, a site of eternal return: "here a sovereign event was taking place and . . . to live consisted for me in being eternally here and at the same time in revolving only around here, in an incessant voyage, without discovery" (CAP55/OW28). Also a space of exigency, that is, a space of passivity or of responsibility isolated from power.

So the narrator's gaze is, to all appearances, Orphic, and the face in the window (if it is a face) occupies the site of Eurydice:

> I thought about it, and I felt the anguish, the sadness, that recalled to me the presence of that figure, riveted to a single point by the fact that I was riveting it with my gaze: it was no longer more than a point, then, an empty, silent point, an empty moment that had become tragically foreign to my gaze at the very moment when my gaze became the error of what rivets, and my gaze itself was empty, did not enter that zone, entered it without reaching it, encountered only the emptiness, the closed circle of its own vision. (CAP74/OW38)

What happens to the gaze of Orpheus after Eurydice vanishes? We may imagine Orpheus staring in fascination at the empty space (empty but not negative). *Celui qui ne m'accompagnait pas* tries to imagine something like this. Near the end the narrator notices that his eyes are "open on something that I didn't at first grasp, a point, not a point, but a blossoming, a smile of the whole of the space, which expressed, occupied all of the space, in which I then recognized precisely what I had wanted to describe to him, a smile that was free, without hindrance, without a face, that radiated softly out from this absence, illuminated it, gave it a semblance, a name, a silent name" (CAP167/OW89). He adds: "I felt . . . how little this view depended on my gaze, how it eluded my gaze without remaining a stranger to it" (CAP168/OW90). Not surprisingly, the smile is (like the cry above) "the tranquil smile of no one, intended for no one, and near which one could not dwell near oneself, not an impersonal smile and perhaps not even a smile, the presence of the impersonal" (CAP168–69/OW91). We may be forgiven for thinking of a smiling Eurydice.

If writing begins with the gaze of Orpheus it is because this gaze no longer unveils what it sees; it is "outside the realm of the visible-invisible" (EI42/IC30): in a region of existence without being. In such a space seeing is reduced to listening.

The last half of *Celui qui ne m'accompagnait pas* (certainly the last half, but quite possibly the whole of it) occurs in a space of this sort, a "neutral expanse" (*une étendue neutre*) in which subjectivity is removed from the site of the *cogito* (CAP89/OW46). The narrator says: "I had always suspected that when I said 'me' it was to oblige him in his turn to say 'I,' to come out of that depth, that sordid sterile neutrality where, in order to be on an equal footing, I would have had to become him for myself. A region I had perhaps approached in an earlier time, without realizing it . . . [where] under the veil of these first persons, shielded by that equality I had to wrest from him each time by a vehement insistence, I thought, at least momentarily, that I was preserved from the danger of hearing the anonymous, the nameless, speak in him" (CAP90/OW47). But now the narrator confronts the anonymous and nameless in himself as well. It is not so much that he speaks as that he cannot help speaking, as when he says (repeatedly): " 'Where we are, everything conceals itself, doesn't it?' " (CAP94/OW50). These words belong to the *étendue neutre* like an echo: "Why, behind everything I said and everything he answered, was there this remark: 'Where we are, everything conceals itself, doesn't it?'—a remark I understood, did not understand, it had no understanding" (CAP99/OW52).

Likewise the companion absurdly or obsessively puts this question to the narrator, "Are you writing, are you writing at this moment?" (CAP102/

$OW54$). The question "passed through space like an avid shiver—'Are you writing? Are you writing at this moment?' Hearing this, I shivered in turn, I understood that what had awakened me, led me back here, was this voracious murmur that I had not ceased to listen to" (CAP102/OW54):

> "Am I writing?
> This slipped out of me more like a sigh than a speech, but weak as this perturbation was, it was enough to disrupt the equilibrium, and right away, as though attracted by this emptiness, his uninterrupted murmur, which had until now wandered at random, turned around impetuously against me, confronted me, while he asked me with an authority that contrasted ridiculously with the weakness of my resources:
> "Are you writing, are you writing at this moment?"
> To which I could not help answering him:
> "But you know very well that I can no longer write and I am almost not myself any longer."
> Words I regretted because of their seriousness, and they were immediately followed, in the furtive manner of a light laugh, from a little farther away, by his own words:
> "Are you writing, are you writing at this moment?" (CAP103/OW54–55)

The question, as it happens, is not so much a question as a demand: the exigency of writing. Occasionally this demand is explicit and—rare moment in Blanchot—comic (recall the companion's preference for the language of facts):

> "You mean I have to talk to you incessantly without stopping?
> "Talk, describe things."
> Which was enough to awaken a spirit of uncertainty.
> "Why describe?" I asked him. "There's nothing to describe, there's almost nothing left." (CAP112–13/OW59)

Certainly this is a parody of Flaubert's *angoisse*. In the space of the *il y a*, of existence without being, *le mot juste* is impossible. Perhaps not quite impossible:

> I listen to this, Who is he addressing? who is involved here? who is speaking? who is listening? who could answer such a distance? this comes from so far away and it doesn't even come, why is he ignoring me? why is this ignorance within my reach? why does it make itself understood? A speech? And yet not a speech, barely a murmur, barely a shiver, less than silence, less

than the abyss of emptiness [*l'abîme du vide*]: the fullness of emptiness, something one can't silence, occupying all of space, uninterrupted and incessant, a shiver and already a murmur, not a murmur, but a speech, and not just any speech, but distinct, appropriate [*juste*]: within my reach. I summoned up my whole being to answer him:

"He wasn't writing, and he mustn't be involved here." (CAP125/OW66–67)

As if *le mot juste* were the murmur of the *il y a*.

Or as if the *il y a* were made of words. At all events the conversation between the narrator and the companion is made of words, but speaking never dissipates them (the words): they circulate through the room in an eternal return, whence the endless or endlessly repeated (infinite) conversation. The narrator imagines words crowding around him, pressuring him to write (CAP128/OW68), and when he finds himself powerless to resist— well, that is what it is to write (that is the meaning of the word, *écrire*). "'Yes,'" he says (repeating the last words of the incessant question), "'at this moment, exactly at this moment'" (CAP130/OW69):

> In this way I understood better why this was what it was, to write: I understood it, I mean this word became completely other, much more demanding even than I had thought it was. To be sure, it was not to my power that it had made its appeal, nor to myself either, but to "this moment" when I could do nothing—and thus it seemed to me that writing had to consist in drawing near that moment, would not give me power over it, but, by some act unknown to me, would make me a gift of this moment, near which, for an infinite time now, I had dwelled without reaching it—far from here and yet here. I clearly perceived the risk I was going to expose myself to: instead of making the words go back over the frontier they had crossed, the risk, on the contrary, of disturbing them more and more, of tormenting them by driving them mad with an empty, unbridled desire, to the point that, at a certain moment, passing through me in their frantic pursuit, they would carry me once again toward a space dangerously open to the illusion of a world to which we would, however, not have access. (CAP134–35/OW71)

The "moment" of writing is an interruption, an interval or *entre-temps* that never passes from future to past (or is it past to future? Which way does time move, if it moves at all?). By a topological conversion this moment duplicates itself as a space of exile: of endless wandering where "here" can never be fixed ("As though the word 'here' had drawn me elsewhere"

[CAP97/OW51]). To write is to inhabit or, more accurately, to traverse this space: the Outside is what Blanchot calls it (where the words are). "To say that I understand these words would not be to explain to myself the dangerous peculiarity of my relations with them. Do I understand them? I don't understand them, properly speaking . . . [but] they don't need that understanding in order to be uttered, they do not speak, they are not interior, they are, on the contrary, without intimacy, being altogether outside, and what they designate engages me in this 'outside' of all speech" (CAP135–36/OW72).

In *L'écriture du désastre* (1980) Blanchot writes: "Theories are necessary (the theories of language, for example): necessary and useless. Reason works in order to wear itself out, by organizing itself into systems, seeking a positive knowledge where it can posit itself, pose and repose and at the same time convey to itself an extremity which forms a stop and a closure" (ED122/WD75–76). Theories belong to the day. *Celui qui ne m'accompagnait pas*, by contrast, registers a "nocturnal" experience of words, a limit-experience that would explode our theories in a twinkling:

> Beautiful hours, profound words which I would like to belong to, but which would, themselves, also belong to me, words empty and without connection. I can't question them and they can't answer me. They only remain close to me, as I remain close to them. That is our dialogue. They stand motionless, as though erect in these rooms; at night, they are the concealment [*dissimulation*] of the night; in the day, they have the transparency of the day. Everywhere I go, they are there.
>
> What do they want? We're not familiar to one another, we don't know one another. Words from the empty depth [*la profondeur vide*], who has summoned you? . . .
>
> I don't know that they press on me, but I sense it. I see a sign of it in the immobility which, even when they seem to wander, even when I leave them, keeps them crowded around me in a circle whose center I am in spite of myself. . . .
>
> Am I their goal, what are they seeking? I will not believe it. But sometimes they stare at me with a power so restrained, a silence so reserved, that this silence points me out to myself; then I have to remain firm, I have to struggle with my refusal to believe. . . .
>
> I didn't invoke them, I am without power over them, and they have no relations with me. . . .
>
> They're always together. No doubt this means I can only see them together, together even though unconnected, motionless around me though

76

wandering. I see them all, never one in particular, never one single one in the familiarity of an undivided gaze, and if, even so, I try to stare at one of them separately, what I'm looking at then is a terrible, impersonal presence, the frightening affirmation of something I don't understand, don't penetrate, that isn't here and that nevertheless conceals itself in the ignorance and emptiness of my own gaze. (CAP139–43/OW74–76)

The "nocturnal" experience of words, in which the cognitive or speaking subject is deprived of its sovereignty and its power, reduced to the passivity of fascination, is one of the most important events in Blanchot's thinking. It resonates everywhere in his texts. (One could already call it the disaster.) Think of it, however, not simply as a moment internal to Blanchot's own intellectual history but as a moment which Blanchot inserts, without malice, into the history of philosophy, that is, the history of the subject whose whole justification consists in the hope of filling its gaze with the absolute. Against this background one could read the paragraphs above as philosophy's nightmare of disaster, an allegory or parody of Hegel's end-of-philosophy story, where, going into its final turn, the philosophical subject encounters, in place of its absolute self-identity, the alien upon whose originary exile its whole history was projected.

PART II

Infinite Conversations

 CHAPTER 4

Blanchot/Celan

Unterwegssein
(On Poetry and Freedom)

Das Fremde
hat uns im Netz,
die Vergänglichkeit greift
ratlos durch uns hindurch . . .
— Paul Celan, *Zeitgehöft*

Poetry and History

Blanchot's poetics (and, of course, not just Blanchot's) presupposes a certain way of framing the following question: To what history (or histories)
does poetry belong? Poetry, after all, is neither a universal nor a natural
kind; that is, it is essentially and empirically invisible. You cannot tell a
poem from a non-poem without the mediation of a theory that is in some
sense constitutive of the thing itself; and all theories are historical. Poetry
stands out as such only against dense cultural backgrounds of concepts,
narratives, archives, and practices in which the writing of a poem is an intelligible event. It presupposes a "poetryworld"; or, in Wittgenstein's idiom, poetry is a form of life, even a multiplicity of such forms.[1]

A convenience of literary history stipulates that the nature of poetry is
internal to the social spaces in which it is composed. So one can address
the question of poetry by studying the history of these spaces—the festival,
the school, the monastery, the court, the alehouse, the theater, the garden,
Grub Street, the countryside (which, when you walk through it, is transformed into a social space), the artist's colony, the jail cell, the closet, library, cafe, workshop, and so on without any definite term.

81

Naturally these discursive spaces are not sealed-off structures but are exposed and vulnerable to the history of disaster. In 1958, replying to a questionnaire, Paul Celan remarked that the German lyric can no longer be written in the language of German poetry (or, for all of that, can no longer be written in a poetic language).[2] As if poetry could only be written in a space outside language or history, assuming one could find it. As Adorno says: "only what does not fit into this world is true" (AT93/AeT86).[3]

On Blanchot's interpretation poetry belongs to the history of philosophy—the history of metaphysics, ontology, reason, or subjectivity—where the task of philosophy is to bring the history of poetry to an end. Here poetry comes into conceptual existence by being excluded from philosophy's self-identity as, in Plato's or Habermas's words, human culture's "guardian of rationality." Ontologically, poetry exists as a product of the logic of exclusion and is henceforward linked conceptually to nondiscourse, or to exile, or to the exile's return (as negotiated, for example, by Aristotle's *Poetics*, which proposes a certain philosophical way of speaking that poets might take up to justify themselves). So for Blanchot literary space is radically exterior: it is the Outside, the nonessential space of the *il y a*.

Blanchot's Plato is Hegel, whose Republic is history itself, where poetry is *vergangen*. In the last part of *L'espace littéraire*—originally an essay from 1952, "L'art, la littérature, et l'expérience originelle"—Blanchot, always looking for a way around Hegel, asks whether art and poetry, being so impossible, can have a future. He thinks at once of Hölderlin (for Blanchot, as for Heidegger, the proper name of poetry)—Hölderlin, "about whom it would not be enough to say that his fate was linked to poetry's, for he had no existence at all except in and for poetry. And yet, in 1799, speaking of the revolution which he saw imperiled, he wrote to his brother, 'And if the kingdom of darkness erupts after all in *full force*, then let us throw our pens under the table and go in God's name where the need is greatest and our presence the most useful'" (EL282/SL213). Imagine poetry trying to resolve a crisis of enlightenment by abandoning itself, disappearing into the light.

Hölderlin in other words seems to throw in with his friend Hegel, for whom art belongs to the *Geistesgeschichte*. It is (or was) part of the history of reason where with each passing epoch reason becomes more completely itself (reflects on itself and eliminates the nonidentical). Poetry, if it is anything, is *geistlich*, a species of *Bildung*, collaborating in the work of humanity as it grows more spiritual, more universal, less relative to this or that epoch or civilization. But on Hegel's telling art has been superseded by philosophy. Philosophy aims for "the universal day" (*EL*281/*SL*213). It is what art and poetry always wanted to be but fell short of; or rather philosophy is what poetry has begun to turn into as consciousness becomes increasingly emancipated from everything it is not. However, all by itself, as such, unphilosophized, poetry—in the celebrated phrase—is "for us a thing of the past." It cannot, by itself, satisfy our desire for the absolute (*EL*284/*SL*214).

The end of art coincides with the development of the museum as the place where consciousness reflects on earlier imperfect representations of itself. One could call this, borrowing from Foucault, the Great Confinement: the confinement of art to the museum and other penitentiaries, that is, to the realm of the aesthetic or to the realm of the private. Henceforward art is a thing set apart from consciousness as such. Perhaps romanticism is a name for this confinement, this removal or retirement of the poem from the objective space of the world to the preconscious or excessive space of imagination. As Blanchot says, useless to the project of the world, useless even to itself as an *art poetique*, "art withdraws into the most invisible and the most interior—into the empty point of existence where it shelters its sovereignty in refusal and the superabundance of refusal" (*EL*285/*SL*215).

Not that art ever loses its ancient desire for absolute consciousness, absolute knowledge or the work to end all works. On the contrary, art is the name for this desire in its most absolute form (the pure form, for example, of the absolute Book: Flaubert's dream of "a book about nothing," or Mallarmé's *Grand Œuvre*).[4] Writing is a pure passion for the absolute. But at the same time it is the recognition that this passion cannot be satisfied within the world, say in the form of a work of art. Poets have always understood this better than Hegel did. Blanchot mentions Hölderlin, Mallarmé, Rilke, René Char. He could (will one day) have added Paul Celan. Or he might have thought of Schlegel's theory of romantic poetry as always on the way (perhaps one could say: incessant, interminable): "Other kinds of poetry are finished and are now capable of being fully analyzed" (*Atheneum Fragments*, no. 116). But romantic poetry, the poetry of modernity (of the future), is incapable of being finished; it cannot be completed. It can only begin and begin again as an untheorizable history of fragments. As if poetry moved with the eternal return. Hölderlin, Mallarmé, Rilke, René Char—each gives a certain interpretation of this insight, to which Blanchot will now add his own.

Error

Two of his own (to start with).

The first, already sketched out in "Littérature et la droit à la mort," is the interpretation of poetry as anarchy. No law rules poetry; its sovereignty takes the form of a refusal of the world and its laws (a refusal of the negative, the movement or history of the spirit). Or as Blanchot now dramatically expresses it: "Art is the subjective passion which no longer wants any part of the world. Here in the world subordination reigns: subordination to ends, to measured proportion, to seriousness and order. On one front science, technology, the state; on another, significance, stable values, the idea of the Good and the True. Art is 'the world turned upside down': insubordination, disproportion, frivolity, ignorance, evil, non-sense" (EL287/ SL216).

As Levinas says, "Expressions such as 'a world in pieces' or 'a world turned upside down,' trite as they are, nonetheless express a feeling that is authentic. The rift between the rational order and events, the mutual impenetrability of minds as opaque as matter, the multiplication of logical systems each of which is absurd for the others, the impossibility of the I rejoining the you, and consequently the unfitness of understanding for what should be its function—these are things we run up against in the twilight of the world, things which reawaken the ancient obsession with an end of the world" (DEE25/EE21). Poetry, we might say, keeps open the rift between the rational order and the anarchy of history; poetry sides with what is outside or on the hither side of every order of things.

Blanchot's second interpretation follows from the first. It is that of poetry as a limit-experience. What is it to experience this outside or limit of the world? This is the question pursued in the last part of *L'espace littéraire*, which is, as it happens, an undisguised theft of much of what Heidegger has to say in "Der Ursprung des Kunstwerkes" about the earthly character of the work as that which is just what it is made of [*"l'œuvre* est *éminemment* ce dont *elle* est fait"] (EL296/SL223). The work is opaque, resistant to clarification, a conspiracy of the earth, "which shows itself only when it remains undisclosed and unexplained" (GA5:33/PLT47). The earth is, radically, a limit-concept. "Earth shatters every attempt to penetrate into it," Heidegger says. "It causes every merely calculating importunity to turn into a destruction. This destruction may herald itself under the appearance of mastery and of progress in the form of the technical-scientific objectification of nature, but this mastery nevertheless remains an impotence of will. The earth appears openly cleared only when it is perceived and preserved as that which is by nature undisclosable, that which shrinks from every disclosure and constantly keeps itself closed up." The work of the work of art is not only to disclose the world; it is to reveal and preserve the undisclosable, self-secluding earth. "The statue glorifies the marble. The painting is not made from material ingredients added to the canvas; it is the presence of this matter, which without it would remain hidden to us. And the poem likewise is not made with ideas, or with words; it is the point from which words begin to become their appearance, and the *elemental depth* upon which this appearance is opened while at the same time it closes" (EL297/SL223).[5]

Blanchot, however, out-Heideggers Heidegger. The work of the work of art is an event, a rifting of earth and world that holds open the opening of the world in a constant condition of exposure to the nonidentical: "This event," says Blanchot, "does not come to pass outside of time any more than the work is simply spiritual. Rather, through the work there takes place in time another time, and in the world of beings that exist and of things which subsist there comes, as presence, not another world but the other of all worlds, that which is always other than the world" (EL303/SL228).

Not another world but the other of all worlds: not a possible world but an impossibility that estranges the world from itself.

The work of art is therefore always external to the world, but not as a separate realm of aesthetic differentiation or, what this term really means, aesthetic noninterference; on the contrary, the work is the endlessly anarchic beginning that never allows the world the repose of self-identity—and this is its politics (a politics of nonidentity, a politics of the impossible). It is perpetual interference. The work is, Blanchot says, "*the* event of history itself. . . . Always it says, in one guise or another, beginning. It is thus that history belongs to it and that nevertheless it escapes history. In the world where it emerges to proclaim that now there is a work—in the usual time, that is, of current truths—it emerges as the unaccustomed, the unwonted [*elle surgit comme l'inaccoutumé, l'insolite*], that which has no relation to this world or with this time. Never is it affirmed on the basis of familiar, present reality. It takes away what is most familiar to us. And always it is in excess [*en trop*]: it is the superfluity of what always lacks. We have called this excess poverty the superabundance of refusal" (EL304/SL228).[6]

85

A refusal to come into the world: as if the withdrawal of the work left open space for a world to enter, a world caught in the work's wake, drawn into being by the draft of the work's retreat.

Blanchot wants to know what it is to experience this originary retreat. This is the poet's experience of poetry: *l'expérience originelle.*

ô *pur langage d'exile*

Blanchot writes:

> When Saint-John Perse named one of his poems *Exile*, he named the poetic condition as well. The poet is in exile; he is exiled from the city, from regular occupations and limited obligations, from everything connected to results, substantive reality, power. . . .
>
> The poem is exile, and the poet who belongs to it belongs to the dissatisfaction of exile. He is always lost to himself [*hors de lui-même*], outside, far from home [*hors de son lieu natal*]; he belongs to the foreign, to the outside which knows no intimacy or limit, and to the separation which Hölderlin names when in his madness he sees rhythm's infinite space. (EL318/SL237)

Exile is an originary political concept, a name for the original division of the world into settlers and nomads.[7] Without exile nothing can be intelligible: it is the nonrecognition from which recognition separates itself and constitutes itself. It is the condition of exclusion that defines the rule of identity and the logic of the same.

Poetry is the name of whatever refuses this rule; it is outside the law of noncontradiction, an outlaw discourse whose inspiration "makes the poet a wanderer, the one always astray [*égaré*], the one to whom the stability of presence is not granted and who is deprived of a true abode. And this must be understood in the gravest sense: the artist does not belong to truth because the work is itself what escapes the movement of the true. For always, whatever our perspective upon it, it revokes the true, eludes signification, designating that region where nothing subsists . . . the *exterior* darkness where man withstands that which the true must negate in order to become possibility and progress" (EL318/SL237). The "exterior darkness": the Outside, the Other Night.

The "movement of the true" is straightforward and propositional; it has a plot and a point that can be fixed beforehand in anticipation of arrival, bringing the point home. It can take the form of discourse. But poetry is nomadic, errant, ambiguous, excessive. "Error is the risk which awaits the poet. . . . Error means wandering [*Erreur signifie le fait d'errer*], the inability to abide and stay. For where the wanderer is, the conditions of a definitive here are lacking. . . . The wanderer's country is not in truth, but in exile; he remains outside, *on the hither side*, apart [*il se tient en dehors, en deçà, á l'écart*]" (EL318–19/SL238). Poetry is not intelligible as a discourse; it is outside of discourse, where discourse is a movement of things being settled into place. (Imagine discourse as a program of confinement.)

It makes sense to think of discourse in terms of narratives and propositions, but poetry's movement is not discursive, it is not a settling into but an abandonment of place. Think of philosophy as a demonstration of what is possible; it is a movement that deposits us somewhere where no more is required to be said or done. Philosophy is all deposit and repose. Poetry is very different from this. It is a movement that begins over and over again: not an *arche* but *an-arche*, beginnings without sequence, beginnings whose only movement is a return that starts over at once, a restless dissemination of beginnings or fragments (EL325–26/SL242–43).

A Poetics of Nonidentity

The conception of poetry as an anarchic movement—as a refusal of philosophy: a withdrawal from every determination—can hardly be clarified within traditional aesthetics where the poem is a stationary formal object that we approach analytically or strategically in order to lay it open to view.[8] How to clarify it then?

Perhaps by way of comparative poetics. Blanchot's thinking is eccentric; but it is neither isolated nor esoteric. For example, in several of his prose writings (which belong very much to Blanchot's conceptual milieu), Paul Celan addressed the question of poetry precisely by separating it, not just from aesthetics and discourse, but from everything that we might recognize as poetic. (*Man kommt uns hier nicht mit "poiein" und dergleichen:* "Don't come here with *poiein* and suchlike" [GW3:177/CP26].) Celan links poetry to exteriority in an astonishing and original way. Poetry is an other-directed movement, a dialogical and topological movement—"Toward what? Toward something open, inhabitable, an approachable you perhaps, an approachable reality [*Auf etwas Offenstehendes, Besetzbares, auf ein ansprechbares Du vielleicht, auf eine ansprechbare Wirklichkeit*]" (GW3:186/CP35).

At the outset of "Der Meridian" (1960), on the occasion of his reception of the Büchner prize, Celan asks, not about art, but about whether there is

87

any sense to the question "What is art?"—which is a question that, as he notes, turns up obsessively and even derisively in Büchner's writings, where art is figured variously in terms of puppets, monkeys or the monkey-shape (*Affengestalt*: gorilla-suit?), automatons, and Medusa heads (GW187–88/CP37–38). Perhaps these figures inscribe Büchner's interpretation of Hegel's picture of what the history of art looks like in the end.

"It is easy to talk about art," says Celan. "But when there is talk of art, there is often somebody who does not really listen"—that is, someone who hears but who doesn't understand. This is not an altogether bad thing. Imagine "someone who hears, listens, looks . . . and then does not know what it was about. But who hears the speaker, 'sees him speaking,' who perceives language as a physical shape, and also . . . breath, that is, direction and destiny [*Der aber den Sprechenden hört, der ihn 'sprechen sieht,' der Sprache wahrgenommen hat und Gestalt und zugleich . . . auch Atem, das heißt, Richtung und Schicksal*]" (GW3:188/CP39). Someone who cannot see through things. Someone on this side, on the skin or fleshly side, of discourse, where language is still visible, or where it can be felt like a breath, where it is an event occurring just now, just this one time.

Celan's reference here is to a character in Büchner's *Dantons Tod*, Lucile, "who is artblind [*Kunstblinde*], for whom language is tangible and like a person [*für die Sprache etwas Personhaftes und Wahrnehmbares hat*]" (GW3:189/CP40). At the end of *Dantons Tod*, Lucile, at the guillotine, cries out (absurdly), "Long live the King." Celan calls this a *Gegenwort*: "It is an act of freedom. It is a step" (GW3:189/CP40).

Celan wants to give this *Gegenwort* the name of poetry: the discourse of the *Kunstblinde*, of those who perceive language as something external to the world of the spirit. But "discourse" is not the right word, or at all events not Celan's word. What makes Celan want to speak of freedom, and of a step (*Schritt*)?

Against the background of Blanchot's poetics we can say (or think, for a moment): Poetry is not a work or process of art; it is a *désœuvrement*: its movement is not toward a point of being finished but a ceaseless, open-ended movement toward what is always elsewhere. Imagine poetry as a name of this elsewhere. Not a movement of the true but of freedom.

(But what is freedom? The concept of freedom in Blanchot's writings, for example, is highly ambiguous. In "Littérature et la droit à la mort" freedom is Hegel's negativity, that is, death, or the movement of the negative that annihilates things by transforming them into concepts and constructs the world over which the spirit presides in absolute sovereignty. Blanchot never relinquishes—one might say, never ceases to exploit—this notion of freedom. However, Celan's use of the word may help to clarify the alternative sense of freedom that emerges in Blanchot's poetics, namely the freedom implicit in poetry's "great refusal" of death or the negative: poetry's freedom from the world or from confinement within totality, which means in turn the freedom of things that poetry refuses to name. This sense of freedom is outside the alternatives of positive or negative freedom. Freedom here is close to Heidegger's sense of *Gelassenheit* or the letting-go of beings: an ontological rather than a subject-centered notion of freedom.)

In Celan's text the relationship between poetry and art is marked out in part by two characters in Büchner's writings: Lucile, the *Kunstblinde*, and Lenz, the artist, a self-forgetting *I*, one "whose eyes and mind are occupied with art" (GW3:193/CP44).[9]

Lenz, who says that "One would like to be a Medusa's head" in order to grasp what is natural, not so much to make it unnatural as to situate it differently as something discernibly *there*: something fixed and self-identical, possessing objectivity and value—but therefore something no longer human, since what is human cannot be fixed or objectified in this way without cost.[10] Art perhaps pays the price by "going [Celan says] beyond what is human, stepping into the realm which is turned toward the human, but *uncanny*—the realm where the monkey, the automatons and with them . . . oh, art, too, seem to be at home [*Das ist ein Hinaustreten aus dem Menschlichen, ein Sichhinausbegeben in einem dem Menschlichen zugewandten und unheimlichen Bereich—denselben, in dem die Affengestalt, die Automaten und damit . . . ach, auch die Kunst zuhause zu sein scheinen*]" (GW3:192/CP42–43).

Art is estrangement, self-estrangement (causing self-forgetfulness) but also estrangement from the human. Art is uncanny in the sense of monstrous, the not quite or no longer human, the almost- or once-human. Poetry is different from this, from art, but not in the way the familiar is different from the strange or the human from the almost-human. Poetry is also uncanny, but differently so, with another sort of strangeness (GW3:195/CP47): not uncanny in the way of art but in the way things are strange when they are no longer subject to our concepts and categories, when they escape us. (Imagine things freeing themselves from the meaningful, becoming, not meaningless, but singular and nonidentical.)

This is how it is with poetry in Celan's text, where the poem is never in place or in view as something self-identical but always something *unterwegs*: on the way, that is, not becoming or in process as if moving toward repose or definition or the objectivity of the work of art but nomadic.

In an earlier address Celan spoke of poetry (or of the poem) explicitly in Heidegger's vocabulary: *Ereignis, Bewegung, Unterwegssein* (GW3:186/ CP34). These are the terms in which Heidegger tries to clarify the question of thinking (*Was heißt Denken?*). Thinking for Heidegger is not a species of reasoning; it is not a conceptual movement or movement of systematic construction. It is an event of language that is irreducible to the propositional form of philosophical discourse. So, like poetry, thinking can be situated outside of discourse. In *Was heißt Denken?* Heidegger emphasizes that thinking is responsive rather than assertive, paratactic (and therefore fragmentary) rather than syntactic and unifying, wayward rather than progressive—incessantly wayward, always on the way, restless even in the moment of pausing, always called out from the familiar into the strange.

The poem for Celan belongs to this ontological condition of *Unterwegssein*: always on the way, leaving an open space behind it. "Perhaps—I am only speculating," Celan says, "—perhaps poetry, like art, moves with the oblivious self into the uncanny and strange to free itself again. Though where? in which place? how? as what? [*vielleicht geht die Dichtung, wie die Kunst, mit einem selbstvergessenen Ich zu jenem Unheimlichen und Fremden, und setz sich—doch wo? doch an welchem Ort? doch womit? doch als was?—wieder frei?*]" (GW3:193/CP44). Open questions.

Clearly *Unterwegssein* is not a discursive or productive movement of *poiesis*. Poetry is on the hither side of discourse and art, as when Celan says: "I believe that I have met poetry in the figure of Lucile, and Lucile perceives language as shape, direction, breath [*nimmt Sprache als Gestalt und Richtung und Atem wahr*]." To which Celan adds: "I am looking for the same thing here, in Büchner's work. I am looking for Lenz himself, as a person [i.e., not as a character in a text but as himself, walking through the mountains on the 20th of January], I am looking for his shape: for the sake of the place of poetry, for the sake of liberation, for the sake of the step [*als Person, ich suche seine Gestalt: um des Ortes der Dichtung, um der Freisetzung, um des Schrittes willen*]" (GW3:194/CP45).

Atem, Ort, Freisetzung (releasement), *Schritt*: an odd vocabulary for a poetics.

Perhaps the most famous line in "Der Meridian" is: "Dichtung: das kann eine Atemwende bedeuten" (GW3:195/CP47).[11] A turning of the breath (if that is what *Atemwende* is) can answer to the name of poetry; or, perhaps, vice versa: this event, this breath, is what poetry responds to. Poetry is perhaps this response or responsiveness, this responsibility for the side of speech that resists reduction or the turning of a breath into a mediation or expression. Possibly the poem is as much the taking of a breath as the expulsion of it ("A breath for nothing," says Rilke, breathing freely, without constriction, not having to speak); or perhaps, as in Levinas's account of *le dehors* in *Autrement qu'être*, freedom is breath, "the breathing of outside air, where inwardness frees itself from itself, and is exposed to all the winds" (AE276/OTB180). Here breathing is nonsubjective: it means taking in the air that belongs to "an outside where nothing covers anything, non-protection, the reverse of a retreat, homelessness, non-world, non-inhabitation, layout without security" (AE275-76/OTB179).

Celan perhaps gives us a glimpse of this outside—this region of the neutral—in "Gespräch im Gebirg" (1959), where two Jews (called "windbags" [*Geschwätzigen*]) encounter one another on alien ground. Levinas himself remains deeply suspicious of this region, which he associates with the *il y a* and Heidegger's dehumanized ontology. To the openness of the Open he opposes the openness of the face, whose breath is "the wind of alterity":

> In human breathing, in its everyday equality, perhaps we have to already hear the breathlessness of an inspiration that paralyzes essence [i.e., self-identity], that transpierces it with an inspiration by the other, an inspiration that is already expiration, that "rends the soul"! It is the longest breath there is, spirit. Is man not the living being capable of the longest breath in inspiration, without a stopping point, and in expiration, without a return? To transcend oneself, to leave one's home to the point of leaving oneself, is to substitute oneself for another. It is, in my bearing of myself, not to conduct myself well, but by my unicity as a unique being to expiate for the other. The openness of space as an openness of the self without a world, without a place, utopia, the not being walled in, inspiration to the end, even to expiration, is proximity of the other which is possible only as responsibility for the other, as substitution for him. (AE278-79/OTB181-82)

Can the term *Atemwende* be clarified in this context? Perhaps only up to a point. Celan thinks of breath as a divergence that turns the poem away from the path of art—or, more exactly, it is the divergence of the strangeness of the one from the strangeness of the other (GW3:196/CP47): think of it (with Levinas's help) as the divergence of the irreducible from the fixed. To catch one's breath one must stop moving, but, for the poet, to listen to one's breathing is to catch the singular, unprecedented movement of a poem (a movement, Charles Olson says, by which the poet departs from the closed form of the metrical phrase into an open field).[12] For Celan this divergence from art is also a movement of freedom. "It is perhaps here, in this one brief moment, that Medusa's head shrivels and the automatons run down? Perhaps, along with the I, estranged and freed *here, in this manner,* some other thing is also set free?" (GW3:196/CP47). The strangeness of the poem is that it is "by necessity a unique instance of language [*Dichtung—das ist das schicksalhaft Einmalige der Sprache*]" (GW3:175/CP23). It is both irreducible and ineffaceable, as if accessible to memory but not to thought.

(Derrida tries to clarify this by saying that the poem is of the same ontology as the date or the *shibboleth;* it is absolutely singular and at the same time never itself. So, as Derrida says: "The date is mad" [S68].)

But the poem is also an event of language (*Ereignis*):

> The poem speaks. It is mindful of its dates, but it speaks. True, it speaks only on its own, its very own behalf [*immer nur in seiner eigenen, allereigensten Sache*].
> But I think—and this will hardly surprise you—that the poem has always hoped, for this very reason, to speak also on behalf of the *strange* [*auch in fremder*]—no, I can no longer use this word here—*on behalf of the other,* who knows, perhaps of an *altogether other* [*gerade auf diese Weise* in eines Anderen Sache *zu sprechen—wer weiß, vielleicht in eines* ganz Anderen *Sache*] (GW3:196/CP48).

Poetry speaks not as a medium but as a thing of its own (the way a person speaks). At the same time, and perhaps precisely because of its withdrawal from the language of mediation, it speaks for another, or perhaps for the other of all others (*eines ganz Anderen Sache*), an otherness more Blanchovian than Levinasian, not just that which is otherwise than being, the ethical, but that which is neither one nor the other, outside even the ethical relation in which an I is turned inside out before the *Autrui.*

In modern tradition (as for Levinas in *Totalité et infini*) freedom is Kantian: it is the free subject, the self-regulating, self-same ego over and against which nothing is free but is rather subject or subjected to cognition and the laws of identity. For Celan, as for Blanchot (and for Levinas in

Autrement qu'être), freedom is the outside, the region of the other, of others near and far, of foreignness itself. The movement of poetry is toward this region, or toward "the 'otherness' which it can reach and be free [*auf jenes 'Andere' zu, das es sich als erreichbar, als freizusetzen*], which is perhaps vacant and at the same time turned like Lucile, let us say, turned toward it, toward the poem" (GW3:197/CP48).

"Movement," however, is a questionable term. Celan's text is not a narrative of a journey or a quest; the poem is not an alter ego but an event of releasement—one could do worse than borrow Heidegger's word, *Gelassenheit*, letting-be or letting-go, which is not a performative that an agent might or might not take up but a condition of openness toward what is outside and uncontainable within our discursive fields. Heidegger calls it *die Offenheit für das Geheimnis*, where *das Geheimnis* is usually translated as "mystery," but which is perhaps better understood topologically as that which is set apart, elsewhere, outside, not what we have made our own but that which is self-standing and alone like the thing (G24). For Heidegger *Gelassenheit* is not a cognitive movement of thinking but the ethical responsiveness of thinking to what withdraws from the world, a responsiveness that is no less ethical for being a *Gelassenheit zu den Dingen*: a releasement turned toward things and not just toward other people.

Gelassenheit is perhaps as much a political as an ethical concept because the condition of openness that it entails is an acceptance or acknowledgment of the other's freedom. This freedom is ontological rather than subjective; that is, it is not the freedom of another subject, freedom as mastery or harmony, but just the anarchic condition of openness in which the singularity or nonidentity of things can take place or, as one should say, can go on. In *L'expérience de la liberté* Jean-Luc Nancy's calls it "the free dissemination of existence"; it is "the an-archy . . . of a singular and thus in essence plural arising whose being *as being* is neither ground, nor element, nor reason, but truth, which would amount to saying, under the circumstances, freedom" (EL16-17/EF13).

Freedom in this sense is not a property or power; it is the separation of existence from essence, identity, or ground. Nor is this separation anything negative. Nancy thinks of it in terms of a "generosity" or "prodigality" of being in which the singular is allowed to exist independently of any justification, without ground or "without why." Freedom is just this groundlessness. Nancy associates it with the *il y a* understood in Heidegger's sense of the free gift rather than in Levinas's sense of the horror of being

(*EL77/EF55*). Nancy's metaphor for freedom is that of "a prodigality of *bursts [d'éclats]*"; "freedom is essentially *bursting*" (*EL80/EF57*). "It is a bursting or singularity of existence, which means existence deprived of essence and delivered to this inessentiality, to its own surprise as well as to its own decision, to its own indecision as well as to its own generosity" (*EL81/EF57*). So there is an internal link between freedom and the excessive. Naturally one thinks of Bataille.

Freedom is not subjective, but it is accessible to subjectivity in some familiar and even comic or utopian ways. In a splendid paragraph Nancy writes:

> "Freedom" cannot avoid combining, in a unity that has only its own generosity as an index, the values of impulse, chance, luck, the unforeseen, the decided, the game, the discovery, conclusion, dazzlement, the syncope, courage, reflection, rupture, terror, suture, abandonment, hope, caprice, rigor, the arbitrary. Also: laughter, tears, scream, word, rapture, chill, shock, energy, sweetness. . . . Freedom is also wild freedom, the freedom of indifference, the freedom of choice, availability, the free game, freedom of comportment, of air, of love, of a free time where time begins again. (*EL79–80/EF56*)

But prior to these freedoms there is the ontological condition of freedom that calls for thinking—thinking as responsibility rather than ratiocination. "Freedom," Nancy says, "is the leap into existence, in which existence is discovered as such, and this discovery is thinking"—thinking *as experience*: "a thought other than understanding, reason, knowledge, contemplation, philosophy, other finally than thought itself. The *other* thought of all thought—which is not the Other of thought, nor the thought of the Other, but that by which thought thinks—is the burst of freedom" (*EL82–83/EF58–59*).

Freedom is a limit-concept. So the fact that we lack a theory or vocabulary for this event in which the singular occurs is not a deficiency but part of the decorum of freedom itself. The task of thinking is not conceptualization but responsiveness, openness, and acknowledgment—"the recognition of the freedom of being in its singularity" (*EL17/EF13*). In a comparable way the reserve or fragmentariness of Celan's discourse in "Der Meridian" is not a deficiency. Like Blanchot, Celan tries to articulate a poetics of nonidentity, of singularity and irreducibility, that remains on the hither side of theory or the clarification of concepts. Poetry is freedom:

without why, without ground, unnameable—perhaps this is already saying too much (GW3:177/CP25).

Elsewhere

At all events, when Celan speaks (strangely) of the self-assertion of the poem—*Das Gedicht behauptet sich* (GW3:197/CP49; Rosemarie Waldrop translates this as "The poem holds its ground")—this event is as much a movement of displacement as of definition. The text reads like a parody of definition or the positioning of an object: "the poem asserts itself on its own margin [*das Gedicht behauptet sich am Rande seiner selbst*]." Imagine the place of poetry as something other than a position to be occupied.[13] Celan in fact deliberately mixes his metaphors, displacing space into time, in order to confound any thought of fixing poetry in its place: "es ruft und holt sich, um bestehen zu können, unausgesetzt aus seinem Schon-nicht-mehr in sein Immer-noch zurück" (GW3:197/CP49; the poem, as Waldrop translates, "calls and pulls itself back . . . from an 'already-no-more' into a 'still-here'"). Put it that the poem's presence is not a self-presence; it never coincides with itself in a moment of self-identity. *Immer-noch* is not a point in which something asserts itself as such; it is rather like the point where the thing, in Heidegger's formulation, stands on its own, alone in its "self-containment" (*Insichruhen*: as if reposing in itself ["Der Ursprung des Kunstwerkes," GA5:11/PLT26]). The poem is singular, not objective but thinglike insofar as it is outside the alternatives of subject and object; or, in other words, free.

A poetics of nonidentity is in Celan's language a poetics of *Ent-sprechung* (GW3:197/CP49), where *Entsprechung* is something like a condition of attunement in which one is turned toward the other in an event of listening. *Entsprechung* describes very well Lucile's response to language as the breath and flesh of what is singular or external to the space that discourse otherwise opens up for our habitation, namely the world of talk and action where things are taken up in the movement of concepts or taken in hand through clarification and description. The poem frees language from this logical domain. It is, in Celan's words, "language actualized, set free under the sign of a radical individuation which, however, remains as aware of the limits drawn by language as of the possibilities it opens [*Sondern aktualisierte Sprache, freigesetzt unter dem Zeichen einer zwar radikalen, aber gleichzeitig auch der ihr von der Sprache gezogenen*

Grenzen, der ihr von der Sprache erschlossenen Möglichkeiten eingedenk bleibenden Individuation]" (GW3:197/CP49).

Individuation is not a term of identity, of naming or nameability; it does not belong to the relation of sameness and difference. Celan clarifies it in terms of what names cannot reach: the *Dasein* and *Kreatürlichkeit* of the poet. The poem actualizes language, but not as if it were a system; actualizing means situating—a movement away from rules and universals. The poem brings language down to earth, situates it in a here and now specific to the *Dasein* and *Kreatürlichkeit* of the one who speaks. *Dasein* and *Kreatürlichkeit* are not features or attributes (Heidegger would say they are onto-logical rather than ontic); Celan calls them *Neigungswinkels*, which is a word made up of nods and winks, irreproducible shapes or turns that belong to the poem as an irreducible event of language (what Lucile perceives: how she reads). Think of *der Neigungswinkel* as a path which a poem opens up to us. The poem is not a species of ostensive discourse: it does not point, rather it inclines, perhaps with a subtlety not easy to register. Whereto? Inclines whereto?

Celan's language is full of Heideggerian nods and winks: "The poem is solitary. It is solitary and on the way [*Das Gedicht ist einsam. Es ist einsam und unterwegs*]" (GW3:198/CP49). Nomadic: always elsewhere. This elsewhere is perhaps already internal to the poem as the hint that it attends to, cares for and follows; it is the other in the poem, not so much a formal or distinctive feature as a fact of its irreducibility to the objective condition of work or text, as if it could be constituted by what it is not. "The poem," Celan says, "intends another, needs this other, needs an opposite. It goes toward it, bespeaks it [*Das Gedicht will zu einem Andern, es braucht dieses Andere, es braucht ein Gegenüber. Es sucht es auf, es spricht sich ihm zu*]" (GW3:198/CP49).

It is difficult to clarify this Other. Certainly it is right to think of the poem in terms of an ethical relation.[14] It is an instance of attentiveness, as if to another human being. *Entsprechung*, after all, does not mean agreement in the sense of *adequatio*; it is a term of responsibility, of listening rather than seeing. It is a dialogical rather than a logical concept. Its attentiveness is not scrutiny, mere attention to details, but an attentiveness of the ear and of memory. So not surprisingly Celan figures the poem as a conversation, where attentiveness is a condition of possibility.

However, Celan's *Gespräch* is neither interlocution nor any sort of *mitsein*. It is both something like and something other than the Levinasian *Dire* in which the subject is turned out of its house: like *le Dire* it "is not a

---

modality of cognition." It is not communication in the sense that "the contents that are inscribed in the said and transmitted to the interpretation and decoding done by the other. It is in the risky uncovering of oneself, in sincerity, the breaking up of inwardness and the abandon of all shelter, exposure to traumas, vulnerability" (AE82/OTB48). However, for Celan this event is at once ethical and more than ethical, a conversation with things as well as with people, a neutral as well as ethical conversation.[15] Celan's *eines ganz Anderen Sache* is neither human nor nonhuman; it is spatial. (What is the upshot of *die Sache* in *eines ganz Anderen Sache*?)[16]

In fact Celan figures conversation explicitly as a space (*Raum*) into which the other, being addressed as a "you," is "brought into the present," with its time now taking place in the here-and-now of the poem (GW3:198/CP50). But the space of this encounter is not fixed; it has no boundaries (no *Gestalt*). One might as well say that the poem is only a traversal of this space, as if this space were a surface, not a volume.

So it becomes difficult to think of the poem as a work or text. "I am talking about a poem that does not exist [*das es nicht gibt*]" (GW3:199/CP51). The poem is a place, not an object—"the place where all tropes and metaphors want to be led *ad absurdam*" (as if to no point: without why and without completion). It is no accident that Celan's later poetry is perhaps the most powerful example we have of what Blanchot calls *désœuvrement*: writing outside the space or totality of the work (EI622/IC424):

Du liegst hinaus über dich,	You lie beyond yourself,
über dich hinaus liegt dein Schicksal,	beyond yourself lies your fate,
weißäugig, einem Gesang entronnen, tritt etwas zu ihm,	white-eyed, it has fled from a song, something comes forth
das hilft beim Zungenentwurzeln,	it's useful in the tearing of tongues from their roots
auch mittags, draußen. (GW3:73)	even in the afternoon, outside (LP159)

(In an undisciplined or lunatic moment one might imagine this as a poem addressed as much to another poem as to a person, a poem elsewhere, or to fragments of a poem; imagine a poem no longer meant to be sung. The violent image of uprooted tongues could be mitigated by thinking of the way words in Celan's poetry are frequently figured as, Yiddishlike, wandering [cf. "Sprich auch Du" [GW1:135]; "Est ist alles anders" (GW1:285)]. In the context opened up by Celan it may not be that we can continue thinking of languages as belonging to nations or of words as belonging to a language—or of letters and syllables as belonging to words:

> ST
> Ein Vau, pf, in der That,
> schlägt, mps,
> ein Sieben-Rad:
>
> o
> oo
> ooo
> O
>
> (GW3:136)

Could one just as well think here of the "oh's" as wheels?)

Certainly Lacoue-Labarthe is not wrong to read "Der Meridian" as, Blanchot-like, a poetics of *désœuvrement*, or a Heideggerian poetics of estrangement, where poetry is "l'interruption du langage, le suspense du langage, la césure. . . . La poésie est le spasme ou la syncope du langage" (*La poésie comme expérience*, p. 74). But as an event of language poetry is also *Unterwegssein*: not catastrophe, but freedom—

> Whenever we speak with things in this way [Celan says] we also dwell on the question of their where-from and where-to [*die Frage nach ihrem Woher und Wohin*], an "open" question "without resolution," a question which points toward open, empty, free spaces [*ins Offene und Leere und Freie weisenden Frage*]—we have ventured far outside [*wir sind weit draußen*].
> The poem also searches for this place. (GW3:199/CP50)

Celan proposes (but with characteristic reserve) the term "topological research" (*Toposforschung*: GW3:199/CP51), as if the poem were a search for a free space or utopia (or a-topia): a place outside the organon of discursive production; or, rhetorically, a free, indeterminate, unconfined, unoccupied, *other* place or *topos* for *die ganz anderen Sache*, whose otherness (or freedom), after all, is what is at stake.[17]

Celan — Blanchot

Mit ihm
wandern die Meridiane (GW1:290)

Blanchot, in his brief essay on Celan, fastens on this "outside" as if it were symmetrical with his own.[18] Not without reason, perhaps. Genealogically both Blanchot and Celan are linked to Heidegger, for example to the "Brief über den Humanismus" (1946), where Heidegger, citing Heraclitus (*ethos anthropoi daimon* [Fr. 119]: sometimes translated as, "character is fate"), gives us the etymology of the word ethics: "*Ethos* means abode, dwelling-place [*Ort des Wohnens*]. The word names the open region in which man dwells. The open region of his abode allows what pertains to man's essence, and what in thus arriving resides in nearness to him, to appear" (W351/BW233). We can think of Celan and Blanchot as giving different interpretations of Heidegger's "open region": not a fixed dwelling-place but a "setting free of places," an "outside" or space of exile or movement where existence is free from essence, identity, and ground.[19]

It was Heidegger, Jean-Luc Nancy says, who separated freedom from "the metaphysics of subjectivity" and refigured it topologically as spaciousness or spatiality. Nancy writes:

> This spatiality, or spaciosity, is the space of freedom, inasmuch as freedom is, at every moment, the freedom of a free space. Which means that it constitutes the spatializing or spacing essence of freedom. Spacing is the general "form"—which precisely has no form, but gives *room* for forms and formations, and which is not general but which gives *room* for singularities—of existence: the spacing, exposure, retrenchment and cutting (decision) of singularity, the *areality* (which is, as we have indicated elsewhere, the character of *air*) of singularity in its difference which relates it to its limit, to others, and to itself: for example, a mouth opened in a cry. (*EL*187/*EF*145)

The experience of freedom, of being free, means being exposed to this open region or "free space" where singularities are given room for existence. Nancy emphasizes that this space is not a place for staying but, borrowing from Deleuze and Guattari (who borrow from Blanchot), a "nomadic space" that opens out in all directions.

A space, in other words, of meridians.

I imagine Blanchot and Celan walking along parallel lines—not, to be sure, on a country or a mountain path, rather in a Paris neighborhood (each of course carrying a copy of Heidegger's *Holzwege* [1950]): but they are not in the event moving along the same meridian. Blanchot, reclusive, speaks of poetry as a movement into exile. Celan, the exile, speaks of poetry as a movement into the Open, the Empty, the Free.

Two interpretations of *Unterwegssein*? Blanchot's seems dystopian ("Art is 'the world turned upside down': insubordination, disproportion, frivolity, ignorance, evil, non-sense"), whereas Celan's is utopian—the most prominent theme of "Der Meridian" is that of *Freiheit* and *Freisetzung*. The two interpretations do not exclude one another. The world is after all already upside down.[20] For Blanchot, moreover, exile does not remain deprivation. In his essay "Être juif" (1962), for example, Blanchot says that the "words *exodus, exile* . . . bear a meaning that is not negative" for the same reason that anarchy is not a negative condition. Exile frees us, and therefore the world, from subjection to principle and rule:

> The words exodus and exile indicate a positive relation with exteriority, whose exigency invites us not to be content with what is proper to us (that is, with our power to assimilate everything, to identify everything, to bring everything back to our I). Exodus and exile express simply the same reference to the Outside that the word existence bears. Thus, on the one hand, nomadism maintains above what is established the right to put the distribution of space into question by appealing to the initiatives of human movement and human time. And, on the other hand, if to become rooted in a culture and in a regard for things does not suffice, it is because the order of the realities in which we become rooted does not hold the key to all the relations to which we must respond (EI185–86/IC127)

Possibly one could say: the world is not all there is. There is also what the exile traverses, where there is nothing to be reached. Blanchot would say: every *Weg* is a detour; history is a "movement of turning and slipping away" (EI28/IC21). Imagine history cut loose from the concept of destiny.

Celan writes in "Der Meridian": "Is it on such paths that poems take us when we think of them [*Geht man also, wenn man an Gedichte denkt, geht man mit Gedichten solche Wege*]? And are these paths only detours [*Um-Wege*], detours from you to you? But they are, among how many others, the paths on which language becomes voice [*auf denen die Sprache stimmhaft wird*]. They are encounters, paths from a voice to a listening You [*zu einem wahrnehmenden Du*], creaturely paths [*kreatürliche Wege*], outlines for existence [*Daseinsentwürfe*] perhaps, for projecting ourselves into the search for ourselves. . . . A kind of homecoming [*Heimkehr*]" (GW3: 201/CP53). Likewise Blanchot writes: "every encounter supposes many paths [*une diversité de chemins*]" (EI472/IC322); but in contrast to Levinas what holds true for Blanchot is the essential solitude—"crossing paths without meeting" (PD51/SNB34). The encounter with alterity leaves one without a relation.

Blanchot figures the exile as outside the world—in the Outside: traversing not this world or another but the other of all worlds. For Celan the world is not so much an inside from which the exile is excluded as it is a surface across which the exile moves indeterminately, with no end in sight nor with any border conceivable. The extension of the concept of the end cannot be closed by a frontier. One is always on the outside as on the skin of the earth or the breath or flesh of language. *Unterwegssein* as a ontological condition is ringed by what Celan, in another but still related context, calls "the sound of the unreachable" (GW3:185/CP34).

The metaphor of the meridian which guides Celan's address puts the *Sache* of homecoming out of reach (makes it an a-topos). The exile's world is a globe measured by imaginary lines unbroken by any fixed points. The meridian is interrupted only by intersections where an encounter might or might not occur. One can come full circle without arriving anywhere. Neither are there points of origin or of departure. "None of these places can be found. They do not exist" (GW3:202/CP54). Every place is elsewhere along the way.

Think of a poem as this movement elsewhere: *Unterwegssein*.

CHAPTER 5

Blanchot/Levinas

Interruption
(On the Conflict of Alterities)

> Now, in this night, I come forward bearing everything, to-
> ward that which infinitely exceeds everything. I progress be-
> yond the totality which I nevertheless tightly embrace. I go
> on the margins of the universe, boldly walking elsewhere
> than where I can be, and a little outside of my steps. This
> slight extravagance, this deviation toward that which cannot
> be, is not only my own impulse leading me to a personal
> madness, but the impulse of the reason I bear with me.
> With me the laws gravitate outside the laws, the possible
> outside the possible. O night, now nothing will make me be,
> nothing will separate me from you.
> —*Thomas l'obscur*

Listening

It was Heidegger's insight that our relation to language is not that of speaking subjects. To be sure, we take up or take over language for our use, and
it appears that all of our theories of it presuppose some such appropriation.
Thus we think of language as a system for framing representations, for thematizing the world, reducing the world to our propositions. But language
remains excessive with respect to our uses of it. It does not, Heidegger says,
"exhaust itself in signifying" (GA5:310/PLT132). Like the thing and the
work of art, language remains outside the world; it withholds itself. If we
communicate by means of language, language itself remains uncommunicative. It is self-standing, reserved, resistant to appropriation.

In his middle years Heidegger would think of language in terms of an event of disclosure that remains itself on the hither side of the world or history that it opens up. Language is an event in which the world manifests itself, but this event is anterior to the world's history. It is an anarchic moment which, however, does not simply recede into an aboriginal past; rather it accompanies the world and exposes its history to the future. Philosophy might end, but not history. Heidegger of course was always tempted by a concept of the future as destiny; but increasingly and perhaps grudgingly he let this concept die away. The history of being, just to call it that, cannot be made into a narrative, and that is because what makes it possible is just that which threatens to turn every narrative into a *Tristram Shandy*. Imagine history as what occurs when the principle of identity withholds itself from the world: history as interruption, history in fragments.

In his later writings Heidegger speaks of undergoing an experience with language, where experience is *Erfahrung*, a reversal of consciousness that leaves consciousness destitute, deprived of its concepts (US159/OWL57). An experience with language is a reversal in which language is no longer an instrument under our control; it is no longer anything we can speak. Our relationship to language has been turned inside out, leaving us speechless and worldless. Countless poems, both before and after Mallarmé's, respond to this event of impossibility. (This is the constant theme of Maurice Blanchot's research.)

For Heidegger, this reversal is not a failure of language but, on the contrary, it is the event in which the truth of language overwhelms and transforms us so that we can no longer comport ourselves with language as speaking subjects. This event occurs precisely as a loss of subjectivity or, better, as an invasion of the subject that deprives it of its self-possession and self-identity. Count it as an event of poetry or madness (or death) that sets the subject apart. Heidegger reads Georg Trakl's poetry as an event that occurs in this apartness. *Abgeschiedenheit* is the place (the elsewhere) of poetry (US52/OWL172).[1]

An experience with language has all the features of a prophetic event in which something transcendental breaks in on us. In fact in "Das Wesen der Sprache" Heidegger cites the story of Pentecost and the tongues of fire as an example of such an experience. But the point of the citation is not anything transcendental; to the contrary, it is that speaking does not originate with subjectivity but is first of all a mode of responsibility. So in "Der Weg zur Sprache" Heidegger identifies speaking with listening; that is, our relation to language is before everything else a relation of listening (where listening [*hören*] is a pun on belonging [*gehören*]). "Speaking is listening to the language which we speak . . . a listening not *while* but *before* we are speaking. . . . We do not merely speak *the* language—we speak *by way of* it [aus ihr]. We can do so solely because we always have already listened to the language. What do we hear there? We hear language speaking [*das Sprechen der Sprache*]" (US254/OWL123–24).

What is it to hear language speaking? The sense of this question is obscured somewhat by the English translation, which evokes the specter of language as a Supersubject or stand-in for the Being of beings whose Godlike voice pursues us across some supersensible space. But of course language does not speak as if it were a kind of speaker. *Die Sprache spricht* ought to be translated as "language languages," because after all there is no one or nothing there: language is not a substantive, nor is speaking a substantive activity. It is an event but not a process. An experience with language is an interruption; it is prophetic in its structure except that nothing is revealed.[2] It is rather that our relation with language (and not just with language) is no longer one of cognition and command. It is now a relation of proximity (*Nähe*) in which, although nothing is revealed, neither can anything be evaded. In "Das Wesen der Sprache" Heidegger speaks of the relation of poetry and thinking in terms of a movement into the proximity of language, where proximity means being face-to-face with others and with things. Think of language as the event in which this proximity occurs. Perhaps language is nothing more than the proximity of others and of things—and (who can say?) of gods as well.

"We tend," says Heidegger, "to think of the face-to-face [*das Gegeneinander-über*] exclusively as a relation between human beings. . . . Yet being face-to-face with another has a more distant origin where earth and sky, god and man reach one another. Goethe, and Mörike too, like to use the phrase 'face-to-face with one another' not only with respect to human beings but also with respect to things of the world. Where this prevails, all things are open to one another in their self-concealment; thus one extends itself to the other, and thus all remain themselves; one is over the other as its guardian watching over the other, over it as its veil" (US211/OWL104). Peculiar how Heidegger construes responsibility and care as guarding and veiling the other. Guarding from what? One wants to say: from philosophy. At all events from knowledge conceived as conceptual grasping.

An experience with language means an interruption of subjectivity in which we find ourselves face-to-face with whatever is otherwise, not just other people but, borrowing Celan's language, *die ganz Anderen Sache.* Being face-to-face means being responsive to and responsible for whatever is encountered, whatever is given (whatever *es gibt*). For Heidegger, nothing is excluded from the *Nähe* (or, alternatively, from the *Gegend*). This "nothing-excluded" is the Fourfold (*das Vier*), that is, the proximity of earth and sky, gods and men.[3]

What matters to Heidegger is whether an experience with language can open the way for thinking as well as for poetry as a mode of responsibility. This is what Heidegger is asking when, in "Das Wesen der Sprache," he (against all reason) characterizes thinking as listening (US180/OWL75–76). If language speaks, it is not as a revelation but as an interruption, a call that calls thinking away from the calculative and cognitive into the proximity of the other. What is it for thinking to be face-to-face with what it thinks, not grasping it or interrogating it but, on the contrary, interrupted by it as if confronted in the open, surprised on the way, no place to hide (deprived of position)? It would not be too much to say that such an event frees thinking from philosophy.

At all events, as Heidegger says, "it is more salutary for thinking to wander in the strange than to establish itself in the intelligible [*es ist heilsamer für das Denken, wenn es im Befremdlichen wandert, statt sich im Verständlichen einzurichten*] (VA218/EGT76). Hence the "weakness" of thinking, which Heidegger says can be summed up in four sentences:

1. Thinking does not bring knowledge as do the sciences.
2. Thinking does not produce usable practical wisdom.
3. Thinking solves no cosmic riddles.
4. Thinking does not endow us directly with the power to act.

(WhD161/WT159)

Thinking with respect to philosophy is evidently on the side of impossibility: that is, thinking, like poetry, can be thought of as a refusal of philosophy. This might be Derrida's angle; it is certainly Maurice Blanchot's.

The Other Discourse

Already in *Sein und Zeit* Heidegger had characterized discourse (*Rede*) nonsubjectively (or, say, passively) so that even "keeping silent" could be counted as a mode of discourse. And at a crucial point he characterized discourse as a call (*Ruf*). The call does not originate with the subject, rather the subject is exposed to the call. Conscience is an event of calling; it is a mode of responsibility.

The call is nonsubjective. In *Sein und Zeit* this nonsubjectivity is obscured by the central place occupied by *Dasein*, where conscience becomes *Dasein*'s responsibility to itself, a call that "summons [*ruft*] Dasein's Self from its lostness in the 'they' [*das Man*]" (SZ274/BT319). But the call itself is nonidentical (neutral): "the caller maintains itself in conspicuous indefiniteness. If the caller is asked about its name, status, origin, or repute, it not only refuses to answer, but does not even leave the slightest possibility of one's making it into something with which one can be familiar when one's understanding of Dasein has a 'worldly' orientation" (SZ274/BT319). The caller is absolutely other: not another subject, nor anything that can be objectified. The call as discourse belongs to the Outside.

Emmanuel Levinas thinks of himself as breaking with Heidegger's "philosophy of the Neuter"—that is, as he puts it, "with the Heideggerian Being of the existent whose impersonal neutrality the critical work of Blanchot has so much contributed to bring out."[4] This break consists of putting a face on the nonidentical (TeI332/TI298). *Gegen-einander-über* becomes, explicitly, *le face à face* (TeI78/TI79). As Levinas says: "it is only man who could be absolutely foreign to me, refractory to every typology, to every genus, to every characterology, to every classification" (TeI71/TI73).

There is an issue to be joined here between Levinas and Blanchot concerning the relation of language and alterity, and beyond this concerning the nature of alterity as such.

The question that needs to be clarified (think of it as Blanchot's question to Levinas) is how the other could be absolutely foreign to me except in virtue of the way language—that is, speaking or writing—can drain me of my self-identity (EI103/IC73). Language is the already-foreign in which the other interrupts me. The other needs language in order to breach my self-sufficiency, because language already has situated me beside myself, turned me out as exposed and waiting. If I were not already breached, no foreignness would ever occur to me.[5]

Levinas seemed inclined this way in "La transcendence des mots: à propos des biffures" (1949), where he speaks of the way sound can fragment the harmonious world composed by the eye (the artist's eye, the philosopher's, or anyone's). "To see," he says, "is to be in a world that is entirely *here* and self-sufficient": the world as work of art, a plenum or totality. "In sound," however, "and in the consciousness termed hearing [*audition*], there is in fact a break with the self-complete world of vision and art. In its entirety, sound is a ringing, clanging scandal. Whereas, in vision, form is wedded to content in such a way as to appease it, in sound the perceptible quality overflows so that form can no longer contain its content. A real rent [*déchirure*] is produced in the world, through which the world that is *here* prolongs a dimension that cannot be converted into vision" (*HS*219/*LR*147). Blanchot is clearly in tune with this idea in "Parler, ce n'est pas voir": "Speaking is not seeing. Speaking frees thought from the optical imperative that in the Western tradition, for thousands of years, has subjugated our approach to things, and induced us to think under the guaranty of light or under the threat of its absence" (*EI*38/*IC*27). Discourse here is not propositional but, let us say, invasive: prophetic-like it breaks in from the outside (turns all insides out).

Philosophy has no place for sound. Sound is foreign. It is always outside the world, threatening to invade it, like anarchy.

We more or less acknowledge this with respect to noise, which like randomness is held in low esteem. The wholeness of the world requires us to exclude or subdue noise, or at least defer it to the background. (Think of the scandal of the avant-garde musician John Cage, who refuses to exclude noise from music.) Noise that takes the form of words, however, is irrepressible, even demonic in the sense of possessive and maddening. "The sounds and noise of nature," says Levinas, "are failed words. To really hear a sound, we need to hear a word. Pure sound is the word" (*HS*219/*LR*148). As if utterances were the medium of sound, not sound of utterances.

The transcendence of words means that words do not originate here, with me, are not mine or part of me; they are always outside of me, raining down on me. Linguistic competence perhaps means no more than that I am able to seal myself off from language, unlike Samuel Beckett's Unnamable who is porous, all ears and mouth, an inside turned inside out, an inside without an outside to protect him from the words that pour through him anarchically, no one knows from where, without beginning or end.

Words are the presence of exteriority, the infinite, the elsewhere, the otherwise or nonidentical as such. So the otherness of the other person is only brought home to me in the word that breaks in on me: "this presence, far from signifying pure and simple coexistence with me, or expressing itself through the romantic metaphor of 'living presence,' is fulfilled in the act of hearing, and derives its meaning from the role of transcendent origin played by the word [*parole*] that is offered" (*HS*220/*LR*148). Language does not unite us, as if it were a bond or a whole that contained us both; rather it separates us because it is itself uncontainable within any totality. It is the interruption of every union.

Language here is irreducible. It is no longer the systematic entity of logic, linguistics, semiotics, and philosophy of language, which try to insulate language—that is, the proposition—from the anarchic exteriority of (among other things) sound. Levinas (like Blanchot and the later Heidegger) appears to take a view entirely contrary to philosophy insofar as he thinks of language as interruptive in the nature of the case. Imagine sounds as words (or words as sounds) rending the world.

For Levinas (at least in this essay from 1949), it is language that introduces the asymmetry between the other and myself—situates the other in its magisterial role—because language is asymmetrical with myself even if I am the one speaking it, as if words were teaching me to speak (an obvious fact when one thinks of it). Anyhow Levinas situates the other, not the speaking subject, at the originary site of language. "The presence of the Other (*Autre*) is a presence that teaches us something; this is why the word, as a form of education, amounts to more than the experience of reality, and why the master of the word is more than a spiritual obstetrician. The use of the word wrenches experience out of its aesthetic self-sufficiency, the *here* where it has quietly been lying" (*HS*220/*LR*148). In virtue of the word we are no longer *here*: as if the word were a mode of alienation or exile, always displacing us from ourselves, a pure tuition without intuition. Beckett's *L'innomable* gives us something like an absolute picture of this condition.

It is plain that "The Transcendence of Words" contains a line of thinking that Levinas has to pursue carefully if (as he thinks) the neutral is an obstacle to ethics. The idea that, all by itself, language is what is absolutely foreign, is the idea that Levinas has to circumvent if ethics (as an ethics of *human* alterity: ethics as a humanism) is to begin. Meanwhile the idea of language as interruption is too good to throw away. So in *Totalité et infini* the face replaces the word (*mot*) as that which signifies the outside, but Levinas retains the idea that discourse is essentially interpellation—"the interpellation of the vocative" (*TeI*65/*TI*69). "The face speaks [*La visage parle*]" (*TeI*61/*TI*66). (Compare *TeI*62/*TI*66: "Discourse is . . . an original relation with an exterior being. . . . It is the frank presence of an existent that can lie, that is, dispose of the theme he offers, without being able to dissimulate his frankness as interlocutor, always struggling openly. The eyes break through the mask—the language of the eyes, impossible to dissemble. The eye does not shine; it speaks.") The face itself is a language without words (*mots*) that works the work of language insofar as it disrupts my self-identity, exposes me to the magisterial claim of someone outside my here and now, situates me elsewhere as if depriving me of immanence. "The relationship of language implies transcendence, radical separation, the strangeness of interlocutors, the revelation of the other to me. In other words, language is spoken where community between the terms of the relationship is wanting, where the common plane is wanting or is yet to be constituted. It takes place in this transcendence. Discourse is thus the experience of something absolutely foreign, a *pure* 'knowledge' or 'experience,' a traumatism of astonishment" (*TeI*71/*TI*73).[6]

A prophetic event.

It is worth stressing that language here is not made of words (*mots*). In "Language and Proximity," language is a word for "the relationship of proximity," or rather this relationship is "the original language, a language without words, propositions, pure communication" (*DHH*228/*CPP*119). Interestingly, as Levinas figures it in this essay, the difference between poetry and ethics is that the one is the "proximity of things" (*DHH*228/*CPP*118) and the other is the proximity of a neighbor. But "the poetry of the world is inseparable from proximity par excellence, or the proximity of a neighbor par excellence," because it is "via the human" that the world impinges on me and, not to put too fine a point on it, obsesses me—the world, via the human, becomes something unevadable, like a prophetic voice (*DHH*228-29/*CPP*119–20). But voice, curiously, is not a Levinasian concept. Language as proximity is not something that carries like a voice but something that contacts like a touch. In fact Levinas does not hesitate to speak of "language as contact" (*DHH*228/*CPP*119). It is at all events a nonlinguistic language or, Blanchot-like, a language outside of language, namely "the possibility of entering into a relationship independently of every system of signs common to the interlocutors. Like a battering-ram, it is the power to break through the limits of culture, body, and race" (*DHH*232/*CPP*122).

The language of words meanwhile belongs to logic and rhetoric, that is, to the monologue of propositions and to my preemption of discourse, where I approach the other as if behind its back in order to deprive it of speech. (The historic task of rhetoric, for example, is to produce silence in the audience.) But all the other has to do is turn round and nothing holds together, everything is taken away: my interior is laid bare, my world is a threshold onto exile. Perhaps one could say that, turning round, the other comes to the aid of language, rescuing it from the discourse of interiority, setting *mots* free by turning them into *paroles*.

The ethical world is noisy in contrast to the interior world of cognition and self-identity, of concepts and representations of fact, the world of the solitary ego for whom, as for the mythical Gyges, "the world is a spectacle" (*TeI90/TI90*). This interior, spectacular world is silent, or almost silent: unfortunately not silent enough. As Levinas (Descartes-like) imagines it the interiority (the self, the same) is always haunted by another sort of Other, evidently nonhuman, an "evil genius [*malin génie*]" who threatens to reduce my representations to travesty, that is, who shadows my experience of the world with the possibility that the world is *mere* spectacle, an Ovid-like world of anarchic metamorphosis in which nothing is what it is but is under a power of enchantment that could dissolve every rational boundary and turn a human world into a world of birds and trees and fixated violent lovers. What is seen is always shadowed by just this uncertainty—which is not, moreover, just a logical uncertainty, a strategic suspension of belief, but a satirical doubt that threatens us with ridicule as if we were always on the verge of being hoodwinked by a magician. "Its equivocation is insinuated in a mockery. Thus silence is not a simple absence of speech [*parole*]; speech lies in the depths of silence like a laughter perfidiously held back. It is the inverse of language [*l'envers du langage*]. . . . The inverse of language is like a laughter that seeks to destroy language, a laughter infinitely reverberated where mystification interlocks in mystification without ever resting on a real speech, without ever commencing. The spectacle of the silent world of facts is bewitched: every phenomenon masks, mystifies ad infinitum, making actuality impossible" (*TeI91–92/TI91–92*).

Of course, whoever imagines this may imagine more, namely that the malign genie is no one other than Maurice Blanchot, who—in a late text, but not for the first time—reminds Levinas that the silent world of fact and knowledge is always unsettled by the sound of the *il y a*—"the incessant insistence of the neutral, the nocturnal murmur of the anonymous, as what never begins (thus, as an-archic, since it eternally eludes the determination of a beginning); it is the absolute, but as absolute indetermination" (*NCC86/OCC49*).[7] For Blanchot, the other as evil genius is not imaginary but inhabits—is the habitation or persistence of—the *il y a*:

there is always another Outside outside the exteriority of other people, an anarchic Outside from which the speech or face of the other cannot entirely emancipate us. The inverse of language is perfidious laughter at the expense of philosophy, that is, an interruption not just of ontology but even of ethics as first philosophy.

The key point is perhaps that Blanchot has always associated this inverse of language—this "talking outside the truth"—with poetry or literature.[8] In fact he calls the speech of the evil genius "a gift of literature, and we do not know if it intoxicates while sobering, or if its speech, which charms and disgusts, doesn't ultimately attract us because it promises (a promise it both does and does not keep) to clarify what is obscure in all speech—everything in speech that escapes revelation, manifestation: namely, the remaining trace of nonpresence, what is still opaque in the transparent": or, in other words, the neuter, or more exactly language or writing experienced as a neutral rather than ethical relation (as in a relation of strangeness in which there is neither one nor the other but simply the presence of what Blanchot calls the *outside* or the *unknown*) (NCC86/ OCC49–50; EI103–4/IC73–74).

This anyhow is essentially Blanchot's question to Levinas: if the ethical relation is a relation of language, a relation in which the other speaks to me, does this not introduce into this relation "certain exigencies that might reverse or overturn speech itself"?—that is, not just overturn speech as *my* discourse, the propositional discourse of the ego or same, but the ethical discourse of the other as well: the discourse that addresses me (addresses me as Blanchot says, not as a *vous* or a *tu* but as an *il*) (NCC82–83/ OCC45). In Blanchot's account of this vocative event—an account that is not so much a dispute with Levinas as a tacit rewriting of ethics as a poetics of the Outside—when the other speaks to me my world is not guaranteed but drains away along with my power to grasp it. When the other addresses me, a fissure or caesura opens up in being—Blanchot calls it explicitly "an interruption of being" (EI99/IC69)—and this interruption, this interval, is our relation: "between man and man there is an interval that would be neither of being nor of non-being, an interval borne by the Difference of speech—a difference preceding everything that is different and everything unique" (EI99/IC69): a difference outside the alternatives of identity and difference, an an-archic difference that Blanchot calls "a relation of the third kind," that is, neither cognitive nor ethical but neutral.

Whereas, in altogether much simpler terms, Levinas thinks that the speech of the other—the magisterial conversation that breaks in on me from the outside—saves me from the evil genius by underwriting the truth (or, at all events, the exteriority) of the world. Language is the guarantor of reality, not reality of language. And if we ask, what language is this, the answer is that Levinas seems to have taken a step back from the language of interruption, or has anyhow reinscribed the discourse of the other in the language of rationality and coherence. That is, Levinas assigns the other's task of reassurance to the sentence (*la phrase*): "The given is the work of the sentence. In the sentence the apparition loses its phenomenality in being fixed as a theme; in contrast with the silent world, ambiguity magnified, stagnant water, water stilled with mystification that passes for mystery, the proposition relates the phenomenon to exteriority, to the Infinity of the other uncontained by my thought" (*TeI*101/*TI*98-99). So it turns out that the other speaks philosophically, in the language of propositions that objectify the world; that is, not to put too fine a point on it, the other is a philosopher (someone who, outside the alternative of true and false, nevertheless does not "talk outside the truth"). Somehow one knew that sooner or later orphans and widows would fall by the wayside in Levinas's philosophy. What saves me, in any event, is not so much the truth as the company of the philosopher. A clandestine company, no doubt, since my relation to him, if "him" is the word, is not cognitive but ethical; but what matter? In my monadic solitude I am prey to misgivings about the given. The presence of the other—"the Master who by his word gives meaning to phenomena and permits them to be thematized" (*TeI*102/*TI*100)—restores my certainty as to the real presence, the objectivity of objects. If I cannot know the other, at least I can know by way of the other. So long as he does not *talk outside the truth* (if "he" [*il*: he or it] is the word).

Plural Speech

So in Levinas's philosophy, the philosopher guarantees the truth of the world: "The world is offered in the language of the Other [*le langage d'autrui*]; it is borne by propositions" (*TeI*92/*TI*92). *Plus ça change. . . .*

Possibly this thought is only a detour in Levinas's philosophy, a turn (or return) that ethics can easily do without, perhaps ought to do without. Or say that vis-à-vis the world language undergoes its customary reduction to propositional form. But ethically language is irreducible: "Language is perhaps to be defined as the very power to break [*rompre*] the continuity of be-

ing or of history" (*TeI212/TI194*). For the other before anything else is an interruption of my interiority, even if only to save me from it; it restores the
world to my knowledge without becoming part of what I know.[9] What interests Blanchot in Levinas's thinking is just this power to interrupt my
power, "turning my highest power into im-possibility" (*EI78/IC54*). Making the other the condition of the world's possibility seems an altogether
needless purchase on the name of philosophy.

However, it is at least true, even for Levinas, that the ethical relation entails a plurality of languages. Certainly by *Autrement qu'être* (1974) language seems no longer reducible to propositional form. Indeed it is hard
for a reader of Blanchot not to see the strong influence of Blanchot here.
At all events ethical language, something like a Saying (*Dire*) addressed to
another and not correlated with a Said (*le Dit*), has always occupied the
site of Blanchot's poetic language insofar as it is "pre-original" (*AE17/
OTB6*), older than naming (*AE60/OTB34*), on the hither side (*en deça*) of
the conceptual movement of negation or the proposition. As if ethics like
poetry were a language without concepts. "Language," says Levinas, is "not
reducible to a system of signs doubling up beings and relations; that conception would be incumbent upon us if the word were the Noun [*si le mot
était Nom*]. Language seems rather to be an excrescence of the verb"
(*AE61/OTB35*). That is, Saying (*Dire*)—speaking a language—is irreducible to the Said (*le Dit*) or the logical construction of identity. It would
not be too much to call this Levinas's version of Blanchot's *le grand refus*,
the refusal of death or of meaning, call it a refusal of thematization or a refusal of the rule of identity. According to this rule, identifying "this *as* that"
removes it from the lived experience of the verb and establishes it in the
"already said" of the noun; that is, in so many words, it kills it. "Language
has been in operation, and the saying that bore this said, but goes further,
was absorbed and died in the said, was inscribed" (*AE64/OTB36*). But language is always in excess of its logical function of predication, and this excess is preserved in the verb which temporalizes the movement of the
proposition, interrupts the "this *as* that, brings it down to the here and
now" (Celan's temporality of the singular).

Language in this context never coincides with itself; it is never self-identical. There is more than one language in language: there is the language
of identity which reduces the other to the same, and there is the language
of temporality or of sensibility in which the *this* breaks down into *that*, that
is, into something other than its selfsame being as such (*AE69–70/*

OTB40). Scratch the idea of being as such: there are only singularities.

Levinas here adumbrates Heidegger's conception of language as an event in which substantives are subsumed by verbs (*Die Sprache spricht; Das Ding dingt*). Strikingly, but perhaps not surprisingly, Levinas associates this verbalization of language with art, where things and the qualities of things resonate with their lived open-endedness: "Through art essence and temporality begin to resound with poetry or song. And the search for new forms, from which all art lives, keeps awake everywhere the verbs that are on the verge of collapsing into substantives. In painting red reddens and green greens, forms are produced as contours and vacate with their vacuity as forms. In music sounds resound; in poems vocables, material of the said, no longer yield before what they evoke, but sing with their evocative powers and their diverse ways to evoke, their etymologies; in Paul Valéry's *Eupalinos* architecture makes buildings sing. Poetry is productive of song and sonority, which are the verbalness of verbs or essence" (AE70/OTB40).[10]

As if, in the work of art, nothing holds still: everything is unsettled, *Unterwegssein*, opaque to the eye that merely sees—in contrast to "the 'listening eye'" (*l'œil qui écoute:* AE67/OTB38) that can hear the sheer noisiness of things as they reverberate throughout their temporal modality, never being just the same but always being in excess, irreducible, on the hither side of being (*en deça*): lesswise than just being-there in the conceptual order of things. In these pages Levinas preserves his old idea of the exoticism of art: the work of art does not reproduce the world; it disseminates worlds (AE71/OTB41). As such it is always, with saying, on the hither side of being or of whatever world is contained within the *already said.* The work of art is always outside *le Dit:* it is unspeakable within the form of the proposition.

The difference between Levinas and Blanchot is that Levinas cannot abandon philosophy, that is, cannot give up the discourse of concepts and definitions.[11] Saying for Levinas is always ambiguously implicated in the said; it is not (as in Blanchot) a refusal of concepts and definition, of mastery and work (of philosophy). To be sure, Blanchot-like, Levinas says, "As soon as saying, on the hither side of being, becomes dictation, it expires, or abdicates, in fables and in writing." But here Blanchot would stop, arguing only that writing (*l'écriture*) cannot be made intelligible as dictation or the mere fixing of saying (*l'écriture* for Blanchot is the freedom of *le Dire*, the impossibility of *le Dit*). Levinas, however, cannot forgo a progress into philosophy. He asks: "Is it necessary and is it possible that the saying on the hither side be thematized, that is, manifest itself, that it enter into a proposition and a book?" Whereas Blanchot would say no ("the great refusal"), Levinas says yes: "It is necessary. The responsibility for another is precisely a saying prior to anything said. The surprising saying which is a responsibility for another is against 'the winds and tides' of being, is an interruption of essence, a disinterestedness imposed with a good violence" (AE75/OTB43). But this saying cannot be thought, cannot be understood as ethical, unless it is in some sense fixed—fixed not just as a said or a theme but as a philosophy. "Philosophy," Levinas says, "makes this astonishing adventure . . . intelligible" (AE75/OTB44).

One can imagine this as the moment at which poetry and philosophy break off from one another, with poetry holding to the outside (the hither side [en deçà] of language), while philosophy institutes its propositional style in order to reduce saying to intelligibility. The ethical relation has, after all, to be formalized as philosophy, and this requires something like a dictation of saying, a writing down, documentation, or exemplification of the "hither side of being." You can't have ethics as first philosophy unless and until you raise or reduce saying to the higher power of a category—an ethical genre. This is why you can have an ethics but not a poetics, since a poetics (in Aristotle's sense: a branch of the Organon) cannot be derived from anything like l'écriture. Ethics as first philosophy is to that extent abusive, but necessary: "The hither side, the preliminary, which the pre-originary saying animates, refuses the present and manifestation, or lends itself to them only out of time. The unsayable saying lends itself to the said, to the ancillary indiscretion of the abusive language that divulges or profanes the unsayable. But it lets itself be reduced, without effacing the unsaying in the ambiguity or enigma of the transcendent, in which the breathless spirit retains a fading echo" (AE76/OTB44). Or, in simple terms, the task of philosophy is to overcome the incommensurability of saying and the said so that the ethical relation, responsibility, can, after all, be said. Philosophy recognizes plural speech only within the framework of the usual hierarchy.

So it is not surprising that Levinas continues to be troubled by the "barbarisms" that philosophy is forced to endure because of the weakness of language, that is, the natural or anyhow historic resistance of language to philosophy (AE273/OTB178: Levinas is in this context apologizing for the title of Autrement qu'être). There is no doubt that for Levinas any depen-dency on language is philosophy's greatest weakness—one can see that Blanchot has never hesitated to harass his old friend on this score, as in "Notre compagne clandestine": "How can philosophy be talked about, opened up, and presented, without, by that very token, using a particular language, contradicting itself, mortgaging its own possibility? Must not the philosopher be a writer, and thus forgo philosophy, even while pointing out the philosophy implicit in writing? Or, just as well, to pretend to teach it, to master it—that is, this venture of a non-mastered, oral speech, all the while demeaning himself from time to time by *writing* books?" (NCC83/OCC45). But it is doubtful that Levinas could recognize himself in this account of the philosopher as *écrivain* (the unmastering figure of the impossible). For at the end of the day Levinas, as if in the grip of a tradition which he otherwise questions, thinks of language as dependent on philosophy. Philosophy is that which strengthens language. In fact philosophy is nothing less than an "exaltation of language in which words, after the event [*après coup: après Dire*], find for themselves a condition in which religions, sciences and technologies owe their equilibrium of meaning" (AE278/OTB181). "Equilibrium of meaning" means, in so many words, transparency of discourse. As if, at the end of the day, Levinas wore the face of Habermas.

In which event one would have to say that an "exaltation of language" for Levinas would be a deracination of language for Blanchot. For Blanchot, the task of poetry is to respond to the strangeness—the Infinity or, in Blanchot's terms, the impossibility, the an-archic interruption—that separates me from the other. The idea is not to conceptualize or make intelligible this strangeness; it is not to allegorize it through some appropriate figure or narrative of adventure. It is rather to allow it to alter our relation to language "such that," as Blanchot says, "to speak (to write) is *to cease thinking solely with a view toward unity*, and to make the relations of words an essentially dissymmetrical field governed by discontinuity; as though, having renounced the uninterrupted force of a coherent discourse, it were a matter of drawing out a level of language where one might gain the power not only to express oneself in an intermittent manner, but also to allow intermittence itself to speak" (EI110/IC77–78). As if what addressed me were no longer another but simply no one: not a person but a *personne*.

L'intermittence (*l'interruption*) is a word for what Blanchot calls "the relation of the third kind" (EI94/IC66), namely the relation of absolute foreignness that puts the other outside every relation that could connect "him" (the *il*) to me, including that of speech. The other is therefore not in any sense another who belongs to language as discursive possibility; rather the *il* is outside language: it is another, Blanchot wants to say, who belongs to the outside, such that the ethical term *Autrui* must be read as "a name that is essentially neutral" (*EI*102/*IC*72). That is, one cannot ask, "Who is '*Autrui*'?" Rather, Blanchot says, this question must be replaced by another, namely:

> "What of the human 'community,' when it must respond to this relation of strangeness between man and man—a relation without common measure, an exorbitant relation—that the experience of language leads one to sense?" And yet this question does not signify that the Other—*autrui*—would be simply a way of being, that is to say, an obligation that each in turn would either fulfill or avoid, whether knowingly or not. There is infinitely more at stake. In this relation, the other—but which of the two of us would be the other?—is radically other, is solely the other and, as such, a name for the nameless whose momentary position on the board—a board upon which he plays when he speaks, and in speaking puts himself at stake—causes him now and again to be designated by the word 'man.' (Just as the pawn can become every piece but the king.) The Other: the presence of man precisely insofar as he is always missing from his presence, just as he is missing from his place. (*EI*101/*IC*71)

The Other: man, but now man is "a name for the nameless"—anonymous, like the murmur of the *il y a*, that space without place.

For Blanchot, the other speaks not from an inaccessible height but from the outside, outside the "speech of power," outside possibility (in a later essay Blanchot takes up the ancient figure of the supplicant, who is so low as to fall outside the relation of high and low).[12] Or, in other words, whereas for Levinas the other occupies the magisterial site of philosophy, Blanchot situates "him" (the *il*) in the space of poetry—space without place: the space of exile, the region of the foreign and the strange, the region of impossibility in which language (as if it were a language without names) can no longer exercise its power of negation, of conceptualization and command.[13] Blanchot does not hesitate to define this outside as the limit of the ethical (the limit, for example, of proximity), for "it follows from this that the Other man who is '*autrui*' also risks being always Other than man, close to what cannot be close to me: close to death, close to the night, and certainly as repulsive as anything that comes to me from these regions without horizon" (*EI*103/*IC*72).

Repulsive.

So, unimaginably, we are to imagine the other not as magisterial but as monstrous, in which event our responsibility with respect to the other might take the form of horror or fascination, that is, of an ecstasy that does not so much substitute us one for the other according to Levinas's model of signification as transform us into the other according to a Bataille-like model of poetry as the perspective of violence, horror, and the sacred.[14] Borrowing Bataille's categories, one might speculate that for Blanchot philosophy belongs to the region of homogeneity where everything is commensurable, capable of being integrated into a common order such that even opposites belong together; whereas poetry implies a region (or regions) of the heterogeneous—where the heterogeneous is not simply a category of disorder or formlessness but a wilderness of the excluded (the monstrous). Heterogeneity here is a social rather than a logical category, that is, it is different from the mere negation of homogeneity as such. The heterogeneous is characterized by what is rejected by a homogeneous society (a society which is rational, purposeful, productive): "Included are waste products of the human body; persons, words, or acts having a suggested erotic value; the various unconscious processes such as dreams or neuroses; the numerous elements or social forms that *homogeneous* society is powerless to assimilate: mobs, the warrior, aristocratic and impoverished classes, different types of violent individuals or at least those who refuse the rule (madmen, leaders, poets, etc.)" (*OC*1:346/*VE*142).[15] So one might say that, in contrast to Levinas's *Autrui*, Blanchot's *other* is not the other of the same; it is what is outside the relation of same and other in the monstrous regions of the heterogenous. What is worth underscoring perhaps is the fundamentally insubordinate character of this alterity; it is (like the fragment) a relation without a context.

Just so. Not for nothing does Blanchot begin his first essay on Levinas's *Totalité et infini* with Bataille's definition of the philosopher as "someone who is afraid" (*EI*70/*IC*49): afraid, not of this or that, but of the condition of being frightened, which is an ecstatic movement that, like poetry, exposes philosophy to this heterogeneous existence, as if turning it out of its house. "Through fright," says Blanchot, "we leave ourselves and, thrown outside, we experience in the guise of the frightening what is entirely outside us and other than us: the outside itself" (*EI*70/*IC*49). There is no possibility of remaining the same in this experience. So in a sense it is an experience, call it a knowledge, that philosophy cannot, as a matter of self-identity or self-preservation, allow itself to have. Philosophy, as Blanchot reminds us, depends on the absolute distance it maintains from whatever would alter it or confuse it with what it is not (*EI*72/*IC*51). The attraction of Levinas for Blanchot is that, like Heidegger, he is willing to test the limits of philosophy's capacity for the strange and the foreign, where these terms refer not to what is merely unusual or unfamiliar but rather define the relation of nonidentity as a relation with what is absolutely without horizon (the monstrous). In fact Blanchot expresses his attraction in just these striking terms: "One of the strongest aspects of Levinas's book is to have led us, through the beautiful, rigorous, vigilantly controlled [*maîtrisé, surveillé*], and yet trembling language that is his—*but in a manner for which we feel ourselves responsible* [italics added]—to consider *autrui* from the basis of separation" (*EI*75/*IC*52–53). Thinking of the other *à partir de la séparation* means thinking precisely about this horizonless condition, which means thinking what Levinas himself leaves unthought but which Blanchot tries to clarify as the experience of foreignness or the experience of the Outside as such.

December 25, 1995: A Note on Friendship

Blanchot asks: "What of the human 'community,' when it must respond to this relation of strangeness between man and man—a relation without common measure, an exorbitant relation—that the experience of language leads one to sense?" (*EI*101/*IC*71). For example, is friendship possible under such conditions, that is, as a nonrelation or relation of the third kind, exorbitant, unmediated by any principle or ideality? Blanchot's answer would be: friendship is nothing other than an impossible relation, that is, it occurs without conditions of possibility (*that*, reason aside, is its condition). There is no such thing as friendship in principle; it is without principle—an anarchic relation that knows neither beginning nor end. It is outside the dialectical relation of mastery—this, indeed, is the upshot. I can never enter into friendship as an "I": or, much to the same effect, the "I" can never survive friendship. Friendship is a mode of survival, of existence without being, which for the human subject means existence without subjectivity or, more exactly, "subjectivity without any subject" (*ED*53/*WD*30). Friendship would be a relation in which it is no longer intelligible to ask, "who is *autrui?*," since the answer could only be both or, more exactly, neither, that is, neither one nor the other: alterity is no longer a relation of one and the other—not just not a relation of subjects any longer, but now a relation of strangeness into which both friends disappear, as if foreignness as such were all that could obtain in this relation. So the whole idea of otherness, of the other as any sort of topic or question for reflection, falls by the way, unless otherness is understood as the relation itself: an anarchic relation that binds nothing together, loosens everything—call it a mode of pure refusal (A130–31).

The "relation of the third kind" is a relation of friendship. It is a relation on which reflection is possible only in the form of a dialogue that, as in so many of the essays in *L'entretien infini*, neither begins nor ends. Neither is it interrupted; it is rather that the dialogue itself is an endless interruption (of, among other things, the dialectic, history, being, possibly even God's own existence). Interruption in any case is the event—the *entre-temps*—of friendship:

> Now, what "founds" this third relation, leaving it still unfounded, is no longer proximity—proximity of struggle, of services, of essence, of knowledge, or of recognition, not even of solitude—but rather the *strangeness* between us: a strangeness it will not suffice to characterize as a separation or even as a distance.
> —Rather an interruption.
> —An interruption escaping all measure. But—and here is the strangeness of this strangeness—such an interruption (one that neither includes nor excludes) would be nevertheless a relation; at least if I take it upon myself not to reduce it, not to reconcile it, even by comprehending it, that is, not to seek to consider it as the "faltering" mode of a still unitary relation.
> And such would be the relation of man to man when there is no longer between them the proposition of a God, the mediation of a world, or the subsistence of a nature.
> What there would be between man and man, if there were nothing but the interval represented by the word "between"—an empty space all the more empty as it cannot be confused with pure nothingness—is an infinite separation, but offering itself as a relation in the exigency that is speech. (EI97/IC68)

Exigency: a claim that exacts more than can be given. Exigency is an excessive demand, a demand outside all reason that deprives one's existence of its justification (my right to be). Blanchot might mean: the demand of the impossible. As if friendship were a mode of responsibility belonging to poetry rather than philosophy or ethics; that is, friendship is no longer a relation of possibility—no longer a relation supported by common ground ("the proposition of a God, the mediation of a world, or the subsistence of a nature").

In "L'amitié," Blanchot speaks of friendship as a renunciation of every form of mediation between myself and my friend—or, rather, the other who is a friend (it is not as if he or she were "mine"). Ours is a relation of "common strangeness" or, better, of infinite discretion—anyhow it is a relation "that does not allow us to speak of our friends, but only to them; it does not allow us to make them the theme of our conversations (or articles), but is the movement of the understanding in which, speaking to us, they keep, even in moments of greatest familiarity, their infinite distance" (A328). It is not just that I keep silent about what I know of the friend, as if ours were a relation of confidentiality or mutual secrets. Our relation belongs to another temporality, namely, "an interval that, from me to this other who is a friend, measures everything there is between us, the interruption of being" (A328). Speaking strictly, the relation between friends is a relation of neither identity *nor* alterity, neither one *nor* the other; or, in other words, it is a neutral relation, where the neutral is not, as Levinas thinks, a word for being but is rather, as Blanchot says, being's interruption. As if friendship could only occur in parentheses.

It must be that the death of the friend destroys this *entre-temps*, as if closing time up like a tomb, restoring the plenum of being, and returning me once more to the subjectivity of the "I" in the isolation of the dialectic that starts up again and where, again, death is everything. To be sure, Blanchot says, I can, in principle, remember the friend, but perhaps only as Orpheus can remember Eurydice, whose oblivion is without horizon. "But thought knows that one does not remember: without memory, without thought, it already struggles in the realm of the invisible where everything falls back into indifference. That is its profound grief. It must accompany friendship into oblivion" (A330). Possibly this means only that there is (or was) nothing in this relation for me to keep. It is (or was) an anarchic relation in the sense that nothing could follow from it, just as, one imagines, Orpheus very likely returned from Hades without so much as an image of his beloved. Friendship, like love, is unavowable, like the anarchic community of which Blanchot would later write that "it must have no part in any kind of duration" (CI56/UC32).

"It is as if he had said to him, saying it in such a friendly way: friendship withdraws from us" (PD117/SNB84).

121

CHAPTER 6

Blanchot/Bataille

The Last Romantics
(On Poetry as Experience)

> The disappearance of Man at the end of History is thus not
> a cosmic catastrophe: the natural World remains what it has
> been throughout eternity. Nor, then, is it a biological cata-
> strophe. Man remains alive as an animal who is in *harmony*
> with Nature or Being as it is given. What disappears is Man
> properly so called—that is, Action which negates the given,
> and Error, or more generally the *opposition* between Sub-
> ject and Object. In fact, the end of Time and of History—
> that is, the final annihilation of Man properly so called or of
> the free, historical Individual—simply means the cessation
> of Action in the strong sense of the term. In practice this
> means the disappearance of wars and bloody revolution—
> and the disappearance of *Philosophy* as well.
> —Alexandre Kojève, *Introduction à la lecture de Hegel*

The Detour of Poetry

For Blanchot poetry is first of all something that happens to language, but
not as a rhetorical tinkering with the formal properties identified by linguistics; rather, poetry is an event that happens before language can do its
work. Poetry is not a work; it is an interruption of the work of language (a
désœuvrement), a detour of language or a turning back or away from the
movement of conceptual determination or the production of meanings,
works, cultures, worlds. By way of this turn language withdraws from itself,
grows mad. Imagine language beside or outside itself, no longer self-iden-

tical but wandering or violent with respect to the scheme of things that it works to construct.

This turn or withdrawal is not an aberration or failure of language. On the contrary: "Language lends itself to the movement of stealing or turning away [*de dérober et de détourner*]—it watches over it, preserves it, loses itself there and confirms itself there." As if language were looking for a way to free itself from its mediations. Blanchot adds: "In this we sense why the essential speech of detour, the 'poetry' in the turn of writing, is also a speech wherein time turns, saying time as a turning [*disant le temps comme tournant*], the turning of time that sometimes turns in a visible manner into revolution" (*EI*31/*IC*23)—ecstatic time. The turn or speech of detour is irreducible to metaphor or figurality; poetry is not simply indirect or self-referential discourse; it is " 'the world upside down': insubordination, disproportion, frivolity, ignorance, evil, nonsense" (*EL*287/*SL*216). But of course one could imagine a world turning side-ways as well.

From the beginning Blanchot's question has been: What is it to experience this detour or turn? The answer takes the form of a poetics of error, of exile, madness, insomnia, the Outside and the Neutral. At the same time, this answer, if answer is the word, also exposes the limits of experience, because this turn is also the turning inside-out of subjectivity, that is, it is a turn that deprives consciousness of its power as an experiencing subject, producing a passivity outside the alternatives of action and lethargy. The subject is no longer an identity, an "I"; it is perhaps no longer even human—neither human nor nonhuman but, in a sense that remains now to be clarified, neutral. Nevertheless, as always Blanchot holds fast to the category of experience. In effect, he asks about experiencing the impossibility of experience. "Can we," Blanchot asks, "delimit the experience of this *neutral* turn that is at work in turning away?" (*EI*32/*IC*24).

The texts that make up *L'entretien infini* can be read in the light of this question. Philosophical traditions of various stripes (Plato, Aristotle, Locke, Kant, Husserl) clarify the concept of experience rigorously in terms of seeing. In fact, mostly everything gets clarified in these terms, including speech and poetry, so that even for Heidegger (even after he drops the idea of *Dasein*) poetry is understood as an originary crossing of light and darkness, disclosure and concealment, showing and saying. ("Being's essence," Levinas says, "is a dissipating of opacity" before "the clairvoyance of the eye" [*AE*53/*OTB*30].) In "Parler, ce n'est pas voir" Blanchot wants to argue against all this: "Speaking is not seeing. Speaking frees thought from the optical imperative that in the Western tradition, for thousands of years, has subjugated our approach to things, and induced us to think under the guaranty of light or under the threat of its absence" (EI38/IC27).[1]

That is, speaking situates thought differently than does sight—or, more accurately, it *unsituates* thought, turns it loose. "Perception is a wisdom rooted in the ground and standing fixed in the direction of the opening; it is of the land, in the proper sense of the term: planted in the earth and forming a link between the immobile boundary and the apparently boundless horizon—a firm pact from which comes peace." Whereas, by contrast, speaking is anarchic, turning everything loose. "For sight, speech is war and madness. The terrifying word passes over every limit and even the limitlessness of the whole; it seizes the thing from a direction from which it is not taken, not seen, and will never be seen; it transgresses laws, breaks away from orientation, disorients" (EI40/IC28). Not for nothing has philosophy always distrusted language. The task of philosophy (but one could just as well say: human culture) is to bring speech in line with seeing, where the goal is to talk straight as one sees directly (without obstruction).

So there is language and language (language outside of language), like two slopes of literature, or two speakings of speech: not so much light and dark as straight and meandering, nomadic and fixed—keeping in mind that these are not category- or genre-distinctions.[2] Blanchot's thought (much like Plato's) is that, left to itself, speech turns (interminably), and that poetry is just the name of this original and endless turning. At all events: "The speech of which we are trying to speak is a return to this first turning—a noun that must be heard as a verb, as the movement of a turning, a vertigo wherein rest the whirlwind, the leap and the fall. Note that the names chosen for the two directions of our literary language accept the idea of this turning; poetry, rightly enough, alludes to it most directly with the word 'verse,' while 'prose' goes right along its path by way of a detour that continually straightens itself out" (EI42/IC30). But the point of the concept of verse (like that of metaphor and figure) is to regularize the turning of poetry, whereas for Blanchot (much as for Plato) poetry is anarchic with respect to every rule: "a vertigo wherein rest the whirlwind, the leap and the fall." Poetry cannot be brought under correction, cannot be straightened (it cannot, as the ancients knew, be reduced to rhetoric).

However, it is (again) important to understand anarchy in its etymological sense of a condition on the hither side of principle and rule. As Levinas says, "anarchy is not disorder as opposed to order. . . . Anarchy troubles being over and beyond these alternatives" (AE159/OTB101). Anarchy means randomness and contingency, to be sure, but only insofar as these events belong to the region of the singular or of things that have not been turned into phenomena or concepts. An-archy is the hither side of being, the Outside or the Night that is outside the movement of day and night, light and darkness, revelation and concealment, speech and silence. In "Parler, ce n'est pas voir," Blanchot associates this outside with Heraclitus's fragment on the speech of the oracle, which *"neither exposes nor conceals but gives a sign* [n'expose ni ne cache, mais indique]" (EI44/IC31). Giving a sign (*sêmainei*), Blanchot says, is neither discursive nor nondiscursive; it is a turn of language away from the whole system of differentiation (speech-silence, word-thing, affirmation-negation) that discourse implies (EI44/IC32). The turn is neutral with respect to these oppositions: neither one nor the other. Poetry is the experience of this turn.

Impossible Experience

"Le grand refus" is Blanchot's rehearsal of perhaps two decades of his thought. Refusal means, first of all, the refusal of death, where death is the movement of negation that annihilates the singularity of things.[3] Speech (my speech, understood now in its straight, logical sense) is "the life of this death" (EI50/IC36; cf. Hegel: "life endures death and maintains itself in it"). Part of what is romantic about Blanchot is his desire to recover what straight speech annihilates ("How can I find it again, how can I, in my speech, recapture this prior presence that I must exclude in order to speak, in order to speak it?" [EI50/IC36]).[4] Or, in other words, how can I experience the "immediate singularity" that experience, being already conceptual, always destroys (EI53/IC37)? This is the question that lies behind the gaze of Orpheus. Can poetry mediate this immediacy? Blanchot, the last romantic, answers no, for reasons which his account of the Orpheus myth tries to capture: poetry is not an alternative form of mediation, that is, it is not a form of mediation that preserves immediacy; it is not any form of mediation at all. "There cannot be an immediate grasp of the immediate. . . . The immediate excludes everything immediate: this means all direct relation, all mystical fusion, and all sensible contact, just as it excludes itself— renounces its own immediacy—each time it must submit to the mediation of an intermediary in order to offer access" (EI53/IC38). The immediate excludes relation of every kind: it belongs to the exigency of the nonrelation.

This means at the very least that our relation to the immediate or the singular cannot be one of knowing; that is, it is not, in Blanchot's idiom, a relationship of possibility. Rather, it is a relation of impossibility, "a relation escaping power" (*EI*54/*IC*38). It is a relation that is closed to me as an experiencing subject, as an "I" who sees, thinks, speaks, acts, or in some sense "has" experiences. For Blanchot, the possible is not merely hypothetical in contrast to actuality. Possibility is a category of power [*pouvoir*]: it means capability and force [*puissance*] (*EI*59/*IC*42).[5] As an "I" capable of speaking I am a force in the world: "I belong, whether or not I know it, to a network of powers of which I make use, struggling against the force that asserts itself against me. All speech is violence, a violence all the more formidable for being secret and the secret center of violence; a violence that is already exerted upon what the word names and that it can name only by withdrawing presence from it—a sign, as we have seen, that death speaks (the death that is power) when I speak" (*EI*59/*IC*42). (Compare "Littérature et la droit à la mort": "Therefore it is accurate to say that when I speak: death speaks in me. My speech is a warning that at this very moment death is loose in the world" [*PF*313/*GO*43/*WF*323–24].)

All speech—my speech—is violence: an extravagant statement, perhaps, but Blanchot's standpoint is deliberately (etymologically) extravagant. Whence he does not hesitate to say, if only in passing ("these things can only be said in passing"—as if from no fixed point of view), that there is an essential link between speech and torture, as if my speech or all speech were a kind of extracted confession: "Torture is the recourse to violence—always in the form of a technique—with a view toward making speak [*de faire parler*]" (*EI*60/*IC*42–43). Blanchot in fact gives this thought another turn of the screw, linking torture and reason, since the torturer, he says, is not interested in empty talk but only in "true speech, free and pure of all violence"—an obvious contradiction, but one that inhabits all of our discourse, and in particular one that calls into question "the truth of our language understood as dialogue, and of dialogue as a space of force exercised without violence and struggling against force. (The expression, 'We will make him see reason' that is found in the mouth of every master of violence makes clear the complicity that torture affirms, as its ideal, between itself and reason)" (*EI*61/*IC*43).[6]

Hence also the violence implicit in the accounts we give of knowledge as "a grasp that gathers the diverse into a unity, identifies the different, and brings back the other to the same through a reduction that dialectical movement, after a long trajectory, makes coincide with an overcoming [*le dépassement*]. All these words—grasp, identification, reduction—conceal within themselves the rendering of accounts that exists in knowledge as a measure: reason must be given. What is to be known—the unknown— must surrender to the known" (*EI*61/*IC*43). So conceptualization as such is violent, as we learn from the word for concept, *Begriff*, from *greifen*, to grasp. By contrast, Blanchot seeks a relation with the unknown (*l'inconnu* or *l'obscur*) that escapes this dialectical movement of negation that aims to make everything transparent. However, this "other relation" would not be mere ignorance or the mere absence of knowing. Against all reason, Blanchot thinks of it as an experience of that which cannot be grasped or reduced or overcome. "What would this experience of the obscure be, whereby the obscure would give itself in its obscurity?" (*EI*62/*IC*44). How can the unknown be experienced without being dissipated? Such an event would be, certainly, "an entirely other experience" (an *Igitur*-experience), as of a time in which events do not simply give way to one another in a perpetual onset of the future: a time of interruption in which the present ceases to pass, a between-time (*entre-temps*) of patience and vigilance.

Blanchot offers the example of physical suffering as a condition in which time is arrested in this way; it is a time in which time and all that it contains (for example, the "I" of experience) is "dispossessed of any future" (*EI*63/*IC*44).[7] In a compelling metaphor, Blanchot speaks of the "hollowing out" of the present, a "hollowing indefinitely distended," as of a present to which we are no longer present. "What has happened?" Nothing like a release, as if we had transcended time, not an epiphany that transports us to the timeless; rather, "we are delivered over to another time—to time as other, as absence and neutrality. . . . A time without event, without project, without possibility; not that pure immobile instant, the spark of the mystics, but an unstable perpetuity in which we are arrested and incapable of permanence, a time neither abiding nor granting the simplicity of a dwelling-place" (*EI*62/*IC*44). Think of this as a time of our undoing, where experience is just that of destitution, of being hollowed out, as in an experience without intentionality. There is nothing any longer to be experienced, and therefore no account to be given of what has happened, unless it were in a Shandy- or Kafka- or Beckett-like narrative in which events are ingeniously deferred or deprived of any possibility of outcome, inevitably at the cost of the subject who remains unborn or unnameable: "So now we see it: the mark of such a movement is that, by the fact that we experience it, it escapes our power to undergo it; thus it is not beyond the trial of experience, but rather that trial from which we can no longer escape. An experience that one will represent to oneself as being strange and even as the experience of strangeness" (EI63/IC45). Blanchot calls this experience le revers de possibilité, or "impossibility" for short (EI64/IC46). The experience of the il y a, for example, is an experience of existence in which nothing happens, the existence of destitution, existence in which time has been evacuated.

Of course Blanchot does not invoke the names of Tristram Shandy, Joseph K., or the Unnamable. In fact it is probably a mistake to do so. The impossible is not to be thought of as out of the ordinary, "the privilege of the exceptional experience" (EI64/IC45), but as that which occurs in every experience, even the most mundane. In fact Blanchot goes so far as to say that "impossibility is nothing other than the mark of what we so readily call experience, for there is experience in the strict sense only where something radically other is in play" (EI66/IC46). No experience without divestiture. This comes out in Blanchot's comment on Simone Weil's saying, "Human life is impossible. But misfortune alone makes this felt." Here it is not a matter of denouncing life as unlivable but of "recognizing in impossibility our most human belonging to immediate human life, the life that it falls to us to sustain each time that, stripped through misfortune of the clothed forms of power, we reach the nakedness of every relation: that is to say, the relation to naked presence, the presence of the other" (EI67/IC47).

Perhaps this means no more than that my relation to the world is, at the end of the day, not one of knowing or of propositions that account the world answerable to my concepts. To put it as bluntly and simply as one can: the world is outside my control, outside my possibilities, "uncommunicative and strange" like Heidegger's thing, not answering to the language of truth (not answerable to the concept of world), but also not just something toward which I can remain indifferent, disengaged, self-contained; rather something addresses me in such a way as to turn me out of my house. What is the character of this other relation, which Blanchot calls "impossibility"?

Blanchot's answer is that this is a relation of dispossession, of separation and foreignness, which cannot be overcome or traversed by any kind of movement whether of action or discourse. For reasons that Blanchot has been trying to articulate since "Littérature et la droit à la mort," where poetry is dissociated from discourse (from naming and predication), this relation of impossibility is one that calls for poetry, or at all events for "that other speech that speaks only when it begins to respond to the other region that is not governed by the time of possibility" (EI68/IC47). The task of poetry is not to illuminate this "relation without relation. Poetry is not there in order to say impossibility; it simply answers to it, saying in responding. Such is the secret lot, the secret decision of every essential speech in us: *naming* the possible, *responding* to the impossible" (EI68/IC48).

Poetry in this event would be irreducible to a text that I can read, or rather my experience of this text would not be that of reading it. It would be a more originary hermeneutics in which speech occurs as an event that situates me in this other "relation without relation," or what Blanchot calls "a relation of the third kind" (EI94/IC66). Poetry is this event; it is the "experience of strangeness" itself. More exactly, it belongs to what Blanchot calls "the non-dialectical experience of speech" (EI90/IC63), or the experience of "writing outside of language," where language is understood in terms of the movement of negation that produces conceptual identity. This experience cannot be adequately characterized as this or that person's experience, say a writer's or a reader's: the experience is not internal to the subject but is what we might crudely call the divesting experience of radical exteriority, that is, the experience of *Autrui* in Levinasian ethics, or, in Blanchot's poetics, the experience of literary space—of separation, exile, waiting, dying, the *il y a*, the Outside or the Neuter.

In "Le rapport du troisième genre: Homme sans horizon," Blanchot calls it "An experience in which the Other, the Outside itself, exceeding any positive or negative term, is the 'presence' that does not refer back to the One, and the exigency of a relation of discontinuity where unity is not implied. The Other, the He [le Il]; but only insofar as this third person is not a third person and brings the neutral into play" (EI101–2/IC71). Elsewhere, in connection with Georges Bataille, it is characterized as a "limit-experience" or the experience of what philosophers of existence used to call a limit-situation (*Grenzsituation*) in which, as in dying, everything is taken away except my ownmost being.[8] For Blanchot, however, my relation to this situation, my experience of it, is no longer mine: it is, so to speak, no longer existential. No more ownmost. "The self has never been the subject of this experience. The 'I' will never arrive at it, nor will the individual, this particle of dust that I am, nor even the self of us all that is supposed to represent absolute self-consciousness. Only the ignorance of

129

the I-who-dies would incarnate by acceding to the space where in dying it never dies in the first person as an "I" will reach it. . . . We speak as though this were an experience, and yet we can never say we have undergone it" (*EI*311/*IC*209–10).

The limit-experience can only be another's, where the other is no longer accessible to me except in a relation to the Outside. For example, in an essay on Camus Blanchot appropriates Sisyphus and his rock as a figure of the limit-experience: "Sisyphus is a solitude deprived of a center not because he is alone, but because he is without relation to himself. And above all: his revolt, this volte-face with which everything (re)commences [i.e., Sisyphus, in a parody of the Eternal Return, must begin and begin again pushing his rock up the hill], is the about face of the rock. All the truth of Sisyphus is bound to his rock; a beautiful image of the 'elementary' that is within him and outside him, the affirmation of a self that accepts being entirely outside itself, delivered over and boldly entrusted to the strangeness of the outside" (*EI*262/*IC*175).[9] Sisyphus (who has lost the right to death [*EI*267/*IC*179]): not the Absurd Man but the Last Man whose dying begins and begins again.

The "last man" is originally one of Nietzsche's creations—the type of human being who appears when the history of masters and slaves has run its course, ridding itself of every shadow of strangeness or difference, flattening us out into something like a prototype of Heidegger's *das Man*, of which Blanchot's "last man" is a kind of parody. In his 1936–37 lectures on Hegel, Alexandre Kojève worked out the history of masters and slaves in such a way that the last man turns out to be Napoleon—as Hegel imagines him ("the man on horseback")—who regards the world with satisfaction (that is, nothing further requires to be negated, viz., overcome).[10] After listening to Kojève's account of the end of history, Bataille wrote an open letter to Kojève ("Letter to X, Lecturer on Hegel"), proposing an alternative ending with himself as the last man:

> If action ("doing") is—as Hegel says—negativity, then there is still the problem of knowing whether the negativity of someone who "doesn't have anything more to do" disappears or remains in a state of "unemployed negativity" [*negativité sans emploi*]: personally, I can only decide in one way, being myself precisely this "unemployed negativity" (I could not define myself more precisely). I admit Hegel foresaw this possibility: at least he didn't situate it at the outcome [*l'issue*] of the processes he described. I imagine that my life—or, better yet, its aborting, the open wound that is my life—consti-

tutes all by itself the refutation of Hegel's closed system. (OC5:369–70/G123; cf. *The College of Sociology*, p. 90)

Following Bataille one could speak of surplus energy—energy which, however, is not stored up like capital but rather expends itself nonproductively in "luxury, war, cults, the construction of sumptuary monuments, games, spectacles, arts, perverse sexual activity" (OC1:305/VE118). Or following Blanchot, one could speak of a surplus of reason (we will see in the next chapter that this is his definition of madness).

In his essay on Bataille, "L'expérience-limite" (1962), Blanchot speaks of a surplus of death, meaning that man has a capacity for dying that cannot be exhausted. Through the power of death, "he has constructed the world, he has put himself to work, he has become a producer, a self-producer. Nonetheless, a strange thing, this is not enough: at every moment he is left as it were with a part of dying that he is unable to invest in activity" (EI305/IC206). It is as if man always remained on the hither side of the work that he completes:

> Most often he does not know this, he hasn't the time. But should he come to sense this surplus of nothingness, this unemployable vacancy, should he discover himself to be bound to the movement that causes him, each time a man dies, to die infinitely, should he allow himself to be seized by the infinity of the end, then he must respond to another exigency—no longer that of producing but of spending, no longer that of succeeding but of failing, no longer that of turning out works and speaking usefully but of speaking in vain and reducing himself to worklessness [*de parler vainement et de se désœuvrer*]: an exigency whose limit is given in the "interior experience." (EI305–6/IC205–6)

Blanchot's last man, in other words, is one who survives the end of history in a tortoiselike temporality that a harelike negativity cannot catch up with: so death withdraws into the interminability of the *il y a*.[11]

Anthropology of the Last Man

In 1957 Blanchot published *Le dernier homme*, which it is difficult not to read as an account of the experience of alterity, or of *autrui* understood as a relation of the third kind—of separation, exile, affliction, dying, and so on. The "last man" is an allegory of strangeness where strangeness means the nonidentical rather than the merely odd or out-of-the-ordinary. As a character in Blanchot's *récit* the "last man" is certainly odd, but the first thing that we learn about him is that "nothing distinguished him from the others" (*DH7/LM1*). This lack of differentiation is the problem—and it is more than a problem of logic: it is an ontological condition of effacement that affects Blanchot's entire *récit*. If nothing distinguishes the last man from other people, soon others, and in particular the narrator, grow indistinguishable from the last man. It is this transformation that concerns Blanchot.[12]

The last man is inaccessible, but not private, withdrawn, introspective, as if something were concealed (one can gloss the last man as "presence of the non-accessible, presence excluding or exceeding any present . . . the infinite presence of what remains radically absent, a presence in its presence always infinitely other, presence of the other in its alterity: non-presence" [*EI54/IC38*]). He is inaccessible even to himself. The narrator quotes him as saying (this is almost his only memorable saying): " 'I can't think about myself [*Je ne puis penser à moi*]: there is something terrible there, a difficulty that slips away, an obstacle that can't be met' " (*DH8/LM2*). The difficulty is perhaps that the last man is a consciousness but not a subject. He cannot, for example, tell his story without plagiary (*DH14/LM6*). There is neither an inner nor an outer, antecedent life to which one could attribute horrors that will not bear looking into. It is quite likely that the last man is simply as external to himself as we are to each other: he is his own *autrui*.

As if he had on himself the same effect that he has on others, for proximity to the last man doubles or displaces one's identity or subjectivity. As the narrator says, it is "as though, confronting him, what had been 'I' had strangely awakened into a 'we' " (*DH9/LM2*). The narrator at all events knows him mainly through this effect: "he turned me away from myself" (*DH21/LM10*); "he made each of us into someone else [*faisait-il quelqu'un d'autre*]" (*DH26/LM12*). Not surprisingly, the face of the last man is "the face of forgetting [*le visage de l'oubli*]" (*DH25/LM12*), as if one could not look at it without disappearing into it; nor, with such a face, could he be anything but dying the endless, unapproachable death of the interminably ill that Blanchot calls dying without a future (*DH56/LM29*). The power of the last man, in other words, is coherent with the "strangeness of his weakness" (*DH34/LM16*), which exerts a quintessential fascination on the narrator (as well as on a young woman who also attends the last man in a protracted vigil): "I think a reverie comes from him to us," says the narrator, "one that agitates us, deceives us, opens us to the suspicion of a thought that won't seem to let itself be thought. I often asked myself if he wasn't communicating to us, without his knowledge and against our wishes, something of that thought" (DH21/LM9).

The narrator asks: "Why do we know that thing of which there is no knowledge?" (DH125/LM70). This is also the regulating question of Blanchot's first essay on Levinas, "Connaissance de l'inconnu." The *autrui* is a thought I am unable to think, that is, "a thought that goes beyond my power; a thought that to the very extent that it is a thought of mine, is the absolute exceeding of the self that thinks it—in other words: a relation with what is absolutely outside myself: the other" (EI75–76/IC53). But the last man is not (or not just) the *autrui* of the ethical relation. "He was present in such a strange way: so completely and so incompletely. When he was there, I could not help coming up against his self-effacement, which made his approach heavier, cruelly disproportionate: maybe insignificant, maybe dominating. As though his presence was all there was of him and did not allow him to be present: it was an immense presence, and even he did not seem able to fill it, as though he had disappeared into it and been absorbed by it slowly, endlessly—a presence without anyone, perhaps?" (DH53/LM28).[13] Or, in other words, a neutral presence, that is, a presence given in the space of separation or of strangeness as such: "A distance that was both fragmented and compact: something terrible without terror, a cold and dry animation, a rarefied, entangled, mobile life which was perhaps everywhere, as though in that place separation itself had assumed life and force, by obliging us to see ourselves only as distant and already separated from ourselves" (DH61/LM32). Sounds very much like an account of the *il y a*.

So perhaps it is not so much that the last man transforms others into others like himself as that one cannot enter into the space that he inhabits, if "inhabits" is the word, without being altered in the direction of nonidentity or of the Neuter, as if the experience of alterity were something like an irreversible detour or turn into a relation of the third kind where man is the other but the other is no longer human (EI102/IC72). The last man is perhaps best understood as a man who is outside the human. His proximity is, so to speak, the Outside itself. *Le dernier homme* is about what it is to be drawn toward this Outside. (Possibly all that Blanchot writes is about this experience of strangeness—in an essay on Brecht's *V-Effekte* Blanchot calls it *une "mauvaise" étrangeté*: whereas the *V-Effekte* frees us from the power of the image, Blanchot's strangeness "arises when the image is no longer what allows us to have the object as absent but is rather what takes hold of us by absence itself: there where the image, always at a distance, always absolutely close and absolutely inaccessible, steals away from us, opens onto a neutral space where we can no longer act, and also opens us upon a sort of neutrality where we cease being ourselves and oscillate strangely between I, He, and no one" [EI536–37/IC366]).

Just so, the second part of *Le dernier homme* becomes a monologue (or rather a conversation—of sorts) in which the narrator, evidently now confined to a room, no longer recites his story of the last man but has himself become the last man who experiences the space of separation as an interval of calm, of waiting, of fatigue, of suffering, dying, and rapt attention, but also as "an endless din [*une rumeur qui ne cessait pas*]," that is, a sort of interminable, incessant, Unnamable-like speech—"a speech untouched by silence. It was at once powerful and empty, authoritarian and docile. It was uttered far away from here, far away even from the space, and as though outside, over there in the useless region, and yet also in me" (DH118–19/LM66). The experience of strangeness (of the *autrui* or, much to same point, of the *il y a*) is an experience of language, or more precisely of "an agitation of speech" of which the narrator says: "I could distinguish myself from it, only hear it while hearing myself in it, this immense speech which always said 'We'" (DH119/LM67). A "we," however, that is not a relation of unity (without mediation and without community: a relation of the third kind): a "we" that is neither "I" nor "He" nor no one but neutral.

In this second part of *Le dernier homme* the narrative voice is turned into the vocative by an inaccessible presence that the narrator addresses, indeterminately, as a space, an image, a thought, and, inevitably, as a "you" (*tu*):

> You are acquainted with shadows. How strange that the darkness [*l'obscurité*] of the night should be this motionless, solitary brightness. I could describe to you the space that you form, perhaps without knowing it, and if I lean outside, I see the hallway lit by the light; if I go out into it, already my steps come to meet me. But I won't go out. All these people I see wandering about, these similar figures obeying the murmur of the night, which says one must come and go, come and go without end: deceptive faith, pointless haste, delusion that is the night's very breathing. Why such haste? Toward what place? Do my words also go toward that place, taking some unknown part of me with them? I sense, in them, that attraction to the vain region,

but why do you prevent me from flowing into this murmur? Why do you save me from being entirely outside myself, why do you separate me from what speaks in me, as though to deflect me, for an instant, from the delusion into which everything goes, from which everything comes back? What part do I have in the words that entreat me with a sweet lure to follow them and that I resist only because you enclose me . . . ? (*DH*134–35/*LM*76)

And as if in a parody of Levinasian ethics the other is at the very end addressed as a face, or as a sort of face, an "invisible face" or a face that the narrator merely desires, perhaps not just the narrator: "I think this is what tempts us both: I, that you be a face, what is visible in a face, and you, to be a face for me once more, to be a thought and yet a face. The desire to be visible in the night, so that it will invisibly fade away" (*DH*150–51/*LM*85). I can't help recalling here two sentences from Levinas: "The unnarratable other loses his face as a neighbor in narration [*L'inénarrable!— autrui perdant dans la narration son visage de prochain*]. The relationship with him is indescribable in the literal sense of the term, uncovertible into history, irreducible to the simultaneousness of writing, the eternal present of a writing that records or presents results" (*AE*258/*OTB*166): lines that, again, one has no trouble imagining Blanchot writing.

Desire is in many respects not a concept in Blanchot's thinking, but the experience of strangeness is something like the experience of desire, where desire is, however, entirely gratuitous: in excess of anything lacking. In his first essay on Levinas Blanchot says that "the thought that thinks more than it thinks is Desire. Such a desire is not the sublimated form of need, any more than the prelude to love. Need is a lack that awaits fulfillment; need is satisfied. Love wants union. The desire that one might call metaphysical is a desire for what we are not in want of, a desire that cannot be satisfied and that does not desire union with what it desires." The word "metaphysical" here is a metaphor of the Outside or the Neutral: it is "the very desire for what must remain inaccessible and foreign—a desire of the other as other, a desire that is austere, disinterested, without satisfaction, without nostalgia, unreturned, without return" (*EI*76/*IC*53). For Blanchot, the other is irreducible to the ethical relation: it is the invisible *visage*. "The very last face, merely manifest, outside waiting and beyond reach [*Le visage ultime, seulement manifeste, hors d'attente et hors d'atteinte*]" (*DH*155/*LM*88).

Negative Phenomenology

In *L'expérience intérieure* Bataille writes: "Blanchot asked me: why not pursue my inner experience as if I were the *last man?*" (*OC*5:76/*ExI*98/ *IE*61).

Plausible suggestion.

Imagine Descartes, having put everything into question except his own indubitability, suddenly bereft of thinking—of doubting, picturing, calculating—that is, a Descartes with nowhere to go, with nothing possible as a prospect, project, or even condition, with nothing to experience except his own subjectivity, which is, however, now a subjectivity without identity, an "I" without past or future, memory or desire, without top or bottom, inside or outside, a boundaryless interiority exposed on all sides to an outside without horizons. This is Georges Bataille as Blanchot imagines him.

In *L'expérience intérieure* Bataille says that by "inner experience" he means something like mystical experience in which the inner is enraptured by what is not itself, that is, by a pure exteriority, an exteriority even more pure than the God of the mystics: a God who is more than dead, who is not just otherwise than being, not just the unknowable, unnameable hyperessential God of negative theology but the unknown and unnameable from the beyond of which God has withdrawn into a magnificent divine annihilation.

In other words not an unknown God but a divine Unknown. Experience is the experience of being laid bare before this *l'inconnu*.[14] Alternatively Bataille calls it an experience of impossibility, impossibility as the end of the possible ("I call experience a voyage to the end of the possible of man [*un voyage au bout du possible de l'homme*" [*OC*5:19/*ExI*20/*IE*7]). In such experience nothing is produced or acquired. It is experience as "expenditure" [*dépense*] or loss. Alternatively, following Nietzsche, Bataille thinks of this as an experience of "life," where life is anarchic. In "La notion de dépense" (1933), Bataille writes: "Human life, distinct from juridical existence, existing as it does on a globe isolated in celestial space, from night to day and from one country to another—human life cannot in any way be limited to the closed systems assigned to it by reasonable conceptions. The immense travail of recklessness, discharge, and upheaval that constitutes life could be expressed by stating that life starts only with the deficit of these systems; at least what it allows in the way of order and reserve has meaning only from the moment when the ordered and reserved forces liberate and lose themselves for ends that cannot be subordinated to anything one can account for" (OC1:319/VE128). Likewise history for Bataille is more Nietzschean than Hegelian. History is not the unfolding of anything. The "movement of existence, which demands a constant distintegration"—the "movement of ruin"—is what creates history (OC1:468/VE198).

Bataille remarks that in German philosophy phenomenology is the tradition that accords "knowledge the value of a goal which one attains through experience" (OC5:20/ExI22/IE8). This would apply, for example, to Husserl, where experience is reducible to intentionality; but it would apply just as well to common sense, which interprets existence as a movement from the unknown to the known, innocence to experience, with empty minds filling as time goes by. But in the romantic tradition experience is often a reversal of this order. In this tradition, experience is *Erlebnis* or *Erfahrung*, experience as living-through or undergoing, as in a trial, transformation, or adventure, or, at the outer limit, as suffering, sacrifice, torture, tragedy, or in short experience as the expenditure of subjectivity. (Suffering, sacrifice, torture, tragedy: this could be a list drawn up by Blanchot; Bataille is more comic than Blanchot: his list includes, apart from torment [*l'angoisse, le supplice*], tickling, laughter, poetry, erotic transport, varieties of religious ecstasy—and moments of sweet felicity ["the sweetness of the outside"] in which the "I" loses itself in the night [OC5:24/ExI174/IE112]).[15] It is true that experience divests us of ignorance, but only because it consumes what we know in the bargain. Not for nothing Hegel called it skepticism in action, the way of despair, consciousness suffering violence at its own hands (*Phenomenologie des Geistes*). What Bataille wishes to do is to pursue this negativity of experience to its limit, to experience experience as the impossibility of knowledge—"the fusion of subject and object, being as subject non-knowledge, as object the unknown" (OC5:21/ExI23/IE9).

A recurring figure in *L'expérience intérieure* is that of the abandoned child: "supreme knowledge leaves one as night leaves a child, naked in the depths of the woods" (OC5:68/ExI88/IE54). There is a threshold here where terror crosses over into rapture.

The experience of the mystics, in which God is experienced as nothing, is for Bataille a prototype of the inner experience, but Bataille's ideal would be to experience the death of God from God's point of view. The perfect motto of divine supplication is the dying Christ's *lamma sabachtani*: God experiencing his own foresakenness, his loss or abandonment, through the mediation of human sacrifice (OC5:61/ExI77/IE47). Not unreasonably, Bataille imagines that God's knowledge of himself is mystical, an experience of nothing: "that is why He is an atheist, profoundly so" (OC5:121/ExI160/IE103). Similarly: "One cannot speak of the knowledge which God has of himself if not by negations — suffocating negations — images of tongues cut out" (OC5:126/ExI167/IE107).

Here is Bataille's version of le dernier homme (Bataille reading a portrait of Hegel as an old man):

> I imagine seeing exhaustion, the horror of being in the depths of things — of being God. Hegel, at the moment when the system closed, believed himself for two years to be going mad: perhaps he was afraid of accepting evil — which the system justifies and renders necessary; or perhaps linking the certainty of having attained absolute knowledge with the completion of history — he saw himself, in a profound sense, becoming dead; perhaps even his various bouts of sadness took shape in the more profound horror of being God. (OC5:128/ExI170/IE110)

This is the face of a Hegel on the verge of the inner experience, which is what occurs when everything possible has been actualized, when nothing remains but impossibility (nothing further can happen: history, like art, is vergangen, all horizons have been surpassed — the Aufhebung has done everything one can ask of it). Blanchot, writing on Bataille, comments: "The interior experience insists upon this event that does not belong to possibility; it opens in this already achieved being an infinitesimal interstice by which all that is suddenly allows itself to be exceeded, deposed by an addition that escapes and goes beyond [un surcroît qui échappe et excède]. A strange surplus" (EI307/IC207). A surplus of the negative, there being nothing left to negate. A surplus that Hegel (as Bataille imagines him) experiences in the form of a looming madness, an approaching horror of being God, on a negative theologian's theory of being God where being such is existence without being — a mystical (that is, absolutely negative) experience: "The experience of non-experience," Blanchot calls it (EI311/IC210).[16] (Just think of it! God: an absolute surplus of negativity; or, the death of God — as God imagines it. It would have to be a death that went on forever.)

"What is a philosopher?," Blanchot asks in "Connaissance de l'inconnu"; and he answers, "borrowing words from Georges Bataille, it is someone who is afraid" (EI70/IC49): afraid of the Outside, of the limit-experience, of what remains irreducible to knowledge, of that which remains unknown when knowledge has no further progress to make, of an existence which, being without being, that is, not being the existence of this or that being, is being that cannot be negated. As Blanchot explains in his essay on Bataille: "Interior experience is the manner in which the radical negation that no longer has anything to negate is affirmed" (EI309/IC208). (To be sure: "This has the air of a joke. But if we will grant that all modern humanism, the work of science, and planetary development have as their object a dissatisfaction with what is, and thus the desire to transform being—to negate it in order to derive power from it and to make of this power to negate the infinite movement of human mastery—then it will become apparent that this sort of weakness of the negative, and the way in which nothingness masks itself in the being that cannot be negated, lays waste at one stroke to our attempts to dominate the earth and to free ourselves from nature by giving it a meaning—by denaturing it" [EI225/IC149].) Imagine therefore a time when the dialectic has overcome everything, which means a time that has ceased to progress, a time without progress or without a future (corresponding to a space without horizon): call it a stop-time or "end of history" when everything has been accomplished or fulfilled.[17]

The difficulty is that for Blanchot temporality does not coincide with history but exceeds it, interminably, as if at the end of history we were "delivered over to another time" (EI63/IC44). ("What remains after the system—the naught left over, still to be expended—is the push of dying in its repetitive novelty" [ED76/WD45].) In his essay on Bataille Blanchot asks us to imagine living our lives twice, once according to the time of the possible "as something we comprehend, grasp, bear, and master . . . by relating it to some good or to some value"—some end or purpose; and another according to an impossible, anarchic time or "time as something that escapes all employment and all end, and more, as that which escapes our very capacity to undergo it, but whose trial we cannot escape. Yes, as though impossibility, that by which we are no longer able to be able, were waiting for us behind all that we live, think, and say" (EI307–8/IC207). The moral is (once more) that "possibility is not the sole dimension of our existence" (EI307/IC207).

Picture therefore Hegel sitting for the portrait that Bataille interprets. This would be Hegel as the last man (a "Hegel living: the travesty of a completed Meaning" [ED79/WD47]); that is, Hegel passive and waiting but with nothing left to wait for: Hegel no longer coinciding with himself, *en detour* to a nonrelation, becoming a visage without site or perspective, framed by exteriority, thinking mad, Nietzsche-like thoughts (the only thoughts left to think: "Nothing ends, everything begins again" [*EI224/ IC149*]; "There is nothing identical except for the fact that everything returns" [*EI418/IC280*]). By rights, or in keeping with the unitary rigor of philosophy, Hegel ought not to have allowed himself to be turned into a portrait ("Hegel the impostor" [*ED79/WD47*]). In the event, availing himself in this fashion, he opened a window in the history of reason, turned himself into a presence that is no longer present: slipped, so to speak, into the Outside. So it is not surprising that, on Bataille's reading, fear is written on Hegel's face.

As if a philosopher were by definition someone who cannot allow himself to be turned into an image without ceasing to be a philosopher. (Supposedly there are no photographs of Blanchot: *visage invisible*. Recall the image as cadaver.) The Hegel whose visage Bataille contemplates is the other Hegel, not the Hegel of the history of philosophy (not Kojève's Sage) but the fugitive Hegel: Hegel excluded from his own thought or his own system, "what is absolutely other and has no place in the whole" (*EI25/ IC19*), Hegel without spirit, Hegel whose subjectivity has been implicated in the death of art and whose face records the awful turning of self-consciousness at precisely this final, possibly ludicrous, moment of expenditure: *comme si j'étais l'Autre et parce que je ne suis rien d'autre que l'Autre: l'inidentifiable, le sans "Je", le sans nom, la présence de l'inaccessible:* "as if I were the Other and because I am nothing other than the Other: the unidentifiable, the 'I'-less, the nameless, the presence of the inaccessible" (*EI100/IC70*). One wonders whether Hegel was inspired at the last moment to take flight, as if to preserve in the final twinkling some passage of faceless identity with respect to the future. But not quite making it. Falling short as if captured or hollowed out once for all by the portrait, that is, by the between-time ("the inhuman and monstrous" [Levinas]) that interrupts the history of the spirit. Henceforward Hegel belongs to the history of fascination or, as in a parallel life, the history of madness.

The Voice of Experience

Between Bataille and Blanchot there is this difference, that for Bataille language is not an important issue in the analysis of "inner experience,"

whereas Blanchot was perhaps the first among French intellectuals coming of age in the 1930s for whom reflection on language became a major
conceptual preoccupation.[18] So in "Le jeu de la pensée" (1963) Blanchot
supplements his texts on Bataille by emphasizing how speech—for example, the everyday speech of conversation—exposes experience to what it
cannot locate or grasp: "What is present in this presence of speech, as soon
as it affirms itself, is precisely what never lets itself be seen or attained:
something is there that is beyond reach (of the one who says it as much as
the one who hears it). It is between us, it holds itself between, and conversation is approach on the basis of this between-two [*l'entretien est l'abord à
partir de cet entre-deux*]: an irreducible distance that must be preserved if
one wishes to maintain a relation with the unknown that is speech's
unique gift" (*EI*315//*IC*212).

Conversation is not reducible to an exchange of speech; that is, in the
exchange something else comes into play, namely the movement of a
speech that is neither mine nor yours, a movement outside the give-and-
take of the dialogue, a speech that interrupts my relation with the other (is
it you?) who addresses me. So "rather than dialogue," Blanchot says, we
should think of conversation as "plural speech"—"a speech that is essentially non-dialectical; it says the absolutely other that can never be reduced
to the same or take place in the whole; as though it were a matter of speaking only at the moment when . . . 'the whole' is supposed to have already
been said" (*EI*319//*IC*215).[19] One thinks of the echo, but Blanchot would
have us imagine an echo that is internal to the speech that you and I exchange: not something ringing in our ears after the fact of our speaking but
an event occurring *while* we speak: an event that forms the *entre-temps* of
the conversation itself. And, what is more, not an echo that either of us
produces, but rather one that is interminable, incessant. As if there were
between us a speech that neither of us could interdict.

The texts from the 1960s in which Blanchot tries to elucidate the nature
of this speech are a constant allusion to madness, where madness is something like speech that cannot be stifled, as in Sade's "frenzy of writing,"
which is horrifying not so much for its obscenities as for its relentlessness:
"Sade's major impropriety resides in the simply repetitive force of a narration that encounters no interdict (the whole of this limit-work recounting
the interdict by way of the monotony of its terrifying murmur) because
there is no other time than that of the interval of speaking [*l'entre-dire*]: the
pure arrest that can be reached only by never stopping speaking"

(*EI*328/*IC*221). Likewise what Blanchot calls "the speech of analysis" is not anything spoken by either the patient or the analyst. Rather the analysis itself is an endless conversation: "The person who submits to analysis enters into a movement whose term is unforeseeable and into a reasoning whose conclusion brings with it, as though it were a new capacity, the impossibility of concluding. For, to say it quickly, what begins to speak here is what is unceasing and interminable: the eternal going over [*le ressassement éternal*], and over and over again, whose exigency the patient has encountered but has arrested in fixed forms and henceforth inscribed in his body, his conduct, and his language" (*EI*353/*IC*236). As if, in a parody of prophecy, the patient had been invaded by a voice from the outside, or from language itself, a voice of the neuter—Blanchot calls it "a speech that is neither true nor false, neither sensible nor senseless but always both [should he have said: neither?] the one and the other: the most profound speech, but speech that speaks as a depth without depth. Perhaps it is the dangerous duty of the psychoanalyst to seek to suppress this speech" (*EI*353/*IC*237). This voice of the neuter is also the voice of "everyday speech," which is speech that escapes interdiction precisely because of its neutrality. "What is proper to the everyday is that it designates for us a region or a level of speech where the determinations true and false, like the opposition of yes and no, do not apply—the everyday being always before what affirms it and yet incessantly reconstituting itself beyond all that negates it" (*EI*361/*IC*242). Blanchot notes that the hero (like, presumably, the philosopher: Heidegger flashes to mind) fears the everyday precisely because the experience of its speech (like the experience of the *il y a*, of which the everyday is a pseudonym) neutralizes subjectivity, turning the hero into *le dernier homme* (*EI*365/*IC*244).

For Blanchot voice is a residual concept of romanticism. He refers to it as the "romantic exigency" (*EI*386/*IC*258), where the voice is restored to its ancient demonic transcendence as a category of hearing and madness: "The voice, but not speech. The voice that is not simply the organ of a subjective interiority but, on the contrary, the reverberation of a *space* opening onto the *outside*." In romanticism this *outside* is no longer the exteriority of the sacred; it is (at least for Blanchot) expressly neutral, neither divine nor human.

This privileging of the voice nevertheless brings to literature a vague experience to which it awakens as though at the threshold of strangeness. The voice sets free from speech; it announces a possibility prior to all saying, and even to any possibility of saying. The voice frees not only from representation, but also, in advance, from meaning, without, however, succeeding in doing more than committing itself to the ideal madness of delirium. The voice that speaks without a word, silently—in the silence of a cry—tends to be, no matter how interior, the voice of no one. What speaks when the voice speaks? It situates itself nowhere, neither in nature nor in culture, but manifests itself in a space of redoubling, of echo and resonance where it is not someone, but rather this *unknown* space—its discordant accord, its vibration—that speaks without speaking. (Hölderlin, in his madness 'declaiming' at the window, gives this voice an organ.) (*EI*386/*IC*258)

Here the original experience, the experience of *l'espace littéraire* or the space of exile, is refigured quasi-romantically as an experience of the voice of the outside, that is, madness. The "experience of vocality" is the preeminent form of the limit-experience or experience of *l'inconnu*, because in the nature of the case the voice can never be objectified or appropriated. It is a "speech that has vanished when it has scarcely been said, always already destined to the silence it bears and from which it comes; a speech in becoming that does not keep to the present but commits itself and the literature it animates to its essence, which is disappearance. The voice is also perhaps always, at least apparently, outside or to the side of rules, as it is beyond mastery, always to be won back, always once again mute" (*EI*387/*IC*259).

Madness: or, what amounts to the same thing, poetry, which has ceased to be a discursive movement and is now rather a mode of responsibility, of listening, patience, and rapture. And if you ask what form poetry as madness will take, the answer is the same as it has been since "Littérature et la droit à la mort": "The impersonality of the voice is a silent appeal to a presence-absence on the hither side of every subject and even every form; anterior to beginning, it indicates itself only as anteriority, always in retreat in relation to what is anterior" (*EI*387/*IC*259).[20] Or, in other words, anarchy: writing that refuses to subordinate itself to the movement of negation, writing that is "foreign to the category of completion" (*EI*228/*IC*153): writing that begins and begins again as an unconfinable murmur—"writing that holds the Work to the disposition of being a surface or a distant evenness, enrolling and unrolling without ceasing to be superficial, turning back upon itself without ceasing to be slack, and in this twisting movement that conceals it, only manifesting the turning about of a space without depth, always entirely outside" (*EI*388/*IC*260). A space without depth is a space for wanderers rather than for grammarians: unthematizable, anarchic, irreducible to wholeness. This would be a space of dispersal rather than of a gathering of entities.

Désœuvrement: "speech of the fragment . . . language still speaking when all has been said [*celui qui parle encore lorsque tout a été dit*]" (*EI*232/*IC*155).

CHAPTER 7

Blanchot/Celan

Désœuvrement
(The Theory of the Fragment)

> La quantité de fragments me déchire.
> —René Char, *Fureur et mystère*

Mad Language

In an essay on Artaud Derrida scolds Blanchot for attempting to forge an essential link between poetry and madness ("La parole soufflée" [*EeD*255–57/*WaD*170–74]). The link is perhaps more topological than essential: from the late 1940s Blanchot has repeatedly situated poetry in the position of madness as that which is outside the life of the spirit—outside the movement of the negative or outside the work of the dialectic on which the edifices of culture and philosophy are raised. Recall the lines from *L'espace littéraire*: "Here in the world subordination reigns: subordination to ends, to measured proportion, to seriousness and order. On one front science, technology, the state; on another, significance, stable values, the ideal of the Good and the True." Poetry is unruly: it is " 'the world turned upside down': insubordination, disproportion, frivolity, ignorance, evil, nonsense" (*EL*287/*SL*216). Insubordination is the watchword of Blanchot's poetics (and, as it happens, of his politics as well). Poetry, he says in his first essay on René Char (1946), is the refusal of submission; its domain is "irreconcilability" (*PF*106/*WF*102).

Poetry, under the sign of madness, is what culture and philosophy cannot reconcile with their self-identity; it is what gets excluded from the history of reason and the work of concepts, from "the negativity of time and productive action" (*EL*287/*SL*216), from propositional style and the "language of continuity" (*EI*7/*IC*7), from the daylight or transparency of a "world completely known and totality transformed" (*ED*118/*WD*73). One has some reason to think that it is from Blanchot that Derrida learned how to resist (or at least distrust) philosophy's exclusionary logic. Derrida has generally insisted that no analysis could justify philosophy's claim to self-identity, that is, its claim to unity, autonomy, or separateness from what it is not. Philosophy is mad to the extent that it cannot be reconciled with itself, but maybe this only means that philosophy is plural and, moreover, porous with respect to every conceivable discourse. No one thing is philosophy. Like everything else it is structured like the weather: this is what the historicity of philosophy means (philosophy's self-refusal). "No one thing" means that philosophy is neutral with respect to itself and perhaps (who knows?) outside its own logic. Anyhow there is nothing from which anything could be excluded as nonidentical with philosophy.

As Derrida suggests with respect to Foucault's great project of writing the history of madness, from the perspective of what philosophy eliminates from its self-definitions (from the *cogito*, for example, or from Hegel's *Geist*), there is no one thing that can be called madness. One could just as well write the history of sleep as that of madness (*EeD*75/*WaD*51). Or, better and more essentially, one could write the history of silence vis-à-vis that of speaking.[1] If anything is philosophical (and what isn't?), speaking is. So long as we can keep speaking (keep making people speak), rationality can affirm itself, which is all that rationality can mean: namely, the assertion that I am not mad. Of course this assertion, which cannot be justified, holds together, constitutes, what we might call the philosophy or garrulousness of the mad. Arguably it is *the* assertion that Bartleby prefers not to make.

Commenting on Foucault's Blanchot-like definition of madness as "the absence of a work," Derrida says, "if discourse and philosophical communication (that is, language itself) are to have an intelligible meaning, that is to say, if they are to conform to their essence and vocation as discourse, they must simultaneously in fact and in principle escape madness" (*EeD*83/*WaD*53).[2] The sentence, for example, is the unit of reason: no reason without sentences. The sentence "carries normality and sense within it, and does so whatever the state, whatever the health or madness of him who propounds it, or whom it passes through, on whom, in whom it is articulated. In its most impoverished syntax, logos is reason and, indeed, a historical reason. And if madness in general, beyond any factitious and determined historical structure, is the absence of a work, then madness is, indeed, essentially and generally silence, stifled speech, within a caesura and a wound that *open up* life as *historicity in general*" (*EeD*84/*WaD*54). Poetry at the very least can hardly be madder than philosophy.

Or, to put it more plainly: philosophy is powerless to exclude from itself whatever is not itself for the same reason that nothing escapes reason (or discourse), that is, no madness is ever sufficiently mad, sufficiently free of philosophy or without sufficient reason, to justify the name of madness. So long as we keep speaking. For (says Derrida) "silence plays the irreducible role of that which bears and haunts language, outside and *against* which alone language can emerge — 'against' here simultaneously designating the content from which form takes off by force, and the adversary against whom I assure and reassure myself by force," that is, by the force of my speech (*EeD*84/*WaD*54). By talking I keep my distance from the mad ("the distance indispensable for continuing to speak and live"); but this distance is not space as extension but is only an exposed surface like one's skin against which madness brushes delicately, or more accurately it is like the breath and flesh of language itself, that side of language which is exposed to madness and inseparable from it. Or in Derrida's words: "Language being the break with madness, it adheres more thoroughly to its essence and vocation, makes a cleaner break with madness, if it pits itself against madness more freely and gets closer and closer to it: to the point of being separated from it only by the 'transparent sheet' of which Joyce speaks, that is, by itself — for this diaphaneity is nothing other than the language, meaning, possibility, and elementary discretion of a nothing that neutralizes everything" (*EeD*85/*WaD*55). Language: neither reason nor madness, as in moments of horror or dread (or of lucidity or writing) when we discover reason, as Blanchot says, "in the very loss into which it is sinking" (*FP*10/*GO*5). Only the mad know what reason is.

Just so, if one were to try to extract from Blanchot's texts a theory of madness, it would not be madness as opposed to reason in the form of delirium or looniness and derangement but madness as the limit of reason: madness as a kind of rigor or exigency rather than the turbulence of the lunatic or genius.[3] In "La folie par excellence" (1951), Blanchot says that madness is not an alternative to reason, much less a lack of it; on the contrary, the mad suffer from too much reason: "sometimes they are remarkable mathematicians or, in the language of the doctors, inclined toward metaphysics."[4] Hölderlin's madness, he says, is mysterious because in its deepest insanity Hölderlin's poetry achieved its greatest simplicity and clarity (as if madness were the freedom of reason rather than the extinction of it). In a late récit, *La folie du jour* (1973), madness is not the darkness of intellect but excessive lucidity: madness free of delusion or bewilderment, not incoherent but merely open (neutral or cool) with respect to the rule of noncontradiction or the integral logic of propositions, narratives, and systems. The narrator of *La folie du jour* finds himself in the care, or keep, of doctors who attempt to extract a story from him (the quintessential speech situation for Blanchot). But the narrator is a sort of Bartleby the Scrivener who prefers silence or something like silence (it is not that he does not speak). When, in the end, he tells his story, it doesn't quite come out in the form of a narrative. The doctors anyhow are disappointed.

> I had been asked: Tell us *"just* exactly" what happened. A story? I began: I am not learned; I am not ignorant. I have known joys. That is saying too little. I told them the whole story and they listened, it seems to me, with interest, at least in the beginning. But the end was a surprise to all of us. "That was the beginning," they said. "Now get down to the facts." How so? The story was over!
>
> I had to acknowledge that I was not capable of forming a story [*récit*] out of these events. I had lost the sense of the story [*l'histoire*]; that happens in a good many illnesses. But this explanation only made them more insistent. Then I noticed for the first time that there were two of them and that this distortion of the traditional method, even though it was explained by the fact that one of them was an eye doctor, the other a specialist in mental illness, constantly gave our conversation the character of an authoritarian interrogation, overseen and controlled by a strict set of rules. Of course, neither of them was the chief of police. But because there were two of them, there were three, and this third remained firmly convinced, I am sure, that a writer, a man who speaks and who reasons with distinction, is always capable of recounting facts that he remembers.
>
> A story? No. No stories. Never again. (*FJ*32–33/*MD*18)[5]

Blanchot traces this state of affairs—this madness of the day (of reason?)—to the Jena romantics, particularly Friedrich Schlegel and Novalis (the original last romantics), in whose texts, Blanchot says, "we find expressed the non-romantic essence of romanticism, as well as all the principal questions that the night of language will contribute to producing in the light of day: that to write is to make (of) speech (a) work, but that this work is an unworking [*désœuvrement*]; that to speak poetically is to make possible a non-transitive speech whose task is not to say things" (*EI*524/*IC*357): not to tell stories, not make statements, not to confess to reason.

It looks as if Jena romanticism were the tradition in which Blanchot would seem most likely to situate himself, and so, in a sense, it is, since it is the tradition of the fragment or of plural speech, that is — "Discontinuous form: the sole form befitting romantic *irony*, since it alone can make coincide discourse and silence, the playful and the serious, the declarative, even oracular exigency and the indecision of a thought that is unstable and divided, finally, the mind's obligation to be systematic and its abhorrence for system" (*EI*526/*IC*358). (Likewise Blanchot links up with Wittgenstein: "To speak of Wittgenstein . . . is to speak of a person who remains unknown. He did not wish — as a philosopher — to be one, nor did he wish to be known" — and then there is "the fact that so many of his investigations are fragmentary, open onto the fragmentary" [*ED*210/*WD*139].) But on Blanchot's reading the romantics tend to reduce madness to a style. "In truth," he says, "and particularly in the case of Friedrich Schlegel, the fragment often seems a means for complacently abandoning oneself to the self rather than an attempt to elaborate a more rigorous mode of writing. Then to write fragmentarily is simply to welcome one's own disorder, to close up upon one's own self in a contented isolation, and thus to refuse the opening that the fragmentary exigency represents; an exigency that does not exclude totality, but goes beyond it" (*EI*526/*IC*359).[6] The fragment, after all, is not the expression of madness, as if madness (or the fragment) were the disintegration, lack, or negation of something. Whatever it is, madness is outside affirmation and negation: neither discourse nor silence, neither system nor incoherence.

What would count as "a more rigorous mode of writing"? For Blanchot writing is not a discursive performance that flows in a single direction, as from inception to result or the work (and then back again). It is a movement that flows in (and from) multiple directions, perhaps simultaneously, so that it is no longer clear how to think of it as a movement at all; perhaps it is only a perturbation or restlessness, a ceaselessness. For example, in an essay on Antonin Artaud, "La cruelle raison poétique" (1958), Blanchot says that Artaud was gripped by "the rigor of poetic consciousness" that demanded "the pursuit of intense movement, a passionate convulsive life and also a moral rigor . . . marked by '*the unbridling of pure forces*,' the shock of what is without limit and without form, '*the initial viciousness*' of that which, while it remains inviolable and safe, never leaves us untouched: a dismembering violence that from out of the open depths makes an ignoble body, at once closed and fissured, and from out of the fragmentary and absolute morcellation by bursts, tearings, organic and aorgic [*aorgiques*] explosions: the prior dissociation or decomposition that is released in the fury—the flesh heap—of writing. Whence this sentence devoid of morality: *all writing is the spilling of guts*" (EI436/IC296). Blanchot's extravagant language here is doubtless a tribute to Artaud; his more lucid point is that Artaud is outside the alternatives of order and disorder in a position of originary anarchy in which nothing occurs that could go to pieces: so the "more rigorous mode of writing," the exigency of the fragment, is not a species of destruction or even of deconstruction but anarchy in the etymological sense of "prior dissociation or decomposition."

In *L'écriture du désastre*, the anarchic character of the fragmentary becomes explicit: "fragmentation is the pulling to pieces (the tearing) of that which never has preexisted (really or ideally) as a whole, nor can it ever be reassembled in any future presence whatever" (ED99/WD60). Maybe one could say: the fragmentary is just historicity—but not as if this were a principle dialectically opposed to the concept of system.[7]

René Char, commenting on one of his texts in *Poème pulvérisé*, writes: "I took my head as one takes a lump of salt, and literally pulverized it."[8] Blanchot does not cite this line in any of his essays on Char, but had he done so he might have remarked that a lump of salt has after all an aleatory structure: imagine one's head as a fragment constituted by the lumping together of fragments. Dada, confronting the accomplished work of art, is inspired to smash it or rip it to shreds, then reassemble the pieces willy-nilly. This is avant-garde, but not madness. Blanchot, confronting the accomplished work of art, looks to Artaud and Char—and, behind Char, to the Surrealists and Jena romantics—for what the accomplished work of art cannot accomplish or contain: "A new kind of arrangement not entailing harmony, concordance, or reconciliation [*d'une concorde ou d'une conciliation*], but that accepts disjunction or divergence as the infinite center from out of which, through speech, relation is to be created: an arrangement that does not compose but juxtaposes, that is, leaves each of the terms that come into relation *outside* one another, respecting and preserving this *exteriority* and this distance as the principle—always already undercut—of all signification. Juxtaposition and interruption here assume an extraordinary force of justice. . . . An arrangement at the level of disarray"

(*EI*452–53/*IC*308). Relation without relation. In Char's language: "Speech as archipelago" (*EI*454/*IC*309).

Here is a rigorous madness, where writing is neither in nor out of control, neither ordered nor disordered but in its way "an extraordinary force of justice." (Justice in what sense, one wonders? Justice as letting-be, perhaps.) Blanchot writes: "It should be understood that the poet in no way plays with disorder, for incoherence knows only too well how to compose and arrange things, albeit in reverse" (*EI*453/*IC*308). As if writing could inscribe a line that did not cut between oppositions but remained indifferent to them: "a line that, withdrawing from discourse any power to totalize, assigns it to multiple regions; a plurality that does not tend to unity (be it vain [that is, a failed unity or mere disruption of order]) nor that is constructed with relation to unity—as lying to its hither side or beyond—but that has always already set it aside" (*EI*457–58/*IC*312).[9] Indifferent or, as Blanchot sometimes likes to say: infinitely different, like a conversation that neither moves nor reposes in silence:

> I recall being present at a conversation between two men who were very different from one another. One would say in simple and profound sentences some truth he had taken to heart; the other would listen in silence, then when reflection had done its work he would in turn express some proposition, sometimes in almost the same words, albeit slightly differently (more rigorously, more loosely, or more strangely). This redoubling of the same affirmation constituted the strongest of dialogues. Nothing was developed, opposed, or modified; and it was manifest that the first interlocutor learned a great deal, and even infinitely, from his own words repeated—not because they were adhered to and agreed with, but, on the contrary, through the infinite difference. For it is as though what he said in the first person as an "I" had been expressed anew by him as "other" [*autrui*] and as though he had thus been carried into the very unknown of his thought: where his thought, without being altered, became absolutely other. (*EI*501/*IC*341)

(Compare *Celui qui ne m'accompagnait pas:* "He listened in silence, but in such a way that his silences were not inert, though no doubt slightly suffocating, as if they consisted in repeating in a more distant world, repeating syllable by syllable, everything one was trying to make him understand" [*CAP*19/*OW*7–8].)

The infinite conversation would be a dialogue without dialectic, a conversation without negation (in its structure conversation is a refusal of negation). So we may imagine once more a discourse outside of discourse, or perhaps one should say discourse in excess of discourse, a surplus of speech which occurs when nothing further is to be said, where the interlocutors neither contest nor supplement one another but have entered into a relation that is structured as an eternal return in which the one is always turning into the other without progress or regression, or where repetition occurs without sameness or identity. The temporality of such a conversation would be (once more) that of the *entre-temps*, the neutral time of the interval or interruption where one's words are neither first nor last, neither original nor final but—as Blanchot phrased it in a *récit* from the 1930s— "like the echo of the words *il y a*" (AC118/VC45).[10] The space of conversation would be (once more) without horizon, a reserve neither here nor there. And what else could the text of conversation be but a fragment, a tissue or lump of fragments?—which for Blanchot is something like the aleatory space of conversation, or of poetry or writing, *as it speaks*. (Of Artaud's poetics of the theater Blanchot says, quoting Artaud, that "poetry is '*a poetry in space*' insofar as it is language that '*aims at encompassing and using expanse, that is space, and by using it, making it speak*'" [EI435/ IC295]). This is Blanchot's anarchic space of literature: "a space that is *other* . . . the very space prior to all language that poetry attracts" (EI435/ IC295). What would it be to enter this space (to go mad)? Evidently it would be the experience of *désœuvrement:* "the experience of an art that is gripped by the violent difference that is prior to all representation and all knowledge" (EI436/IC295).

Perhaps one could say: Not a cognitive experience or experience of seeing or meaning, rather one of listening, or (so far as this goes) of madness. "Hear, simply hear"—which is Blanchot's advice on how to read Samuel Beckett's *Comment c'est*, which is a text (in fragments) about a voice without origin, a sort of parody of prophecy in which speaking has neither beginning nor end, is neither subjective process nor objective product, neither *le Dire* nor *le Dit*. To which Blanchot (writing in voices) adds:

> "—And this goes for the pure movement of writing.
> "—And with what clarity and in what a simple manner the voice offers itself to the one who holds himself or herself with the space of such a book, ready to hear; how distinct the rumor is in the indistinct. Reduced to the essential, but rejecting only words that are useless to listening, with a simplic-

ity that at times divides and redoubles itself, the voice speaks eternally." (*EI*482/*IC*329)

Characteristically, Blanchot turns Heidegger inside out. Imagine rumor, not as *Gerede*, but as an infinite conversation: "The power of rumor is not in the force of what it says, but in the fact that it belongs to the space where everything that is said has always already been said, continues to be said, and will not cease being said. What I learn through rumor I have necessarily already heard, it being what is simply related and what, for this reason, requires no author, no guarantee or verification. Rumor is what abides no contestation since its sole, its incontestable truth is to be related in a neutral movement wherein the relating seems reduced to its pure essence —a pure relation of no one and nothing" (*EI*26/*IC*19-20). In rumor, as in conversation, no one speaks.

Maurice Blanchot: nous n'eussions aimé répondre

One sees that in Blanchot's first essay on René Char (1946) his anarchist poetics or poetics of the fragment is already clearly articulated. "Language speaks wrongly of poetry in general," he says (*PF*105/*WF*100). There is no essence of poetry, and neither is poetry a genre-distinction, one discourse among others. It is outside the organon of discourse just in the sense that "the poem is division, vexation, torment. It does not come from a higher reality, capable of guaranteeing it; it does not refer to a truth that would last longer than it; it is not rest, for it does not rest on anything, and the poet receives only the anxiety of a movement without beginning or end from it" (*PF*106/*WF*101). The poem is outside all foundations; it belongs to an anarchic temporality, that of the interruption (*le pas au-delà*), which is an event in which nothing takes place. "The poem," Blanchot says, "is never present. It is always on the hither side or beyond [*Le poème n'est jamais présent. Il est toujours en deça ou au-delà*]" (*PF*107/*WF*103). Logically, or according to the rules of logic or the temporality of the proposition, one must speak of a "fundamental poetic contradiction" (*PF*108/*WF*103), which Blanchot characterizes in these terms: "The search for totality, in all of its forms, is the poetic claim [*prétention*] par excellence, a claim in which the impossibility of being accomplished is included in its condition, so that if it ever happens to be accomplished, it is only as something not possible, because the poem aims [*prétend*] to include its impossibility and its nonrealization in its very existence" (PF108/WF104). Here is *désœuvre-ment* already in play: "the poem stands unjustified; even realized, it re-mains impossible [*le poème reste injustifié; même réalisé, il demeure impos-sible*]" (PF109/WF105).

How to clarify this impossibility? Possibly by recurring to the idea that the experience of language in Blanchot's thinking is a limit-experience—not an experience of integral rationality (such as logic, linguistics, and phi-losophy of language try to describe) but of *désœuvrement*. For example, a recurring theme in Blanchot's writing is the anxiety or fear (or perhaps only a momentary thoughtfulness, or maybe an odd pleasure or depen-dency) aroused by words which, being neither nouns nor verbs—that is, not names of any sort—ordinarily draw no one's attention.[11] For example, in *Celui qui ne m'accompagnait pas*—whose narrator seems immobilized in an interminable conversation, or perhaps in a space set apart or neu-tralized by writing—words like "except," "at least," "then," "here," "so far," "really," "soon," "at one time" (*autrefois*), "perhaps," are opaque little pieces of disturbance, inquietude, or madness. In a fragment of a *récit* that occurs in *Le pas au-delà*, a narrative voice almost detaches the word "al-most" from the rest of language: "almost" detaches, but not entirely, since similar words trail in its wake, as if draining from the whole—certain "*ways of speaking, maybe, barely, momentarily, unless, and many others, signs without signification*" (PD15–16/SNB7)—words that are not quite words: neutral words, neither/nor or in-between words. "Almost" at all events be-longs to the *entre-temps*, the time of *no longer* and *not yet* that parallels or traverses the space of *too much* and *not quite*, the space of quotation marks and parentheses, a reserved space or space of reserve, where everything seems "completely immobile as in a place where nothing happens [*un place où rien ne ce passe*]" (CAP40/OW20). This is literary space, the space of writing, or the space in which *la folie d'écrire* occurs (EI323/IC217).

Perhaps it is too much to say that Blanchot inserts Char's *œuvre* into this space, or the context of this space, but he begins his essay "René Char et la pensée du neutre" (1963) by listing words in Char's vocabulary that are of this space, that is, "are grammatically neutral or border on the neu-tral"—for example, the word *attenants* (bordering) (EI439/IC298); and, with Heidegger-like concentration (or obsession), he cites the opening line of the Argument to *Poème pulvérisée*: "*How can we live without the un-known* [inconnu] *before us?*" where the unknown is that which is outside the relations of ignorance and cognition (OC247/PRC97). Blanchot says:

"the unknown is neuter. . . . [It] is that which cannot be assigned to any genre whatsoever: the non-general, the non-generic, as well as the non-particular [where the particular is an instance of the universal, that is, something other than the singular]" (*EI*440/*IC*298-99). The neuter is not a term in a relation, but neither is it nothing; it supposes another relation, a relation without relation, "a relation in which the unknown would be affirmed, made manifest, even exhibited: disclosed—and under what aspect?—precisely in that which keeps it unknown. In this relation, then, the unknown would be disclosed in that which leaves it under cover" (*EI*442/ *IC*300).

To which Blanchot adds the somewhat rhetorical question: "Is this a contradiction?" That is, is it madness? For he is speaking of disclosure without light: the unknown or the neuter "does not belong to light, but rather to a 'region' foreign to the disclosure that is accomplished in and through light. The unknown does not fall before a gaze, yet it is not hidden from it: neither visible nor invisible; or, more precisely, turning itself away from every visible and every invisible" (*EI*443/*IC*300: the term "region" is enclosed in quotation marks in the French text, the word "foreign" in the English—possibly it is redundant to place the word "foreign" in quotation marks).

The upshot is that the task of this disclosure outside the light, outside the alternatives of light and darkness, falls to poetry—poetry as it has been understood since "Littérature et la droit à la mort": "To speak the unknown, to receive it through speech while leaving it unknown, is precisely not to take hold of it, not to comprehend it [*ne pas prendre, ne pas le comprendre*]; it is rather to refuse to identify it even by sight, that 'objective' hold that seizes, albeit at a distance. To live with the unknown before one . . . is to enter into the responsibility of a speech that speaks without exercising any form of power" (*EI*445/*IC*302). Whereas earlier this speech was characterized as *le grand refus*, the refusal of death or negation, now it is characterized expressly as *neutral* speech—*l'acte littéraire qui n'est ni d'affirmation ni de négation* (*EI*448/*IC*304): speech which is neither sense nor non-sense but which works like brackets or quotation marks insofar as these figures of speech (figures of neutralization) function by placing words outside the movement of discourse, excluded from language, in the region of the neither/nor. (A fragment in *Le pas au-dèla* begins: "Madness: let us suppose a language from which this word would be excluded" [*PD*65/*SNB*44]. Derrida, in both his essays on Foucault and Artaud, explains that *folie* is a classical concept: modernity, in the form of psychiatry, does not have the word madness in its vocabulary, unless it is between quotation marks: a premodern citation. Blanchot perhaps does not speak a modern language: "His reduction of the clinical reduction is an essentialist reduction" [*EeD*257/*WaD*172].)

A poem of Char's, "Possessions extérieures," might, if we read it through Blanchot's eyes, be said to speak to such a region:

> Parmi tout ce qui s'écrit hors de notre attention, l'infini du ciel, avec ses défis, son roulement, ses mots innombrables, n'est qu'une phrase un peu plus longue, un peu plus haletante que les autres.
>
> Nous la lisons en chemin, par fragments, avec des yeux usés ou naissants, et donnons à son sens ce qui nous semble irrésolu et en suspens dans notre propre signification. Ainsi trouvons-nous la nuit différente, hors de sa chair et de la nôtre, enfin solidairement endormie et rayonnante de nos rêves. Ceux-ci s'attendent, se dispersent sans se souffrir enchaînes. Ils ne cessent point de l'être. (*OC*453)

> [Among everything that writes itself beyond our attention, the sky's infinitude, with its challenges, its rumbling, its innumerable words, is only a sentence slightly longer, of quicker breath than others.
>
> We read it on our way, in fragments, with eyes worn out or freshly born, giving its sense what seems irresolute and suspended in our own meaning. So we find night different, outside its flesh and ours, solidly asleep and radiant with our dreams. These await each other, scatter while not suffering to be restrained. They do not cease to be so.] (*PRC*213; translation slightly amended)

This is a poem to catch Blanchot's eye, because it is a poem about poetry — not, however, about poetry as such; rather it is no one's poetry. Imagine writing as an adverbial movement, irreducible to pronomial identities or indices. Such writing cannot be said to originate; it is not expression but rather something found or encountered, a poem that falls not so much from the sky as from the infinity of the sky, which is a bit like falling through the cracks in the firmament. Mallarmé would have thought *l'infini du ciel* excessive or redundant, since for him "sky," or *le ciel*, is already the most indeterminate of nouns: not the name of anything, at most the distance or yawning that makes *l'azur* inaccessible or the vast nocturnal page on which constellations strew themselves. Blanchot would define the sky as that which is outside every horizon, and therefore, as Char says, *hors*

156

de notre attention: the unknown that we always have before us.

But for Char the sky's infinity is not simply a background; it is itself writing, writing itself. Perhaps this as much as anything makes his poem vulnerable to a Blanchovian allegory. The sky is refractory (*ses défis*), incessant and interminable like the murmur of the *il y a* (*ses roulement*), irreducible to a totality—*ses mots innombrables* do not constitute an ensemble or a language from which a word (for example, madness) might be excluded; rather they are each of them singular, external to one another and to any imaginable totality: each forms, if anything, a mere fragment, a sentence only slightly longer than any other, a breath. (And as in Celan and in Levinas, breath is linked with freedom where space is a surface rather than a container: "Its word [*la liberté*] was not a blind battering-ram but rather the canvas where my breath was inscribed" [OC148/PRC63].)[12]

How to read the sky? Not as one regards a landscape. Not from an astronomer's fixed perspective but as nomads, sailors, or augurs do: *unterwegs*. As if the sky were, like language (or everything), structured like the weather. Imagine by contrast if nothing moved. As Levinas says, *apropos* of Blanchot, "Poetry can be said to transform words, the tokens of a whole, into unfettered signs, breaching the walls of immanence, disrupting order. . . . Without this, the world would know only the meanings which inspire official records or the minutes of the board meetings of Limited Companies" (*SMB39/LR156–57*). So the sky is poetry, a space of fragments.

Char, or a lover of Char, might protest that the "we" in his poem are lovers, not a Blanchot-like "we" where, Joyce-like, no one is anything, that is, neither the one nor the other; to which Blanchot might reply that the world of lovers is a *communauté désœuvrée*—or, more accurately, the relation between lovers is more interval than unity. In his commentary on Marguerite Duras's *La maladie de la mort*, Blanchot thinks of love as a scandal to ethics just in the sense that it is outside all bounds, a neutral relation, a relation of strangeness, possibly "a return to the wilderness that does not even transgress prohibitions, given that it ignores them, or to the 'anogistic' [*aorgique*] (Hölderlin) which unsettles any social relationship, just or unjust, and, contumacious to any third party, cannot be satisfied with a society of two where the reciprocity of the 'I-you' would reign, but prefers to invoke the original, precreational chaos, the night without end, the outside, the fundamental unhinging" (*CI68/UC40*). So Blanchot, persisting in his allegory, might say: the night of the lovers is the other night, *le nuit différente, hors de chair et de la nôtre*; and likewise it is a space of fragments where dreams *s'attendent, se dispersent sans se souffrir en-chaînes*. And so on without end. The thing to remember (remember the lesson of Blanchot vis-à-vis Celan) is that literary space is not a nullity. Blanchot concludes *La communauté inavouable* by remarking that Marguerite Duras's book "carries an exacting political meaning and . . . does not permit us to lose interest in the present time which, by opening unknown spaces of freedom, makes us responsible for new relationships . . . between what we call *œuvre* and what we call *désœuvrement*" (CI93/ UC56).

Note the phrase "opening unknown spaces of freedom": imagine this as the task of poetry or of writing outside of language ("We can't do anything with an object that has no name" [PF312/GO42]). Or of love. A poem by Celan ends with

Die Liebe löscht ihren Namen: sie	Love blots out its name: to
schreibt sich dir zu.	you it ascribes itself.
(GW1:220)	(PPC165)

No One's Voice, Again

It seems important to repeat again that *désœuvrement* is not a catastrophic concept in which something whole goes to pieces; perhaps it is a response to catastrophe. At all events it is not a species of deconstruction; it is not the undoing of metaphysics, it is older than metaphysics. It is that which is on the hither side of doing, of philosophy or *poiesis* or worldmaking, where a voice sounds intransitively. Let's repeat it again: "The voice sets free from speech; it announces a possibility prior to all saying, and even to any possibility of saying. The voice frees not only from representation, but also, in advance, from meaning, without, however, succeeding in doing more than committing itself to the ideal madness of delirium. The voice that speaks without a word, silently—in the silence of a cry—tends to be, no matter how interior, the voice of no one [*la voix de personne*]" (EI386/IC258). Recall the terror of being forced to speak (EI60–61/IC42–43) or the "fear of speaking" (PD84–85/SNB59). The voice is outside the economy of discourse, therefore outside the workings of construction and catastrophe.

Adorno, author of a famous saying about the relation of poetry to catastrophe, says that the poems of Paul Celan respond to catastrophe in the way of windowless monads. They "articulate unspeakable horror by being silent. . . . They emulate a language that lies below the helpless prattle of human beings—even below the level of organic life as such. It is the language of dead matter, of stones and stars" (AeT477/AT444).[13] We can imagine Celan, for whom stones and stars are not dead matter, replying to Adorno (or to the end of history) very simply:

es sind	there are
noch Lieder zu singen jenseits	still songs to be sung on the other
der Menschen.	side
(GW2:26)	of mankind.
	(PPC227)

With *Sprachgitter* (1959) and *Niemandsrose* (1963), to be sure, Celan's poems grow increasingly spare and reserved, like "Ein Auge, Offen":

Stunden, maifarben, kühl.	Hours, May-coloured, cool.
Das nicht mehr zu Nennende, heiß,	The no more to be named, hot,
hörbar im Mund.	audible in the mouth.
Niemandes Stimme, wieder.	No one's voice, again.
Schmerzende Augapfeltiefe:	Aching depth of the eyeball:
das Lid	the lid
steht nicht im Wege, die Wimper	does not stand in its way, the lash
zählt nicht, was eintritt	does not count what goes in.
die Träne, halb,	The tear, half,
die schärfere Linse, beweglich,	the sharper lens, moveable,
holt dir die Bilder.	brings the images home to you.
(GW1:187)	(PPC133)

What is our relation to such a poem? It is not an analytic one of glossing and parsing. Analytically, a text can only be glossed by an insider—a stand-in who is privy to the secrets of the text (as if the text were made of references).[14] Otherwise the reader is something of a bystander or eavesdropper, someone in front of (*en deçà*) rather than behind the text. Recall Lucile in "Der Meridian": "somebody who hears, listens, looks . . . and then does not know what it was about"; someone who perceives language from the outside, as flesh or breath (GW3:188/CP39). The translator of "Ein Auge, Offen" renders *heiß* in the second line as "hot," corresponding to the word *kühl* in the first. This is grammatically coherent. But hearing is often incoherent with respect to reading; that is, it cannot, for example, tune out the discursiveness of *heiß*, as if it were a fragment of the word for calling (*heiße, heißt*). As if the ear could never be brought fully under the control of the eye.

Ein Ohr, abgetrennt, lauscht.

(GW2:19)

Imagine an eye as vulnerable as the ear, exposed to the outside, unable to close or even to focus, tearing-up, unable to keep out images. In "Ein Auge, Offen," the eye is not simply open; it is no longer part of a body. It is itself a porous body with tears for eyes.

Celan's world, or his poetry, is made of detachments: syllables from words, words from sentences, names from persons, things, gods, voices from speakers, eyes (especially eyes, but also fingers, hands, teeth—most horribly, teeth—hearts, mouths, tongues, breaths, souls) from bodies, stars from the firmament, stones from mountainsides, hours from the day, colors from the spectrum, pronouns from subjects, objects, interlocutors.[15] As if unity did not hold the key to all the relations to which we must respond.

der Name Ossip kommt auf dich zu	the name Osip walks up to you, and
du erzählst ihm	you tell him
was er schon weiß, er nimmt es,	what he knows already, he takes, he
er nimmt es dir ab, mit Händen	accepts it from you, with hands,
du löst ihm den Arm von der	you detach an arm from his
Schulter, den rechten, den linken	shoulder,
du heftest die deinen an ihre Stelle,	the right, the left,
mit Händen, mit Fingern, mit	you attach your own in its place,
Linien	with
(GW1:284)	hands, with fingers, with lines.

(PPC217)

Osip Mandelstam, who thought "the law of identity the most fruitful of all poetic laws"![16] In Celan's poetry this law finds its limit. The effect, however, is not of dismembered randomness or of particles indifferent to one another; rather what is in play now is a relation other than unity, namely, interruption, *entre-temps*, a rift of proximity and separation:

Zu beiden Händen, da	On either hand, there
wo die Sterne mir wuchsen, fern	where stars grew for me, far
allen Himmeln, nah	from all heavens, near

160

allen Himmeln:	all heavens:
Wie	How
wacht es sich da! Wie	one's awake there! How
tut sich die Welt uns auf, mitten	the world opens for us, right
durch uns!	through the midst
	of ourselves!
Du bist,	You are,
wo dein Aug ist, du bist	where your eye is, you are
oben, bist	above, are
unten, ich	below, I
finde hinaus.	find my way out.
O diese wandernde leere	O this wandering empty
gastliche Mitte. Getrennt,	hospitable midst. Apart,
fall ich dir zu, fällst	I fall to you, you
du mir zu, einander	fall to me, fallen away
entfallen, sehn wir	from each other, we see
hindurch:	through:
Das	One
Selbe	and the same
hat uns	has
verloren, das	lost us, one
Selbe	and the same
hat uns	has
vergessen, das	forgotten us, one
Selbe	and the same
hat uns—	has—
(GW1:219)	(PPC163)

It is not as if the absence of the principle of identity were to be thought of as a loss or deprivation—anyhow it is not our loss: the last lines of "Zu beiden Händen" have it that selfsameness, *das Selbe*, has been deprived of us, creatures of the between where nothing is fixed or resolvable into a whole. The loss of unity or totality is not a lack but a freedom where the law of noncontradiction, although not exactly abrogated, no longer has any coherent application. The between—O *diese wandernde leere / gastliche Mitte*—is an opening rather than a gap or void: it is a neutral space, neither near nor far, neither high nor low, "a breath between there and not-there [*ein Atem zwischen / Dort und Nicht-da*]" where we are neither bound nor lost to one another.

161

Think of the paradoxical intimacy that characterizes Blanchot's "relation of the third kind": "no longer proximity—proximity of struggle, of services, of essence, of knowledge, or of recognition, not even of solitude—but rather the *strangeness* between us: a strangeness it will not suffice to characterize as a separation or even as a distance" (*EI*97/*IC*68), as in the closing lines of Celan's "Soveil Gestirne":

ich weiß	I know,
ich weiß und du weißt, wir wußten	I know and you know, we know,
wir wußten nicht, wir	we did not know, we
waren ja da und nicht dort,	were there and not there
und zuweilen, wenn	and at times when
nur das Nichts zwischen uns stand,	only the Nothing stood between us
fanden,	we got
wir ganz zueinander.	all the way to each other.
(GW1:217)	(PPC159)

Das Nichts is not nothing; it is, in a way that Blanchot helps us to understand, outside negation, outside the alternatives of there and not-there, in the no-one's space of neither/nor, where the encounter with the other is neither a relation of identity nor an I-Thou relation of intersubjectivity but a relation of alterity, neither immediate nor mediated: neutral, but not in the rational sense of disinvolvement. As if there were no room in the neutral for neutrality.

Celan's "space of conversation [*der Raum des Gespräch*]" (GW3:198/ CP50) is full of complications like this. "Gespräch im Gebirg," for example, describes a space of noncoincidence in which everything (including the elements of Celan's prose) remains slightly disconnected from itself and its surroundings:

> One evening, when the sun had set and not only the sun, the Jew—Jew and son of a Jew—went off, left his house and went off, and with him went his unspeakable name [*und mit ihm ging sein Name, der unaussprechliche*], went and came, with a stick, came over stones, do you hear me, you hear me, I am, I, I, and whom you hear, whom you think you hear, I and the other [*ich und der andre*]—so he went off, you could hear it, went off one evening when various things had set, went under clouds, went in the shadow, his own and not his own [*dem eignen und dem fremden*: his own and alien]—because the Jew, you know, what does he have that is really his own, that is not borrowed, taken and not returned—so he went off and walked along this road, this beautiful, incomparable road, walked like Lenz

through the mountains, he who had been allowed to live down in the plain where he belongs, he, the Jew, walked and walked. (GW3:169/CP17)

Or perhaps one should say that here nothing is anchored or fixed, everything is loose, disjointed, or estranged—the sun sets but not just the sun, the narrative voice wanders grammatically into the vocative or accusative, the Jew sets off (goes and comes) as if his unspeakable, detachable name were a clandestine companion, as he is to another (if it is he who speaks): "ich bins, ich, ich und der, den du hörst, zuhören vermeinst, ich und der andre."

The name, especially the Jewish name, has a deeply ambiguous place in Celan's poetry, which is in many respects a poetry of anonymity; it is as if the name were and were not a name.[17] Imagine an anonymous name, as God's name is in some sense the name of the unnameable: no-one's name. Names are not just designations; they belong to the named as to their flesh, which is why "Solve" is such a chilling poem (if only everyone had been unnameable):

Entosteter, zu	De-Eastered, grave
Brandscheiten zer	tree split into
spaltener Grabbaum:	logs for burning:
an den Gift-	past the poison-
pfalzen vorbei, an den Domen	palatinates, past the cathedrals,
stromaufwärts, strom-	floated upstream,
abwärts geflößt	downstream,
vom winzig-lodernden, vom	by the tinily flaring, the
freien	free punctuation marks of
Satzzeichen der	sequestered writ that
zu den unzähligen zu	has dis-
nennenden un-	persed
aussprechlichen	into the
Namen aus-	countless, un-
einandergflohenen, ge-	utterable,
borgenen	to be uttered
Schrift.	Names.
(GW2:82)	(PPC257)

But who is the other in "Gespräch im Gebirg"? Perhaps the Jew's walking-stick, or perhaps his shadow, which is his own and a stranger's, but if

163

one is anonymous, as this Jew is, one is always otherwise than someone: someone and no one. Doubly so if one is referred to, as here, as *der Jud*, "the Jew."[18] The Jew, as always, is out of place, not just in these mountains, but even on the lowlands where, as if confined, "he belongs." (Later the narrator adds: "Because the Jew and nature [*die Jud und die Natur*] are strangers to each other, have always been and still are, even today, even here" [GW3:169/CP18]).

Along the way the Jew meets his older, taller cousin, whose shadow is also not his own: the cousins are now identified as Jew Klein and Jew Gross (is not a shape "as good as a name?" Or a breath?).[19] Many commentators think the two are simply younger and older, smaller and larger versions of the same self, but perhaps it were better to say, as the poem cited above suggests, *das Selbe* is a category lost on them. They are the same and not the same, there and not there.[20]

There and not there, moreover, in the additional sense of seeing and not seeing what surrounds them (worldblind), although it is not easy to say how this is to be understood. The narrator takes care to name the flowers that adjoin the path (the flowers are perhaps all that is not anonymous in the tale)—"On the left, the turk's cap lily [*Türkenbund*] blooms, blooms wild, blooms like nowhere else. And on the right, corn-salad [*die Rapunzel*] and Dianthus superbus, the maiden pink [*die Prachtnelke*], not far off"—then adds, strangely:

> But they, those cousins, have no eyes, alas [*Aber sie, die Geschwisterkinder, sie haben, Gott sei's klagt, keine Auge*]. Or, more exactly, they have, even they have eyes, but with a veil hanging in front of them, no, not in front, behind them, a moveable veil. No sooner does an image enter than it gets caught in the web, and a thread starts spinning, spinning itself around the image, a veil-thread; spins itself around the image and begets a child, half-image, half veil. (GW3:170/CP18)

"Flower—a blindman's word [*Blume—ein Blindenwort*]" (GW1:164/PPC115). Perhaps the process described here is the formation of the mysterious *Augenkind* mentioned in "Eis, Eden."[21] The ancients thought of names as veils, where the veil was understood as a figure that conceals in order to disclose, on the principle that the unadorned thing itself would be invisible (or perhaps maddening) to merely human cognition. Think of the painful, lidless eyeball in "Ein Auge, Offen," where a tear works like a veil as well as a lens. "Zuversicht" (translated as "Confidence," but the word is a pun) begins:

Es wird noch ein Aug sein,	There will be another eye,
ein fremdes, neben	a strange one, beside
dem unsern: stumm	our own: unspeaking
unter steinernem Lid.	under its stony lid.
(GW1:153)	(PPC105)

Or, again, if "You are / where your eye is," the cousins are nowhere.

Which may be somewhat to the point. In Blanchot's dialogue "Parler, ce n'est pas voir," one of the voices says, "For sight, speech is war and madness" (EI40/IC28). The same voice continues: "I am seeking a way, without getting there, to say that there is a speech in which things, not showing themselves, do not hide. Neither veiled nor unveiled: this is their nontruth" (EI41/IC29). Poetry is this sort of speech: outside the movement of *aletheia*—outside of language: neither veiled nor unveiled.

The cousins—*die Geschwisterkinder*, but also garrulous *Geschwätzigen*—are perhaps outside in this sense. They are at all events not observers of the passing show. When they encounter one another, their walking-sticks cease their dialogue with stones, and a stillness settles over the scene that Heidegger would have listened for, perhaps chiefly to his disappointment:

> Poor lily, poor corn-salad. There they stand, the cousins, on a road in the mountains, the stick silent, the stones silent, and the silence no silence at all. No word has come to an end and no phrase, it is nothing but a pause, an empty space between the words, a blank—you see all the syllables stand around, waiting. They are tongue and mouth as before, these two, and in their eyes hangs a veil, and you, poor flowers, are not even there, are not blooming, you do not exist, and July is not July. (GW3:170/CP19)

Neither/nor: the silence is no silence, the flowers are there and not there, July is not July. Obviously this is not a space ruled by logic. It is a neutral space or space of interruption, of waiting, of Celan's own *Atempause* (GW3:197/CP48): as in an infinite conversation, the relation of words forms "an essentially dissymmetrical field governed by discontinuity" (EI110/IC77).

The subject of the cousins' conversation is, initially, language, a certain kind of language. One of the cousins says:

"You know. You know and see. The earth folded up here, folded once and twice and three times, and opened up in the middle, and in the middle there is water, and the water is green, and the green is white, and the white comes from even farther up, from the glaciers, and one could say, but one shouldn't, that this is the language that counts here [*die hier gilt*: literally, "that is current here"], the green with the white in it, a language not for you and not for me—because, I ask you, for whom is it meant, the earth, not for you, I say, is it meant, and not for me—a language, well, without I and without You, nothing but He, nothing but It, you understand, and She, nothing but that. (GW3:170–71/CP19–20)

In his essay on Celan Levinas comments on this passage and interprets this language immediately as the Heideggerian "Langue du neutre": a language that, like the peal of stillness, is no longer human. But one could just as well say that what Celan is thinking of is simply the language of philosophy, a language built for framing representations, a language of designation and combination, a third-person language of references and rules, a language without voices, ghosts, or pneumatic movements: a language of names rather than of persons, of Lenz the character (the "he") as against Lenz the singular and irreproducible "I" whose epitaph is nameless and inaccessible.[22]

This way of figuring language would at least be consistent with "Edgar Jené und der Traum von Traume," whose narrator remembers a conversation with a friend about Kleist's *Marionette*, which oddly turns into a conversation about the beginning and the end of history: How to recapture a consciousness purified of contingency (that is, of history)? The friend is a foundationalist who believes in the metaphysical unity of words and things. For him the idea is to set history aside in order to recover the foundations of language, reason, consciousness, history. "It was, my friend argued, by letting reason purify our unconscious inner life that we could recapture the immediacy of the beginning. . . . But what must we do now, in our own time, to reach timelessness, eternity, the marriage of tomorrow-and-yesterday? Reason, he said, must prevail. A bath in the *aqua regia* of intelligence [*mit dem Königswasser des Verstandes reinwusch*] must give their true (primitive) meaning back to words, hence to things, beings, occurrences. A tree must again be a tree, and its branch, on which the rebels of a hundred wars have been hanged, must again flower in the spring" (GW3:156/CP4–5).

But what, the narrator wonders, "could be more dishonest than to claim that words had somehow, at bottom, remained the same [*was war unaufrichtiger als die Behauptung, diese Worte seien irgendwo im Grunde noch dieselben*]!" (GW3:157/CP6). What if words are not for naming (what if names are not names)? What if meanings are local and transitory, as if words lived as humans do—only once in a lifetime, not forever in a purely logical space but only here and now in a space of traversal or eternal return? So in place of names and concepts the narrator imagines "words and figures [*Gestalten*] coming, images and gestures, veiled and unveiled as in a dream [*traumhaft verschleiert und traumhaft entschleiert*]. When they meet in their heady course, and the spark of the wonderful is born from the marriage of the strange and the strange [*da Fremdes Fremdesten vermählt wird*], then I will know I am facing the new radiance" (GW3:157–58/CP6). Blanchot would mark the odd fact that the light of this radiance "is not daylight [*ihr Licht ist nicht das Licht des Tages*]" (GW3:158/CP6). In this light the narrator does not so much recognize things as encounter them for the first time, seeing them not under the category of the same but in their singularity and irreproducibility.

And in this strange light the narrator himself undergoes some astonishing disconnections: "its colour speaks to the new eyes which my closed lids have given to one another; my hearing has wandered into my fingertips and learns to see; my heart, now that it lives behind my forehead, tastes the laws of a new, unceasing, free motion. I follow my wandering senses into this new world of the spirit and come to know freedom" (GW3:158/CP6–7). One wants to say that against the philosophical language of naming and representation, of order, fixity, and identity, Celan opposes the poetic language of *désœuvrement*, the language of dislocation, wandering—and freedom.

With respect to "Gespräch im Gebirg" there might be a looser way of constructing this distinction. Say that in contrast to a philosophical language of names and things there is a language (not of dialogue exactly, but) of movement—a language that opens a space that is not to be filled with relations but to be traversed, which is what occurs in the event of the murmur, the cry, the breath, the sigh or gasp, which is to say the event of the poem as *unterwegs* (GW3:186/CP35). In "Gespräch im Gebirg" this distinction is formulated as a difference between speaking (*sprechen*) and talking (*reden*)—the sticks and stones "do not talk, they speak" (GW3:171/

CP20) — where speaking is something like solitary singing in contrast to speech that opens a space for another, a space into which another can walk and talk and be heard. This space would be as much for listening as for speaking. Speaking, as such, is not aimed at listening, whereas talking belongs to the open reserve of responsibility.[23]

We shouldn't let Levinas talk us out of characterizing this reserve as a *neutral* space: that is, an open, empty, free space without conditions that the other must meet, without relations to be entered or names to be borne. A space, Blanchot would say, for the relation of the third kind: a relation without relations, "an interruption of *being*" in which I encounter the other in its otherness, outside of language. This is the space of neither/nor whose alterity makes the other "neither another self for me, nor another existence, neither a modality or a moment of universal existence, nor a superexistence, a god or a non-god, but rather the unknown in its infinite distance" (*EI*109/*IC*77). No-one's space.[24]

For both Blanchot and Celan the no-one (*la personne, Niemand*) is many-sided, but in different if perhaps symmetrical ways, starting with the difference between French and German. Martine Broda, thinking of the translation of Celan's *Niemandsrose* into French (*La rose personne*), notes that *Niemand* is "purely negative," whereas *personne* has a "double valence": no man or a person (*Dans la main de personne*, p. 67). But in Celan's writings the German, without ceasing to be German, begins to resonate with the French, so that *Niemand* takes on the ambiguity (Blanchot would say: the neutrality) of *personne*. One could clarify this by saying that in Celan's texts — for example, "Niemand schnitt uns das Wort von der Herzwand" (*GW*1:193) — *Niemand* takes on the character of anonymity that belongs to *personne*: not "no one," but someone outside the alternatives of identity/difference, and therefore outside the possibility of designation and belonging — like the Jew's shadow in "Gespräch im Gebirg": "my own and not my own [*dem eignen und dem fremden*]." Whereas, by contrast, Blanchot achieves for *personne* the ontological indeterminacy of *Niemand:* not "no one," but *autrui*, the one outside the alternatives of there and not-there, presence/absence, entity/nonentity, one and not-one.

One could deepen the context of this difference by asking whether it makes sense to say that Blanchot's *personne* is Greek (no one is anyone), whereas Celan's *Niemand* is unmistakably Jewish, as (famously) in "Psalm," where it defines the relation between Jews and the God of the Jews as a relation of the third kind:[25]

Niemand knetet uns wieder
    aus Erde und Lehm,
niemand bespricht unsern Staub
Niemand.
	No one moulds us again
	    out of earth and clay,
	no one conjures our dust.
	No one.

Niemand knetet uns wieder
  aus Erde und Lehm,
niemand bespricht unsern Staub
Niemand.

Gelobt seist du, Niemand
Dir zulieb wollen
wir blühn
Dir
entgegen.

Ein Nichts
waren wir, sind wir, werden
wir bleiben, blühend:
die Nichts-, die
Niemandsrose.

Mit
dem Griffel seelenhell,
dem Staubfaden himmelswüst,
der Krone rot
vom Purpurwort, das wir sangen
über, o über
dem Dorn.
(GW1:225)

No one moulds us again
  out of earth and clay,
no one conjures our dust.
No one.

Blessed be your name, no one.
For your sake
we shall flower,
Towards
you.

A nothing
we were, are shall
remain, flowering:
nothing-, the
no one's rose.

With
our pistil soulbright,
with our stamen heaven-ravaged,
our corolla red
with the crimson word which we
sang
over, O over
the thorn.
(PPC175)

"Gelobt siest du, Niemand"; "Loué sois-tu, Personne": a prayer, like a breath for nothing, for no-one.[26] No one is addressed—and no one speaks: that is, the voice of the poem (as of many of Celan's poems) is precisely no-one's voice. A relation of the third kind is not an I-Thou or intersubjective relation but a nonrelation, a relation without unity or relation of separation or foreignness that binds two *personnes,* two no ones, together—a neutral relation that for Celan is nevertheless not neutral with respect to feeling but, psalmlike, is traversed by an existential sense of disconnection and abandonment. This is a sense whose pathos Blanchot tries to neutralize by not taking *personne* personally, impersonalizing it, as he does most explicitly in his essay "La voix narrative (le 'il', le neutre)," where the narrative voice "marks the intrusion of the other . . . in its irreducible strangeness and perversity": not a remote *autrui,* in other words, but a proximate and, one might even say, prophetically invasive one: "The other speaks. But when the other is speaking, no one speaks [*personne ne parle*] because the other [*l'autre*], which we must refrain from honoring with a capital letter that would determine it by way of a majestic substantive, as though it had some substantial or even unique presence, is precisely never simply the other. The other is neither the one nor the other, and the neutral that indicates it withdraws it from both, as it does from unity, always establishing it outside the term, the act, or the subject through which it claims to offer itself" (*EI*564–65/*IC*385).

Just so, "Psalm" figures our relation with God as a relation of *désœuvrement*: it is, so to speak, a unity that does not occur, an impossible community formed out of death.[27] Precisely for his reason we can think of it as a relation of *exigency* in Blanchot's sense of this word, as in "the exigency of strangeness" (*EI*189/*IC*129): it is the impossibility to which no-one's voice responds with its psalm or cry of destitution. Imagine a poem composed in a language whose names had been extinguished, a poem in which nothing (or only nothing) could be designated: a burnt-out language or language no longer capable of use (in which Mallarmé could no longer say, "Je dis: une fleur")—a language for nothing or for poetry of the kind that "Psalm" bears witness to, an anonymous, absolute poem of intransitive evocation in which there occurs neither appearance nor disappearance, neither visibility nor invisibility, neither presence nor absence: *désœuvrement*—a flowering nothing, *die Niemandsrose*.

"Psalm" is a sort of complication of "Gespräch im Gebirg." To the question of why he has walked into the mountains, one of the cousins answers:

"Because I had to talk, maybe, to myself or to you, talk with my mouth and tongue, not just with my stick. Because to whom does it talk, my stick? It talks to the stones, and the stones—to whom do they talk?"

"To whom should they talk, cousin? They do not talk, they speak, and who speaks does not talk to anyone, cousin, he speaks because nobody hears, nobody and Nobody [*niemand und Niemand*], and then he says, himself, not his mouth or his tongue, he, and only he, says: Do you hear me?"

"Do you hear me, he says—I know, cousin, I know . . . Do you hear me, he says, I'm here. I am here, I've come [*Hörst du, sagt er, ich bin da. Ich bin da, ich bin hier, ich bin gekommen*: I am there. I am there, I am here, I am come]. I've come with my stick, me and no other, me and not him, me with my hour, my undeserved hour, me who have been hit, who have not been hit, me with my memory, with my lack of memory, me, me, me [*ich, ich, ich*] . . . ."

"He says, he says . . . Do you hear me, he says . . . And Do-you-hear-me
[*Hörstdu*] does not say anything, does not answer, because Do-you-hear-me
is one with the glaciers, is three in one, and not for men." (GW3:171/CP20)

On close reading it does not appear certain that the speech of the cousins
is finally different from that of the sticks and stones, who speak without
talking because nobody hears. Of course the apposition of *niemand und
Niemand* prevents nobody from being purely negative, turns nobody into
a *personne*, and as the conversation develops the speech of the sticks and
stones merges with the talk of the *ich*. The question is, perhaps, what language does "Hörstdu"—*Niemand*, the unnameable, God—speak? Perhaps
he speaks only a philosophical language—the language of the glaciers—or
perhaps only the language of the theologians: a Greek language rather
than a Jewish one, that is, a language of reference and identity but not of
address. In any event there is no reaching him in the language of "three-
in-one," because this language does not belong to the existential mode of
listening. Perhaps this mode has been lost or destroyed, reducing us to
sticks and stones, which would be why talking, like poetry, always sounds
like a cry of destitution.

Having said this, however, one should try to reflect on the irony of
Celan's text, which could be said to bring God into the space of conversation despite his inability to answer.[28] The cry of "Hörst du!" interrupts the
logical space in which the "three-in-one" remains aloof and theological.
Likewise in "Psalm" God [*Hörstdu*] is summoned in spite of himself, as if
his death did not release him from responsibility to those whom he abandoned.

A final discrimination among anonymities is suggested by "Es ist nicht
mehr," which one might read as a poem of the neutral:

Es ist nicht mehr	It is no longer
diese	this
zuweilen mit dir	heaviness
in die Stunde gesenkte	lowered at times together with you
Schwere. Es ist	into the hour. It is
eine andre.	an other.
Es ist das Gewicht, das die Leere	It is the weight holding back
zurückhält	the void
die mit-	that would
ginge mit dir.	accompany you.

Es hat, wie du, keinen Namen.	Like you, it has no name.
Vielleicht	Perhaps
seid ihr dasselbe. Vielleicht	you two are one and the same.
nennst auch du mich einst	Perhaps
so.	one day you also will name
(GW1:238)	me so.
	(PPC185)

The opening line has the character of the *il y a* or *es gibt:* weight without substance. Think of this anonymous weight or weightliness, the weight or inertia of this hour (or this present), as the movement of eternal return: an event which, in a certain sense, does not occur. The interval of this event (*nicht mehr/einst*) is perhaps the space in which the no-one's voice of this poem addresses itself (interminably, ceaselessly) to the other, the eternally approachable, nameless "du." This interval can never complete itself. It is the repeatable/unrepeatable moment of *désœuvrement:* "Let there be a past, let there be a future, with nothing that would allow passage from one to the other, such that the line of demarcation would unmark them the more, the more it remained invisible [*de telle sorte que la ligne de démarcation les démarquerait d'autant plus qu'elle resterait invisible*]: hope of a past, completed of a future. All that would remain of time, then, would be this line to cross, always already crossed, although not crossable, and, in relation to 'me' [*moi*], unsituable [the English text misprints this as "unsuitable"]. Perhaps what we would call the 'present' is only the impossibility of situating this line" (*PD22/SNB12*). This present is the time of the poem, of writing, the time of infinite conversation in which the proximity and separation between past and future, between the voice of the poem and the "du" that it endlessly addresses, can never be effaced by any predicate.

PART III

The Temporality
of Anarchism

CHAPTER 8

Infinite Discretion

The Theory of the Event

Merci pour tous ces mots qui n'ont pas été dits.
—*Le pas au-delà*

Words without Language

Foucault, with evident insight, praises Blanchot for replacing man with language.[1] Naturally thoughts fly at once to *le dernier homme*, whose death would mean the end of history ("Could it be that he is dying at this moment?" [*DH*156/*LM*88]). Certainly it is true that Blanchot was among the first of his generation of French intellectuals to acknowledge the reality and the primacy of language—or, to be more exact, its *historicity*.[2] Historicity, as against (what is the word?) *systematicity*. For it is not as if Blanchot could ever sponsor a theory in which language circumscribes, subsumes, and effaces everything that is not itself. The refusal of such a theory—the refusal of every form of structuralism, the refusal to think of history in terms of structure—is already the moral of "Littérature et la droit à la mort." We are not *parlée plutôt que parlant*. Better to say that no one speaks (*"Voice of no one, once more"* [*ED*121/*WD*75]). Blanchot's thought is of a moment of speech that is not part of the succession of operations by which silence is dissipated, but neither can such a moment be excluded (or filled up) in order to protect language from not working. It is a nondialectical moment within discourse, corresponding perhaps to the moment of historicity within history (Blanchot might say: the moment of *infinity*, the *infinitude* of history) when an event occurs contingently without respect to positions in a scheme—for example, before and after, beginning and end, past and future, not to mention depth and surface, cause and effect, matter and idea: an event which is perhaps the not-happening of these things: — "An event: what nevertheless does not arrive, the field of non-arrival and, at the same time, that which, arriving, arrives without gathering itself in some definite or determinable point—the sudden arrival of what does not take place as either a single or a general possibility" (EIxix/ICxviii-xix). Think of this as either the interruption of history, or again as the excessiveness or proliferation of a history in flight, branching endlessly and impassively down multiple, intersecting, contradictory streets; history as disarray, confusion (unable to trace itself back or resolve itself into a whole). In *L'écriture du désastre* it is called "the *other* history . . . wherein nothing of the present ever happens" (ED209/WD138). There is a moment at the end of *Au moment voulu* (1951), which I can't help thinking of here, when the narrator, who realizes that he can never be part of a narrative, imagines his days turning into "a pure dissipation" where "each event [becomes] the image of a displaced episode (an episode that is not in its place, a sort of farce of time, belonging to a different age [*in-actuel*], a lost and baffled fragment of history)" (AMV157/WTC69–70).[3]

In *L'écriture du désastre* Blanchot writes: "Lassitude before words is also the desire for words separated from each other [*le désir des mots espacés*] — with their power, which is meaning, broken, and their composition too, which is syntax or the system's continuity (provided the system be in some way complete in advance and the present a *fait accompli*). This lassitude, this desire is the madness which is never current, but the interval of un-reason [*folie qui n'est jamais de maintenant, mais le délai de la non-raison*], the 'he'll have gone mad by tomorrow' — madness which one mustn't use to elevate, or to deepen, or to lighten thought" (ED18–19/WD8). Words separated from one another: words without language—one must under-stand such things if one is to understand Blanchot at all.

Recall the "nocturnal" experience of words in *Celui qui ne m'accom-pagnait pas*, where words induce the passive and empty Orphic gaze. Or recall the theory of metaphysical desire: "Such a desire is not the subli-mated form of need, any more than the prelude to love. Need is a lack that awaits fulfillment; need is satisfied. Love wants union. The desire that one might call metaphysical is a desire for what we are not in want of, a desire that cannot be satisfied and that does not desire union with what it desires" (EI76/IC53). Not, in other words, desire that inspires action and move-ment (or, obversely, asceticism and otherworldliness); on the contrary, this is desire that possesses the radically passive structure of fear, fascination, or fatigue, that is, the structure of affliction (*malheur*), or of attention and waiting (*l'attention et l'attente*).

In his essay on Simone Weil, Blanchot says that "the further thought goes toward expressing itself, the more it must maintain a reserve somewhere within itself, something like a place that would be a kind of uninhabited, uninhabitable non-thought, *a thought that would not allow itself to be thought*" (EI173/IC119). As a word might not allow itself to be pronounced, a word set apart from language (in *Le pas au-delà* Blanchot thinks of *folie* and *angoisse* as examples of such a word [PD65–66/SNB44–45, PD89/SNB62–63])—a forbidden or forgotten word that nevertheless is loose in our discourse, turning it into an event in which nothing is said, a nonevent or, more exactly, an event that separates into past and future without realizing itself: an interval or arrest that would not be merely a gasp or a sigh or a pause for breath but an interminable delay—a disaster— that language (conceived as a logical condition of possibility, a system for constituting states of affairs) would be powerless to overcome.

In the early *récit* "Le dernier mot" (1935), which one can already read quite happily as an anarchist's tribute to *désœuvrement*, there is a splendid moment when the narrator finds himself in the midst of "a chaotic celebration." Crowds of people flow back and forth through the streets, shouting. "At some intersections the earth trembled, and it seemed that the people were walking over the void, crossing it on a footbridge of cries. The great consecration of *until* [jusqu'à ce que] took place around noon. Using only little scraps of words, as if all that remained of language were the forms of a long sentence crushed by the crowd's trampling feet, they sang the song of a single word that could still be made out, no matter how loud the shouting. This word was *until*" (AC112–13/VC43). Until: a word for the *entre-temps*: a word set apart, consecrated, while the rest of language is disposed of like so many old newspapers.

Until, more than thirty-five years later: *Le pas au-delà* (1973). This is a text divided heterogeneously into roman and italicized fragments. The first roman fragment says, simply and appropriately, if deceptively, "Let us enter into this relation" (PD7/SNB1), a narrative or discursive relation that turns out to be a relation of the third kind (a nonrelation). The italicized fragments meanwhile often, but neither exclusively nor coherently, take the form of *récits* and dialogues, or rather bits and pieces of such things. The first of these begins: "*In this city, he knew there were people who did not see anyone* [de gens qui ne fréquentaient personne: imagine a city of reclusives, a *communauté désœuvrée* of Blanchots]" (*PD*9/*SNB*3). One might just as well think of it as a city of pronouns—for example, *ils:* they. The (or a) narrative voice pauses to inquire of itself (presumably of itself but just as likely of another) as to how he (*il*) could possibly know anything of them (*leur*), for example that there are, roughly speaking, several of them (*plusieurs*, neither one nor many: *"Several—perhaps this only helped him not to think of them in an overly determined way* [d'une manière trop déterminée]: *some people* [des gens]"). "Several" (like *until*): not a deep-structure word but one that floats on the surface of language like a piece of debris; a word without justification.

Not, at any rate, *le mot juste*, rather a common word, as in the sentence: *"But when he had decided, as though under the pressure of common words* [paroles communes] *to ask, 'Do you think I know them?', he was surprised by the frivolity of the answer. 'How could that be, you don't see anybody'"* (*PD*10/*SNB*3). The *pressure* of words: at least since *Thomas l'obscur* words have always been active as against the passivity of the subject. Recall *Celui qui ne m'accompagnait pas*, where writing is understood as a passivity or weakness vis-à-vis the pressure of words: "I think I have to write. I think all the words we have exchanged are crowded around me and I won't resist their pressure for very long, that probably for a long time now, an infinite time, I haven't really been resisting them any longer" (*CAP*128/*OW*68). However, this pressure is not a pressure to speak: the words do not work like a muse that demands or produces an irrepressible expression. The narrator in *Celui qui ne m'accompagnait pas* puts it this way: "even when I hear them, I do not hear them, and when I speak them, nothing is said, even though everything may be said in them forever" (*CAP*138/*OW*73). What condition is this? Negation without negation—a neutralization: the narrator is no longer a speaking subject nor is he merely passive vis-à-vis *active* words. His condition is that of a passivity outside the alternatives of action or passion. In *L'écriture du désastre* Blanchot coins the term *le subissement* "in an attempt to name the inert immobility of certain states said to be psychotic, the *patior* in passion, servile obedience, the nocturnal receptivity of mystics—dispossession, that is, the self wrested from the self, the detachment whereby one is detached from detachment, or again the fall (neither chosen nor accepted) outside the self. Still, these situations, even if some are at the limit of the knowledge that designate a hidden face of humanity, speak to us hardly at all of what we seek to understand by letting this characterless word be pronounced, *passivity*" (*ED*30–31/*WD*15).

But what of a "pressure of *common* words"? Whole theories of language go by without anyone noticing common words—as opposed not only to proper names ("God," "Nietzsche") but to generic nouns and verbs as well, not to mention the tedious business about signs or signifiers.[4] ("The fragmentary expresses itself best, perhaps, in a language that does not recognize it" [*PD62/SNB43*].) But now what happens (what happens to language or speech) when a common word gets loose, asserts itself, impresses itself as if it were a secret or a sacred word, that is, a word apart, something secretly sublime or magical in the sense of exerting fascination? *Le pas audelà* returns Blanchot once more to this (one wants to say: foundational) question. For example:

> *It was almost easy for him* [Il lui était presque facile], *there where he lived, to live almost without a sign, almost without a self* [presque sans signe, presque sans moi], *as if at the border of writing; close to this word, barely a word, rather a word too many, and in that nothing but a word from which, one day in the past, gently welcomed, he had received the salute that did not save, the summons* [l'interpellation] *that had awakened him. That could be told, even if, and especially if, nobody were there to hear it. In a certain way, he would have liked to be able to treat it with the gentleness he had received from it, a gentleness that held him at a distance, because of the excessive power it gave him over himself, and, by way of him, over all things. Over almost all things: there was always this slight restriction, implied, which obliged him—sweet obligation—to go back, often and as if by a ritual at which he smiled, to these ways of speaking, almost, maybe, barely, momentarily, unless, and many others, signs without signification that he knew very well (did he know it?) granted him something precious, the possibility of repeating himself—but no, he did not know what would come to him through them, "maybe" the right to cross the limit without his knowing it, "maybe" the anxious, slovenly retreat in face of the decisive affirmation from which they preserved him in order that he still be there not to hear it." (PD15–16/SNB7)

One understands that the word initially in question—"barely a word, rather a word too many"—is *il:* the word which, as the early roman fragments take some pains to explain, is outside the rule of identity, neutral with respect to sameness and difference, neither one nor the other, likewise neither "he" nor "it," a word which escapes language, almost. The *il* occupies the site of the *moi*, the self, which (the text says) "is not a self but the same of myself [*n'est pas moi, mais le même du moi-même*], not some personal, impersonal identity, sure and vacillating, but the law or rule that conventionally assures the ideal identity of terms and notations. The self is therefore an abbreviation that one could call canonical, a formula that regulates and, if you like, blesses, in the first person, the pretention of the Same [du Même] to primacy. Whence, perhaps, the sacred character that is attached to the self and that egoism confiscates, giving it the privilege of the central place it would occupy, and making it the fundamental trait of any movement to bring together, to associate, to group, to unify, or even, negatively, to disunify, to dissociate, to disassemble" (PD12/SNB4). So the site of the *moi* is the site of the rule of identity, the center that makes possible the construction of systems and the operations of the whole. The *il* occupies this site, however, not as a stand-in and interpreter, that is, not philosophically, but as the invasion of the other in the same, where the other is not Levinas's *Autrui* but Blanchot's *le Neutre*: the *il* (which in English takes the indeterminate form of "he/it") is neither the one nor the other, neither identity nor difference, neither me nor not-me. The *il* thus designates an "infinite and discontinuous" relation, a "relation always in displacement"—a relation of the third kind. So the *il* in this respect is inaccessible to language understood as a conceptual system ruled by the law of noncontradiction. "A word perhaps, nothing but a word, but a word in excess, a word too many, which for that reason is always lacking. Nothing but a word" (PD12–13/SNB5). Nothing but a word, but uncontainable within language (almost).

Just so, the word that begins to impinge on the *il*, to echo or haunt it, is *presque*, which is a word (appropriately, a vagabond word) for the neutral space or border that the *il* occupies or, more accurately, traverses and keeps open as if preserving it from occupation. Almost is (like the *il*) "nothing but a word," "barely a word," a word that says nothing but exerts a kind of daimonic restraint upon speech or, at any rate, upon the power of language. A word of discretion; a word that holds language back. In spite or because of this it is strangely evocative—"one day in the past" it had interrupted ("interpellated") the *il*, as if awakening it from a dogmatic slumber, or maybe simply introducing into it the infinite distance that separates the "he" or the "it" from each other or the same. The power, or rather sovereignty, of the word *almost* is remarkable ("sovereignty of the accidental" [ED11/WD3]: more powerful than the rule of identity). It presides over almost everything just insofar as everything is, according to the meaning of historicity, only a qualified version of itself, whence there can be no thought of grasping it as such but only as *"almost, maybe, barely, momen-*

tarily, unless": words which are neither positive nor negative, whose task is to open the space in which things (not just things, you and I as well) are neither self-identical nor different from themselves. It is a moment of grace (like that of chance)—a grace period in which the law of the same is (not transgressed but) diverted and confused. *Almost* is perhaps even more powerful in its generosity than *es gibt*: the *il* at all events receives it as "*something precious, the possibility of repeating himself*"—without, however, actually doing so. The relation between identity and difference has, in effect, been transformed into an "infinite and discontinuous" pause, a space that logical relations cannot fill.

The word, "barely a word, rather a word too many, and in that nothing but a word," maps a region of listening onto the logical space of designation. Or, alternatively, innocent word that it is, it exposes this space to something anarchic, like the reverberating, muffled sound of the *il y a*. However, in this context it is nothing horrible (although "horribly [terrifyingly] ancient" [*PD*33/*SNB*21]).[5] On the contrary, it "interpellates" the *il*, Augustine-like, like the cries of children: "*As if there had reverberated, in a muffled way, this call, a call nevertheless joyful, the cry of children playing in the garden: 'who is me today?' 'who holds the place of me?' and the answer, joyful, infinite:* lui, lui, lui" (*PD*16/*SNB*7). Imagine this as a call to conversion, where the seat of identity is converted into something else ("a space infinitely empty," like an echo chamber in which sounds die away endlessly without producing silence). A later text in *Le pas au-delà* (in roman type) says: "All words are adult. Only the space in which they reverberate—a space infinitely empty, like a garden where, even after the children have disappeared, their joyful cries continue to be heard—leads them back towards the perpetual death in which they seem to keep being born" (*PD*31/*SNB*19).

Anonymity

The narrator of "Le dernier mot" is, to his shame (or so he says), a judge. His mere presence is an occasion of order, as when he enters a schoolroom:

> Upstairs, the children were noisily playing ball in a wide-open classroom. When I entered, everyone became silent. Each child went to his place quietly, and, as the veil fell over the statue of the teacher, their heads lined up hypocritically on their desks. . . . Right away, they asked me the traditional

question that is asked in the schools: "Are you the teacher or God?" I looked at them sadly. There were so many ways to answer them, but first I had to bring order to the class. (AC119–20/VC45–46)

Order is (or used to be) the order of discourse: "It's in both our interests," says the narrator, "to see if we speak the same language. But first, you have to learn the alphabet." Whence the narrator writes this strange text on the blackboard: "*Fear is your only master. If you think you are no longer afraid of anything, reading is useless. But it is the lump of fear in your throat that will teach you how to speak*" (AC120–21/VC46). (Cf. *Le pas au-delà*: "fear is a piece of language" [PD84/SNB59].)

In keeping with the unreasoning logic of the *récit*, the students turn out to be more orderly than the narrator ("'So you're logicians, like everyone else'" [AC121/VC46]. As if in a hermeneutical ritual ("'Let's move on to the commentary'") one of them hands the narrator a book:

> I couldn't stop trembling. I read the sentences and broke up their meaning by replacing some of the words with gasps and sighs. After a few moments the clamoring of pupils merged with my groans, and I wrote out the passage on the blackboard, so that everyone could become familiar with it. *When the census of the population was taken, it happened that an individual by the name of Thomas was not included in the general list. He therefore became superfluous, and others began treating him as if, in relation to humanity—which was itself insane—he had lost his mind.* Then, according to custom, I asked the youngest child to pronounce each word along with me as loudly as he could. (AC122–23/VC47)

Imagine (as Deleuze has done) a language of gasps and sighs, or of stammering: that is, a language of interruptions—or, if "language" is not the right word, imagine a discourse or phrase in which the positions appointed by grammar are occupied by something unpronounceable.[6] Perhaps in this same spirit the proper name *Thomas* (the most famous in Blanchot's *œuvre*) has become unpronounceable, a word too many, or a word for *folie* ("Madness: let us suppose a language from which this word would be excluded" [PD65/SNB44]). Suppose there were a list of all possible names, an absolute end-of-history list of everything and everyone—in which you find your own name missing: a leftover name, no one's name. Would a list of pseudonyms be possible? Or a list of *personnes* (*lui, lui, lui*)?

Or, again, imagine a list, or *récit*, in which no one is named, or in which names, as if voluntarily restraining themselves, no longer exercise their prerogative of designation. In *Le pas au-delà* the question of naming arises under circumstances of roughly this bizarre sort:

> "We would give them a name." — "They would have one." — "The name we would give them would not be their real name [leur vrai nom]." — "All the same, able to name them." — "Able to make it known that, the day they would recognize that they were ready, there would be a name for their name." — "A name such that there would be no place for them to feel summoned by it, nor tempted to respond to it, nor even ever denominated by this name." — "However, have we not assumed that they would have one name that would be common to them?" — "We have, but only so that they might more easily pass unnoticed." — "Then how could we know we could address ourselves to them? They are far away, you know." — "It is for this that we have names, more numerous and more marvellous than all those that one commonly uses." — "They wouldn't know it was their name." — "How could they know it; they don't have one." (PD16/SNB8)

The "they" (*ils*) here are the people of the city, or words to that effect: those who frequent no one, whom no one sees, that is, whom the narrator neither sees nor doesn't see. Heidegger asked who Dasein is—or, more exactly, who the *who* of Dasein is—in its everydayness, and his answer was that the *who* "is *not* the 'I myself'" (SZ115/BT150). Nor is the who a *we*. "The 'who' is not this one, not that one, not oneself [*man selbst*], not some people [*einige*], and not the sum of them all. The 'who' is the neuter, *the* '*they*' [*das Man*]" (SZ126/BT164). "They" is not a category, that is, not a place of predication or identity; rather it is entirely otherwise. In the "they," as Heidegger says, "Everyone is the other, and no one is himself" (SZ128/ BT165). "They" are, to that extent, outside of language, or more accurately in a separate or excluded portion of it, set apart from the rest of language — apart, Heidegger might say, from the authentic portion of language in which unique individuals can be singled out from everyday ones (made narrative subjects).

If only we could think clearly about discretion, the kind of discretion that we show a word (or whatever) when we enclose it in quotation marks, as if holding something back; or when we address a thing only by way of adjectives and question marks. In this respect we could think of *Le pas au-delà* as a text inscribed entirely within the space of qualification in which the task of writing is to keep everything (no saying what, exactly) at a certain distance, neither here nor there.[7] Certainly the narrative voice of the italicized fragments is infinitely reserved: the people about whom *il* speaks or writes are not at all under the usual sort of third-person surveillance that, as narrators or readers, we are used to experiencing ("The novelist lifts up the rooftops and gives his characters over to a penetrating gaze" [EI40/IC29]):

> It was like an eternal subject of pleasantry, an innocent game. "You met them in the street?"—"Not exactly in the street: near the river, looking at books, then leaving or losing themselves in the crowd."—"That could not but be so; and, rather young, aren't they?"—"Young?" One had to stop at this word which involved, demanded, and promised too much; he did not concede it willingly until he let himself go ahead and answer: "Yes, young, there was no other word; and yet, young without anything that makes their age a moment of themselves, or youth a characteristic of age; young, but as in another time, thus not so young, as if youth made them ancient or too new to be able to appear only young." (PD17/SNB8)

Imagine a narrator under interrogation. Young? "One had to stop at this word": it isn't the right one, but no other word will do. Nothing is said which is not also unsaid—without, however, being canceled: neither young nor old without being middle-aged.[8] Perhaps we could call these texts fragments of a narrative of lassitude whose affirmations are nondialectical: outside the movement of negation that compels one to speak strictly, that is, in the definite terms of one or the other, where the one or the other are meant to cancel each other out.

One has to think again of the critique of the name in "Littérature et la droit à la mort," where murder is not too strong a word for the name of the name, as if the right to identity were the right to death. Foucault remarks that, prior to modernity, "ordinary individuality—the everyday individuality of everybody [or in other words Heidegger's or Blanchot's "they"] remained below the threshold of description. To be looked at, observed, described in detail, followed from day to day, was a privilege. The chronicle of a man, the account of his life, his historiography, written as he lived out his life formed part of the rituals of his power." The life of the antique hero was determined by the relation between name and fate, in contrast to the endlessly surviving comic rascals who never went by their right names. Modernity, however, erased the comic when it lowered the threshold of description and reconstituted the workings of language—naming, predication, description, narration—"as a means of control and method of domination. It is no longer a monument for future memory but a document for possible use."[9] As Blanchot says: "We can't do anything with an object that has no name" (*PF*312/*GO*41).

Here is testimony by the Israeli poet Dan Pagis:

THE ROLL CALL

He stands, stamps a little in his boots,
rubs his hands. He's cold in the morning breeze:
a diligent angel, who worked hard for his promotions.
Suddenly he thinks he's made a mistake: all eyes,
he counts again in the open notebook
all the bodies waiting for him in the square,
camp within camp: only I
am not there, am not there, am a mistake,
turn off my eyes, quickly, erase my shadow.
I shall not want. The sum will be all right
without me: here forever.[10]

A victim too many. Anonymity is an instance of *désœuvrement*: it enables something not to take place. The "I" is a name without a name, parentheses in the regime of signs that cannot be filled by death. Since the system has no other function than to keep itself systematic, the anonymous lives on, "here forever," in a present without presence that can never be terminated (an incessant, interminable memory lodged within language). The weakness of this event is its contingency. It cannot be turned into a program of salvation. In the Holocaust, for example, death is systematic; life is accidental.

I think of the calling of the names in the camps. Naming carries the mortal play of the word. The arbitrariness of the name, the anonymous that precedes or accompanies it, the impersonality of nomination bursts forth in the manner of *something terrible* [d'un terrible] in this situation in which language plays its murderous role. The proper name — a number [*un chiffre*] — is disappropriated by the very power that designates it and by the power of interminable language. What does "proper name" signify here? Not the right to be there in person; on the contrary, the terrifying obligation by which what would like to preserve itself in the name of a private unhappiness [*malheur*] is drawn out into the public square, into the cold and the impoverishment of the outside, with nothing that can assure any refuge. The prohibition against having anything of one's own and against keeping anything having to do with oneself is pronounced by the proclaiming of the name or of that which holds its place. The call in the camps makes appear, certainly in a way that leaves no room for any decent camouflage, the meaning of any civil-state formality (as of any verification of identity, which gives place, in our refined civilizations, to all police violences and deprivations of liberty). Language does not communicate, it makes naked and according to nakedness—the placing outside—that is proper to it and that one can only temper, that is to say, pervert, by the detour which is the game of this always oblique outside, a game that is also and in the first place a game of language without right or direction, indirect as though a *game*. (PD56–57/SNB38–39)

In the camps the deep structure of the spirit rises to the surface: "Work, death: equivalents" (*ED*129/WD81). The place to take up this matter is the next chapter.

One could quickly sketch in here, without digressing, the outline of a hermeneutics of the fragment: a world of random particles cannot be described or represented; it can only be reproduced, particle by particle. (Todd May says that "the central theme of anarchism [is] the rejection of representation."[11]) A world of random particles would be an excessive world, a world in which a single particle would be one too many (the impossibility or *désœuvrement* of the world: in the end one would have to reconceptualize the particle away from an atomistic theory toward a theory of the particle as an event).[12] Imagine the book of such a world (*Le pas au-delà* reads like such a book). Commentary in this event would be powerless, reduced (as in "Le dernier mot") to idle or baffled quotation, repetition without identity, as if the relation between text and context were now a relation of the third kind. In *L'écriture du désastre* Blanchot says: "the fragment without a text, or any context, is radically unquotable" (*ED*64/WD37).

Or perhaps it is merely a relation of infinite discretion, of speaking forgetfully, or by way of endless detours, reserving names, deferring the period:

> He desired to say it to him: *this way of thinking about what he wanted to say even in saying it—to whom? or in saying that he would say it—to whom? even though he had gotten this way of thinking or thought that he had gotten it* [bien qu'il la reçût ou crût la recevoir] *from this point where it seemed he could fictitiously situate it, helped to hold him back from saying it. For he had to be there—in this place where it was given him to stay, like an assigned residence, in order for the other to be over there, immobile, immovable, yet always hard to recognize, as if the right to identity had been refused him at the same time it was granted him.* (PD18/SNB9)

In the 1940s Blanchot gave application to the term *irreal* as that which is neither real nor unreal. Now this concept becomes, among other things, the site or interval of the "would." Imagine a subjunctive history: what prevents its events from happening? (*"We would give them a name."* But we can't: they live on without us.) The (*il*) is given the right to an identity that (*il*) is powerless to assume, winning thereby a comic immortality outside modernity.

That is, as Blanchot tries to explain, the anonymous is not the negation of the name (it is not brute namelessness, the non-name; it is neither the one nor the other: "the neuter—the name without name" [*PD*162/ *SNB*118], the name that cannot be pronounced). The anonymous is inscribed in the same logical space in which naming occurs, but as a hesitation or reserve, possibly a gasp or cry, at all events an interruption of the dialectic, a discretion or secretion of the name: "The anonymous puts the name in place, leaves it empty, as if the name were there only to let itself be passed through because the name does not name, but is the non-unity and non-presence of the nameless [*la non-unité et la non-présence du sans nom*]" (*PD*52/*SNB*35). The mind sticks on this last phrase, but "non-unity and non-presence of the nameless" is a neutral relation rather than a double negative.

This is roughly how the *il* works, which is perhaps why Blanchot inscribes the word discreetly/discretely, within parentheses (*il*), which one could just as well picture as a place whose interior has been removed ( ): (*il*) *l'ouverture interdite*: "(he/it) the hidden opening" (*PD*32/*SNB*20). Interestingly, *interdite* also carries the note of confusion or bewilderment, as when one is suddenly bereft of one's presence of mind: a momentary nonpresence, "the interval of unreason," self-interruption—"this was what the name that was barely a word indicated and that designated him so eminently in designating nobody" (*PD*32/*SNB*20). Alternatively: "Forbidden opening [*Ouverture interdite*]" (*PD*32/*SNB*20): less a threshold one cannot cross than a position one cannot fill. The (*il*) is the phantom subject of the *il y a* and the *il pleur*: "The fact that (he/it), even in the most simple sentence, is somewhat apart from the sentence, but rather in each empty moment that the articulation sets aside for its play, discharges it from the role of the subject that it seems to accept" (*PD*32/*SNB*20). Think of the sentence as a stand-in for language: it is a totality, but a totality with a hole in it, a hole which is as much an excess as a deficiency or gap, as if the sentence contained a word too many—but it is not "as if." In addition to being neither "he" nor "it," neither the one nor the other, the *(il)* is neither something nor nothing: it is neither there nor not there: "*(il)* pronounces itself without there being a position or deposition of existence, without presence or absence affirming it, without the unity of the word coming to dislodge it from the between-the-two in which it disseminates itself. *(il)* is not 'that one,' but the neuter that marks it (as *(il)* appeals to the neuter), leads it back towards the displacement without place that robs it of any grammatical place, a sort of lack in becoming [*sorte de manque en devenir*] between two, several or all words, thanks to which these interrupt each other, without which they would signify nothing, but which upsets them constantly to the very silence in which they extinguish themselves [*mais qui les dérange constamment jusque dans le silence où ils s'éteignent*]" (*PD*52–53/*SNB*35). So we may think of the *(il)*, for example, as the occasion or inspiration (or even exigency) of a "lassitude toward words," which, remember, is the same as "the desire for words separated from one another—with their power, which is meaning, broken, and their composition too, which is syntax or the system's continuity." The *(il)* is, so to speak, older than grammar: *l'effroyablement ancien*. It is a word, the archvagabond, that is uncontainable within a language. The anarchist's word.

It is thus a *disastrous* word in the sense that Blanchot will give this term in *L'écriture du désastre*, where "disaster" is, not surprisingly, not a name:

> If someone pronounces this word, the *disaster*, we feel that it is not a word, not the name of anything; indeed, we feel that there never is a separate, nominal, predominate name, but always an entire complex or simple sentence, where the infinitude of language—of language in its unfinished history [*son histoire non achevée*] and its unclosed system—seeks to let itself be taken in hand by a sequence of verbs, and yet seeks at the same time, in the never resolved tension between noun and verb, to fall, as if immobilized, outside language—without, however, ceasing to belong to it. (*ED*120/ *WD*74–75)

Disaster means: "break with every form of totality" (*ED*121/*WD*75). The disaster is, however, an *anarchic* break, that is, an event older than every form of totality (as if Nietzsche were older than Hegel): it is the *désœuvrement* of language, history, or the world—not a catastrophe that reduces to ruin but a ruin that already haunts every beginning like a prophecy murmuring constantly in one's ears, a rumbling of something that never occurs, disturbing sleep and work alike.[13] Think of anarchism not as a position that might or might not be adopted but as a state of affairs, that is, a fact of the matter that cannot be done away with.

In *Le pas au-delà* the disastrous word is *folie:* madness, in particular Nietzsche's madness, which is, like Hölderlin's, an exigent madness—"the *other* madness—that which has no name to enclose it" (PD34/SNB21). It is the noncoincidence of reason with itself rather than its breakdown or failure. In place of "reason" one might say "presence" or "the same" or *Moi:* madness means I am always beside myself, outside myself, dispersed, wandering, declaiming before an empty mirror. Think of the present (or the self) as a magic looking-glass through which everything (the whole of time) disappears and from which nothing can be recalled: "the past is empty, and only the multiple play of mirroring, the illusion that there would be a present destined to pass and to hold itself back in the past, would lead one to believe that the past was filled with events, a belief that would make it appear less unfriendly, less frightening: a past thus inhabited, even if by phantoms, would grant the right to live innocently (in the narrative mode, which, once, twice, as many times as one time can repeat itself, makes evocation usable) the very thing which, nevertheless, gives itself as revoked forever and, at the same time, as irrevocable" (PD23/SNB13).

But the story of time (that is, history) is really the story of Eurydice, who gives back to our gaze the noncoincidence, the endless interruption, that separates past and future. She is the allegory of the event. Eurydice, dying, does not recede into the past. She vanishes into what Blanchot calls " 'the terrifyingly ancient [*l'effroyablement ancien*],'" which is an anarchic temporality, an siteless, limitless, interminable space of time (infinitude between parentheses: the *entre-temps* or time without movement) "where nothing was ever present" (PD24/SNB14). One can easily imagine a story in which Orpheus goes mad when he recognizes that Eurydice was never present to him, nor, for that matter, was he ever coincidental with himself (an Orpheus too many, as allegorized in the dismemberment scene). We might imagine him, as he goes to pieces, reasoning thus: "If, in the 'terrifyingly ancient,' nothing was ever present, and if, having barely produced itself, the event, by the absolute fall, fragile, at once falls into it, as the mark of irrevocability announces to us, it is because (whence our cold presentiment) the event that we thought we had lived was itself never in a relation of presence to us nor to anything whatsoever" (PD25/SNB15). Eurydice was never there for Orpheus in the way he desired: that is precisely the weakness of his otherwise overwhelming desire (Plato called it the "weakness of the logos").

In *Le pas au-delà* the proper name of Orpheus is interchangeable with Nietzsche's, or the fate of Nietzsche's, which Blanchot locates at the moment before writing: "What I live today opens time to the depths, giving it to me in this unique present as the double infinity that would come to re-unify itself in the present; if I have lived it an infinite number of times, if I am called upon to relive it an infinite number of times, I am there at my table for eternity and to write eternally: all is present in this unique instant that repeats itself, and there is nothing but this repetition of Being in its Same"—and in that moment, in that absolute twinkling, Nietzsche encounters *his* Eurydice: "there was no one at his table" (PD44/SNB29).

One of Blanchot's words for this twinkling, this infinite interval or time without presence, is *l'irrévocable* (the Eurydice-word), which has its customary meaning of irreversibility, but in addition "it is perhaps the means —strange, I admit—for the past to warn us (preparing us) that it is empty and that the falling due [*l'échéance*]—the infinite fall, fragile [*la chute infinite, fragile*]—that it designates, this infinitely deep pit into which, if there were any, events would fall one by one, signifies only the void of the pit, the depth of what is without bottom" (PD24/SNB13). *L'irrévocable* thus belongs to the same family as forgetfulness, absolute forgetting, where there is no communication whatsoever between past and future. Time is not a totality in which events participate; it is multiple and fragmented in the sense that each event is an *entre-temps:* a disaster. Possibly one could say, after Deleuze, that the whole of time occurs in the disaster. In *Différence et répétition* Deleuze writes:

> In the first place, the idea of a totality of time must be understood as follows: the caesura, of whatever kind, must be determined in the image of a unique and tremendous event, an act which is adequate to time as a whole. This image itself is divided, torn into two unequal parts. Nevertheless, it thereby draws together the totality of time. It must be called a symbol by virtue of the unequal parts which it subsumes and draws together, but draws together as unequal parts. Such a symbol adequate to the totality of time may be expressed in many ways: to throw time out of joint, to make the sun explode, to throw oneself into the volcano, to kill God or the father. This symbolic image constitutes the totality of time to the extent that it draws together the caesura, the before and the after. (DeR120/DR89)

The caesura here looks very much like Heidegger's rift, which is not a principle of unity but rather an anarchic relation in which adversaries are drawn together in an irresolvable—originary, once and future—conflict. Instead of caesura or rift, however, but as part of the same family of unclarifiable concepts, Blanchot tries to think Nietzsche's thought of the Eternal Return, where time is "an infinite game with two openings (given as one, and yet never unified): future always already past, past always still to come, from which the third instance, the instance of presence, excluding itself, would exclude any possibility of identity" (*PD21/SNB11*).[14]

Nietzsche's madness: a once and future affliction ("he'll have gone mad by tomorrow").

The Infinitive

The propositional style of philosophic discourse, on which our picture of speech is modeled, presupposes an Aristotelian/Hegelian temporality, a logical time or narrative with plot and hero (the concept) who achieves self-identity by overcoming (*Aufhebung*) the random and contingent, subsuming them into his destiny as purposeful and justified after all. Here events are states of affairs governed by a law of obsolescence. The thought of the Eternal Return cannot be framed in this language. On Blanchot's interpretation, it was Nietzsche's attempt to do so that drove him mad, but with a different madness, his reason not so much shattered by its failure to think the unthinkable as by its success in crossing over "to another language removed from the ordinary forms of temporality" (*PD59/SNB40*). Nietzsche, in his madness, becomes reconciled to the irreconcilable, equal to the unequal, congruent with the incongruent, speaking a *langage fou* (*PD66/SNB45*): a language of writing that dispenses with the negative or embraces its weakness.

In 1958 Blanchot had called this "crossing the line," where nihilism nihilates or reverses itself:

> Nietzsche expressed it in this way: "Let us think this thought in its most terrible form: existence, as it is, without meaning or aim, yet recurring inevitably without any finale of nothingness: the eternal recurrence"—"the most extreme form of nihilism." What do we learn from this remark? Until now we thought nihilism was tied to nothingness [*néant*]. How ill-considered this was: nihilism is tied to being. Nihilism is the impossibility of being done with it and of finding a way out even in that end that is nothingness. It

says the impotence of nothingness, the false brilliance of its victories. (EI224/IC149)

The thought (or experience) of eternal recurrence frees the will-to-power from its "dissatisfaction with what is, and thus the desire to transform be-ing—to negate it in order to derive power from it and to make of this power to negate the infinite movement of human mastery. . . . [The] weak-ness of the negative, and the way in which nothingness unmasks itself in the being that cannot be negated, lays waste at one stroke to our attempts to dominate the earth and to free ourselves from nature by giving it a meaning—that is, by denaturing it" (EI224/IC149). So history is liberated from its progressive movement of overcoming the past in the name of the future, and time spreads itself out into the eternal (incessant, inter-minable) recurrence of the *il y a*.

But we should not think of this as Nietzsche overcoming Hegel, or of one sort of temporality giving way to another, but rather of multiple di-mensions that allow us—as Blanchot put it in 1962 while trying to clarify the concept of the limit-experience—"to 'live' each of the events that is ours by way of a double relation. We live it one time as something we com-prehend, grasp, bear, and master . . . by relating it to some good or to some value, that is to say, finally, by relating it to unity" (EI307–8/IC207). Blan-chot had already learned how to call this the time of the day when day passes into night and then returns to continue on its way without having missed a step: the time of the possible. But, as Bataille taught, "possibility is not the sole dimension of our existence." Existence occurs otherwise: "we live it another time as something that escapes all employ and all end, and more, as that which escapes our very capacity to undergo it, but whose trial we cannot escape" (EI308/IC207): the time of the impossible, the be-tween-time of the night that no longer passes, in which the "I" is no longer the subject of experience and experience is of "presence without anything being present," the experience of what does not take place, "thought think-ing that which will not let itself be thought," the event or between-two (*en-tre-deux*) that cannot be overcome (EI310/IC209): the interval of madness, for short. Almost nothing can be predicated of this event. "This is all one can say about it: it does not unify, nor does it allow its own unification. Hence it would appear to be in play on the side of the multiple, and in what Georges Bataille names 'chance'" (EI310/IC209).

The fragmentary—fragmentary writing—is speech of the between-time that cannot be overcome (the step/not [*pas*] or word too many that interrupts the work of the negative). It is, as Blanchot put it in his third essay on Nietzsche, "a non-dialectical experience of speech," say of "a lassitude toward words" (*"I am not the master of language. I listen to it only in its effacement, effacing myself in it, toward this silent limit where it waits for one to lead it back in order to speak, there where presence fails as it fails there where desire carries it"* [*PD46/SNB30*]). The fragmentary is not an alternative, aphoristic or formally multiple, discontinuous, unfinished style of discourse; it is rather other than discourse, "neither negating nor (in this [dialectical] sense) affirming, and yet allowing the unlimited in difference to play between the fragments by its interruption and arrest [*laissant jouer entre les fragments, dans l'interruption et l'arrêt, l'illimité de la différence*]" (*EI231/IC154*). The unlimited here is the nonobjective, noneventful event that divides infinitely into past and future, endlessly separating them. This seems to be the crucial point: "The fragmentary: There is no experience of it, in the sense that one does not admit it in any form of present, that it would remain without subject if it took place, thus excluding every present and all presence, as it would be excluded from them" (*PD71/SNB49*; cf. *ED36/WD18–19*). Fragmentary writing belongs to this event, not as its realization, but in the form of its aleatory effects: it "invisibly destroys surface and depth, real and possible, above and below, manifest and hidden" (*PD72/SNB50*). The fragmentary is thus anarchic with respect to language, or what we think of as language—deep-structured, rule-governed, semiotic, hierarchical, productive, etc. However, it is not an aboriginal chaos that language must struggle to subdue. The fragmentary is not dialectically opposed to language as totality; rather it is language in a different temporality, which Blanchot calls "language's rupture with itself" (*PD67/SNB46*), that is, its rupture with the temporality of propositions and narratives, or of systems and rules, that otherwise constitute it.

We can think of this other temporality as the temporality of the infinitive: "To write [*écrire*]: work of the absence of work, production which produces nothing except (or out of [*ou à partir de*]) the absence of a subject, mark that unmarks, infinitive in which the infinite would like to play itself out even to the neuter: to write does not depend on the present and does not make it raise itself [*écrire ne relève pas du présent et ne le fait pas se lever*]" (*PD79/SNB55*). The infinitive (*écrire*) is outside past, present, and future, that is, outside the temporality in which the realization of states of affairs is possible. To write, Blanchot says, "tends . . . to maintain itself in a conditional without condition," uneventful, not as if suspended in space or in an ideal that waits to be realized, but as that which separates time between past and future: neither one nor the other (PD79/SNB55). The infinitive is elliptical rather than hypothetical: to write . . . , where writing separates into the not yet and the always already (mad writing). Interestingly, the infinitive is close to the interrogative just in the sense that the interrogative belongs to the open and impassable space echoed by words like *until, almost,* and *(il).* To be in question is not a state of affairs; it is an event, an *irréalisation,* neither active nor passive, like being in play or tossed like dice. It is a kind of ecstasy with respect to the temporality in which things resolve their differences and contradictions. Think of it as an event or ecstasy akin (1) to madness: "Madness would thus be a word in perpetual incongruence with itself and interrogative throughout, such that it would put into question its possibility and, through it, the possibility of the language that would admit it, thus would put interrogation itself into question, in as much as it belongs to the play of madness" (PD65–66/SNB45). And, of course, (2) to exigency: the claim, the condition of responsibility or answerability to a demand (to write, to die).

No More Texts

Give me an example of the fragmentary.

Blanchot would say that none can be extracted from literary history, nor even from the history of philosophy. Naturally thoughts fasten upon Heraclitus, *Tristram Shandy,* Nietzsche, Gertrude Stein, Wittgenstein—but these texts are at most, in a manner of speaking, effects of the fragmentary rather than instances of it. Likewise *Le pas au-delà,* to all appearances a book of fragments, does not offer itself as an illustration of what it tries to think ("not every fragment is related to the fragmentary" [ED72/WD42]). The fragmentary cannot be engaged by any sort of reading (it is "radically unquotable" [ED64/WD37]). Instead, as examples of the fragmentary, Blanchot proposes—fear (*peur*) and dread (*angoisse*).

> When he crossed it, the city murmured in him constantly: I am afraid, be the witness of fear.

> He carries fear, fear does not belong to him: intransportable fear, without anyone to feel it, destitute of all, fear, the lack of fear [la manque de la peur].

> Fear for the one who is afraid, who does not know it: the collapsed center of empty fear.

Fear, that which does not have death as a limit, even the infinite death of others; nevertheless I am afraid for the others who are afraid of dying, who will die without me, in the distancing of this self which would vainly replace theirs.

Let fear leave me to interrogate fear: "But why are you afraid?"—"Don't ask me: I'm afraid."—"Are you afraid, in this way, even to the point of fear?"— "You ask me this, you shouldn't have asked me this."—"But I ask it in the same way that you're afraid: my question is your fear."

Fear, as if he recalled this word that made him forget everything.

Fear, it is this gift that they would give us in the posthumous city; the possibility of being afraid for them: fear given in the word fear, fear not felt.

Neither of them was given to using tricks: he, being a part of his plans that supposed a life that was still intact, the everyday life promised to all, and he, hearing nothing but the speech that was already failing, incapable of speaking except by default. Between them, the responsibility of fear.

"It's true, I am afraid."—"You say this so calmly."—"Saying it, however, does not alleviate the fear: on the contrary, it is the word fear that henceforward makes me afraid; having said it no longer allows me to say anything else."—"But, 'I am afraid', I also: because of this word, spoken so calmly: as no one, as if no one were afraid."—"From now on, it is the whole language that is afraid."(PD82–84/SNB57–59)

This is the other fear: like madness, it is not a subjective condition (recall the horror of the *il y a*, which evacuates subjectivity). Fear: "there is no experience of it." It is a mode of responsibility rather than of feeling (it is the relation with *autrui*). It is anonymous, neutral, no one's fear. Recall that it is what gives the definition of the philosopher, who fears the ecstasy that turns philosophy into poetry (that is, makes it impossible: think of the thought that will not allow itself to be thought [*EI*70/*IC*49]). Fear is the companion of the Orphic gaze.[15] It is, finally, nothing but a word, barely a word, a word too many that (like madness) shatters language the way the eternal return shatters Nietzsche, removing him to another temporality in which language is suddenly beside itself, no longer of one piece:

This fear of language, it was incumbent upon him not to see in it anything but the possibility, always open, that any word, belonging to the order of words that are only such by their belonging to language, could turn on this language in order to detach itself from it and to raise itself above it in mastering it, perhaps in shattering it, at least in pretending to assign it a limit. Fear does not signify that language would be afraid, even metaphysically, but that fear is a piece [*morceau*] of language, something that it would have lost and that would make it entirely dependent on this dead piece: entirely, that is, precisely in reconstituting itself without unity, piece by piece, as something other than a collection of significations. (*PD84/SNB59*)

Mad language: language outside of language, reconstituted as something other than a vocabulary—reconstituted on the basis of a "dead word": something unpronounceable, like the name of God ("God is thus a name, pure materiality, naming nothing, not even himself. Whence the perversion, magical, mystical, literal, of the name, the opacity of God to any idea of God. And still, like fear, like madness, it disappears, if only as a messenger of another language" [*PD85/SNB60*]). Blanchot has a name for this other language: namely, dread, the word of the impossible (or of poetry). "There are no words in the language of dread to say: that is possible" (*PD95/SNB68*).

For Blanchot, dread (*angoisse*)—the hoary old word of Kierkegaard and the existentialists—has always been what shadows and attenuates will-to-power.[16] In *Le pas au-delà* it is a word of infinite discretion (another word too many): "Dread—horror of all that names it, and, naming it, identifies it, glorifies it. It wants this: that one not speak of it, and that, since as soon as one speaks it is it that speaks, one says nothing. . . . Dread—this word that cannot be pronounced [*ce mot imprononçable*]" (*PD89/SNB62-63*). On a certain view, dread is a hole through which the whole of poststructuralism drains away: "Dread makes reading forbidden (the words separated, something arid and devastating about them; no more texts . . .)" (*PD89/SNB63*).

No more narratives; no more texts.

But in this word (*angoisse*) Blanchot seems to allow the whole of his thought to resonate. Two fragments read like an inventory of Blanchovian obsessions:

> A word chosen by the dread foreign to any choice in its immense oscillating work, the work of dread, its hammer of ruin, dread seeking refuge in dread.
>
> The distant always near to dread, its trace effaced, retraced: never whole, morcellated, hammered, with something young about it that is frightening. Sparse brevity, persevering, become slowness that interrupts itself, like a suffering has always returned and that does not recognize me. Its arrogance is my supplication.

The smallness of my dread, my whole is always surpassed — that which keeps me from being whole with myself, with you. The incessant intermittence. (PD92/SNB65)

"The incessant intermittence": the infinite discretion. Recall the solitude, lassitude, and calm of the last man: "The most anguishing idea [*idée la plus angoissante*]: he cannot die, because he has no future" (*DM56/ LM29*). Death belongs to the temporality of the dialectic; the other temporality (of Nietzsche, or of Igitur) is that which death excludes: "Whence the appeal to a morcellating repetitive demand [*exigence*]: the three knocks of the traditional theater that would seem to announce that something is going to happen, while instead they reverberate in the eternal empty tomb" (*PD122/SNB88*).

Man Disappears

In "Nietzsche et l'écriture fragmentaire" Blanchot distinguishes between the philosopher and the last man. The one is "the man of permanence, of substance," the other is the man who disappears. The one is the master of death, the other is not. This distinction corresponds to another between, on the one hand, "an integral discourse, the logos that says the whole, the seriousness of philosophical speech . . . : a speech that is continuous, without intermittence and without blanks, the speech of logical completion that knows nothing of chance, play, or laughter" (*EI233/IC155*); and, on the other, fragmentary speech, speech of the between-two, in which the disappearance of man is announced. One could think of these two figures in terms of a dialectical relation in which the one overcomes the other: the man who disappears is subsumed in the one who "*synthesizes, who totalizes and justifies*" (*EI233/IC155*), that is, the one who finds a place for everything. But for Blanchot the philosopher and the last man are not opposed to one another; rather, the last man is (let us say) one man too many. How to make sense of this? What does disappearance mean?

The longest fragment in *Le pas au-delà* begins: "We can always ask ourselves about the neuter" (*PD101/SNB72*). Notice that the question is reflexive: we are ourselves the space opened up by the question. The neuter as such cannot be directly interrogated. It is preeminently the thought that will not allow itself to be thought, "indicating in the form of a noun, a verbal way of holding back the demand to speak" (*l'exigence de dire*)

(PD103/SNB73). Blanchot, always the philologist, gives us the derivation: "The Neuter [why does he capitalize the first letter here?] derives, in the most simple way, from a negation of two terms: *neuter*, neither the one nor the other. Neither nor the other [*Ni ni l'autre*], nothing more precise" (PD104/SNB74). This is (something like) a nondialectical negation, that is, not a negation at all, not a double negation, but a pure affirmation that leaves everything each to itself (self-standing)—"does not put them together for a dialectical reversal" (PD105/SNB75). One and the other, where the relation between the two is not binary (nor, let us say, friendly in the usual Aristotelian sense), but a relation of the third kind: "one, yes, this can be indicated with the finger; but other [*autre*] is the other, entirely other and always the other; it flees itself in fleeing us" (PD104/SNB74). The neuter (or Neuter) holds open the question, "'Which of the two?'— 'Neither one nor the other, the other, the other,' as if the neuter spoke only in an echo, meanwhile perpetuating the other by the repetition of that difference" (PD108/SNB77). So the neuter is nonstructural or nonrelational: "Something is at work by way of the neuter that is immediately the work of worklessness [*désœuvrement*]" (PD105/SNB75). It is the event, the time of writing that suspends or exceeds the *Aufhebung*; it is the between-time of dying that separates past and future, the distant and near, the young and old; it is the difference without identity of which Deleuze has given us the most lucid philosophical account: "difference in itself."[17]

Blanchot, however, does not appear to think of himself as a philosopher of difference. Philosophy, always opening up and laying bare, is nothing if not indiscretion. Whereas Blanchot is a thinker of painful discretion.

Sometimes I allow myself the thought that *Le pas au-delà* contains a self-portrait (but I imagine this of all of Blanchot's texts). For example, in the second longest fragment in the book (italicized), someone (*il*, without parentheses) pays a visit, one of an endless number ("the usual visit" [PD110/SNB79]), to an old friend, if friend is the word, someone horribly ancient, to all appearances the last man: *"very old—like a reminiscence rather than a memory—shrunken, as someone who had waited too long might have shrunk, without one's knowing to what wait he still hoped to respond"* (PD110/SNB79).[18] A man, at all events, of the event, neither mortal nor immortal—I do not, in the event, call him "Blanchot"; one could as well call him "Bataille," or, better, "Levinas," or perhaps simply the "clandestine companion": waiting, weary, attentive—and, not to put too fine a point on it, neither there nor not there (*"It is true that this friend had dis-*

appeared. Since when, he could not say; they had for so long been used to speaking to each other from afar, from near, through the rumors of the city, or even through the repetition of an ancient language, always ready to give them a place in its game" [PD109/SNB78]).

However, recall (from chapter 5) that friendship is no longer a relation of possibility—no longer a relation supported by common ground. In another fragment, for example, the shrunken friend is *"the strange man—the man whom he had not decided in what terms it would be appropriate to call to"* (PD118/SNB85). The relation between the two friends is a relation of the third kind in which the other is the limit of the human—he speaks, for example, in no one's voice: *"he was startled to hear him speak with his usual voice, clear, neuter, so that one would have had to say that it stressed and cut off every word, if what it said so clearly had not failed to correspond to any particular word. 'It's the impeded speech, he said to reassure himself, a long animal sob'"* (PD118/SNB85). Say only that their relation is *"exceptional"*—*"this word resonated like a low-pitched sound in several registers at once, always below the lowest vibrations, those which he still liked to muffle"* (PD109/SNB78)—but of course the two have only agreed to act as if this were the case, although perhaps not deliberately.

> *That was not deliberate, at least on his part—but what was his part, what did he get outside of his role, which was, moreover, interchangeable, in exchanges that were never imposed on him except in his being haunted by memories over which he had so little control that he began to believe that they did not belong to him, memories of nobody, perhaps* [souvenir de personne, plutôt]? (PD109–10/SNB78)

Nobody's memories, to be sure: the two friends, as if at history's end, have been drained of identity. Each is perhaps what Blanchot, in *L'écriture du désastre*, calls "a borrowed, happenstance singularity [*une singularité d'emprunt et de recontre*]" (ED35/WD18). One or the other of the two, perhaps the visitor, worries that he is late, but in the temporality (or infinity) of their conversation there is neither early nor late: *"'Late, you are always perfectly punctual.'"* Someone anyhow comes as if to the point, which not surprisingly concerns the possibility of a breach of discretion, the risk of speaking (which is to say speaking aloud, actually pronouncing words):

> *"Still, lagging behind my memory: as if it happened that, following the eternal straight road, I found myself alone and suddenly, as, however, I had al-*

ways feared would happen, tested by the risky words that we had intentionally pronounced about them [leur]: dangerous words, words of the blind [paroles d'aveugle]." (PD110–11/SNB79)

Words of the blind, as if there were any other: speaking is not seeing (a later fragment of *Le pas au-delà* speaks of "the practice of writing" as "impracticable, sovereign, blind, pitiable in every case" [*PD127/SNB92*]).

Recall "Parler, ce n'est pas voir," where Blanchot formulated, not for the first time, the exigency of discretion—of *not* being the "novelist who lifts up the rooftops and gives his characters over to a penetrating gaze" (*EI40/IC29*). In place of the novelist's discourse we may imagine the speech of Orpheus: "A speech such that to speak would no longer be to unveil with light" (*EI41/IC29*). This would be a speech outside the alternatives of veiling-unveiling, that is, "a rare speech; it knows no precipitation. . . . It is most open in its obliqueness, through interruption always persisting, always calling upon detour, and thus holding us as though in suspense between the visible and the invisible, or on the hither side of both [*en deça de l'un et de l'autre*]" (*EI43/IC31*). This describes very nicely the language of *Le pas au-delà*.

Speech without precipitation, or, alternatively, "the speech of the waiting [*la parole d'attente*] wherein things are turned back toward latency. Waiting: the speech of detour without digression, of errancy without error" (*EI43/IC31*). We can trace this speech back to "Littérature et la droit à la mort," where literature (a certain side of literature), by refusing to name things, "by turning itself into an inability to reveal things," responds to (for the sake of) "the presence of things before the *world* exists" (*PF317/GO47/ WF328*). Or, in other words, like poetry, it responds to the impossible: to the *il y a*, existence without being, where presence, like "a great instantaneous fire, consumes itself endlessly"—that is, disappears (PD111/SNB80).

In *Le pas au-delà*, the fragment of the two friends arrives at a moment of indiscretion (perhaps we can call it *"a moment in the life of a man—consequently in the life of men—when everything is completed, the books written, the universe silent, beings at rest. There is left only the task of announcing it"* [EIxii/ICxv]):

"*Say it, be brave, tell me what happened* [ce qui serait arrivé].*"—"It's that you had disappeared." To his surprise, he did not take this lightly: he remained silent, pushing this answer, already completely prepared, away, and only saying, a little later, with some agitation: they arrive, they arrive* [ils arrivent]. *It is from this that he got the feeling he should no longer leave him.* (PD111/SNB80)

The exigency of narrative: "tell me what happened." The direct answer (*"already completely prepared"*) is a sort of death sentence which, like much in *Le pas au-delà*, one doesn't know how to read, as if the sentence were divided (infinitely) in two. (1) We already know what happened, and we know that the fact is strangely inconsequential: *"It is true that this friend had disappeared. Since when, he could not say"*: as if the disappearance had been uneventful, or something one pretends not to notice. (2) But of course the friend responds as if it were a matter of some seriousness, possibly an omen—or does he have the sense of having been cheated, as if the sentence had been incapable of being carried out ("all it brings to the person who was trying to prepare an unstoried death for himself is the mockery of immortality" [PF328/GO58/WF340])? Anyhow he does the human thing: *"he remained silent, pushing this answer . . . away."*[19]

The fragments that follow multiply the ways in which one can take the answer ("like a junction of all kinds of decisions having different meanings" ([*de signes différents*] [PD113/SNB81]). There is no hope of assembling these fragments into something plotlike; each fragment is a branching of the text, a breaking-free of every context. So discretion of a certain kind is imposed upon commentary, where saying anything is saying too much. If one wanted a model of how *Le pas au-delà* is put together, one could do worse than borrow Deleuze's conception of the rhizome. "A rhizome is composed not of units but of dimensions, or rather directions in motion. It has neither beginning nor end, but always a middle (*milieu*) from which it grows and which it overspills. It constitutes linear multiplicities with n dimensions having neither subject nor object, which can be laid out on a plane of consistency, and from which the One is always subtracted (n-1). When a multiplicity of this kind changes dimension, it necessarily changes in nature as well, undergoes a metamorphosis." It seems worth emphasizing, in the context of Blanchot, that the rhizome is not a structuralist concept: "Unlike a structure, which is defined by a set of points and positions, with binary relations between the points and biunivocal relationships between the positions, the rhizome is made only of lines: lines of segmentarity and stratification as its dimensions, and the line of flight or deterritorialization as the maximum dimension after which the multiplicity undergoes metamorphosis, changes in nature" (MP31/TP21).

Prudence urges that we attend mainly to the briefest fragment: "*But what shadow of presence would I have if I had not at each moment already disappeared?* What a strange emptiness is the lack of an answer" (*PD*111/ *SNB*80). Recall Blanchot's conception of the double death in *L'espace littéraire*: "There is one death which circulates in the language of possibility, of liberty, which has for its furthest horizon the freedom to die and the capacity to take mortal risks; and there is its double, which is ungraspable. It is what I cannot grasp, what is not linked to *me* by a relation of any sort. It is that which never comes and toward which I do not direct myself" (*EL*129–30/*SL*104). The one death is narratable, is a form of action, a suicide: Empedocles leaps into the abyss; the other is not, that is, the leap is "not the irreversible step beyond which there would be no return [*n'est pas le passage irréversible au-delà duquel il n'y aurait pas de retour*], for it is that which is not accomplished, the interminable and the incessant" (*EL*133/ *SL*106). Here "death disappears, discreetly, into itself" (*EL*201/*SL*154)— withdraws, so to speak, from the determinacy and objectivity of a consummation: withdraws, let us say, into "the *other* history . . . wherein nothing of the present ever happens" (*ED*209/*WD*138).

Suppose, against the background of this theory, we say that the two friends share, or occupy, not a relation, certainly not a common ground, but two different temporalities, or rather two asymmetrical sides of time, one serial, the other not, one composed of determinable states of affairs (either definitely alive or dead, for example), the other endured as the pure passivity of dying—the impossible nonpresence of the present (compare *EI*307–8/*IC*207). Presence is what disappears, but this is not an event that can "be fixed or included in the game of a relation" (*PD*113/*SNB*81). So disappearance as a statement of what happened cannot (as yet) have occurred; it belongs to a "wild, unnarratable history having no meaning in the present [*l'histoire sauvage, inénnarable, n'ayant pas de sens présent*]" (*ED*49/*WD*28).[20] The friend therefore lives on, but not as it were in uninterrupted transit from the future to the past, rather in the interval of dying: "*That this friend had disappeared, carried, carried off, by the great wave of his perpetual memory, did not prevent him, with his usual benevolence, from answering for the disappearance himself, both as if nothing had happened and as if he had had to draw out, in his presence, all the consequences of his unfortunate admission*" (*PD*114/*SNB*82).[21]

In place of "the interval of dying" one could (still borrowing from *L'espace littéraire*) think of "death's space." We know that in the world's space "things are transformed into objects in order to be grasped, used, made more certain in the distinct rigor of their limits" (EL182/SL141): this is the task of speech. By contrast, in death's space everything loses definition (that is, everything fragments). Interestingly, in the world (in "the language of the living" [PD118/SNB85]) it is possible to speak of death—to use the word death as if it were a proper name—but in death's space the word has no place or use: death is unnameable. Likewise speech has no place (hence the shrunken friend's stammer, his "long animal sob" (PD118/SNB85). In Blanchot's equation, speech is to death as writing is to dying (PD123–24/SNB89–90). And in the end it looks for all the world as if the visitor were drawn into this equation:

> While it seemed to him that he would from now on have to make an effort to join him, as the other was maintaining himself in a fiction of distancing even when he was present, it would be his person that bore the intensity, be it as a being unalterably shrunken, he saw him behind his table, seated comfortably and sumptuously, majestic character [personage majestueux] who greeted him with his customary good will, although this time a little frozen with immobility. But what was most extraordinary was that by reason of his grandeur called majestuous [qualifée de majestueuse]—another way (he soon noticed), no less miserable, of ending up removed from space—he had to be aware of the impeded speech that henceforth, like a grave profoundly opened around him, a failure of words in words, seemed destined to preserve his isolation. Who was responsible for it? Must he linger over such a thing happening? Should he, speaking of it to him, confiding it to him as an element of their relationship and perhaps a sign of life, sign of death, risk lessening its importance? As discretion necessarily meant saying everything in advance, how could he, in the game of their discreet silence, introduce this new indiscretion that claimed, in some form, by some wild muteness, to modify the course of what had been said? Impeded speech that found its equivalent in silent ease, inexorable, leaving room only for the continuous murmur of the river crossing the room between immobile hills. Ease as of a thing already written and nevertheless always still to be written and always not writing itself. "There you are—this time it's you—sovereign over speech."—"For the benefit of age." According to his conviction, the monumental character that was suddenly visible, that of a dead sovereignty, of a name sovereignly alive . . . (PD114/SNB82)

Here Blanchot's text seems to have achieved a perfect decorum with "*the non-arrival of what comes about*" [l'inarrivée de ce qui advient] (PD132/

SNB95). Reading cannot repair the disaster. At most one might remark how odd it seems that, as the shrunken companion withdraws further into death's space, he becomes, not smaller or more clandestine but larger, or at all events more "majestuous"—not a word one runs across much in English: one might have said, "more grave," were it not that in Blanchot's economy death is heavy in contrast to dying, which is light, fragile, unserious, without consequence, infinitely gentle, invisible, calm, discreet (PD136/SNB98; PD168/SNB123; PD179/SNB131).

Commentary is reduced by fragmentary writing to its most ancient form, which is to allow what is elsewhere plain to illuminate what is here obscure. Two texts will serve.

(1) In an essay called "La douleur du dialogue" (1956), apropos of a conversation in a *récit* by Marguerite Duras (*Le square*), Blanchot characterized dialogue as a species of impossible discourse. Dialogue would therefore be neither Socratic nor hermeneutical; it is perhaps no more than idle talk, where the interlocutors (two old men, as we imagine them, but of course one could imagine a man and a woman, or two women, just as well) simply want "to make use of the one faculty they are still lucky enough to possess and which they cannot be sure of having for long. It is this last feeble and threatened resource which gives an element of gravity to the simple exchange. From their first words we sense that, for these two people, and more especially for one of them, the space and air required to make talking possible are all but exhausted" (LV214/SS203). Conversation in this sense is a limit-experience, that is, it is shadowed by "the imminent threat of reaching a point beyond which a person is finally isolated in silence and violence [*limite en deçà de laquelle le mutisme et la violence fermeront l'être*]." When, in the event, "the frontier [*limite*] has been crossed, it is the language of solitude and exile that we hear, the language of extremity, focusless and almost partnerless, impersonal too, but for lack of a person [*privée de centre et donc sans vis-à-vis, impersonnelle à nouveau, par perte de la personne*]" (LV214/SS204).

For Blanchot, however, the limit is not really a kind of frontier; it is, in its way, already in excess of anything that could be crossed. One's relation to the limit is no longer narratable, no longer a movement but rather a radical immobility, a passivity more passive than simply the absence of action. As, for example—(2) in "L'expérience-limite," his most important essay on Bataille, where Blanchot says that the limit-experience offers to thought something like "an essential gift, the prodigality of an affirmation; an affir-

mation, for the first time, that is not a product (the result of a double negation), and thereby escapes all the movements, oppositions, and reversals of
dialectical reason." The statement *"It's that you had disappeared"* can be
read as an (anarchic) affirmation, what Blanchot calls "the decisive Yes":

> Presence without anything being present. Through this affirmation, an af-
> firmation that has freed itself from every negation (and consequently from
> every meaning), that has relegated and deposed the world of values, that
> consists not in affirming, upholding, and withstanding what is, but rather
> holds itself above and outside being, and that therefore does not answer to
> ontology any more than to the dialectic, man sees himself assigned—be-
> tween being and nothingness, and out of the infinite of this between-two
> that is entertained as relation—the status of his new sovereignty: the sover-
> eignty of being without being in the becoming without end of a death im-
> possible to die. (*EI*310/*IC*209)

So the *"dead sovereignty"* of the shrunken friend is precisely that of the last
man, the one who disappears as if into the *il y a*, existence without being.
Sovereignty here is freedom from the dialectical narrative of negation,
from the rule of logic, from the law of the same.

Of course one could try to account for the majesty of the shrunken
companion by thinking of the friendship between the two as a relation between the *moi* and *Autrui*, where the relation is asymmetrical in Levinas's
sense. In *L'écriture du désastre*, Blanchot gives a somewhat exaggerated
turn to this asymmetry:

> The Other: the Separate, the Most-High which escapes my power—the
> powerless, therefore; the stranger, dispossessed. But, in the relation of the
> *Other to me*, everything seems to reverse itself: the distant becomes close-by,
> this proximity becomes the obsession that afflicts me, that weighs down
> upon me, that separates me from myself . . . dis-identifying me, abandoning
> me to passivity, leaving me without any initiative and bereft of present. And
> then, the other becomes rather the Overlord, the Persecutor, he who over-
> whelms, encumbers, undoes me, he who puts me in his debt no less than he
> attacks me by making me answer for his crimes, by charging me with mea-
> sureless responsibility which cannot be mine since it extends all the way to
> "substitution" (*ED*36/*WD*19).

It is plausible that one of the two friends is a philosopher and therefore
magisterial according to the usual explanations. However, *Le pas au delà*
holds to Blanchot's theory of alterity where the relationship between the

two is symmetrical just in the sense that, in the same event, the visitor is himself altered (if himself is the word), as anyone would be who enters into the space of the other, call it the space of the neutral—or, alternatively, into the time of the other: the time of dying. In either case the friendship perhaps absorbs the two; one anyhow grows indistinguishable from the other, is now neither one nor the other:

> Immobile before this unmoving friend, still he is never immobile enough; the feeling of a threat comes from this, and the fear—the fear that nothing provokes; one of the two moves, it is not completely life; one goes to get up perhaps, it will be night, the other will continue to mount guard with these vacillating words.

> "You torment yourself in speaking."—"If not, I would torment myself in not speaking."

> While they waited on the threshold, far away, yet perhaps already leaning towards us, and watching us as if we were a single thing, he saw, falling over the face of the young girl, as the night falls, the dark hair that completely hides it.

> "We speak, we speak, two immobile men whom immobility maintains facing one another, the only ones to speak, the last to speak."—"Do you mean that from now on we speak because our words are without consequence [sans suite], without effect, a stammering from the depths of ages?"—"Stay calm, look how I'm calm."—"You're not calm, you're as afraid as I'm afraid, fear makes us majestuous, solemn."—"Solemn, majestuous." (PD126–27/SNB91–92)

One can't help wondering what the young girl (her hair falling across her face in a gesture of infinite discretion) sees when she looks at the two men. We know only that she watched them as if they were "*a single thing,*" not an entity of sorts but only the relation (or nonrelation) that separates them—"Friendship: friendship for the unknown without friends [*Amitié: amitié pour l'inconnu sans amis*]" (PD181/SNB133).

A final thought: the friends, for all of that, need not be old, as subjects go. Doubtless they have been friends for many years (fifty or more, let us say), but their relation cannot be figured in terms of the passage of time. They inhabit (perhaps calmly, perhaps not) the *effroyablement ancient* (PD24/SNB14), the time of dying that death cannot bring to a completion (the time of survival). Imagine someone young, a child perhaps, inhabiting an ancient temporality, a *pas au-delà*.

CHAPTER 9

Blanchot's "holocaust"

The completion of time is not death, but messianic time,
where the perpetual is converted into the eternal.
— Emmanuel Levinas, *Totalité et infini*

Concluding the Disaster

"Let there be a past, let there be a future, with nothing that would allow
the passage from one to the other" (*PD22/SNB12*). If Blanchot's theory of
the event makes sense, the disaster can never be concluded. "We are on
the edge of disaster without being able to situate it in the future: it is rather
always already past, and yet we are on the edge or under the threat, all for-
mulations which would imply the future — that which is yet to come — if
the disaster were not that which does not come, that which has put a stop
to every arrival" (*ED7/WD1*). The disaster is nonapocalyptic. It is what
keeps history from ending, or from forming or being formed by any period
or unity. It interrupts the transition from beginning to end, leaving us with
only a "wild unnarratable history without any meaning in the present"
(*ED49/WD28*). So basically it is a concept that only an anarchist could
have ("the idea of totality cannot delimit it" [*ED9/WD2*]). It is the event
which does not happen ("there is no time or space for its accomplishment" [*ED8/WD2*]) — whence none of our historical categories has application any longer, not even concepts of crisis and revolution, or obsolescence and the new: no more *au-delà*. "The *Aufhebung* turns inoperable,
ceases" (*ED69/WD40*; cf. *ED158–60/WD101–3*).[1]

Perhaps the disaster is only historicity itself, not so much what happens
as that which prevents the succession of past into future. (Or is it future
turning into the past? No one has ever figured out which way time moves.)
This is to say nothing against past or future but only that the disaster is not

a turning point where the possible begins to realize itself; it is (the) impossible. Being an-archic, nothing can follow from it, possibly not even memory. Blanchot writes: "The disaster is related to forgetfulness [*du côté de l'oubli*] — forgetfulness without memory, the motionless retreat of what has not been treated [*le retrait immobile de ce qui n'a pas été tracé*] — the immemorial perhaps" (ED10/WD3): that is, the *il y a*. Narrative, for example, is rooted not in memory but in forgetfulness: "It is narrative (independent of its content) that is a forgetting, so that to tell a story is to put oneself through the ordeal of this first forgetting that precedes, founds, and ruins all memory. Recounting, in this sense, is the torment of language" (EI564/IC385).

Perhaps Blanchot means no more than this, that memory is nondialectical and therefore not in a binary relation with forgetfulness (it is not what forgetfulness is not). In "Oublieuse mémoire" (1962) Blanchot speaks of forgetting as a power (EI461/IC316), but this is not the power of the negative: "forgetting is not nothing. Forgetting is the very vigilance of memory, the guardian force thanks to which the hidden of things [*le caché des choses*] is preserved" (EI460/IC315).[2] "Forgetful memory" is not the obliteration of memory but rather that which opens a neutral space — a between-time outside of presence and absence, the far and the near — in which memory abides: "There is in memory a relation we can no longer term dialectical, since it belongs to the ambiguity of forgetting that is at once the mediating site and a space without mediation — indifferent difference between depth and surface" (EI462/IC316). This means, at the very least, that memory is not structured as a language or discourse and cannot be simply retired or retrieved and spoken at will. Discourse, Blanchot says, "is active; it unfolds and develops according to the rules that assure it a certain coherence. [It is] synthetic, conforming to a certain unity of language and to a time which, always the memory of itself, maintains itself in a synchronic whole" (ED32/WD16). But memory is outside discourse and, therefore, never self-identical: there is no form that it can take, except perhaps that of the fragmentary (which is not a form). The problem with memory is not so much that it recedes into oblivion as that, on the contrary, there is too much of it. Its temporality is excessive; it cannot be gathered together or contained. It ruins history (it "refers us to nonhistorical forms of time, to the other of all tenses, to their eternal or eternally provisional indecision, bereft of destiny, without presence" [ED134–35/WD85]). Like the fragmentary, it can never be part of a panorama. It endlessly repeats itself, a fascination or obsession, bearing down on us again and again, and maybe forgetting is what mediates this eternal return. To put it another way: Our relation to the disaster cannot be mediated "from the perspective of terminated history, already seated by the river, dying and being reborn, content with the contentment of the universe, and thus of God, through beatitude and knowledge" (*EI*303–4/*IC*204). The experience of the disaster is not a subjective possibility but a limit-experience, which means that it cannot be objectified or thematized; on the contrary, it drains away our subjectivity, turns us into no one ("we live it another time as something that escapes all employment and all end, and more, as that which escapes our very capacity to undergo it, but whose trial we cannot escape" [*EI*308/*IC*207]). In *L'écriture du désastre* this becomes: "We feel that there cannot be any experience of the disaster, even if we were to understand disaster to be the ultimate experience [*expérience-limite*]. This is one of its features: it impoverishes all experience, withdraws from experience all authenticity; it keeps its vigil only when night watches without watching over anything" (*ED*85/*WD*51). We recognize this night as the other night, the *entre-temps* of insomnia that turns me inside out: "Wakefulness is estrangement.... Something wakes, something keeps watch.... The disaster watches"—that is, "no one watches. Watching is not the power to keep watch—in the first person; it is not a power, but the touch of the powerless infinite, exposure to the *other* of the night, where thought renounces the vigor of vigilance, gives up worldly clearsightedness, perspicacious mastery, in order to deliver itself to the limitless deferral of insomnia, the wake that does not waken, nocturnal intensity" (*ED*82/*WD*48–49).[3] No one's endless vigil: imagine this as a (nonmessianic) theory of history.

Just so, the temporality of the disaster is that of the *il y a* or the *es gibt*: "The disaster is the gift; it gives disaster: as if it took no account of being or not-being. It is not advent (which is proper to what comes to pass): it does not happen. And thus I cannot ever happen upon this thought, except without knowing, without appropriating any knowledge. Or again, is it the advent of what does not happen, of what would come without arriving, outside being, and as though by drifting away? The posthumous disaster?" (*ED*13/*WD*5). Think of it (as of the *il y a*) as both a haunting and a premonition, always already past and always to come, something without definition that hovers and looms, holding us in thrall, saturating us with a fascination of horror that sets us apart, "out of reach" (*ED*7/*WD*1).

So it is no surprise to read: "The disaster is separate; that which is most separate" (ED7/WD1). The disaster is a concept of exteriority rather than of catastrophe (it is "foreign to the ruinous purity of destruction" [ED9/WD2]). Emerging as it does late in Blanchot's *œuvre* it becomes a kind of grand finale in which changes are rung on all of his themes: the Outside, the Other Night, the Neutral, the fragmentary: "*He does not believe in the disaster* [Il ne croit pas au désastre]. *One cannot believe in it, whether one lives or dies. Commensurate with it there is no faith, and at the same time a sort of disinterest, detached from the disaster. Night; white, sleepless night—such is the disaster: the night lacking darkness, but brightened by no light* [Nuit, nuit blanche—ainsi le désastre, cette nuit à laquelle l'obscurité manque, sans que la lumière l'éclaire]" (ED8/WD2). Insomnia, affliction (*le maleur*), waiting, attention, vigilance without desire or purpose—our relation to the disaster is a nonrelation: "We are passive [*passifs*] with respect to the disaster—but the disaster is perhaps passivity, and thus past, always past, even in the past, out of date [*en cela passé et toujours passé*]" (ED9/WD3: the original is given a double translation). As always, passivity is not an attitude but a hyperpassivity that "has abandoned the level of life where *passive* would simply be the opposite of *active*" (ED28/WD13).

Or, in other words, there is passivity as disengagement and passivity as *an-archism*: "There is the passivity which is passive quietude (suggested, perhaps, by what we know of quietism); and then there is the passivity which is beyond disquietude, but which nevertheless retains the passiveness of the incessant, feverish, even-uneven movement of error which has no purpose, no end, no starting principle [*initiative*]" (ED31/WD15–16). Passivity is the ontology of disaster, of existence without being, of space without place (the space of exile), of "a time without present" (ED29/WD14), of "*subjectivity without any subject*" (ED53/WD30), of responsibility without reason, selfhood, or identity.

Responsibility is a keyword in *L'écriture du désastre*, which continues the endless conversation with Levinas in which the philosopher's (philosophy's) terms of art (for example, "responsibility") are inscribed "as though from an unknown language which we speak counter to our heart and to life, and unjustifiably" (ED47/WD26).[4] To be sure, already in Levinas "responsibility—my responsibility for the other, for everyone, without reciprocity—is displaced; it is not an activating thought process put into practice, nor is it even a duty that would impose itself from without and from within" (ED45/WD25). In Levinas responsibility is not an imperative, not a form of action or disposition (a liberal sensitivity or compassion, for example) rooted in law or principle, but is already an-archic. But in Blanchot's thinking responsibility is something more than (without perhaps altogether ceasing to be) an ethical concept. More exactly, its ethical meaning consists precisely in the encounter with the foreign that "separates me from myself (from the 'me' that is mastery and power, from the free, speaking subject) and reveals the other *in place* of me"; or (in so many words) it turns me into *autrui* (*ED46/WD25*), situates me on his site as an exile or outsider face to face with something other than a face. In the Outside responsibility is no longer to another, that is, it is no longer strictly or philosophically ethical; it is now a "response to the impossible" (*ED46/WD26*), which is how Blanchot has long since characterized the responsibility of poetry to the exigency of writing (*EI69/IC48*).

Blanchot never hesitates to turn Levinas inside out on just this point: "in the relation of *the Other to me*," he says, "everything seems to reverse itself" (*ED36/WD19*), by which he appears to mean that I become the other to the other's Same: "When the other crushes me into radical alienation, is my relation still a relation to the other? Is it not rather a relation to the 'I' of the master, to absolute egotistical force, to the dominator who predominates and ultimately wields the force of inquisitorial persecution?" (*ED38/WD20*). If so, then my response to the other must be one of "refusal, resistance, combat" (*ED38/WD20*). However, this refusal, this resistance or combat, is not a counterattack; it is nondialectical, like Bartleby's "I would prefer not to," which Blanchot thinks of as "the core of refusal" (*ED33/WD17*). This, Blanchot explains, "is why there must always be at least two languages, or two requirements [*exigences*]: one dialectical, the other not; one where negativity is the task, the other where the neutral remains apart, cut off both from being and from not-being" (*ED36/WD20*). In other words: there is language and language (language outside of language, or writing—recall Nietzsche's attempt to think the Eternal Return, and going mad in the bargain—that is, crossing over "to another language removed from the ordinary forms of temporality" [*PD59/SNB40*]).

In *L'écriture du désastre* Blanchot says that in trying to clarify this (impossible, Bartlebyan) sense of responsibility, "I can no longer appeal to any ethics, any experience, any practice whatever—save that of some counterliving, which is to say an un-practice, or (perhaps) a word of writing [*parole d'écriture*]" (*ED47/WD26*). But there is no language in which this appeal or counterappeal can be registered. "One would have thus to turn toward some language that has never been written—a language never inscribed but that is always to be prescribed—in order that this incomprehensible word [*responsibilité*] be understood in its disastrous heaviness and in its way of summoning us to turn toward the disaster without either understanding it or bearing it. That is why responsibility is itself disastrous" (ED47/WD26–27). It is the facing of disaster: *that*, let us say, is what writing is—and also, perhaps, conversation, since Blanchot is quick to add that "it is in *friendship* that I can respond" (ED47/WD27), as if friendship were something like a condition of possibility for responding to the impossible, or to the disaster. Something *like* a condition, perhaps, but responsibility, Blanchot insists, is an-archic: unconditional, without foundation, without beginning or end—like one's involvement in an infinite conversation. And we know (this seems roughly the upshot of Le *pas au-delà*) that in such a conversation friendship is very strange, since it is (once more) a nonrelation, absolutely without filiation, more Jewish than Greek: "a friendship unshared, without reciprocity, friendship for that which has passed leaving no trace. This is passivity's response to the un-presence of the unknown" (ED47/WD27).

Impossible friendship: or, as Blanchot once expressed it in a letter to Bataille, "J'ajoute que l'amitié est aussi la vérité du désastre."[5] One might as well be a suppliant before one's enemy—"For responsibility is the extreme of *submissement*" (ED41/WD22). It is, Blanchot says, "through awkward *weakness* alone . . . that I am called upon to enter into this separation, this other relation. I am called to enter it with my selfhood gangrened and eaten away, altogether alienated (thus it is among lepers and beggars beneath the Roman ramparts that the Jews of the first centuries expected to discover the Messiah)" (ED42–43/WD23). The Messiah, a concept "that would imply the future—that which is yet to come—if the disaster were not that which does not come, that which has put a stop to every arrival" (ED7/WD1).

No more narratives, no more Messiahs—unless messianism is understood not as a coming (a coming yet to come) but as a waiting, that is, an infinite patience that no longer grasps the future.

The Metaphysics of Being Jewish

L'écriture du désastre is usually perceived as a book about the Holocaust.[6] This is not especially wrong, but the perception sometimes obscures an dissymmetry between terms ("an essential discordance between the 'terms' that come face to face" [EI611/IC416]): disaster and Holocaust are not reciprocal. To be sure, Blanchot's book resonates with the historical and cultural context in which it was published. In 1980 France was in the midst (as perhaps it still is) of a complex and traumatic awakening to its past half-century, that is, to the years of Occupation during World War II, but also to the years of crisis that preceded it as well as to the years of denial and bad faith that followed—the so-called "Vichy syndrome."[7] This meant an awakening to the consequences of French fascism (or fascisms) and to the realities of the Vichy regime's collaboration with the Nazis, and in particular it meant acknowledging Vichy's initiatives in the deportations of French Jews (and "foreign" Jews in France) to the extermination camps in Eastern Europe. "Initiatives" is obviously a euphemism.[8] Vichy's policies toward the Jews were neither merely strategic nor bureaucratic but an obsession rooted in "French anti-semitic traditions" (*The Vichy Syndrome*, p. 7).

Until the 1980s the Holocaust was not a subject of much or, indeed, any interest in French intellectual or cultural life—this despite the fact that one of the earliest and still one of the most important studies of the Holocaust, Leon Poliakov's *Bréviaire de la haine*, was published in France in 1951.[9] Henry Rousso's argument in *The Vichy Syndrome* is that the Holocaust had no meaning in either Gaullist or Communist memory of the Vichy years, and he indicates that in France Jewish memory itself did not really awaken systematically to the Holocaust until the 1970s.[10] It was not until the early 1980s that the fate of the Jews during the Occupation began to receive anything like concerted scholarly attention.[11] (Holocaust studies as a university discipline meanwhile is itself a development of the 1980s— and of course what this discipline confronted at once is the exteriority of memory, its irreducibility to history.)

L'écriture du désastre can be read as a contribution to (or effect of) this awakening, but there may be no straightforward way of doing so because of the elusive, problematical nature of the relation between the Holocaust and the disaster. It is not a logical relation, that is, for Blanchot the Holocaust is *not a species* of the disaster. The disaster is not generic of anything—it is neutral with respect to every relation (it is neither negative nor positive)—which may be Blanchot's point in distinguishing it from catastrophe. But what to make of this distinction, since the word disaster must surely mean what it says? Allan Stoekl puts the problem very well: "We should recall at once the formulation with which *The Writing of the Dis-*

aster opens: 'The disaster ruins everything, all the while leaving everything intact.' In this sense the disaster is out of history, unrecuperable within a dialectical framework. And yet, if the Holocaust is an example of the disaster, an emblem of it—even if it is the major example—how can we say that it leaves or that it left 'everything intact'?"[12] The difficulty is that the relation between the disaster and the Holocaust is not one of exemplarity (not a type-token relation). It is neither a relation of synonymy nor one of specific difference.

Another way to put this would be to say that the Holocaust is irreducible to any term or concept, and if the disaster is a term or concept, the Holocaust is irreducible to the disaster. But perhaps the disaster is just this condition of singularity or irreducibility ("The disaster: break with every star, break with every form of totality" [ED121/WD75]):[13]

> If someone pronounces this word, the *disaster*, we feel that it is not a word, not the name of anything; indeed, we feel that there never is a separate, nominal, predominant name, but always an entire complex or simple sentence, where the infinitude of language—of language in its unfinished history and its unclosed system—seeks to let itself be taken in hand by a sequence of verbs, and yet seeks at the same time, in the never resolved tension between noun and verb, to fall, as if immobilized, outside language—without, however, ceasing to belong to it. (*ED120/WD74–75*)

Surely the word *disaster* means what it says? But no: "there is . . . practically nothing disastrous in this disaster: this is what we must surely learn to think, without, perhaps, ever knowing it" (*ED99/WD60*). The disaster is neutral: a word and not a word, neither one nor the other, outside of language without ceasing to belong to it, as if it were in excess of language, or perhaps only an expression of the excessiveness of language with respect to itself as a totality ("language in its unfinished history and its unclosed system"). A word too many.

This may help to explain an earlier, very puzzling fragment, which begins with the statement: "The disaster is not somber; it would liberate us from everything if it could just have a relation with someone; we would know it in light of language and at the twilight of a language with a *gai savoir*." How not somber? As if the disaster could in some sense be a comic event? The fragment continues: "But the disaster is unknown; it is the unknown name for that in thought itself which dissuades us from thinking of it, leaving us, through its proximity [*nous éloignant par la proximité*],

alone. Alone, and thus exposed to the thought of the disaster which disrupts solitude and overflows every variety of thought, as the intense, silent
and disastrous affirmation of the outside" (*ED*14/*WD*5).[14] Not somber, but
calm, as (evidently) opposed to frightened—recall the two friends in *Le
pas au-delà*: "*We speak, we speak, two immobile men whom immobility
maintains facing one another, the only ones to speak, the last to speak.*"—
"*Do you mean that from now on we speak because our words are without
consequence, without effect, a stammering from the depths of ages?*"—"*Stay
calm, look how I'm calm.*"—"*You're not calm, you're afraid as I'm afraid,
fear makes us majestuous, solemn.*"—"*Solemn, majestuous* [Solennels, ma-
jestueux]" (*PD*127/*SNB*91–92). And remember that fear in Blanchot's
thinking is the disposition of the philosopher toward impossibility or the
unknown (*EI*70/*IC*49), in contrast (say) to the poet's response: "If we
could, through a reduction or preliminary dissidence, separate death and
dying, speech and writing, we would obtain, although at great expense and
at great pains, a sort of theoretical calm, theoretical happiness [*bonheur*]"
(*PD*127/*SNB*92). *Reste calme:* neither joyful nor melancholy, as if being
calm were a kind of limit-experience in which one's feeling or disposition
could no longer be thought of exactly as one's own; rather it belongs to the
situation (the outside) into which one has been cast. Claude Lanzmann's
Shoah has a very Blanchovian ending in this respect: the last to speak is a
member of the Jewish underground who recalls his return to the Warsaw
ghetto only hours after its final evacuation by the SS: "Yes, I was alone all
the time. Except for that woman's voice, and a man I met as I came out
of the sewers, I was alone throughout my tour of the ghetto. I didn't meet
a living soul. At one point I recall feeling a kind of peace, of serenity. I
said to myself: 'I'm the last Jew. I'll wait for morning, and for the Germans.'"[15] Compare the fragment from *L'écriture du désastre*: "*Le calme, la
brûlure de l'holocauste, l'anéantissement de midi—le calme du désastre*"
(*ED*15/*WD*6).

The Holocaust is not a species of the disaster, but the disaster clarifies
the question of how we stand with respect to the Holocaust—clarifies, one
might say, the *exigency* of the Holocaust. The Holocaust exposes us to
what the philosopher has always feared, as in an ecstatic movement of divestiture (sometimes called "tragedy") that leaves us in an "uninhabitable
world" where "everything is the face to face of incompatibilities [*tout est
affrontement d'incompatibilités*]" (*EI*142/*IC*99). So there is no such thing
as a proper, correct, or (for all of that) *any* approach to the Holocaust.

It is as a limit of philosophy—as an unnameable or unpronounceable name (or, indeed, as a cry)—that the Holocaust enters into Blanchot's text, where (like *autrui*) it remains in lower case:[16]

> *The unknown name, alien to naming:*
> *The holocaust, the* absolute *event of history—which is a date in history—* *that utter-burn* [toute-brûlure] *where all history took fire, where the movement of Meaning was swallowed up* [le mouvement du Sens s'est abîmé], *where the gift, which knows nothing of forgiving or of consent, shattered without giv-ing place to anything that can be affirmed, that can be denied—gift of very passivity, gift of what cannot be given. How can it be preserved, even by thought? How can thought be made the keeper of the holocaust where all was lost, including guardian thought?*
> *In the mortal intensity, the fleeing silence of the countless cry.* (ED80/ WD47)[17]

"How can it be preserved, even by thought?" The Holocaust is opaque, outside the "the optical imperative" *(EI38/IC27)*. Images often obscure the event, since it is an event of memory rather than of history—that is, an event in Blanchot's radical sense of that which the disaster sets apart as something that cannot be delimited by language or cognition; it is not ac-cessible to subjectivity or representation, that is, to the construction of con-cepts.[18] There is no point of view from which it can be grasped or eluci-dated; or, alternatively, there are too many points of view.[19] The question would be why we approach the Holocaust as if it were accessible, or as if knowledge were proper to it. But this is hardly a question, since it isn't as if we knew any other way to approach it (we cannot get out from under the metaphor of approach: we cannot cease to be modern). Blanchot mean-while is asking: How can a scream be preserved? It can be staged, repre-sented by means of art, but Blanchot is thinking of a voiceless scream that sounds endlessly in the night that the day cannot dissipate. This is a sound that cannot be registered, but neither can one ever close one's ears to it; it is a scream that sets one apart. Like the scream, the Holocaust is an unap-proachable, unappeasable memory—or, more accurately, a heterogeneous array of memories, fragments of memories—whose temporality is that of the *il y a* or the disaster.

Interestingly, Blanchot first engaged this issue in an essay published in 1962, "Être juif," which he later reprinted in *L'entretien infini* as the first part of a larger text, "L'indestructible." (The second part of this text, "L'espèce humaine," is an essay on Robert Antelme's memoir of Buchenwald, *L'espèce humaine* [1946–47], which first appeared in 1962 under the title "L'indestructible.") "Être juif" begins as an attempt to locate "Jewish difference" outside every set of categories that would characterize "Being-Jewish . . . [as] essentially a negative condition" (*EI*181/*IC*124). This means arguing principally against Sartre's famous essay that defined Jewish difference as "the negative of anti-Semitism" (*EI*181/*IC*124). Blanchot's argument, however, is not so much against Sartre or even against anti-Semitism as it is against the negative as such. It is not just that being Jewish is not a negative condition; being Jewish is existence *outside the negative*, with all that this expression entails in virtue of the position (or history) of the negative in Blanchot's thinking as the dialectical movement of conceptual determination that destroys the singularity of things and events in behalf of a totality of meaning. So we may recall once more that in "Littérature et la droit à la mort" (1948) naming is nothing less than murder, and in "Le grand refus" (1959) it is "the speech of death"—"the infamous death that is the beginning of the life of the spirit" (*EI*49/*IC*35). Being Jewish is outside all this, an affirmation unmediated by negation or destruction.[20] For most of his career Blanchot has pursued something like an affirmation not predicated upon a prior destruction—"an affirmation . . . that is not a product (the result of a double negation), and that thereby escapes all the movements, oppositions, and reversals of dialectical reason" (*EI*310/*IC*209). And if we ask, An affirmation of what?, the answer here seems to be: Of being human, where being means occupying a certain space ("l'espace/espèce humaine") rather than being in possession of a certain essence. Imagine literary space as, of all things, human—but this is exactly what Blanchot asks us to imagine: being human means being in a certain relation of human to human that is not marked by identity or a common possession but rather by the "experience of strangeness" (*EI*183/*IC*125). Being Jewish (like poetry, perhaps) opens up this other humanism.

Being Jewish is otherwise than being Greek or pagan, where the difference is between the nomadic and the fixed, and where being Jewish is "an affirmation of nomadic truth" (*EI*183/*IC*125). "To be pagan is to be fixed, to plant oneself in the earth, as it were, to establish oneself through a pact with permanence that authorizes sojourn and is certified by certainty in the land." So paganism is a metaphor of the proper, of a self-possession that brings all that it beholds under its logical extension. The nomadic is not the absence of this, not dispossession, but a separate and independent norm of residence or of being human. "Nomadism," Blanchot says, "answers to a relation that possession cannot satisfy" (*EI*183/*IC*125), namely a relation of nonidentity that is, however, not a lack of identity but rather "a new relation with the 'true'" (*EI*185/*IC*127)—one might think of it as an emancipation of the true from the rule of identity (from naming or the negative). For it is not "as if truth itself were necessarily sedentary" (*EI*186/*IC*127). Truth here is not reducible to "the word Being—in its identity" (*EI*186/*IC*127); rather, it is outside the alternatives of Being and non-Being, that is, outside the logical determinations of presence and absence. Hence the resonance of the metaphors of exile and traversal. "The words *exodus* and *exile* indicate a positive relation with exteriority, whose exigency invites us not to be content with what is proper to us (that is, with our power to assimilate everything, to identify everything, to bring everything back to our I). Exodus and exile express the same reference to the Outside that the word existence bears" (*EI*186/*IC*127). So being Jewish opens onto the order of existence without being, the *il y a*; but notice that in this context there is no experience of horror—or, more exactly, the horror of existence without being is not part of the Jewish experience of being Jewish (why not joy?). Rather the horror, one might say, is what is felt by the Greek. It is what inspires anti-Semitism; it is what anti-Semitism imposes on being Jewish.

Blanchot makes no attempt to characterize the *Jewish* experience of being Jewish—except to say (as part of his dialogue with Levinas) that "Jewish thought does not know, or refuses, mediation or speech as mediating" (*EI*187/*IC*128).[21] Jewish thought is ethical rather than conceptual, and therefore it is nondialectical, that is, its orientation is toward others rather than toward being or toward the relation of self and world, which is why Blanchot does not hesitate to characterize Judaism as a humanism (*EI*188/*IC*128), specifically a humanism of the third kind or a humanism without horizon. "To speak to someone," he says, "is to accept not introducing him into the system of things or of beings to be known; it is to recognize him as unknown and to receive him as foreign without obliging him to break with his difference" (*EI*187/*IC*128).[22] What interests Blanchot, of course (in contrast to Levinas), is, once more, the relation of foreignness that sets this humanism apart, but whereas Levinas would characterize this foreignness theologically in terms of God (*EI*187/*IC*127), for Blanchot it is the Neutral or the Outside: "To speak is to seek the source of meaning in the prefix that the words *exile*, *exodus*, *existence*, *exteriority*, and *estrangement* are

committed to unfolding in various modes of experience; a prefix that for us
designates distance and separation as the origin of all 'positive value'"
(*EI*187/*IC*128). As if meaning (say the meaning of the word human) were
anarchic; or as if "all 'positive value'" (say being human) could never be
derived from anything given but only from the *es gibt* (or the *il y a*: the
Outside) as such.

It needs to be stressed that a metaphysics of being Jewish is not a theory
of it. Metaphysics is to be understood in Levinas's sense of exteriority
rather than in Heidegger's and Derrida's sense of totality. Levinas writes:
"Metaphysics, transcendence, the welcoming of the other by the same, of
the Other by me, is concretely produced as the calling into question of the
same by the other, that is, as the ethics that accomplishes the critical
essence of knowledge. And as critique precedes dogmatism, metaphysics
precedes ontology" (*TeI*33/*TI*43). Blanchot tries to clarify his use of the
word metaphysics in a long footnote to "Être juif," where he says that the
"question that being-Jewish poses is a universal question" (*EI*191/*IC*447),
meaning that it is not the historical (and historic) "Jewish question" that assimilation was thought to answer or that Hitler tried to solve once for all.
The term *question* here has to be understood in Blanchot's sense of *exigency*, that is, "being Jewish" confronts those of us who are not Jews with
something like a demand or a claim, and this claim is of such a kind that
our response to it cannot be one of knowing, that is, it cannot be answered
with a concept—a theory, for example, as to what constitutes Jewishness.
Blanchot's idea is that the question of what counts as a Jew should remain
open—should not in any event be answered with a definition, which is always governed by a logic of negation whose murderousness is all too concrete and historical, as in Vichy's *Statut des juifs* of October 1940, a leg-
islative order (made independently of any Nazi edict concerning the Jews)
issued first to identify those who were to be excluded from political, mili-
tary, or professional positions, and then later to identify those who were to
be deported. (Recall the fragment from *Le pas au-delà:* "I think of the calling of the names in the camps . . . the impersonality of nomination bursts
forth in a manner of *something terrible* in this situation in which language
plays its murderous role" [*PD*56/*SNB*38].)

A metaphysics of being Jewish is not a representation of it but a reflection upon the radical alterity that Judaism exposes us to: "Whoever wishes
to read the meaning of the history of the Jews through Judaism," Blanchot
says, "ought to reflect upon the distance that separates man from man

when he is in the presence of *Autrui*. Jews are not different from other men in the way racism would have us believe; they rather bear witness, as Levinas says, to this relation with difference that the human face . . . reveals to us and entrusts to our responsibility; not strangers, but recalling us to the exigency of strangeness; not separated by an incomprehensible retribution, but designating as pure separation and as pure relation what, from man to man, exceeds human power—which is nonetheless capable of anything" (*EI*189/*IC*129). Jews are not strangers to non-Jews; it is rather that their relation is irreducible to categories of being and non-being, unity and diversity, identity and difference, same and other: it is a relation of separation outside every totality, an-archic, without the mediation of any principle or ideality.

It follows (and, of course, thirty years after Blanchot's essay this has become a familiar theme) that anti-Semitism is not any sort of aberration but is a matter of principle, a logic: "Anti-semitism . . . is in no way accidental; it gives a figure to the repulsion inspired by the Other, the uneasiness before what comes from afar and elsewhere: the need to kill the Other, that is, to submit to the all-powerfulness of death what cannot be measured in terms of power" (*EI*189/*IC*129). In *L'écriture du désastre* this becomes: "Judaism is the sole thought that does not mediate. And that is why Hegel, and Marx, are anti-Judaic, not to say anti-Semitic" (*ED*104/*WD*63). Anti-Semitism is the attempt to negate what is outside negation; it is the attempt to destroy the indestructible. "The anti-Semite, at grips with the infinite, thus commits himself to a limitless movement of refusal. No, truly, excluding the Jews is not enough, exterminating them is not enough; they must also be struck from history, removed from the books through which they speak to us, just as the presence that inscribed speech must finally be obliterated: the speech before and after every book and through which, from the farthest distance where all horizon is lacking, man has already turned toward man—in a word, destroy '*autrui*'" (*EI*190/*IC*130).[23]

Perhaps this text can help us to begin to understand the relation between the Holocaust and the disaster, a relation that is outside the alternatives of identity and difference. " 'Already' or 'always already' marks the disaster, which is outside history, but historically so: before undergoing it we (who is not included in this we?) will undergo it. It is a trance, motionless transgression, the passiveness of the passage beyond" (*ED*68/*WD*40). The Holocaust is not outside history. It is a historical consequence of the attempt to destroy the indestructible—"in a word, destroy '*autrui*' "—and the attempt is, historically, successful: "Man is the indestructible that can be destroyed" [*EI*192/*IC*130]). At the same time, however, the Holocaust is not a historical event like another. Blanchot clearly thinks of it as a limit of historical consciousness, something uncontainable within a history defined by the temporality of this consciousness. So Blanchot thinks of it as an interruption of history, a lesion in the history the spirit. A fragment from *Le pas au-delà* articulates this with a powerful clarity:

> That the fact of the concentration camps, the extermination of the Jews and the death camps where death continued its work, are for history an absolute which interrupted history, this one *must* say, without, however, being able to say anything else. Discourse cannot be developed from this point. Those who would need proofs will not get any, even in the assent and the friendship of those who have the same thought, there is almost no affirmation possible, because any affirmation is already shattered and friendship sustains itself with difficulty in it. All has collapsed, all collapses, no present resists it. (*PD*156/*SNB*114)[24]

But there remains the question of what it is to live through or within (or outlive) this collapse, to bear and bear witness to it. It is possible that the disaster, so far from being a category-event to which the Holocaust belongs, is internal to the Holocaust, a fragment of it, an endless array of fragments — not the whole story, therefore, perhaps not even a story within a story, but an event whose temporality is of a different order altogether from the one (ours, let us say) that tries to grasp the enormity of the Holocaust by appropriating it *as* history.

Work/Death: Affliction

Blanchot at all events does not seem to think of the Holocaust globally as a massive death-event; or, rather, he thinks of this event in terms of affliction in which annihilation is interminable and incessant, as if the death-event could be reconceptualized according to the temporality of dying (that "non-arrival of what comes about" [*PD*132/*SNB*95]). In "L'expérience de Simone Weil" (1957), Blanchot writes: "Affliction has a relation to time. Through affliction we endure 'pure' time, time without event, without project and without possibility; a kind of empty perpetuity that must be borne infinitely, and at every instant (just as fatigue and hunger must be borne in the extreme destitution of need). Let it be over. But it is without end" (*EI*176/*IC*121). For whom is it without end? An essay on Camus from the same period says: "It is intolerable but always borne, because the one who bears it is no longer there to undergo it in the first person" (*EI*259/ *IC*173). The afflicted is no one: "anonymous, impersonal, indifferent" (*EI*175/*IC*120).

Can one speak of the Shoah (annihilation) in these terms?[25]

Blanchot's thinking has been shaped by a longstanding preoccupation with what he calls "the society of the camps" (*EI*191/*IC*130), by which he means (as if indiscriminately) both concentration or labor camps like Buchenwald and extermination camps like Auschwitz. He seems to run the two together, partly perhaps because his first (and lasting) picture of the camps came from his friend Robert Antelme, a member of the Resistance who was a prisoner of war at Buchenwald and later at Dachau, and whose *L'espèce humaine* (1946–47) is an account of his experience at the hands of the SS. *L'espèce humaine* is not part of the canonical literature of the Holocaust. Antelme was not Jewish, although once in his memoir he characterizes himself and his fellow prisoners as stand-ins made to substitute for Jews, there being none left, as he imagined, in Buchenwald ("Around here the SS don't have any Jews to hand. We take their place").[26] The dedication of *L'espèce humaine* reads: "To my sister Marie-Louise, deported, killed in Germany" (p. 1).

However, in Blanchot's work Buchenwald and Auschwitz, like labor and death, are linked by an internal and comprehensive logic.

> Concentration camps, annihilation camps, emblems wherein the invisible has made itself visible forever. All the distinctive features of a civilization are revealed or laid bare ("Work liberates," "rehabilitation through work" [Auschwitz mottos]). Work, in societies where, indeed, it is highly valued as the materialist process whereby the worker takes power, becomes the ultimate punishment: no longer is it just a matter of exploitation or of surplus-value; labor becomes the point at which all value comes to pieces and the "producer," far from reproducing at least his labor force, is no longer even the reproducer of his life. For work has ceased to be his way of living and has become his way of dying. Work, death: equivalents. (*ED*129/*WD*81)

"Work, death: equivalents"; or, in the same manner of speaking, history is the equivalence of Marx and Hegel ("Thus is history formed, say Hegel and Marx—by work which realizes being in denying it, and reveals it at the end of the negation" [*PF*305/*GO*33/*WF*313–14]). What is it to fall into

human hands, or human history, when "human power is capable of anything [*le pouvoir humaine peut tout*]" (EI192/IC130)? One is, as ever, made
to work, that is, one is absorbed into the dialectic of labor (or its equivalent,
discourse) that transforms existence into something else: the domain of the
subject, civilization, the world ("the life of the Spirit is not the life that
shrinks from death and keeps itself untouched by devastation, but rather
the life that endures it and maintains itself in it" [Hegel]). But in the
camps the "invisible has been made visible": the life of the Spirit—the
philosophical discourse of modernity that otherwise embellishes the dialectic—is stripped away. Labor is essentially a process in which the la-
borer slowly (perhaps not so slowly) dies of hunger, disease, cold, or (in the
bargain) exhaustion and the inevitable beating when one's strength disappears. Antelme's memoir brings this home: "For the essentially deported
person, the one who no longer has either a face or speech, the work he is
forced to do is designed only to exhaust his power to live and to deliver
him over to the boundless insecurity of the elements. Nowhere any recourse: outside the cold, inside hunger; everywhere an indeterminate violence" (EI193/IC131).

Auschwitz was, as we know, a labor as well as a death camp—Jewish
prisoners, for example, were used to construct the crematoria ("The law's
scheme: that prisoners construct their prison themselves. This is the cul-
mination of the concept, and the concept is the mark of the system"
[ED76/WD45])—but even more to the point, I. G. Farben, the industrial
giant of the Third Reich, established a factory within the camp (artificial
rubber and synthetic gasoline) and utilized Jewish prisoners as workers;
later it was joined by Krupp. Raul Hilberg notes that the relations between
the "I.G." and the SS were superb, and that the factory very quickly
"adopted . . . the methods and mentality of the SS":

> Even during the construction stage I. G. foremen adopted the SS "work
> tempo"—for instance, the unloading of cement at a trot. One day in 1944 a
> group of arriving inmates were greeted with a speech in which they were
> told that they were now in the concentration camp of the I. G. Farben-
> industrie. They had come not in order to live there but "to perish in con-
> crete." This welcoming speech referred, according to a survivor, to an I. G.
> Farben practice of throwing the corpses of inmates into ditches which had
> been dug for cables. Like the ancient children of Israel, these corpses were
> then covered as concrete was poured over them.
> How completely the SS mentality had taken hold even of I. G. Farben di-

rectors is illustrated by the following story. One day two Buna inmates, Raymond van den Straaten and Dr. Fritz Löhner-Beda, were going about their work when a party of visiting I. G. Farben dignitaries passed by. One of the directors pointed to Dr. Löhner-Beda and said to his SS companion, "This Jewish swine could work a little faster [*Diese Judensau könnte auch rascher arbeiten*]." Another director then chanced the remark, "If they can't work, let them perish in the gas chamber [*Wenn die nicht mehr arbeiten können, sollen sie in der Gaskammer verrecken*]." After the inspection was over, Dr. Löhner-Beda was pulled out of the work party and was beaten and kicked until, a dying man, he was in the arms of his inmate friend, to end his life in I. G. Auschwitz.[27]

Likewise, Hilberg says, the SS was powerfully influenced by the I. G. and began to develop plans for the industrialization of the camps. The idea had some plausibility on paper, but since the labor force was worked according to the SS model their mortality rate was both too swift and too high, and in the end it was plain that there would never be enough Jews to make the system work (pp. 596–98). Not that plenty of Jews weren't arriving daily in "the East," the SS euphemism for the death camps, but they were mostly women, children, and old men.

Of course, most of those killed in "the East" never really became members of the "society of camps": they were processed from train to gas chamber to incinerator in a matter of a few hours—especially at the "pure killing centers" (Hilberg, p. 580), Treblinka, Sobibor, Belzec, and Kulmhof. Could anyone experience this event? So few victims realized what was happening; only those watching—the SS, the Jewish prisoners (Kapos) made to work in the extermination process—knew that the new arrivals were already dead. But experience here is not knowledge; it is, Blanchot would say, "non-knowledge" (*EI*309/*IC*208). In *L'écriture du désastre* Blanchot writes:

I think of that young prisoner of Auschwitz (he had suffered the worst, led his family to the crematorium, hanged himself; after being saved at the last moment—how can one say that: *saved?*—he was exempted from contact with dead bodies, but when the SS shot someone, he was obliged to hold the victim's head so that the bullet could be more easily lodged in the neck). When asked how he could bear this, he is supposed to have answered that he "observed the comportment of men before death" [*observait le comportement des hommes devant la mort*]. I will not believe it. As Lewental, whose notes were found buried near a crematorium, wrote to us, "The truth is always more atrocious, more tragic than what will be said about it." Saved at the last minute, the young man of whom I speak was forced to live that last instant again and each time to live it once more, frustrated every time of his own death and made to exchange it every time for the death of all. His response ("I observed the comportment of men . . . ") was not a response; he could not respond. What remains for us to recognize in this account is that when he was faced with an impossible question, he could find no other alibi than the search for knowledge, the so-called dignity of knowledge: that ultimate propriety which we believe will be accorded us by knowledge. And how, in fact, can one accept not to know? We read books on Auschwitz. The wish of all, in the camps, the last wish: know what has happened, do not forget, and at the same time never will you know. (*ED*130–31/*WD*82)

This is an odd fragment, made of two anecdotes. The first is a moral allegory of Stoic impassivity (seeing without experiencing? without witnessing?). The young man who has endured the worst is asked (by whom? someone outside of Auschwitz, a disengaged punctual ego), "How did you bear it?" And "he is supposed to have answered" (but maybe did not), "I observed [that is, followed] the comportment [that is, conduct] of men before [that is, facing] death": warriors and philosophers. But the second anecdote, that of a piece of writing left behind, an underground message from the other side of Auschwitz ("found buried near a crematorium"), testifies to the implausibility or bad faith of the first, the idea being that philosophy ("he could find no other alibi than the search for knowledge, the so-called dignity of knowledge") cannot respond to the unknown or the impossible. In any event Blanchot does not believe the young man but instead projects him into the temporality of the disaster—the between-time of dying ("death's space"), "the *pas au-delà* that does not belong to duration, that repeats itself endlessly" (*PD*145/*SNB*105)—as if to trap him inside the moment of survival (as if in fact he had not yet experienced the worst): "Saved at the last minute, the young man . . . was forced to live that last instant again and each time to live it once more, frustrated every time of his own death and made to exchange it every time for the death of all." So he commits suicide—which we know from *L'espace littéraire* is philosophy's response to the impossible: "Voluntary death is the refusal to see the other death, the death one cannot grasp, which one never reaches" (*EL*134/*SL*106).[28] What is it to see the other death?

"The suffering of our time: '*A wasted man, bent head, bowed shoulders, unthinking, gaze extinguished*'" (*ED*129/*WD*81).

"They crowd my memory with their faceless presences," writes Primo Levi, "and if I could enclose all the evil of our time in one image, I would choose this image which is familiar to me: an emaciated man, with head dropped and shoulders curved, on whose face and in whose eyes not a trace of thought is to be seen."[29]

In Auschwitz it was called "Moslemization":

> When they could still walk, they moved like automatons; once stopped, they were capable of no further movement. They fell prostrate on the ground; nothing mattered any more to them. Their bodies blocked the passageway. You could step right on them and they wouldn't draw back their arms and legs an inch. No protest, no cry of pain came from their half-open mouths. And yet they were still alive. The Kapos, even the SS men, could beat and push them, but they would not budge; they had become insensible to everything. They were men without thoughts, without reactions, without souls, one might say. Sometimes, under blows, they would suddenly start moving, like cattle, jostling against each other. Impossible to get them to tell their names, much less the date of their birth. Even gentleness was not enough to make them talk; they would only give you an expressionless stare. And when they tried to answer, their tongues could not touch their dessicated palates to produce sounds. You smelled only a poisonous breath, as though it issued from entrails already in a state of decomposition.[30]

Here, for Blanchot, is the true "society of the camps." "Their life is short," Primo Levi says, "but their number is endless; they, the *Muselmänner*, the drowned, form the backbone of the camp, an anonymous mass, continually renewed and always identical, of non-men who march and labour in silence, the divine spark dead within them, already too empty to really suffer. One hesitates to call them living: one hesitates to call their death death, in the face of which they have no fear, as they are too tired to understand" (p. 90). Recall from *Le pas au-delà* the inhabitants of the "posthumous city" (PD83/SNB58), the anonymous *ils*, the neutral and fatigued, who do not see anyone, who "exist at the limit of existence, surviving in survival" (PD178/SNB131).

Affliction, Blanchot says, is a form of suffering "that has lost time altogether. It is the horror of a suffering without end, a suffering time can no longer redeem, that has escaped time and for which there is no longer recourse; it is irremediable" (EI257/IC172). It is outside the history which brings it about (outside explanation: an-archic, without why); it is outside the history that would atone for it (outside, once for all, salvation history).

As Geoffrey Hartman might say, there is poetry but no redemption after
Auschwitz.[31] What could redeem the time of affliction? Affliction is the
mode of existence of survival, the survivor's mode of existence, living on as
if the death-event had no terminus. It a form of existence without being:
separate, foreign, without horizon. Nothing follows survival. No more narratives, no more utopias. No after-life, no Messiah.

At least, no Christian Messiah, arriving (this time, the second time, on
a cloud) with the end of history in his wake. Affliction is not despair, not nihilism. It is not empty time, as of unfulfilled prophecies; rather it is a time of
infinite patience, of passivity without passion, a time without duration whose
Messiah is, without reason (without why), already present—as if freed from
the narrative of history. *L'écriture du désastre* contains a fragment (on messianism) with this warning: "it would be wrong to speak of the Messiah in
Hegelian language" (ED215/WD142). Jewish messianism, Blanchot says,
concerns "the relation between the event and its nonoccurrence" (ED214/
WD141). By contrast, Christian messianism—or its secular equivalent, political millennialism—functions as a distancing factor: it is a mechanism
for transporting ourselves out of the without-end (escaping Auschwitz).
Perhaps it is not too much to think of it as a kind of suicide, a refusal or inability to witness (but witness before whom?). In any case Blanchot's question is: "Can one maintain any distance at all when Auschwitz happens?
How is it possible to say: Auschwitz has happened?" (ED216/WD143)—
that is, how can one say (thank God) it is over and done with?

Blanchot writes: "He who has been the contemporary of the camps is
forever a survivor: death will not make him die" (ED217/WD143). Being
contemporary: what category of being is this? Suppose it means: belonging to the temporality of the camps, whence Auschwitz is interminable,
endless?

The Writing of the Disaster

Go back to the young prisoner at Auschwitz who hangs himself. Why does
he do it? We say: there is something he cannot face—namely, survival, the
"other death," the *entre-temps* in which the sovereignty of the cognitive
subject drains away into "the sovereignty of a being without being in the
becoming without end of a death impossible to die" (EI310/IC209). But
what if this is not right (or, at all events, not enough)? What if it is rather
that, having witnessed the impossible, the young man is then required to

reflect on it and to speak of it as if he were still a subject of experience?

It is reported that when Robert Antelme was set free he could not stop talking—"he experiences a kind of drunkenness of speech. Antelme talks, narrates everything he has seen, undergone, and his full memory unwinds like a skein."[32] Perhaps this simply means that he had not suffered the worst. But who speaks here, if anyone? Blanchot remarks that Antelme's book is not (or not just) a prisoner's memoir: "It is not . . . simply a witness's testimony to the reality of the camps or a historical reporting, nor is it an autobiographical narrative. It is clear that for Robert Antelme, and very surely for many others, it is a question not of telling one's story, of testifying, but essentially of *speaking* [parler]" (*EI*198/*IC*134). As if Antelme had become a "narrative voice," the voice of the other according to Blanchot's theory of alterity where, "when the other speaks, no one speaks . . . neither one nor the other" (*EI*564/*IC*385). Autobiography, self-reference, remains the work of the negative: "To write one's autobiography," Blanchot says, "is perhaps to seek to survive, but through a perpetual suicide" (*ED*105/ *WD*64). The voice of the other, the voice of affliction, emanates not so much from a self as from a nowhere or elsewhere, because "the one afflicted no longer has any identity other than the situation with which he merges" (*EI*194/*IC*131). Antelme's garrulousness, his inability to stop talking, is the form that responsibility takes: it is speech that escapes the dialectic ("responsibility of a speech that speaks without exercising any form of power" [*EI*445/*IC*302]; cf. Bartleby: "Bartleby copies; he writes incessantly, and cannot stop long enough to submit to anything resembling control" [*ED*219/*WD*145]). What comes out at all events is not a narrative but something closer to a cry:

> —Yes, one had to speak: to entitle speech in responding to the silent presence of the other that is *autrui*. The unique authority of this speech coming directly from this very exigency.
> —It was, in fact, the most immediate exigency that can be. I have to speak. An infinite demand [*Revendication infini*] that imposes itself with an irrepressible force. And it was as well an overwhelming discovery, a painful surprise: I speak, am I speaking? Could I now truly speak? Nothing more grave than this being able to speak from the basis of the impossible, the infinite distance to be "filled" by language itself. "*And yet,*" says Robert Antelme, "*it was impossible. We had hardly begun to speak and we were choking.*" (*EI*199/*IC*135)

In "Réflexions sur l'enfer" (1954) Blanchot associates this speech ("speech which speaks outside all power to represent and to signify") with the "song of Orpheus: a language that does not push hell back, but makes its way into it, speaking at the level of the abyss and thereby giving word to it; giving a hearing to what can have no hearing" (*EI*274/*IC*183–84). The next thought would therefore have to be: No poetry after Auschwitz? Only if you think, as philosophers do, that poetry is just happy-talk. Recall the motto of Blanchot's "great refusal": *Nommant le possible, répondant à la impossible* (*EI*68/*IC*48): so if poetry is the language of affliction, that is, of survival, then there could only be poetry after Auschwitz.

In order to understand the agony (and suicide) of the young prisoner, it is important to understand the link between the "impossibility of ever stopping [*l'impossibilité de s'arrêter jamais*]" (*EI*302/*IC*202), the impossibility of keeping silent (*ED*51/*WD*29), and the "great refusal," the refusal of death or of philosophy—Bartleby's refusal, the "I prefer not to," which is (to repeat) not a counterattack but a passivity outside all active or passive resistance: Blanchot calls it a resistance "no dialectical intervention can take hold of" (*ED*33/*WD*17). "How did you bear it?" is a philosopher's question, a dialectical intervention from someone who wants to know how something is possible, to which the young man gives the correct answer (the only answer the interrogator would know how to hear). "How did you bear it?" The question conceals a fatal recrimination: it says, "You had no right to bear it." The young prisoner, in a desperate effort of self-justification, philosophizes himself—*J'observais le comportement des hommes devant la mort:* I followed the model of Socrates, he says. And he continued to do so: "the true philosophical act is the putting to death of oneself" (*ED*56/*WD*32).[33]

Antelme's speech by contrast is almost entirely without self-reference: the "I" of *L'espèce humaine* is almost always submerged in a "we," or (increasingly) in an empty body—"I chewed slowly. The bread resisted a little. I was chewing—that's all I did, doing it with my whole body. Cologne captured or not captured, I was chewing. Whether the war ended in two months or a year, right now I was chewing. I knew that hunger would not part company with me, that I would still be hungry, but I chewed: that was what was called for, that and that alone" (p. 82). Later: "I am two trudging feet, one dragging after another; I am a drooping head" (p. 237). Toward the end, there is only "a kind of deaf, blind memory of consciousness" (p. 264).

However, there is a remarkable moment when one of the prisoners at Buchenwald produces a mirror. Everyone crowds around, asking to borrow it: "We wanted to look at ourselves" (p. 51). Antelme hadn't seen himself for months. When his turn comes, he hesitates, then looks: "First of all I saw a face appear. I had forgotten about that" (p. 51). A face is an anomaly, that is, in the camps a face is something one ceases to have. "The SS man's stare, his behavior toward us—which never varied—meant that for him no difference existed between one prisoner's face and another's" (pp. 51–52). Moreover, one is not allowed to present one's face to the SS:

> No one, by means of his face, was to express to the SS anything that might have been the beginning of a dialogue and that might have been able to bring into being upon the SS man's face anything else than the permanent and impartial negation reserved for everyone. Thus, as a face was not only useless but also, in spite of itself, rather dangerous, in our relations with the SS we reached the point where we made an effort to negate our faces ourselves, an effort which perfectly matched the negation practiced by the SS. Denied, doubly denied, or else as laughable and as provocative as a mask— for indeed it was nothing else than to provoke a scandal, this carrying of our one-time face, the mask of a human being—our face had, for us, finally become absent from our life. For even in our relations with other prisoners our life remained burdened by this absence; our life had almost become that absence. Of the same striped outfits, of the same shaved heads, of our progressive emaciation, of the rhythm of our life here, for each of us what finally appeared generally amounted to a collective, anonymous face. (p. 52)

The mirror works as a kind of magic looking-glass. In the camp, one is faceless, or a face without features, but in the mirror one returns to the remains of an ethical world. "Only the [face] in the mirror was distinct. It alone signified something that couldn't be accepted here. This piece of glass opened out upon a mirage. We weren't that way here; we were only that way all alone in the mirror" (p. 52). Antelme finds his own face "dazzling," but exposed and vulnerable to the camp-face: "Even if I hadn't had to pass the mirror on to somebody else who was waiting for it avidly, I would have let it go, because I was already contaminating the face in it. It was getting old; it was going to model itself on the standard face around here, sagging, wretched, like a pair of hands one stares at hollow-eyed" (p. 53). The camp is no place for a face. Having a face produces an unwanted, intolerable subjectivity—"It could only provoke a radical despair. . . . What it presented was not a past state, which, like other past states, one would

have had only to remember, and which like all the others might simply
have been wrenching. What was presented here was exhausting. It was
what one could—really could—become again tomorrow, and that was impossibility itself" (p. 53).

The voice of *L'espèce humaine* is a voice from behind a camp face—
"voice of no one, once more" (ED121/WD75)—not the voice of a face in the
mirror. In 1962 Blanchot reads or hears it as a human voice for all that: "So
now we understand this reserved speech of *autrui*; a speech unheard, inexpressible, nevertheless unceasing, silently affirming that where all relation is lacking there yet subsists, there already begins, the human relation
in its primacy. It is this truly infinite speech that each of those who had
been handed over to the impossible experience of being for himself or herself the 'other' [*autrui*] felt called upon, now back in the world, to represent to us in speaking endlessly, without stopping, for the first time"
(EI199/IC135). The affirmation outside possibility—outside the negative,
outside language—is of "the human relation in its primacy," that is, of the
other humanism irreducible to identity, community, or shared ground: an
anarchic humanism, humanism without principle, humanism freed from
the rule of value, obviously not the humanism of humanists.

In *L'écriture du désastre* the affirmation outside negation is an event of
(among other things) skepticism, where skepticism is no longer Carte-
sian—no longer a position occupied by a doubtful subject: "it is not simply nihilist negation: rather, irony" (ED123/WD76), call it a last romantic
or anarchic irony. (Cf. the irony of the *il y a* [ED108/WD65].) For Blanchot, skepticism occupies the site of poetry (and madness) vis-à-vis reason
or the negative; that is, it is not in a dialectic relation with the negative,
which is why, vis-à-vis philosophy, it cannot be refuted or, more accurately,
it can be and is endlessly refuted (perpetually destroyed, like the indestructible): "Skepticism is the return of the refuted, that which erupts anarchically, capriciously, and irregularly each time . . . that authority and
the sovereignty of reason, indeed of unreason, impose their order upon us
or organize themselves definitively into a system" (ED123/WD76). Being
nondialectical, skepticism is an-archic, neutral or without principle or
rule, rather than chaotic or disintegrative: "Skepticism does not destroy the
system; it destroys nothing" (ED123/WD76). Anarchy is comic, not tragic
—Blanchot thinks of it as "a sort of gaiety without laughter" (ED123/
WD76: nowhere in Blanchot is there any laughter).

Here one remembers Levinas's remarks concerning "the inanity of the "man-as-principle, the inanity of principle [*l'inanité de l'homme-principe, l'inanité du Principe*]" (*HAH*81/*CPP*132). The humanism of humanists is a humanism *au-delà*, a humanism of the higher ground, a humanism that overcomes whatever stands in its way—for example, the more- or less-than-human, the monstrous or the *autrui* "who risks being always Other than man, close to what cannot be close to me: close to death, close to the night, and certainly as repulsive as anything that comes to me from this region without horizon" (*EI*103/*IC*72). Perhaps one could speak of a humanism of survivors, not, obviously, as if they occupied a special place or held a special set of beliefs that would set them apart (say from nonhumanists, whatever that could mean), but because they are separated from me by a distance that I cannot overcome or by a relation that cannot be filled in by any ideality or transformed into any form of mediation. They are marked—set apart—by this distance, this separation or foreignness. They are (the) outside, the reverse or an-archic side of being. ("Zombies, pariahs, infidels [*morts-vivants, parias, musulmans*]: such is the truth of life" [*ED*131/*WD*82].) A disastrous humanism—which is what Blanchot affirmed in 1967 as a humanism without identity, outside the logos, outside language, in the space of "the cry—that is to say, the murmur; cry of need or of protest, cry without words and without silence, an ignoble cry—or, if need be, the written cry, graffiti on the walls" (*EI*392/*IC*262). Or the *nachlass* of Auschwitz: "As Lewental, whose notes were found buried near a crematorium, wrote to us, 'The truth was always more atrocious, more tragic than what will be said about it'" (*ED*131/*WD*82).

In *L'écriture du désastre* Blanchot writes: "We read books on Auschwitz. The wish of all, in the camps, the last wish: know what has happened, do not forget, and at the same time never will you know" (*ED*131/*WD*82). We read books on Auschwitz, as if knowledge could redeem the claim the event has on us, but the higher humanism (or, say, philosophy) fails us. "Whence the temptation to appeal to ethics, with its conciliating function (justice and responsibility)." This is the temptation of Levinas's ethics as a first philosophy or philosophy without reason (without why). "But when ethics goes mad in its turn, as it must, what does it contribute if not a safe-conduct which allows our conduct no rights, leaves us no space to move and ensures us of no salvation? [*un sauf-conduit qui ne laisse à notre conduite nul droit, nulle place, ni aucun salut*]" (*ED*48/*WD*27). Mad ethics, an ethics of disaster, would be an ethics of nonredemption.

Or, much to the same point, it would no longer be an ethics of responsibility (at least not in Levinas's sense of responsibility as substitution). If I have it right, it would be an ethics of patience — of "double patience . . . speakable, unspeakable patience [*patience mondaine, patience immonde*]" (*ED48/WD27*), but perhaps it were better to speak of infinite patience, like the patience of the Jews beneath the Roman ramparts who await the nonarrival of the Messiah. Mad ethics is the ethics of *le pas au-delà*, or of "the passivity of a time without present" (*ED29/WD14*): "Patience opens me entirely, all the way to a passivity which is the *pas* ["not"] in the utterly passive, and which has therefore abandoned the level of life where passive would simply be the opposite of active" (*ED28/WD13*). A mad ethics, an ethics of passivity, could just as well be called an ethics of madness, since "passivity is, perhaps (perhaps), that 'inhuman' part of man which, destitute of power, separated from unity, could never accommodate anything able to appear or show itself. . . . [E]scaping our power to speak of it as well as our power to test it (to try or experience it), passivity is posed or deposed as that which would interrupt our reason, our speech, our experience" (*ED32/WD16*). Let us call this an ethics, not of silence, but of refusal, keeping instead an endless vigil.

What drives ethics mad?

Perhaps the same thing that draws Blanchot obsessively to the image of the *musulman* of the camps, a figure whose abjection or exteriority is so pure or so absolute that no relation with him is possible, as if our response to him could no longer take the ethical form of responsibility but required (as in our encounter with the last man) a turn or detour in our relation to being and time.

Dull, extinguished eyes burn suddenly with a savage gleam for a shred of bread, "even if one is perfectly aware that death is a few minutes away" and that there is no longer any point in nourishment. This gleam, this brilliance does not illuminate anything living. However, with this gaze which is a last gaze, bread is given us as bread. This gift, outside all reason, and at the point where all values have been exterminated — in nihilist desolation and when all objective order has been given up — maintains life's fragile chance by the sanctification of hunger — nothing "sacred," let us understand, but something which is given without being broken or shared by him who is dying of it (*"Great is hungering,"* Levinas says, recalling a Jewish saying). But at the same time the fascination of the dying gaze, where the spark of life congeals, does not leave intact the need's demand [*l'exigence du besoin*], not even in a primitive form, for it no longer allows hunger (it no longer allows bread) to be related in any way to nourishment. In this extreme moment when dying is exchanged for the life of bread, not, any longer, in order to satisfy a need and still less in order to make bread desirable, need—in need—also dies as simple need. And it exalts, it glorifies—by making it into something inhuman (withdrawn from all satisfaction)—the need of bread which has become an empty absolute where henceforth we can all only ever lose ourselves. (ED133–34/WD84)

Need, Levinas says, "is the primary movement of the same" (TeI119/TI116). In the metaphysics of the *musulman,* need is no longer a movement but a passivity. If, as Levinas says, the "distance intercalated between man and the world on which he depends constitutes the essence of need" (TeI120/ TI116), the *musulman* now regards the world with something like the gaze of Orpheus, that is, with a gaze freed from the good, a gaze that (in the extreme moment of its look) frees the good from its objective status within or atop the order of value. But evidently we must be careful not to confuse need and desire (this is Levinas's instruction), and, just so, the *musulman* converts ("exalts") need into desire, where desire is metaphysical, that is, "a desire for what we are not in want of, a desire that cannot be satisfied and that does not desire union with what it desires" (EI76/IC53).

Perhaps the calm of the disaster—*"the undesirable calm"* (ED138/ WD87)—is registered in the *musulman,* who belongs to something like a "negative community" ("the community for those who have no community" [CI46/UC25]): a community without communion and without redemption, a community without principle or foundation—a community constituted, if that is the word, simply by everyone else's death.

CHAPTER 10

The Anarchist's Last Word

Wittgenstein's all too famous and all too often repeated pre-
cept, "Whereof one cannot speak, there one must be
silent"—given that by enunciating it he has not been able to
impose silence on himself—does indicate that in the final
analysis one has to talk in order to remain silent. But with
what kinds of words? That is one of the questions this little
book entrusts to others, not that they may answer it, but rather
that they may choose to carry it with them, and, perhaps, extend it. Thus one will discover that it also carries an exacting
political meaning and that it does not permit us to lose interest in the present time which, by opening new spaces of
freedom, makes us responsible for new relationships, always
threatened, always hoped for, between what we call work,
œuvre, and what we call unworking, désœuvrement.
                    —*La communauté inavouable*

Refusal/Survival

What is survival? In the simplest possible language, it is *le grand refus*—the
refusal of "the infamous death that is the beginning of the life of the spirit"
(EI49/IC35). In *L'écriture du désastre* Blanchot asks: "*What does to survive
mean, if not to be sustained by an assent to refusal* [acquiescement au re-
fus], *by the exhaustion of feeling, and to live withdrawn from any interest in
oneself, disinterested, thinned out to a state of utter calmness, expecting
nothing?*" (ED179/WD116). It is important to stress here the condition of
being "withdrawn" from any subjective existence. Refusal is not (or not
just) an attitude of individual rebellion (A131).

The context of Blanchot's definition of survival in *L'écriture du désastre* is given by a half-dozen fragments that gloss and embellish a proposition paraphrased from the French Lacanian Serge Leclaire: "According to him, one lives and speaks only by killing the *infans* in oneself (in others also); but what is the infans?" (*ED*110/*WD*67). Blanchot had already answered this question in his essay on psychoanalysis, "La parole analytique" (first published in 1956 under the title "Freud"), where he unhesitatingly identified the infant with the *il y a*, existence without being: "To be born is, after having had everything, suddenly to lack everything, and first of all being, inasmuch as the infant exists neither as an organized, self-contained body nor as a world. For the infant, everything is exterior, and he himself is scarcely anything but this exterior: the outside, a radical exteriority without unity, a dispersion without anything dispersing" (*EI*346/*IC*231–32). The killing of the infant (in oneself or others: suicide or murder) is therefore the "primal scene," the "primary event," in the constitution of being human (so infanticide replaces parricide and fratricide in the foundation of things). This scene or event corresponds to the transition in Lacan's theory from the specular to the symbolic, and to the dialectical movement in Hegel from the singular to the conceptual (the one is already modeled on the other—Lacan was a regular participant in Kojève's seminar on Hegel's *Phenomenologie*). In Blanchot's analysis, however, there is more than a symmetry between the work of psychoanalysis and the work of the negative that produces meaningful speech, because in the psychoanalytic project speech must, in effect, be extracted from a patient who remains on the hither (infantile) side of language. Psychoanalysis is in this respect an instrumental branch of the dialectic; it is a species of the confessional: it "becomes under these conditions an *institution* (whether or not willingly), risks serving the institutional forms that alone, historically, have a hold on speech" (*EI*354/*IC*455).[1] As a discourse of possibility, psychoanalysis is, like philosophy, unresponsive, that is, structurally repressive with respect to the impossible or indestructible. Its job is to negate what is outside the negative.

"La parole analytique" highlights the paradox that in Lacanian analysis this extraction of speech from the other is achieved through the method of silence. The analyst does not speak but draws the patient out by withdrawing behind a mask of neutrality (he is "the most negligent and absent of auditors, someone without a face, scarcely someone; a kind of anyone at all . . . who, like a hollow in space, a silent emptiness, is, nonetheless, the real reason for speaking" [*EI*348/*IC*233]): "For the [patient], there is the freedom to say anything at all; for the other, that of listening without attending, as though without knowing it and as though he were not there. And there is this freedom that becomes the cruelest of constraints"—the patient is, in effect, forced to speak, "little by little speaking as though on the basis of the impossibility of speech; an impossibility that is always already in the words as much as on their hither side, an emptiness and a blank that is neither a secret nor something passed over in silence but rather something always already said" (EI348/IC233). As if the impossibility of speaking were not a defect in the patient, not something accessible to a cure but something internal to language—which is in fact how Blanchot expressed it in Le pas au-delà: "Behind discourse the refusal to discourse speaks, as behind philosophy the refusal to philosophize would speak: speech not speaking, violent, concealing itself, saying nothing and suddenly crying out" (PD158/SNB116). Refusal in this respect is not a subjective possibility but an exigency: a break-in or interruption, like Bartleby's passivity, which brings work to a halt.

Just so, the last section of "La parole analytique" raises the question, "When, then, is the cure over?," and the answer is that it is never over, because the impossibility of speaking can never be completely destroyed (for the same reason that exteriority, the il y a, is "indestructible"); it can only be experienced as an impossibility of concluding, which is why the psychoanalytic dialogue, however structured dialectically as a philosophical dialogue aimed at true speech ("the supreme contentment that is the equivalent of death, as Socrates already suggested"), remains, ironically, a species of infinite conversation (EI353/IC236). The patient, in effect, never quite dies but merely speaks madly, that is, à la Sade, "never stopping" (EI329/IC221). Analysis, being interminable and incessant, is thus something like a mode of survival, that is, a "movement that is not dialectical, that threatens every dialectic, and that also speaks in language itself—a speech that is neither true nor false, neither sensible nor senseless but always both one and the other: the most profound speech, but speech that speaks as a depth without depth" (EI353/IC236–37). To which Blanchot adds: "Perhaps it is the dangerous duty of the psychoanalyst to seek to suppress this speech, suppressing that which in fact opposes all supposedly normal conduct and expression—but also suppressing himself, thereby meeting up again with death, his truth" (EI353–54/IC237).

"La parole analytique" is in fact a tribute to Lacan's refusal to suppress this speech of the other, which famously—perhaps endlessly—interrupted his own seminars. In her history of pyschoanalysis in France, Elisabeth Roudinesco gives this account of Lacan's seminars during the 1950s:

> There [in the ampitheater at Sainte-Anne], over a period of ten years, he held forth in a vacillating voice, alternately faltering and thunderous, laced with sighs and hesitations. He would note down in advance what he would say, and then, in the presence of his audience, improvise like an actor from the Royal Shakespeare Company who might have had Greta Garbo as diction coach and Arturo Toscanini as spiritual guide. Lacan played false because he was speaking true, as though through the rigor of a voice perpetually on the verge of cracking, he was, like some ventriloquist, effecting the resurgence of the secret mirror of the unconscious, the symptom of a mastery endlessly on the brink of collapse. A sorcerer without magic, a guru without hypnosis, a prophet without god, he fascinated his audience in an admirable language effecting, in the margins of desire, the revival of a century of enlightenment.[2]

(Here one should consult a fragment of conversation in *Le pas au-delà* that begins: "I refuse this speech by which you speak to me" [*PD*159/ *SNB*116]. One can easily imagine this fragment as a dialogue between analyst and patient, where the difference between the two gradually turns from a logical relation, say a relation of mastery and submission, into a relation of foreignness in which the two have become neither one nor the other, neither analyst nor patient. One can just as easily imagine that this same dialogue occurs in Lacan's seminars. Anyhow when listening with Blanchot's ears one can hear in Lacan's ludic monologue the refusal of discourse that in *Le pas au-delà* speaks as follows: "I am there in your logic also, denouncing the oppression of a coherence that makes itself the law and I am there with my violence that affirms itself under the mask of your legal violence, that which submits thought to the grip of comprehension" [*PD*159–60/*SNB*117].)

In *L'écriture du désastre* Blanchot returns to this analytic paradox in order to reflect on the child whose death is, on the one hand, a logical necessity (a given)—namely the condition of possibility on which the life of the spirit depends—and, on the other, an impossibility, a death that slips away: the interminable, incessant *entre-temps* or interruption (*le pas au-delà*) that puts paid to the dialectic, rendering "the *Aufhebung* null and void" (*ED*113/*WD*69). Blanchot has been fixated on this paradox since his first essays on Kafka (*PF*16–17/*WF*7–9). It is the subject of chapter 5 of

Thomas l'obscur. In *L'espace littéraire* it is the paradoxical impossibility of suicide, "the fact [that] dying . . . includes a radical reversal, through which the death that was the extreme form of my power only becomes what loosens my hold upon myself by casting me out of my power to begin and even to finish, but also becomes that which is without any relation to me, without power over me—that which is stripped of all possibility—the unreality of the indefinite"; or, in other words, impossibility (*EL*133/*SL*106; cf. *ED*114/*WD*70). In "Le grand refus" the paradox is figured in terms of the double death of Lazarus, whose corpse is assigned to the tomb only to be summoned back by an act of naming that murders him: "But what does this Lazarus saved and raised from the dead that you hold out to me have to do with what is lying there and makes you draw back, the anonymous corruption of the tomb, the lost Lazarus who already smells bad and not the one restored to life by a force that is no doubt admirable, but that is precisely a force and that comes in this decision from death itself?" (*EI*50/*IC*35-36). Naturally this leaves open the question of where, when all is said, Lazarus is: perhaps neither here nor there. Perhaps he returns as a philosopher, fearful of the impossibility he has experienced; or as an endlessly aging conversationalist ("As if death, through him, distracted itself" [*PD*181/*SNB*133]).

In its longest fragment *L'écriture du désastre* recapitulates the whole history of Blanchot's dialectical obsession, starting with Hegel (that is, as always, Kojève's Hegel): "Yes, let us remember the earliest Hegel," and the idea "that only the act of confronting death . . . could found the sovereignty of masterhood: the mind and its prerogatives" (*ED*112/*WD*68).[3] But what the master experiences is the withdrawal or inaccessibility of death, and (in turn) the fear which anyone can see is etched on his philosophical face: "It remains, however, that if death, murder, suicide are put to work, and if death loses its sting by becoming powerless power and then negativity, there is, each time one advances with the help of *possible* death, the necessity not to advance any further, not to approach the death without expression, the death without any name, the death outside the concept—*impossibility* itself" (*ED*112/*WD*68).[4] Impossibility cannot be overcome: the child (in us, in others) whom we destroy is "indestructible" (*ED*111/*WD*67), as if finally there were no beyond beyond impossibility—as if the dialectic were, not a monumental fraud perhaps, but only one more supreme fiction (*ED*113/*WD*71). There is no beyond beyond impossibility: this is what *le pas au-delà* means—Paul Davies calls this the "logic of the

désastre," a logic that belongs to a different (an-archic, a-logical) temporality from that of the dialectic and which implies therefore an alternative
future (if "future" is the word) to that projected by the logic of the *Aufhebung.*[5] The logic of the disaster—only a philosopher would think to use
the word "logic" in this context—is the "logic" of survival, which Blanchot
commemorates in the central fragment of *L'écriture du désastre:*

> (A primal scene?) *You who live later, close to a heart that beats no more, sup-
> pose, suppose this: the child—is he seven years old, or eight perhaps?—stand-
> ing by the window, drawing the curtain and, through the pane, looking. What
> he sees: the garden, the wintry trees, the wall of a house. Though he sees, no
> doubt in a child's way, his play space, he grows weary and slowly looks up to-
> ward the ordinary sky, with clouds, grey light—pallid daylight without depth.*
>
> *What happens then: the sky, the same sky, suddenly open, absolutely black
> and absolutely empty, revealing (as though the pane had been broken) such
> an absence that all has since always and forevermore been lost therein—so
> lost that therein is affirmed and dissolved the vertiginous knowledge that noth-
> ing is what there is, and first of all nothing beyond* [rien est ce qu'il y a, et
> d'abord rien au-delà]. *The unexpected aspect of this scene (its interminable
> feature) is the feeling of happiness that straightaway submerges the child, the
> ravaging joy to which he can bear witness only by tears, an endless flood of
> tears. He is thought to suffer a childish sorrow; attempts are made to console
> him. He says nothing. He will live henceforth in the secret. He will weep no
> more.* (ED117/WD72)

Living henceforth in the secret might mean: the child will live henceforth
in vigilance, possibly like the Jewish outcasts of the first centuries who
awaited the Messiah beneath the Roman ramparts—who for all we know
may be waiting still (ED43/WD23). The starless (disastrous) sky is without
augury: "nothing is what there is, and first of all nothing beyond." Not surprisingly, some pages later Blanchot quotes Paul Celan to just this same
point: " '*Poetry, ladies and gentlemen: an expression of infinity, an expression of vain death and of mere Nothing*' (Celan)," where infinity is to be
understood in the sense of the interminable (the "infinite conversation,"
for example, or whatever continues after everything has been said), and
where death is vain because it no longer belongs to the same economy as
work (ED143/WD90).[6] (And this of course was Bataille's insight: death is a
nonproductive expenditure.)

Suppose, in other words, a child discovers that it (*il*) has escaped the
death in which the life of the spirit maintains itself. Of course, the child is

now no longer an infant: at seven or eight, it is already beyond its years, is already in the world, progressing (to all appearances) normally, except that something has been held back, kept in reserve, call it a "secret," it doesn't matter of what—"The secret alluded to is that there is none, except for those who refuse to tell" (ED177/WD114). Let us suppose a secret life rather than a secret message: "Life without any of the surpassing indicated by the prefix of 'survival'—life in the absence of any relation of temporal necessity, life which is without any present and which universal duration (the concept of time) does not govern, any more than the intimate singularity of a lived time affirms it": this is just le pas au-delà all over again—"pure difference, the lapse of time, the unbridgeable interval which, crossed, becomes limitless by virtue of the impossibility of any crossing (it is impossible to cross, inasmuch as it is already crossed)" (ED162–63/WD105). The secret, like the prophecy, belongs to the temporality of survival (ED134/WD85); it is like the lèthé in Heidegger's alèthéia—although Blanchot himself parses this term as alè-théia, "uncovering a meaning which could be translated as divine wandering," as of gods in exile (ED148/WD94), and then again as a-lèthéia, that is, "de-sheltering" or exposure to the outside (ED149/WD95): "Whence the precaution of not overemphasizing the too-well-known phrase: 'language is the house of being.'" Imagine truth as "the revelation of the outside" (ED178/WD115), a revelation neither of being nor of nonbeing, like a prophecy neither empty nor fulfilled: a prophecy or revelation that bears the same nondialectical structure as all the rest of Blanchot's impossible expressions: "presence without anything present," "experience of non-experience," "knowledge of the unknown," "thought thinking that which will not let itself be thought," and so on ad infinitum. The child evidently experiences such a revelation through the broken windowpane (ED178/WD115).[7]

The revelation is not important, bears neither repeating nor anything repeatable, is not news good or bad, anyhow is not memorable, cannot be made into a story; a cult or secret society will not form around it (unless Blanchot is really Bataille in disguise). What matters is that the child does not speak of it, meaning that he does not so much keep the secret to himself, as if secrecy had anything to do with privacy, as that he already finds himself in that other world—the other of all worlds, histories, spaces, etc.—that the "assent to refusal" affirms. The survival of the child is not progressive, not a triumph of life over death. "The transcendence that living is," Blanchot says, "cannot be satisfactorily expressed in life itself as survival (a surpassing of life [*sur-vie, dépassement de la vie*])." It can never be as if one had escaped the end. Rather survival is a response to "the exigency of an *other* life, the life of the other" (*ED*163/*WD*105): life outside of life.

Accordingly, near the end of *L'écriture du désastre* Blanchot quotes Guy Lardreau and Christian Jambert: "'The ethics of revolt is opposed to all classical notions of the Sovereign Good, and to all moral or immoral claims, for it constructs, protects, maintains an empty place, letting another history come to us'" (*ED*209/*WD*138). Revolt, Blanchot explains, or adds, is not rebellion but a "turning point where time changes" (*ED*209/*WD*138), that is, turns upside down in an insubordination that will never yield to the future into which the millennialist projects the Sovereign Good. "This does not mean," Blanchot says—for whose benefit, one wonders?—"that one should not struggle against the master with the instruments of his mastery" (*ED*209/*WD*138). As if Blanchot's anarchism were not opposed to the classic "performance" of the demolition expert—Blanchot can still pay homage to what Arthur Redding calls "the dream life of political violence." One suspects that Blanchot would read the history of anarchism as a history of futility in much the way that Redding does in his account of the American labor movement, where most often "proponents and perpetrators of violence within the union halls were plants, double agents, private detectives, the hired guns of industry itself, who wished either to provoke strikers or to prove afterwards in court that violence was the intent of the strikers. Violence in any form generally culminated in a rhetorical and economic victory for industry; the language of the disenfranchised became the political instrument of their overlords, for, in a sort of ironic reversal of Sorel, it galvanized the public consciousness with the fear of anarchy."[8] Dialectical anarchism always loses because the dialectic always serves the order of things. This is what Blanchot teaches; it is perhaps what his early experience of fascism taught him.

So alongside the history of the possible—Pascal's, Kierkegaard's, Sartre's, or Bakunin's and Sorel's possible—Blanchot locates a history of the impossible: "Foreign to the succession of moments . . . the other history is the deployment of a plurality which is not that of the world or of numbers. It is history in excess, a 'secret,' separate history, which presupposes the end of visible history, though it denies itself the very idea of beginning or end" (*ED*209/*WD*139). In other words, in contrast to the history of the spirit or the history of being—and even the history of anarchism—there is anarchic history, where revolt is nondialectical, like Bartleby's "I prefer not to"—or, to change the example, Wittgenstein's, who (as Blanchot imagines him) "did not wish—as a philosopher—to be one, nor did he wish to be known, any more than he taught out of choice; likewise, the majority of his published works is unauthorized. Whence—perhaps—the fact that so many of his investigations are fragmentary, opening onto the fragmentary" (ED210/ WD139). Whether Bartleby's, Wittgenstein's, or Blanchot's, insubordination is unmediated by principle or ideality; the present is not refused in behalf of past or future or anything universal. Refusal is without why.

A short list of survivors would include (besides Bartleby and Wittgenstein) Hölderlin, Nietzsche, and Kafka—"What Kafka gives us—the gift we do not receive—is a sort of combat through literature for literature: a struggle which is—and is at the same time escaped by—its aim. It is so different from what we know by the name 'combat' or by any other name, that even the term 'unknown' does not suffice to make it perceptible to us, since it is as familiar as it is strange to us" (ED213/WD141). *Combat*: the very word is like a bell, recalling that one can compose many lists of survivors, with Thierry Maulnier heading the one on which Blanchot's name appears. But the theme of Blanchot's career is the attempt, perhaps somewhat after the fact, to situate combat in another, nondialectical history (a history of the third kind).[9]

This is the moral he draws from Robert Antelme's story. "The man of the camps is as close as he can be to powerlessness," writes Blanchot in "L'espèce humaine." "All human power is outside him, as are existence in the first person, individual sovereignty, and the speech that says 'I.'" But powerlessness is inaccessible:

The Powerful One is the master of the possible, but he is not master of this relation that does not derive from mastery and that power cannot measure: the relation without relation wherein the 'other' is revealed as '*autrui*'. . . . Hence the furious movement of the inquisitor who wants by force to obtain a scrap of language in order to bring all speech down to the level of force. To make speak, and through torture, is to attempt to master infinite distance by reducing expression to this language of power through which the one who speaks would once again lay himself open to force's hold; and the one who is being tortured refuses to speak in order not to enter through the extorted words into this game of opposing violence, but also, at the same time, in order to preserve the true speech that he very well knows is at this instant merged with his silent presence—which is the very presence of *autrui* in himself." (*EI*194–95/*IC*132)

Here is Blanchot's "primal scene" (his worst fear and longstanding obsession): the forced confession, the extraction of speech. The dialectic of master and slave requires the slave to come inside, show the mastery (the universality) of reason. The true slave belongs to the outside: unassimilable. In *Le pas au-delà* Blanchot writes: "Let us think of the obscure combat between language and presence. . . . Perhaps here only he who does not fight wins" (*PD*46–47/*SNB*31). So the most important thing about the child in *L'écriture du désastre* would be that it does not speak. "He will henceforth live in the secret" (*ED*117/*WD*72).

What does "living in the secret" mean, actually?

The Community of Lovers

In *La communauté inavouable* (1983), Blanchot recalls May 1968, to which he gives an anarchist's interpretation, thinking of it as a moment of revolution "without project," that is, not as a political movement on a field of concerted action but as an event in his disastrous sense of the *entre-temps* in which people came together without unity and to no end or purpose (a nondialetical community). "Contrary to 'traditional revolutions,'" he says, "it was not a question of simply taking power to replace it with some other power. . . . It was not even a question of overthrowing an old world" (*CI*52/ *UC*30). For Blanchot, what made this event political—the only meaning of political to which he could ever respond—was its impossibility: its refusal of power, its refusal to act against a regime that, as it appeared, the slightest breath would topple. Dystopian by every standard of coherent political theory or practice (one cannot help thinking here of Habermas and the claims of purposive rationality), it was for Blanchot a utopian moment, but only in the anarchist's sense that *nothing could follow from it*: "without future, therefore without present: in suspension as if to open time to a beyond of its usual determinations [*en suspens comme pour ouvrir le temps à un au-delà de ses déterminations usuelles*]" (*CI*54/*UC*31). Imagine time opening not to the future but inside out, opening as interruption: time without possibility (*le pas au-delà*). In Bataille's language: time as ecstasy.

Blanchot has repeatedly asked us, against all reason, to distinguish between a philosophic temporality, in which time (in the style of the proposition) is disposed toward the future (that is, messianically, toward the end), and a disastrous, anarchic temporality in which time (like the fragmentary) is dispersed and therefore interminable. "I believe," Blanchot says, thinking of a procession in remembrance of demonstrators killed years earlier during the Algerian crisis, "that a form of community happened then, different from the one whose character we had thought to have defined, one of those moments when communism and community meet up and ignore that they have realized themselves by losing themselves immediately. *It must not last, it must have no part in any kind of duration.* That was understood on that exceptional day: nobody had to give the order to disband. Dispersal happened out of the same necessity that had gathered the innumerable. Separation was instantaneous" (*CI*56/*UC*32).[10] So what counts as an ideal community—a utopia—for Blanchot is one in which a body politic does not form, rather the way writing does not produce a work of art:

> The people (do not translate it as *Volk*) . . . are not the State, not any more than they are the society in person, with its functions, its laws, its determinations, its exigencies which constitute its most proper finality. Inert, immobile, less a gathering than the always imminent dispersal of a presence momentarily occupying the whole space and nevertheless without a place (utopia), a kind of messianism announcing nothing but its autonomy and its *désœuvrement* (on the condition that it be left to itself, or else it will change immediately and become a network of forces ready to break loose): thus are mankind's people whom it is permissible to consider as the bastardized imitation of God's people. (*CI*57/*UC*33)

The "people," in other words, belong to the metaphysics of "being Jewish": they are like nomads whose movement is nondialectical—or, much to the same point, whose space is a surface, a pure exteriority without depth, on which a rhizome describes itself as an endless meandering (unconfinable: a "network of forces ready to break loose").

As if anarchy were, in some impossible way, constitutive of community—a thought that Jean-Luc Nancy tries to clarify in *La communauté désœuvrée* when he says that "community cannot arise from the domain of *work*."[11] Community cannot be objectified as an edifice, although much of politics is an attempt to define community in terms of groups, places, buildings, rules, institutions, and nations. Nancy writes: "Community necessarily takes place in what Blanchot has called *désœuvrement*, referring to that which, before and beyond work, withdraws from the work, and which, no longer having to do either with production or with completion, encounters interruption, fragmentation, suspension" (CD78–79/ICy31). Community, Nancy says, is a sharing (partage), not of something held in common like a set of beliefs, but of something passed from one hand to another. There is "no entity or hypostasis of community because this sharing, this passage, cannot be completed. Incompletion is its 'principle,' taking the term 'incompletion' in an active sense, however, as designating not insufficiency or lack, but the activity of sharing, the dynamic, if you will, of an uninterrupted passage through singular ruptures" (CD87/ICy35). Sharing is, in this respect, anarchic precisely because it resists the reduction of human relations to the immanent communion of a coherent body or intersubjective relationship ("Only the fascist masses tend to annihilate community in the delirium of an incarnated communion"). Community, Nancy says, "is resistance itself: namely, resistance to immanence . . . to all the forms and all the violences of subjectivity" (CD87/ICy35). So community must be understood in terms of events and movements rather than in terms of structures and meanings. Concepts of task and struggle have greater application to community than do concepts of rules, beliefs, ideals, or spirit. And of course it is easier to share a pleasure than a space.[12]

The interpretation of May 1968 serves Blanchot as a prelude to his brief commentary on Marguerite Duras's La maladie de la mort, where the "community of lovers . . . has as its ultimate goal the destruction of society" (CI80/UC48). Of course, the antisocial character of love is a commonplace as old as the troubadours. Blanchot in fact mentions Tristan et Iseult, but really he is only talking again about Orpheus and Eurydice. The lovers' communauté désœuvrée is not a chaos of destructive passion; it is, once more, a space set apart where time is without duration and where, like death, the union that occurs "takes place by not taking place" (CI82/UC49). Love is a relation of the third kind, where the man is a creature of action ("he is nothing except a constant 'doing'" [CI66/UC39]), and the young woman is—in a word (how could she be otherwise?)—"refusal" (CI83/UC50). Refusal (she refuses, for example, to refer to her lover by name)—but refusal is not a stubborn willfulness, not the work of an autonomous other constructing an alternative world. Blanchot (the last romantic) figures the young woman under the title l'absolument féminin, but quite apart from the transcendental category (his list includes Aphrodite, Eve, Lilith, Beatrice, but not, oddly, Eurydice) she embodies for him the alterity of absolute powerlessness—and as such she seems to summarize all of his most cherished themes. She is someone "who is indeterminate, un-known, unreal, thus ungraspable in her passivity" (CI60/UC35).[13] She is "forever separate"; "her difference . . . is that of another species, of another type, or that of the absolutely other" (CI65/UC38); "she escapes what would turn her into a graspable whole, a sum that would integrate the in-finite and thus reduce it to an integratable finite. Maybe that is the mean-ing of that combat lost in advance" (CI66/UC39). She is therefore (like the Jews, like the child) indestructible—"due to her very weakness, due to her very frailty, she cannot be killed, preserved as she is by the interdiction which makes her untouchable in her constant nakedness, the closest and most distant nakedness, the inaccessible intimacy of the outside" (CI63/UC37).

In this event love is perhaps not something one would necessarily want for oneself, that is, it is the preeminent condition of incommensurability (existence without reason, without being: no good, nothing lasting, can come of it). It is, as Jean-Luc Nancy says of the heart, the "place where the power of the dialectic is suspended (or shattered)" (PFi235/ICy89). So it is no wonder, Nancy continues, that "we represent love as foreign to the city and to religion": "for itself, in its living essence, love is . . . rebellious, fugi-tive, errant, unassignable, and inassimilable . . . at once the promise of completion—but a promise always disappearing—and the threat of de-composition, always imminent" (PFi /ICy93).

It may be that here at last is the context in which one can try to make sense of Thomas l'obscur, which in its revised version (1950) turns out to be, on close reading, a love story or, more exactly, a story about what it is to experience the nonrelation—the noncommunicative, nonproductive, nondurable community—of lovers. Possibly love is not the word you would choose, but it is not as if there were a word for this state of affairs. The principal event in the story is Anne's death or, say, Thomas's exposure to her death. But prior to this event there is the strangeness of Anne's ex-perience, or nonexperience, of Thomas.

One has to feel one's way carefully through this narrative, because it is made of many astonishing twists, with plots interrupting one another with-out notice. With respect to the love story, all that is certain is that Thomas and Anne keep company, and Anne, for her part, experiences "a few days of great happiness" (TO49/TTO47). Thomas seems to have abandoned himself to her without reserve. Anyhow, she plays with "this strange body as if it belonged to her," but his passiveness turns out to be a radical impassivity that makes him inaccessible to her (the opening chapters show why: Thomas has been invaded, or at this stage at least frightened, by the other night; he is like one returned from the dead).[14] The person who rolls his head on her lap is "a man she could not approach, whom she could not dream of making speak" (TO49–50/TTO47). (One may be forgiven for thinking of Thomas as a stand-in for Blanchot himself: it is impossible "to get information about him" [TO51/TTO48].) Not that Anne does not try — aggressively: "The more he withdrew within himself, the more she came frivolously forward. . . . Her stare was fixed on him" (TO51/TTO47). So their relationship entails a gender-switch. Anne is not the absolutely feminine but the philosopher.

She begins, naturally enough, to interrogate him: "Really, who could you be?" "She looked him right in the face: 'But, what are you?'" Yet it is hard to know what she might recognize as an answer. The longer she experiences the interrogative mood, the less she can be contained by it ("it was such a crude way to treat the impossible)" (TO52/TTO48). She senses a difference, or so it appears, between someone who has something to conceal and someone who is simply impervious: "it never came into her head . . . that there might be, in what she called the character of Thomas, duplicity . . . she perceived him to be so impenetrable [infranchissable] that she saw how ridiculous it would have been to call him insincere" (TO54–55/TTO50). He is not dissimulating for the very reason that his impenetrability is not a subjective position; that is, it is not something of his own making (not a mask). Anne is perhaps at first not clear about this. She attributes "penetrable motives [to] the difficulties of her relationship with him, thinking, for example, that what was abnormal was that nothing could be discovered about his life and that in every circumstance he remained anonymous and without a history" (TO56/TTO55). However, it is evident that what is secret about Thomas is not something that he keeps to himself (a past like Blanchot's, for example); the secret is rather the distance, sometimes called indifference — "the indifference that flowed the length of Thomas like a lonely stream" (TO67/TTO62) — that separates him from her (and, as it happens, from himself as well).

Perhaps it is at this very point of noncommunication that Thomas and Anne enter into the community of lovers. If the relation between Thomas and Anne is incommensurable (she is all curiosity and desire, he is all enigma), it has not been for subjective reasons; rather, the decisive fact is that they have occupied different temporalities (recall the distinction from

"L'expérience-limite": we live our lives according to "a double relation. We live it one time as something we comprehend, grasp, bear, and master . . . by relating it to some good or to some value, that is to say, finally, by relating it to Unity; we live it another time as something that escapes all employ and all end, and more, as that which escapes our very capacity to undergo it, but whose trial we cannot escape" [*EI*307–8/*IC*207]). Anne belongs to the order of possibility and the logic of propositions. She holds to "the perspective of time" (*TO*63/*TTO*59). She is "carried along by a feeling of duration" (*TO*64/*TTO*60). She is a creature of narrative (of desire, knowledge, action, accomplishment, of beginning, middle, and end); she is "the impersonal cadence of all things" (*TO*65/*TTO*60). She is, not to put too fine a point on it, "the time of men" (*TO*65/*TTO*60). Whereas Thomas belongs to the impossible temporality of incompletion—time "eternally immobilized, unable to come from the depths of the future" [*TO*66/*TTO*61]. Chapter 5 figures him as Lazarus, not so much returned from the dead as death itself resurrected and walking about, "a painted mummy" (*TO*42/*TTO*37). In other words, a figure of disaster.

But now (at the end of chapter 8) a crucial thing appears to happen. Thomas begins to think "with the enemy . . . his perfect antagonist, this *time*, Anne, and mysteriously receiving her within himself he found himself for the first time in the grip of a serious conversation" (*TO*64/*TTO*61). He becomes almost rationative. And as for Anne: "It was within this situation that she penetrated as a vague shape into the existence of Thomas" (*TO*66/*TTO*61). What is it to penetrate into this existence? Here is what Anne sees:

> Everything there appeared desolate and mournful. Deserted shores and deeper absences, abandoned by the eternally departed sea after a magnificent shipwreck, gradually decomposed. She passed through strange dead cities where, rather than petrified shapes, mummified circumstances, she found a necropolis of movements, silences, voids; she hurled herself against the extraneous sonority of nothingness which is made of the reverse of sound, and before her spread wondrous falls, dreamless sleep, the fading away which buries the dead in a life of dream, the death by which every man, even the weakest spirit, becomes spirit itself. (*TO*66–67/*TTO*61)

As if Thomas were, Bataille-like, a "surplus of emptiness, of 'negativity,'" a pure "passion of thought" (*EI*308/*IC*207).[15] For Anne, his existence is a limit-experience, an experience of absences within absences within absences structured like so many circles of the Inferno: it is like falling end-lessly into a "vacuum machine" (*machine aspirante*) (*TO69/TTO63*). "But at this limit Anne became conscious of the madness of her undertaking" (*TO69/TTO63*)—too late. Thomas is a looking-glass into which (howling her own name) she disappears (*TO70/TTO64*).

Anne collapses, and when she awakens (chapter 9) it is clear that she is becoming, quite as much as Thomas, a creature of the other night (im-mobile, impassive, secretive, ungraspable, insomniac, fatigued). She is "touched with the feeling of letting go, with the absence of consciousness into which she leapt with the greatest abandon. From this moment on, not a single desire came to her to elucidate her situation in any way, and love was reduced to the impossibility of expressing and experiencing that love" (*TO75/TTO69*). Thomas is no longer a real person to her (in this respect she could be said to be undeceived): "Thomas came in. But the presence of Thomas no longer had any importance in itself. On the contrary, it was terrible to see to what extent the desire to enjoy this presence, even in the most ordinary way, had faded" (*TO75–76/TTO69–70*). She turns away from him, "the least obscure man in the world . . . a trivial character" (*TO76/TTO70*). No one.

One might try to think of Anne as a Eurydice-figure (in a garden, sur-rounded by the souls of the dead, she sees "her mortal pain coming to meet her" (*TO79/TTO72*]). Like Eurydice, she dies twice (*TO97/TTO85*) —or, more exactly, she dies once for all following an *arrêt de mort*, "this trap into which those who have nearly vanquished death fall, ultimate re-turn of Eurydice, in looking one last time toward the visible" (*TO97/ TTO85*). Of course, for Blanchot the relation between life and death, be-ing dialectical as well as ontological, has always been ambiguous or, how should one say, neutral. Recall "Littérature et la droit à la mort" ("I say, this woman . . ."): it seems plausible to say that Anne dies because proper names are fatal, whence it is precisely "when her story and the story of her death had faded away together and there was no one left in the world to name Anne" that Anne achieves immortality (*TO102/TTO91*). Dialecti-cally, she remains identical with her cadaver, and quite possibly she was never logically more coherent with herself than in this rigorous state, as Thomas testifies by treating her corpse "as if she were alive," kissing her forehead, holding her hand (has he ever been so affectionate? But then he is himself, Lazarus-like, indifferent with respect to life and death): "Did she appear alive, then? Alas, all that prevented her from being distinguished from a real person was that which verified her annihilation. She was entirely within herself: in death, abounding in life. She seemed more weighty, more in control of herself. No Anne was lacking in the corpse of Anne. . . . At her end, she seemed to need more being to be annihilated than to be, and, dead precisely from this excess which permitted her to show herself entirely, she bestowed on death all the reality and existence which constituted proof of her own nothingness. Neither impalpable nor dissolved in the shadows, she imposed herself ever more strongly on the senses" (*TO*100/*TTO*89–90).

But why does she die?

Confessions of the Everyday

Recall that in his essay on Bataille, "L'expérience-limite" (1962), Blanchot says that a limit-experience occurs when one puts or finds oneself in question (*EI*302/*IC*203). But what is it to be in question? "What," he asks in *La communauté inavouable*, "calls me most radically into question? Not my relation to myself as finite or as the consciousness of being before death or for death, but my presence in the proximity of another who by dying removes himself definitively, to take upon myself another's death as the only death that concerns me, this is what puts me beside myself, this is the only separation that can open me, in its very impossibility, to the Openness of a community" (*CI*21/*UC*9).

So it is not strange that Thomas experiences Anne's death not as a loss but as an exigency, or agony, of self-reflection, an "inner experience" whose drama is recited in the form of a confession. Without leaving the room in which her body reposes, Thomas begins speaking, not privately or randomly but as if making a formal statement—"One might think that what he was saying to himself could in no way allow itself to be read, but he took care to speak as if his words had a chance of being overheard" *TO*99/*TTO*89). Thomas gives an account of a sort of mirror-experience— "I found myself with two faces, glued one to the other" (*TO*111/*TTO*96)— in which one self of Thomas is present as the negation of the other, as if Thomas's relationship with himself were dialectical: "With one hand showing that I was indeed there, with the other—what am I saying?—without the other, with this body which, imposed on my real body, depended entirely on a negation of the body, I entered into absolute dispute with my-self [*je me donnais la contestation la plus certaine*]" (*TO*111/*TTO*96–97).

"Dispute" is perhaps not quite the right word. When Thomas looks in "the strange face" of himself, he sees, Narcissus-like, someone desirable, but also inaccessible: "a marvelous companion with whom I wished with all my might to blend myself, yet separate from me, with no path that might lead me to him. How could I reach him? By killing myself: absurd plan. Between this corpse, the same as a living person but without life, and this unnameable, the same as a dead person but without death, I could not see a single line of relationship" (*TO*112/*TTO*97). His relationship with himself is one of incommensurability, or at all events of irreducibility, as if Thomas were neither one nor the other of himself. Thomas evidently makes every effort to coincide with himself—"But if I advanced within myself, hurrying laboriously toward my precise noon, I yet experienced, as a tragic certainty, at the center of the living Thomas, the inaccessible proximity of that Thomas which was nothingness [*ce Thomas néant*], and the more the shadow of my thought shrunk, the more I conceived of myself in this faultless clarity as the possible, the willing host of this obscure Thomas" (*TO*113/*TTO*97–98).

Who (or what) is Thomas the obscure (this clandestine companion)? He is not an alter ego whom psychoanalysis might expose. Interiority is not a space of subjectivity. Thomas's guess is that he belongs to a dialectical relation (as between existence and nothingness) whose movement, if it could be suspended, would produce something like self-possession ("Harpagon suddenly catching his thief and grabbing his own arm" [*TO*114/*TTO*99]). His guess is not completely wrong—the dialectic of sameness and difference *is* suspended—but the consequences of this interruption cannot have been foreseen: "It was then that, deep within a cave, the madness of the taciturn thinker appeared before me and unintelligible words rung in my ears while I wrote on the wall these sweet words: 'I think, therefore I am not.' These words brought me a delicious vision" (*TO*114/*TTO*99). It is (so far as I can make out) the vision of a *cogito* outside the order of possibility, "a monstrous I" figured as a lens that reflects the sun with such an intensity that it can exist without being: "I think, it said, I am subject and object of an all-powerful radiation; a sun using all its energy to make itself night, as well as to make itself sun. I think: there at the point where thought joins with me I am able to subtract myself from being, without diminishing, without changing, by means of a metamorphosis which saves me for myself, beyond any point of reference from which I might be seized" (TO115–16/TTO99). If I understand: I am, said the *cogito*, not I.

Two things about this vision. The first is that it is not mystical, not otherwordly, not a prophetic communication that sets Thomas apart or discloses his difference from the rest of us. Rather, the point is that his strangeness, his self-estrangement or nonidentity, is not strange. "I think, said Thomas, and this invisible, inexpressible, non-existent Thomas I became meant that henceforth I was never there where I was, and there was not even anything mysterious about it" (TO116/TTO100). Being without identity is not a problem to be solved, but fact to be acknowledged. Recall that Blanchot's conception of the everyday is precisely that it is not governed by the rule of identity (or by the law of noncontradiction); it escapes the dialectic—it is the realm of the anarchic *par excellence*. "The everyday," Blanchot says, "is the movement by which man, as though without knowing it, holds himself back in anonymity. In the everyday we have no name, little personal reality, scarcely a figure, just as we have no social determinations to sustain or enclose us" (EI361–62/IC242). It is, in this respect, a refuge. "The everyday where one lives as though outside the true and the false is a level of life where what reigns is a refusal to be different, a still undetermined stirring: without responsibility and without authority, without direction and without decision, a storehouse of anarchy in that it discourages all beginning and dismisses every end" (EI362/IC243). Not a place for philosophers.

The second thing about this vision is that Anne may well have had it, and couldn't bear it: "When she saw that there was nothing abnormal about me she was seized with terror. I was like her. My strangeness had as its cause all that which made me not seem strange to her. With horror she discovered in everything that was ordinary about her the source of everything that was extraordinary about me. I was her tragic double" (TO117/TTO100). This wants careful reading. Thomas says: "I offered this girl the experience of something absurd, and it was a terrible test." But absurd in what sense? "I was absurd," Thomas says, "not because of the goat's foot which permitted me to walk with a human pace, but because of my regular anatomy, my complete musculature which permitted me a normal pace, nevertheless an absurd pace, and, normal as it was, more and more absurd" (TO118/TTO101).

But what could be absurd about the normal? The answer is that the normal is the region of nonidentity or, in Blanchot's language, the neutral. Recall Heidegger, who (we have seen this) asked who Dasein is, that is, who the *who* of Dasein is—in its *everydayness*. The *who* of *Dasein* is not an I but a no one: "The 'who' is not this one, not that one, not oneself [*man selbst*], not some people [*einige*], and not the sum of them all. The 'who' is the neuter, the 'they' [das Man]" (SZ126/BT164). In the "they," as Heidegger says, "everyone is the other, and no one is himself" (SZ128/BT165).

Thomas helps us to understand that the "they" are not the masses or the crowd, although Heidegger perhaps did not make such a distinction. The point is rather that Thomas occupies a region of existence that is inaccessible to philosophy. One could say, thinking of Bataille, that he is *l'inconnu*, but it must be understood, perhaps against Bataille, that this is not because Thomas is a mystery ("I brought her the one true mystery, which consisted of the absence of mystery" [TO118/TTO101]). His obscurity is not an obscurity of depths but of surfaces. "Everything was clear in me, everything was simple: there was no other side to the pure enigma. I showed her a face with no secret, indecipherable"—but Thomas is not a text, and neither is he a cipher. His opacity is perhaps no more than the opacity of the everyday (that is, the obvious). Anne in any case has nothing to decipher since all is plain: "She read in my heart as she had never read in any other heart; she knew why I had been born, why I was there"—and this, it appears, is the problem: "The more she reduced the element of the unknown in me, the more her discomfort and her fright increased. She was forced to divulge me, she separated me from my last shadows, in the fear of seeing me with no shadow. She pursued this mystery desperately; she destroyed me insatiably" (TO119/TTO101). What was being destroyed was Thomas's anonymity.

Bad Conscience

It might be appropriate to conclude, or to stop, with "Les intellectuels en question," a tortuous essay that Blanchot published in 1984 when controversies over French fascism and the Vichy years were at their most intense. Blanchot had himself been called out by the appearance of Jeffrey Mehlman's essay "Blanchot at *Combat*," which he had seen as early as 1979, and, more generally, by the publication of Sternhell's *Ni droit ni gauche* in 1983.[16] So perhaps it is not surprising that "Les intellectuels en question" is not a very straightforward text. At every turn it seems to have application to Blanchot's own career, but the text breaks off whenever this application becomes explicit. So in reading one has to negotiate a number of substitutions for what might have been a self-criticism, or even self-defense. For example, in a footnote Blanchot indicates that the provocation that compelled him to write was an accusation (by Boris Souveraine, who had been editor in the 1930s of the journal *La critique sociale*) that Georges Bataille had been a closet fascist who would have openly collaborated during the Vichy years had he had the courage to do so. Blanchot protests: "Since I had the privilege, from 1940 onwards . . . of seeing Georges Bataille on an almost daily basis and discussing a whole range of subjects with him, I can vouch for his horror of Nazism, as well as of the Pétain regime. . . . He came to regret the pages he wrote on 'The Psychological Structures of Fascism' (published of course in *La critique sociale*), and which could have lent themselves to misunderstanding" (IQ20/ BR226).

It's a good guess that Bataille here is a stand-in for Blanchot himself, and that "La structure psychologique du fascisme" is cited as an archetype of the writings of conflicted young intellectuals in the 1930s whose common experience, whatever their ideological background or fellowship, was the despair of politics. But Bataille is not the only stand-in. "Intellectuels en question" is, on one level, an attempt to give the concept of the intellectual a certain application. For example, no one is an intellectual as such or all the time. There are only poets and writers, philosophers and historians, painters and sculptors, scientists and teachers. Each of these types is, in the nature of the case, in retreat, apart from the world—but not turned away from it. On the contrary, he (or she) is something like a Kantian spectator, "a look-out who is there solely to keep watch, to remain watchful, to wait with an active attention, expressive less of a concern for himself than of a concern for others" (IQ6/BR208). The intellectual is one who, owing to the exigency of justice or liberty, steps out of this space of retreat and intervenes in the world of decision and action.

What is the justification of such interventions? Appeals to justice and liberty are in themselves not enough. Blanchot tells the story of Paul Valéry's involvement in the Dreyfus affair—the event in which "intellectuals recognized themselves as such" for the first time (IQ8/BR210); that is, artists and writers, philosophers and academics responded in protest, and as a social group, against the injustice of the verdict and in particular the anti-Semitism that seemed to have inspired it. "For the first time, an appeal against the verdict in a rigged trial gives rise to an 'Intellectuals' Manifesto'" (IQ9/BR210). Blanchot lays great stress on the anti-Semitism of the affair, "during which were uttered against the Jews and those who stood by them, words as violent as the most violent of those with which the Nazis worked themselves up in order to justify the final solution ('we must roast the Jews')," and this virulence had the "sombre merit . . . of obliging intellectuals to reveal themselves to themselves, and of entrusting them with a simple demand [exigence] (the demand for truth and justice, the call for freedom of the mind against fanatical vehemence) from which they drew a new authority and sometimes a moral gain" (IQ10–11/BR211–12).

But Paul Valéry sided with the anti-Dreyfusards and anti-Semites. Why? Blanchot emphasizes Valéry's silence on this question, not to mention his forgetfulness. There is only a brief notebook entry, thirty years after the fact, in which Valéry complains of the extravagance and insincerity of those who claimed to speak and act in the name of Justice and Humanity. He will not take part in such a "charade." Better to be unjust than to act justly in bad faith. A "paltry explanation," says Blanchot (IQ11/BR212). Indeed, Blanchot is, to all appearances, unsparing in his judgment against Valéry: "I can find nothing that can justify his allowing his name to be associated with the names of those who called, in the worst terms, for the death of the Jews and the elimination of their defenders." To which he immediately adds, however, the following: "There would thus seem to be a moment, in every life, when the unjustifiable prevails and the incomprehensible is given its due" (IQ13/BR213). As who should say.

The incomprehensible, in other words, is not merely a feature of Valéry's subjective decision, although of course it is that, the more so since Valéry's master, Mallarmé, had sided with the Dreyfusards, and so did his friend André Gide, whom Valéry tried to persuade otherwise. "A painful memory and a painful enigma" (IQ13/BR214). To be sure; but there is more. The incomprehensible—this is Blanchot's argument—is structural and pervasive; it is not a subjective failing but a condition that attaches to the situation of the intellectual as such. Blanchot cites the case of Charles Péguy, who had championed Dreyfus and then vilified him for not being, after all, both as an individual and as a certain type, worth the deep moral investment the intellectuals had made in him. Péguy had written: "Consecrated a hero in spite of himself, consecrated a victim in spite of himself, consecrated a martyr in spite of himself, [Dreyfus] was unworthy of that triple investiture. Historically, truly unworthy. Inadequate, below standard, incapable, unworthy of that triple consecration, of that triple investiture" (quoted in IQ14/BR214). Blanchot's comment: "Words which, read carefully, are absurd, and which show what *debasement* the intellectual exposes himself to in becoming the messenger of the absolute, the substitute for the priest, the superior being bearing the mark of the sacred" [IQ14/BR214]). As if, in the end, Péguy were more invidious than Valéry.

However, the moral of Valéry's story is deferred. "Intellectuels en question" is a critique of the intellectual, that is, it is less a criticism of intellectual malfeasance (Valéry) or presumption (Péguy) than a reflection on the double exigency, and indeed the asymmetry, of writing and justice. What is the nature of the transformation by which the writer becomes an intellectual? It is all very well to ask what, after all, the writer can contribute to the pursuit, or cause, of justice — "he who, despite his name, often does not know very much, but who at least sticks by a simple idea, which says that there is a requirement [*exigence*] that must be sustained, come what may" (IQ17/BR216–17). But what exactly is this exigency, and what are its limits? This looks as if it were the regulating question of Blanchot's essay.

It is important to notice that Blanchot frames (and pursues) this question in a complicated way. He remarks that "in a society based on right there are specialists in justice" whose task is to keep the system in order (IQ17/BR216). Presumably the exigency of the intellectual comes from outside this system and situates him at something like a transcendental level of responsibility. For example: "There is Luther, who stands where he is and cannot do otherwise. There is Socrates, who says yes to death, and calmly refuses the way out that would allow him to escape his sentence. There is the stiff-necked Jew [Jesus?]. There is the obligation to come to the assistance of others which, according to Hermann Broch, takes precedence over everything to do with one's own work" (IQ17/BR217). But then Blanchot adds another figure to this list, a Blanchot-figure, "the person whose vocation is to remain in retreat, far from the world (in that place where speech is the guardian of silence)": there is, for this person, "the pressing necessity to expose himself to the 'risks of public life' by discovering a responsibility for someone who, apparently, means nothing to him, and by joining in the shouting and the clamour, when, on behalf of that which is closest, he has to give up the sole exigency that is properly his own: that of the unknown, of strangeness and of distance" (IQ17/BR217). What about this "pressing necessity"? "What . . . is this command from without, to which he must respond and which obliges him to take his place in the world again and assume an additional responsibility which may lead him astray?" (IQ17/BR217). It is this last phrase that is Blanchot's concern.

For example, in an apparent digression Blanchot asks whether there is a link of sorts between socialism (that is, the desire for the millennium of a just and free society) and war. There is, he says, "no firm socialist concept of war" (IQ19/BR218), but there has always been, or so it appears, "the vague idea that war and social emancipation go together" (IQ19/BR218), as if violence and catastrophe could serve as a conditions of possibility, as foundations, for justice (Sorel's basic doctrine). "For the decisive characteristic of justice (justice for others [*autrui*]) is that it brooks no delay, so that as a consequence it can let slip no opportunity—be it dangerous or doubtful—to fulfill itself. (Levinas pertinently cites this line from Bialik: 'And if justice exists, let it immediately appear')" (IQ20/BR219). From Martin Buber Blanchot summons the "Seer of Lublin, the great Hasidic master," who "sensed in Napoleon a demonic force capable of raising up the abyss and, through the excess of evil he represented, of cooperating in the hope for salvation, and even hastening the coming of the Messiah" (IQ20–21/BR219–20). As if the question of the exigency of justice could be reformulated as follows: "ought one to promote Evil, bring it to a paroxysm, and hence precipitate catastrophe, so that at the same time deliverance may draw nearer?" (IQ21/BR220).

In other words, can violence or terrorism serve as a method of public salvation?

Blanchot recalls that in the 1930s "Fascism . . . was greeted with few misgivings." The odd thing about it (to the eye, presumably, of a young French nationalist) was that it had become international—spreading "like an epidemic and [presenting] itself as a universal model"—in contrast to Communism, which, originally international, more and more had become identified with Soviet interests (IQ22/BR220). "What is it about Fascism," Blanchot asks—putting the question in the present tense—"that is so attractive? [*Qu'est-ce qui attire dans le fascisme?*]" (IQ22/BR220). The short answer is the Sorelian one Walter Benjamin gives, namely, "the irrational, the power of spectacle and a hybrid resurgence of certain forms of the sacred: in other words, precisely what is needed by a society wishing once more to open itself to myths; something that seemed cruelly lacking then in the democratic regimes" (IQ22/BR220). This is not a wrong answer. In fact it is one that, Blanchot says, helps to account for the special nature of Hitler's hatred of the Jews: "In the Jew, in the 'myth of the Jew,' what Hitler wanted to annihilate was, precisely, man freed from myths" (IQ22/BR221). But no one saw national socialism clearly at the time. Hitler's racism was seen in much the same light as "the fashionable anti-Semitism which reigned in Vienna" (IQ23/BR221). Blanchot's suggestion is that the reality of Hitler was masked by the coherence of fascism with the broad contempt for democratic government that dominated Europe at the time. "Democracy was worn out, so to speak; it had lost its radiance, it was identified with day-to-day mediocrity; and its disastrous weaknesses were highlighted by economic difficulties created by the war. It was to require considerable merit on the part of intellectuals, or the majority of them, to gather round and defend a regime for which they felt no respect, and in order not to yield to the fascination of the irrational, the fecundity of which was often demonstrated by their works and their art (Surrealism). They were anti-Fascists out of a love of freedom and an innate sense of justice" (IQ22/BR221). Here one wonders where Blanchot would locate himself, but he remains in the shadows.

The question is, or was: How to act against fascism? Blanchot distinguishes between two groups. There were those like Simone Weil and Alain for whom violence could never be a method and who remained staunch pacifists. Others were ready to take up arms, as in Spain and, again, during the Resistance, presumably on the principle (which, Blanchot says, remains "resolutely true") that the "intellectual should not just judge or take sides: he is someone who puts himself at risk, and answers for his decisions, if necessary, with his freedom and his existence" (IQ24/BR222). But there is more to risk than imprisonment or death. The intellectual, Blanchot says, "constantly incurs a twofold danger: that of giving up his 'creative' powers by giving up his solitude; that of involving himself in support of a public declaration which he is not even sure can justify his 'sacrifice'" (IQ24/BR222). If I understand, Blanchot seems to be arguing that there is no categorical imperative that can justify the intellectual in advance. The concepts of justice and liberty ("vague words, and powerful, unclear assertions" [IQ25/BR223]) are not, of themselves, guarantors of right action. In an interesting turn, Blanchot replaces Kant with Adorno:

From the Dreyfus affair to Hitler and Auschwitz, the proof is there that it was anti-Semitism (along with racism and xenophobia) which revealed the intellectual most powerfully to himself: in other words, it is in that form that concern for others obliged him (or not) to abandon his creative solitude. The categoric imperative, losing the ideal generality given to it by Kant, became the one which Adorno formulated more or less thus: *Think and act in such a way that Auschwitz may never be repeated*; which implies that Auschwitz must not become a concept, and that an absolute was reached there, against which other rights and duties must be judged. (IQ25/BR223)

Notice that Auschwitz does not function as a concept; that is, it cannot be used as a principle upon which anything can be based or from which something must follow. It is in this sense anarchic. But how to think and act after Auschwitz?

The answer seems to be twofold, and concerns the limits of the exigency that transforms the writer into the intellectual. The first is a rejection of violence as a method of salvation. This is the lesson that Blanchot extracts from the war in Spain and from the Resistance (as well as perhaps from Simone Weil and Alain, or again perhaps from his own attraction to violence): "It is that intellectuals, attached as they generally were to the principle of freedom, did not heed the fact that the good (the liberation of the people) would be gravely compromised, the day it required or even tolerated that evil (war) should hasten or ensure its advent" (IQ25/BR223).[17]

The second is "that the writer, the artist and the scientist divert and misappropriate the influence they have acquired, and the authority they owe to their particular activity, in order to employ them in the service of political choices or moral options" (IQ26/BR223). He mentions Zola, Sartre, and "an actor of renown," but principally Sartre, who became a sort of permanent intellectual and a parody of the Kantian guardian of rationality presiding over the lifeworld—"he felt there was vested in him a responsibility which obliged him to take sides far beyond anything he had the right to pronounce upon, speaking and writing according to his dreams or his hopes, until the moment when he was forced to recant in the face of what was self-evident" (IQ26/BR224). In Sartre we can see the contradiction of the intellectual writ large: the writer and the guardian are, so to speak, incommensurable, nor is there any way to remove this contradiction. "But it can be alleviated," Blanchot says, "if the intellectual manages to make it clear that he is one only momentarily and for a fixed cause, and that, as a supporter of that cause, he is merely one among others, with the hope (be it vain) of losing himself in the obscurity of everyone, and becoming one with an anonymity which is, in fact, his profound yet constantly thwarted goal as a writer or an artist" (IQ26/BR224). ("The vain struggle for the anonymous . . ." [PD53/SNB36].)

Here, let us say, is an anarchist's theory of the intellectual—an intellectual who speaks in no one's voice and acts from the bottom up rather than from the top down, that is, without principle and without hope, whose cause is not to bring about the future but only to keep something from recurring. The point must be that this is the only way the writer can become an intellectual without ceasing to remain a writer ("there is no biography for writing" [PD51/SNB34]), as if it were only through the mediation of anonymity and in behalf of a community that does not last that the writer could respond to the double exigency of writing and justice. If "justice" is the word.

"Les intellectuels en question" ends in remembrance of three moments of struggle. The first is of 1968, which is (as we have seen) the event that Blanchot thinks comes closest to what a revolution should be, first because it was an "anti-authoritarian movement" in which "the unknown and the too-well known" became indistiguishable, that is, anonymous, neutral (neither one nor the other); and second because nothing came of it (it was not a messianic event): "It provides no solution, even if it gives an idea of a revolution that does not need to succeed or achieve a fixed goal, since, whether it endures or does not endure, it is sufficient unto itself, and since the failure that eventually rewards it is none of its concern" (IQ27 /BR224). It is as if a revolution were like a work of writing (that is, a dés-œuvrement).

The second moment was the Algerian crisis and the "déclaration des 121," where "those who declared themselves made no claim to announcing a universal truth (insubordination for its own sake and in all cases)" (IQ27/BR225). Subordination is not a principle or rule that justifies actions in advance. At most it is a principle of insufficient reason, that is (in defiance of contradiction), an anarchic principle in the sense that, in the nature of the case, nothing follows from it; rather it is a way of summarizing, in parody of Leibniz, the incompleteness of things, the deficiency of structures (perhaps one could say the freedom) that can never be eliminated or overcome, and which therefore necessarily sets a limit to every exercise of power, whether of reason or the state.

The third moment occured in 1943. Here Blanchot's reference is much more elusive. He cites the following from René Char, and calls it his "personal confession":

*I want never to forget that I have been forced to become—for how long?—a
monster of justice and intolerance, a cooped-up simplifier, an arctic individual with no interest in the fate of anyone who is not in league with him to kill
the hounds of hell. The round-ups of Jews, scalpings in the police-stations, ter-
rorist raids by Hitler's police on stunned villages, lift me off the ground, strike
my chapped face with a red-hot slap of molten iron.* (IQ28/BR225)

Obviously there is no way of knowing what is being confessed here. All we
have is a voice from the underground, the voice of "a monster of justice,"
the voice of someone Valéry, for example, refused to become. We may
never know whether Blanchot was one of these or not. The question is,
What is it to issue a "personal confession" in another's voice, signed with
another's name? Perhaps this is the only way the contradiction of writing
and justice can be negotiated. Figure this evasion as you will—as the
rhetoric of the scoundrel, for example—Blanchot at any rate maintains a
certain consistency: he has summoned René Char, as he summoned
Valéry and Bataille, to bear witness for him (or is it to him?), as if his own
voice could not be embodied, could not bear him out; as if he were no
more than a sharing, or division, of voices. This line of thought has a certain conceptual coherence.

In a footnote to his essay on the narrative voice, Blanchot (thinking of a
novel by Marguerite Duras), speaks of an "indescribable event . . . that
cannot be recalled and cannot be forgotten" (*EI*567/*IC*462). Imagine this
as, in a nutshell, the story of someone's life. "Recounting," Blanchot has
said, "is the torment of language" (*EI*564/*IC*385), as survival is the torment
of being questioned (*CI*21/*UC*9; IQ28/BR225). Or, again, and much to the
same point, suppose one's relation to one's self, one's life, were like the relation of Orpheus and Eurydice. There would always be "the nocturnal
desire to turn around in order to see what belongs neither to the visible nor
the invisible, that is, to remain for a moment, through one's gaze, as close
as possible to strangeness where the rhythm of revealing-concealing has
lost its rectifying force [*sa force rectrice*]" (*EI*567/*IC*462). But is self-reflection a possibility of reason? Or is the confession a limit-experience that the
"I" could not survive?

Levinas, in an essay written for a volume devoted to Blanchot, recalls
that the "I" is always "forgetful of the indirectly lived and the nonintentional and its horizons, forgetful of what accompanies it" (*MC*109/*BC*36).
What would it be for reflection to bring this forgotten companion to con-

sciousness, that is, to intentionality and objectivity? No doubt it would be the Orpheus-Eurydice encounter. "The critique traditionally applied to introspection has always suspected a modification that the consciousness called 'spontaneous' would undergo under the scrutinizing, thematizing, objectivizing, and indiscreet eye of reflection, as a violation and misappreciation [*méconnaissance*] of some secret. This critique is always refuted, but it is always reborn" (MC110/BC36).

The secret, if there is a secret, is that the "I" of intentionality is always accompanied by another, call it a *discreet*, nonintentional consciousness—consciousness which is neither active nor capable of rest but is outside the ego's modality of cognition and action in the condition of pure passivity. Perhaps one could think of it as consciousness without why: "It is bad conscience: without intentions, without aims, without the protective mask of the character [*personnage*] beholding himself in the mirror of the world, reassured and posing. Without name, without situation, without titles" (MC110/BC37). Here is Blanchot as I imagine him, as Levinas did, too, since it is clearly a Blanchot-like effigy that Levinas opposes to the good conscience of philosophy, that is, to the "I" that stands upright and can look itself squarely in the eye because it has every right to exist, who walks abroad in the world without the least sense of being out of place, who glories in the light of being as in the possession of a good name. Nothing can rattle it: its right to be cannot be questioned. Whereas the other is careful to remain out of sight: "Bad conscience or timidity: accused without guilt, responsible for its very presence. Reserve of the noninvested, the nonjustified, the 'stranger on the earth,' according to the expression of the Psalmist, without country or abode, who does not dare to enter"—someone only Kafka could adequately picture or put into words (MC111/BC37).

In fact this companion, this other in me (this Blanchot), will not let me rest. He is always there, exposing me to "being as bad conscience; being in question, but also having to respond to the question—the birth of language; to have to speak, to have to say 'I,' to be in the first person, to be precisely me; but, then, in the affirmation of the ego's being, to have to respond to its right to be [*droite à l'être*]" (MC111/BC38). Suddenly, inevitably, this right is no longer self-evident but in question, together with my right to speak and my position in the world (my titles, my identity). "My 'in the world,' my 'place in the sun,' my at homeness, have they not been the usurpation of the places belonging to the other man already oppressed and starved by me?" (MC111/BC38). What is happening? Perhaps something like a philosophical limit-experience (an experience of the limit of philosophy): "Fear of all that my existing, despite its intentional and conscious innocence, can accomplish of violence and murder. Fear that rises up behind my 'self-consciousness' and whatever, towards good conscience, are the qualms of pure perseverence in being. Fear that comes to me from the face of the Other" (MC111/BC38).[18] Only now this Other is the face in the mirror: no longer my mirror-image but now every face that bad conscience exposes me to, including my own, "putting into question my presence and my responsibility" (MC112/BC38). My "I," for its part, is in pieces. Imagine Oedipus as a bourgeois intellectual caught up by his past: Oedipus as Kafka might have imagined him.

"The subject in responsibility," Levinas says, "is alienated in the depths of its identity with an alienation that does not empty the same of its identity, but constrains it to it, with an unimpeachable assignation, constrains it to it as no one else, where no one could replace it. The psyche, a uniqueness outside of concepts, is a seed of folly, already a psychosis. It is not an ego, but me under assignation" (AE222/OTB142). Being under assignation is different from being interrogated. It is being under a claim (*exigence*) rather than under a charge (that is, under the summons of those in charge of laws, rules, and account books). It is therefore not a condition in which one can defend or justify oneself; one is, in the nature of the case, unjustified and unredeemable, that is, one is in question in the sense of exposed, without shelter or refuge, abandoned, no longer in the world, no longer an "I." ("The writer," Blanchot has said "gives up saying 'I'" [EL21/SL26].) How to respond to this exigency? Levinas figures this answer in terms of the biblical *me voici* ("here I am"), where the "I" is no longer an ego but only a bad conscience. Blanchot would perhaps figure it as a stammer. Bad conscience is a mode of survival, that is, it is the survivor's recognition that existence can no longer be justified, and that the future will bring no redemption. Bad conscience has perhaps always been a condition of historical existence (ED217/WD143). However that may be, Blanchot thinks of the Holocaust as the event that has interrupted messianic time, perhaps for good. What remains is a temporality of survival in which vigilance becomes a species of memory, a watchfulness without hope (ED179/WD116).

Blanchot's thought seems to be this: there is poetry after Auschwitz, and also philosophy, but it is no longer possible for these things to go on in good conscience. Of course poetry (since Plato's time a discourse of survival) is interminable, incessant; that is, thinking of poetry in terms of its place in the history of philosophy, Blanchot has always understood it (as he has understood everything else, perhaps himself as well) in bad conscience. Bad conscience, just to summarize, is internal to the exigency of writing. The question is whether philosophy could ever respond to this exigency, becoming, in effect, anarchic ("without intentions, without aims, without the protective mask of the character beholding itself in the mirror of the world, reassured and posing. Without name, without situation, without titles"). This question is Blanchot's provocation, or perhaps his gift, to philosophy.

Notes

Preface

1. The phrase "rationalization of the world" is Max Weber's, and it is one of the great themes of the Frankfurt School. See in particular Max Horkheimer and Theodor Adorno, *The Dialectic of Enlightenment* (1944), trans. John Cumming (New York: Seabury Press, 1972). Jürgen Habermas gives a critical account of the development of this problematic in volume one of *The Theory of Communicative Action: Reason and the Rationalization of Society*, trans. Thomas McCarthy (Boston: Beacon Press, 1984), esp. pp. 339–99.

2. "Philosophy as Stand-in and Interpreter," *Moral Consciousness and Communicative Action*, trans. Christian Lenhardt and Shierry Weber Nicholson (Cambridge: MIT Press, 1990), esp. pp. 17–20.

3. Zeev Sternhell, *Neither Left Nor Right: Fascist Ideology in France* (Berkeley: University of California Press, 1986), p. 4.

4. See Robert Wohl, "French Fascism, Both Right and Left: Reflections on the Sternhell Controversy," *Journal of Modern History*, 63 (March 1991), 91–98.

5. See Jacques Julliard, "Sur un fascisme imaginaire: à propos d'un livre de Zeev Sternhell," *Annales: E. S. V.* 39, no. 4 (1980), 850–52. See also Roger Austin, "The Conservative Right and the Far Right in France: The Search for Power, 1934–44," *Fascists and Conservatives: The Radical Right and the Establishment in Twentieth-Century Europe*, ed. Martin Blinkhorn (London: Unwin Hyman, 1990), pp. 176–99. Against Sternhell, Austin's essay stresses "the need to examine *Realpolitik* as well as ideology. It represents a deliberate attempt to shift the discussion away from the realm of ideas, where conflicting definitions of fascism are unlikely to be resolved, towards an examination of the means by which different groups on the right competed for power through a combination of parliamentary and extra-parliamentary methods" (196). Fascism here is essentially a "mass politics" in behalf of right-wing interests. Robert Soucy's recent *French Fascism: The Second Wave, 1933–39*, cited in chapter 1 below, is an excellent example of the sort of study Austin calls for.

6. *The Blanchot Reader* (*BR5*). This excellent collection makes available some of Blanchot's social and political writings as well as his literary criticism, and brings together as much biographical and historical information as we have so far.

7. See Todd May, *The Political Philosophy of Poststructuralist Anarchism* (University Park: Pennsylvania State University Press, 1994), esp. chap. 5 ("Steps Toward a Poststructuralist Anarchism"), pp. 87–119. Foucault and Deleuze are May's principal subjects of study, but much of what he has to say has application to Blanchot, whose influence on both Foucault and Deleuze is not difficult to see. May is particularly helpful in connecting poststructuralist anarchism to the classical anarchism of Bakhunin and Proudhon.

267

8. The late Rainer Schürmann's book *Heidegger on Being and Acting: From Principles to Anarchy*, trans. Christine-Marie Gros (Bloomington: Indiana University Press, 1987), has been of great help to me, although I think he would have been suspicious of Blanchot's anarchism as being, finally, an "anarchism of power" that would undermine not just a cybernetic culture of self-regulating technologies but also the practical rationality of everyday life, which proceeds without rules without, however, being irrational. See chapter 5 of Schürmann's book, esp. pp. 251–303, and particularly pp. 289–92. I think in fact that Blanchot's anarchism belongs to the rationality of everyday life, but it would perhaps take another book, and someone more adept than I, to give this argument the force that it would require.

9. See Herman Rapaport, *Heidegger and Derrida: Reflections on Time and Language* (Lincoln: University of Nebraska Press, 1989), and Timothy Clark, *Derrida, Heidegger, Blanchot: Sources of Derrida's Notion and Practice of Literature* (Cambridge: Cambridge University Press, 1992).

10. "On Deconstructing Nostalgia for Community within the West: The Debate between Nancy and Blanchot," *Research in Phenomenology*, 23 (1993), 7.

11. See Jon Elster, *Solomonic Judgments: Studies in the Limits of Rationality* (Cambridge: Cambridge University Press, 1989), p. 17. Probably not many people working in the humanities (including especially Anglo-American philosophers who recoil against the "irrationalism" of Continental thinking) realize how thoroughly the social sciences—economics, political science, sociology—have embraced rational choice theory, which is an unembarrassed reduction of rationality to a logic of calculation aimed at maximizing payoffs (a rational choice is one that most efficiently serves my interests). Basically the theory analyzes collective action on the model of the strategic behavior of individuals. It assumes, for example, that political decisions try to maximize the production of power and judicial decisions try to maximize the production of wealth. The theory excludes axiomatically any conception of noninstrumental relations between or among human beings, whence ethics, for example, reduces to the question of how far it pays to treat people decently. See *Rational Choice*, ed. Jon Elster (Washington Square, N.Y.: New York University Press, 1986); and Donald P. Green and Ian Shapiro, *Pathologies of Rational Choice Theory: A Critique of Applications in Political Science* (New Haven: Yale University Press, 1994), which is a critique of rational choice theory from a rigorously (or narrowly) empirical standpoint, giving the theory high marks as a theory of politics but low marks as a source of explanations that can be empirically tested. There is also a nice discussion of rational choice theory by Jon Elster, Martin Hollis, and Michael Hechter in the *Times Literary Supplement* for 29 March 1996, pp. 12–15.

Chapter 1: This Way Out

1. "Wittgenstein 'After,'" *Political Writings*, trans. Bill Readings and Kevin Paul (Minneapolis: University of Minnesota Press, 1993), p. 21.

2. Françoise Collin gives a brief account of Blanchot's sense of the anarchic in *Maurice Blanchot et la question de l'écriture* (Paris: Gallimard, 1971), pp. 43–44.

3. Mallarmé writes:

Écrire—
L'encrier, cristal comme une conscience, avec sa goutte, au fond, de ténèbres relative à ce que quelque chose soit: puis, écarte la lampe.

Tu remarquas, on n'écrit pas, lumineusement, sur champ obscur, l'alphabet des astres, seul, ainsi s'indique, ébauché ou interrompu; l'homme poursuit noir sur blanc. (OC370)

I tried to give an account of Mallarmé's typological poetics some years ago in *Modern Poetry and the Idea of Language: A Critical and Historical Study* (New Haven: Yale University Press, 1974), pp. 101–37, esp. pp. 114–16. See also Jacques Derrida, "Mallarmé," *Tableau de la littérature française: De Madame de Staël à Rimbaud* (Paris: Gallimard, 1974); trans. Christine Roulston, *Acts of Literature*, ed. Derek Attridge (London: Routledge, 1992), esp. pp. 115–16, on the nonmetaphoricality of Mallarmé's poetry, where (for example) the "white" of the white-space is not one figure among other *blancs*: "The white of the spacing has no determinate meaning, it does not simply belong to the plurivalence of all the other whites. More than or less than the polysemic series, a loss or an excess of meaning, it folds up the text toward itself, and at each moment points out the place (where 'nothing will have taken place except the place' [*Un coup de dés*, pp. 474–75]), the condition, the labor, the rhythm. As the page *folds in* upon itself, one will never be able to decide if *white* signifies something, or signifies only, or in addition, the space of writing itself."

4. See "Le Livre, instrument spirituel":

Un miracle prime ce bienfait, au sens haut ou les mots originellement, se réduisent à l'emploi, doué d'infinité jusqu'à sacrer du langue, des quelque vingt lettres—leur devenir, tout y rentre pour tantôt sourdre, principe—approchant d'un rite la composition typographique.

Le livre, expansion totale de la lettre, doit d'elle tirer, directement, une mobilité et spacieux, par correspondances, instituer en jeu, on ne sait, qui confirme la fiction.

[A miracle, in the highest sense of the word: words led back to their origin, which is the twenty-four letters of the alphabet, so gifted with infinity that they will finally consecrate Language. Everything is caught up in their endless variations and then rises out of them in the form of the Principle. Thus typography becomes a rite.

The book, which is the total expansion of the letter, must find its mobility in the letter; and in its spaciousness must establish some nameless system of relationships which will embrace and strengthen fiction.] (OC380/SP26–27)

Cf. "La Musique et les lettres" (OC646/SP47). Blanchot discusses Mallarmé's *Le livre* in *Le livre à venir* (LV303–32/SS227–28).

5. Letter to Eugène Lefébure, 17 May 1867: "C'est bien ce que j'observe sur moi—je n'ai créé mon œuvre que par *élimination*, et toute vérité acquise ne naissait que de la perte d'une impression qui, ayant étincelé, s'était consumée et me permettait, grâce à ses ténèbres dégagées, d'avancer profondément dans la sensation des Ténèbres absolues. La destruction fut ma Béatrice" (C1: 245–46).

6. Letter to Georges Rodenbach, 25 March 1888: "Aussi faut-il des doigts délicats,

faits à indiquer sans toucher, puisque ne reste aucune réalité; elle s'est evaporée en écrit." (C3:177.)

7. OC178: "tout, au monde, existe pour aboutir à un livre"; "une trou foré dans l'Etre" ("a hole in being") is Sartre's phrase, in *Mallarmé: La lucidité et sa face d'ombre* (Paris: Gallimard, 1986), p. 162. Blanchot gives an extended account of the Mallarméan theory of the book in "L'absence de livre" (1969), where *l'écriture* is figured as a "gap [vide] in the universe" (EI620/IC422).

8. In one of his most important texts, "Le grand refus" (1959), Blanchot clarifies the concept of possibility as follows:

> We say something is possible when a conceivable event does not run up against any categorical impediment within a given horizon. It is possible: logic does not prohibit it, nor does science or custom object. The possible, then, is an empty frame; it is what is not at variance with the real, or what is not yet real, or, for that matter, necessary. But for a long time we have been alert to another sense. Possibility is not what is merely possible and should be regarded as less than real. Possibility, in this new sense, is more than reality: it is to be, plus the power to be. Possibility establishes and founds reality: one is what one is only if one has the power to be it. Here we see immediately that man not only has possibilities, but is his possibility. Never are we purely and simply, we are only on the basis of and with regard to the possibilities that we are; this is one of our essential dimensions. The word possible becomes clear, then, when it is placed in relation with the word power [*pouvoir*], first in the sense of capacity, then in the sense of a power that is commanded or a force [*puissance*]. (I am simplifying a great deal.) (EI59/IC41–42)

9. This is the upshot of my discussion of Heidegger's poetics in *Heidegger's Estrangements: Language, Truth, and Poetry in the Later Writings* (New Haven: Yale University Press, 1989), esp. pp. 43–51. I try for a somewhat shorter and more pointed account (one which points directly from Heidegger to Blanchot) in *Hermeneutics Ancient and Modern* (New Haven: Yale University Press, 1992), pp. 229–46 ("Against Poetry: Heidegger, Ricoeur, and the Originary Scene of Hermeneutics"). Contrast Gianni Vattimo's discussion of Heidegger's aesthetics in *The End of Modernity*, trans. Jon R. Snyder (Baltimore: Johns Hopkins University Press, 1988), pp. 51–89.

10. "The world is the self-disclosing openness of the broad paths of the simple and essential decisions in the destiny of an historical people. The earth is the spontaneous forthcoming of that which is continually self-secluding and to that extent sheltering and concealing. World and earth are essentially different from one another and yet are never separated. The world grounds itself on the earth, and earth juts through the world. But the relation between world and earth does not wither away into the empty unity of opposites unconcerned with one another. The world, in resting upon the earth, strives to surmount it. As self-opening it cannot endure anything closed. The earth, however, as sheltering and concealing, tends always to draw the world into itself and keep it there" (GA5:35/PLT48–49). The work of art can be thought of as an event in which the earth strives to draw the world into itself. The work is structured as a rift of earth and world; the strife of earth and world is inscribed in the work as its basic *Gestalt* (GA5:51/PLT63–64).

11. That is, the work is thingly just in the sense in which Heidegger speaks of the resistance of the thing to our efforts to grasp its essence: "The unpretentious thing evades thought most stubbornly. Or can it be that this self-refusal [*Sichzurückhalten*] of the mere thing, this self-contained independence, belongs precisely to the nature of the thing? Must not this strange and uncommunicative feature of the nature of the thing [*jenes Befremdende und Verschlossene im Wesen des Dinges*] become intimately familiar to thought that tries to think the thing? If so, then we should not force our way to its thingly character" (GA5:17/PLT31–32).

12. The English text of this last sentence contains a longstanding error: it misprints "stronger" for "stranger" [*befremdlicher*].

13. I give a brief account of Ricoeur's hermeneutics in *Hermeneutics Ancient and Modern*, pp. 235–41. See also Gianni Vattino, *The End of Modernity*, pp. 70–71. And see section 2 of chapter 2 below, "The Aristotelian Argument."

14. Sartre modified his conception of the exteriority of poetry somewhat as the years passed, particularly in virtue of his study of Mallarmé and his reading of Lacan. See Christina Howells, "Sartre and the Language of Poetry," *Philosophers' Poets*, ed. David Wood (London: Routledge, 1990), pp. 140–52.

15. Joseph Libertson has remarked, quite perceptively, that when one reads the texts of Bataille, Levinas, and Blanchot from the 1940s, it is extremely difficult to tell them apart. "The anomaly which haunts these disparate and exceptionally private texts is the following: each of these thinkers has the capacity and the inclination to speak in the voices of the other two thinkers. This inclination is perceptible not only in the occasional thematic or lexical congruences which link these texts, but also at the most solitary level of their definitions and predications. Underneath the thematic disparity which distinguishes Bataille's world of excess, irony, and violence, Blanchot's economy of impersonality and nocturnal dispersion, and the Levinasian universe of gravity, dissymmetry, and responsibility, a single configuration of communication exists." *Proximity: Levinas, Blanchot, Bataille, and Communication* (The Hague: Martinus Nijhoff, 1982), pp. 2–3.

16. *The Philosophical Discourse of Modernity*, trans. Frederick G. Lawrence (Cambridge, Mass.: MIT Press, 1987), p. 208. See also Habermas, "Philosophy as Stand-in and Interpreter," *Moral Consciousness and Communicative Action*, trans. Christian Lenhardt and Shierry Weber Nicholson (Cambridge, Mass.: MIT Press, 1990), pp. 1–20, esp. pp. 17–20.

17. "Three Dialogues," *Disjecta: Miscellaneous Writings and a Dramatic Fragment*, ed. Ruby Cohn (London: John Calder, 1983), p. 139.

18. *Selected Letters of Gustave Flaubert*, trans. Francis Steegmuller (New York: Farrar, Strauss, and Cudahy, 1953), pp. 127–28.

19. See, however, Simon Critchley's important discussion of "De l'angoisse au langage" in "Il y a — A Dying Stronger than Death (Blanchot with Levinas)," in *Oxford Literary Review*, 15, nos. 1–2 (1993), esp. 86–94. Critchley writes: "Note here that the condition of possibility for literature is a certain silence, the silence of solitude. Silence is then equated by Blanchot with the theme of the Nothing (*le rien*), the silent essence of solitude is a nothingness. Nothing, then, is the material of the writer and *the writer has nothing to express*: a statement that must be read in the same way as Heidegger reads Leibniz's Principle of Sufficient Reason, with the emphasis on *nothing* and *ex-*

press. The writer has an obligation to bring to language, to literature, the nothing or silent solitude that is the source of literature" (88–89). To which Critchley adds, quite rightly: "Such is the tragic-comic situation of the writer (one is reminded of Beckett, although this essay precedes the publication of the first volume of the *Trilogy* by seven years), 'having nothing to write, of having no means of writing, and of being forced by an extreme necessity to keep writing it.'"

20. See chapter 2 below, and Simon Critchley's "*Il y a*—A Dying Stronger than Death (Blanchot with Levinas)," esp. 86–94. See also John Gregg's *Maurice Blanchot and the Literature of Transgression* (Princeton: Princeton University Press, 1993), esp. pp. 10–17. Gregg's discussion is very useful for its account of the coherence between Blanchot and Georges Bataille, from whom Blanchot perhaps learned that "possibility is not the sole dimension of our existence" (*EI*307/*IC*207).

21. Compare Samuel Beckett's writings in this matter. It is easy to read much of Beckett's fiction against the background of the years 1940–44, whence the spies, refugees, and prisoners forced to talk who highlight his inventory of characters. The Beckett world is an occupied country in which people are under surveillance, awaiting orders, confined, picked up and interrogated, in flight or hiding. Without knowing why, people gather information and give it within vast networks presided over by ominous superiors and nameless committees. Watt speaks in increasingly complex codes that Sam, a mole of sorts, is finally unable to break. It is precisely under these conditions that Molloy, a harmless derelict, would be regarded as a suspicious character requiring systematic investigation. Moran meanwhile is an operative turned out into the cold, his son perhaps having informed on him. The Unnamable may have fallen into the hands of the Gestapo, and may be outwitting them still.

See Allan Stoekl's discussion of Blanchot's novel *Le très-haut* (1948), whose hero, Henri Sorge, is a minor bureaucrat in a totalitarian state, "Blanchot and the Silence of Specificity," *Politics, Writing, Mutilation: The Cases of Bataille, Blanchot, Roussel, Leiris, and Ponge* (Minneapolis: University of Minnesota Press, 1985), pp. 22–36; and also John Gregg, who gives a detailed reading of this text in *Maurice Blanchot and the Literature of Transgression*, pp. 72–126, esp. pp. 121–26. See also Stoekl's introduction to his English translation of *Le très-haut*, "Death at the End of History," *The Most High* (Lincoln: University of Nebraska Press, 1996), pp. vii–xxxii.

22. See "Le refus" (A130–31), where "refusal" is not an act of the disengaged subject but an anonymous response to structures of sovereignty and control that speech reflexively affirms. See Leo Strauss, *Persecution and the Act of Writing* (Chicago: University of Chicago Press, 1952), pp. 22–37. Strauss imagines the case of an intellectual in a totalitarian state who knows that certain forbidden opinions are importantly true, and so he writes a book denouncing them, taking care to do so, however, in the dreariest language possible. But of course in order to denounce these views he has to lay them out, and this he does very briefly but in a passionate and unforgettable style that makes their truth emphatic and thus creates an underground audience among those few intelligent enough to have grasped his method. Meanwhile the dull-witted censor and the literal-minded majority join together in missing the point. Derrida tacitly appeals to a model of double writing much like Strauss's in defending his friend Paul de Man against the charge of collaboration. See "Like the Sound of the Sea Deep within a Shell: Paul de

Man's War," trans. Peggy Kamuf, *Responses: On Paul de Man's Wartime Journalism* (Lincoln: University of Nebraska Press, 1989), pp. 127–64.
The best account of double writing that I know of is given by the Polish writer Czeslaw Milosz, in *The Captive Mind* (New York: Vintage Books, 1949). For many Eastern European writers after World War II, becoming the voice of the state was the only alternative to silence or exile, but Milosz describes a third option, namely the practice, or institution, of *Ketman*, which is an old Arabic word for deceiving one's powerful adversaries by seeming to say all that they want to hear. After the war, Milosz says, Eastern European writers became adepts at a practice of writing in which one does not so much express forbidden truths as resist the truths one is bound to reproduce in the cultural documents that one produces in behalf of the state. Milosz distinguishes among various sorts of *Ketman*—I won't elaborate them here, but what they come down to is an art of writing that consists in the disfiguration of official texts. The intellectual contained within a totalitarian structure disguises his thought, not allegorically by expressing alien ideas in a veiled language, but by altering in a material way the thought expressed in the official text—"by removing a comma, inserting an 'and,' establishing this rather than another sequence to the problem discussed" (p. 79). The point is not to convey a secret message but to interrupt the ready-made message of the system that has discourse under its control. This has very much the structure of Blanchot's refusal of philosophy.

23. See Jean-François Sirinelli's discussion of "the generation of 1905" (to which Blanchot, b. 22 September 1907, could be said to belong), in *Génération intellectuelle: Khâgneux et normaliens dans l'entre-deux-guerres* (Paris: Fayard, 1988). A concise history of the "French intellectual," from the Dreyfusards of 1898 to the *intellecrates* of the 1980s, is given by Jeremy Jennings in his introduction to *Intellectuals in Twentieth-Century France: Mandarins and Samurais*, ed. Jeremy Jennings (New York: St. Martin's Press, 1993), pp. 1–32. See also Pascall Ory and Jean-François Sirinelli, *Les intellectuels en France de l'affaire Dreyfus à nos jours* (Paris: A. Colin, 1992), esp. 93–113. A very interesting piece of research is Diane Rubenstein's study *What's Left? The Ecole Normale Supérieure and the Right* (Madison: University of Wisconsin Press, 1990).

24. (Paris: Éditions du Seuil, 1969), esp. pp. 37–77.

25. See Robert Schalk, *The Spectrum of Political Engagement: Mounier, Benda, Nizan, Brasillach* (Princeton: Princeton University Press, 1979), pp. 82–83. Schalk's book is quite well done, but his study of "fascist engagement" confines itself to "self-proclaimed fascists" (p. 77).

26. See "Fascist Ideology," *Fascism: A Reader*, ed. Walter Laqueur (Berkeley: University of California Press, 1976), pp. 315–76, which contains a valuable bibliographical discussion of the renewal of research on fascism since the 1960s, pp. 360–71; *La droite révolutionnaire, 1885–1914: Les origines françaises du fascisme* (Paris: Éditions du Seuil, 1978), and (with Mario Sznajder and Maia Asheri), *Naissance de l'idéologie fasciste* (Paris: Librairie Arthème, 1989); *The Birth of Fascist Ideology: From Cultural Rebellion to Political Revolution*, trans. David Maisel (Princeton: Princeton University Press, 1994). Sternhell's most important study for our purposes is *Ni droite ni gauche: L'idéologie fasciste en France* (Paris: Éditions du Seuil, 1983). The English translation by David Maisel, *Neither Right nor Left: Fascist Ideology in France* (Berkeley: University of Cal-

ifornia Press, 1986), is an enlarged and revised version of the French text. See especially chapter 7, "Spiritualistic Fascism," pp. 213–65, which is a detailed account of the confusion and intensity that characterized the intellectual culture of Paris during the 1930s, where individuals of widely disparate ideological positions joined together in condemning materialism, capitalism, liberalism, bourgeois society, and the decay of culture that these traditional political concepts had come to represent. Not everyone rejecting Marxism and liberalism was a fascist, but, as Sternhell says in his conclusion, "the existence of quasi-fascist channels of transmission [which is where Blanchot begins his intellectual career]—people, movements, journals, study circles—devoted to attacking materialism and its byproducts—liberalism, capitalism, Marxism, and democracy—created a certain intellectual culture which was to undermine the moral legitimacy of an entire civilization" (pp. 302–3). See also Eugen Weber, "France," *The European Right: A Historical Profile*, ed. Hans Rogger and Eugen Weber (Berkeley: University of California Press, 1965), pp. 71–127.

27. See Georges Bataille's "Popular Front in the Street" (1935), a polemic that attacks the leadership of the Popular Front for having abandoned "the anticapitalist offensive" and placed the antifascist movement at the "disposal of socially conservative elements" (OC1:406/VE164).

28. Cf. Robert Soucy, "The Nature of Fascism in France," *International Fascism: New Thoughts and Approaches*, ed. George Mosse (London: Sage, 1979), pp. 243–72, esp. pp. 264–65: "Like Drieu [La Rochelle] most French fascists conceived their revolution to be essentially a spiritual revolution. They argued that France suffered from a declining birthrate, from egoism and individualism and materialism, from a lack of vitality and force, not so much because of economic conditions (French fascist thinkers unanimously rejected a strictly economic or materialistic explanation of history and society), but because of certain philosophical conceptions, especially democratic and liberal philosophical conceptions, which had misled the French people. Once these conceptions were replaced by superior conceptions, French society would be regenerated." Cf. Soucy, "French Fascist Intellectuals in the 1930s: An Old New Left?," *French Historical Studies*, 8, no. 3 (1974), 445–58, esp. 452–53.

Soucy's more recent studies regard French fascism in more social and economic terms and only marginally as an intellectual phenomenon. In *French Fascism: The First Wave, 1924–33* (New Haven: Yale University Press, 1986), and even more so in *French Fascism: The Second Wave, 1933–39* (New Haven: Yale University Press, 1995), Soucy argues explicitly against Sternhell's interpretation of fascism as a revolutionary ideology that was "essentially leftist in . . . its intellectual origins" (p. 10). If one studies groups like the Solidarité Française, the Croix de feu, and the Parti populaire Français, French fascism appears rather straightforwardly as a reactionary movement of right-wing, anti-Semitic nationalists that depended heavily on capitalist interests threatened by Marxism. Soucy defines fascism as "primarily a new variety of authoritarian conservatism and right-wing nationalism that sought to defeat the Marxist threat and the political liberalism that allowed it to exist in the first place. Most fascists therefore shared with the traditional right a fundamental social and economic conservatism that was strongly opposed to Marxism" (p. 17).

29. See Steven Ungar's account of *Combat*, and Blanchot's contributions, in *Scandal and Aftereffect: Blanchot and France since 1930* (Minneapolis: University of Min-

nesota Press, 1995), pp. 104–10; and Jeffrey Mehlman, "Blanchot at *Combat:* Of Literature and Terror," *Legacies of Anti-Semitism in France* (Minneapolis: University of Minnesota Press, 1983), pp. 6–22, and also appendix 2, pp. 107–9. See also Eugen Weber, *Action Française: Royalism and Reaction in Twentieth-Century France* (Stanford: Stanford University Press, 1962), esp. pp. 501–16; and Michael Holland and Patrick Rousseau, "Topographie-parcours d'une (contre)revolution," *Gramma*, 5 (Winter 1976), 8–43. See also Diane Rubenstein, *What's Left?*, esp. pp. 103–36 ("The Ecole Normale Supérieure and the Scene of Writing").

30. With respect to collaboration, Blanchot seems to have somewhat less care than Maulnier to avoid explicit association with Vichy, since (as Bayle noted) he served briefly as Directeur littéraire de Jeune France, nor did he hesitate to write literary essays for a pro-Vichy periodical, the *Journal des débats*. In a postscript Mehlman indicates that he sent a typescript copy of his essay to Blanchot, whose "reaction, in a letter of 26 November 1979, was one of utter disagreement with my argument" (p. 117). In the portion of the letter that Mehlman generously cites, Blanchot rejects any suggestion that he was a collaborator, and in particular he denies Mehlman's statement that, in 1942, he had agreed to serve as a sort of nominal editor of the NRF under the direction of the renowned collaborator Drieu la Rochelle ("the collaborator of a collaborator" is how Blanchot refers to him [p. 22]). Blanchot says he rejected this offer out of hand. Of his post as Directeur littéraire de Jeune France, Blanchot mentions in his letter to Mehlman that he resigned after "only a few weeks (having seen, with a few friends, how naive and dangerous it was to want to use Vichy against Vichy)" (*Legacies of Anti-Semitism*, p. 117).

See Michael Holland's introduction to his edition of *The Blanchot Reader*, pp. 1–15, which offers a few more details about Blanchot's early career. Holland thinks it is wrong to reconstruct Blanchot's politics in terms of those with whom he was associated during the prewar years and the Occupation. Blanchot's virtual anonymity during much if this period, and the lack of biographical and historical information, is, Holland thinks, not an accident, but is already a political position that Blanchot will maintain throughout his career (see esp. pp. 4–5).

31. See Carroll's excellent chapter on Maulnier in *French Literary Fascism: Nationalism, Anti-Semitism, and the Ideology of Culture* (Princeton: Princeton University Press, 1995), pp. 222–47. On Carroll's view, which is close to Sternhell's, Maulnier's was "not the fascism of direct collaborators but of someone who attempted both to stand above the politics of the left and the right and to direct the nation and nationalist politics toward the extremist, antidemocratic culturalist position he derived from a radical, Nietzschean form of classical humanism. Maulnier's aesthetics, which were the foundation for an ultranationalist politics, thus represented one of the most uncompromising, rigorous, intellectual forms of literary fascism, a *literary* fascism beyond fascism" (p. 247).

32. One might compare the Action Française in this respect. Sternhell writes:

The total lack of any real will to action in the Action Française, its flavor of a literary salon, its royalism could only be repellent to the genuine fascists. The Action Française was singularly unattractive to them: from Valois in the days of the Cartel to Bucard, Déat, and Doriot in Paris under the Occupation, the fascists loudly proclaimed their profound contempt for the very narrow social power base of the Action Française, its association with one social class, its character as a movement that existed only in its journalistic publications, and its resulting incapacity for action. The fascists, or simply the men of action, were not deceived. They knew that the surly disposition, inflammatory style, and invectives of the Action Française ill concealed the truth, which was that, comfortably installed in their editorial offices, Maurras and his journalists were happy under a liberal regime—a regime that provided them with the perfect setting for the development of their talents. Not only did the Action Française not think of moving into action, but it was also totally incapable of it, never having envisaged the setting up of any structures other than those necessary for putting out its publications. (*Neither Right nor Left*, p. 100)

33. Stoekl's characterization of Blanchot as basically a bourgeois liberal is worth thinking about. Bourgeois as opposed to what? Neither Marxists nor fascists fall from the sky or well up from the depths; they are products of the culture and society that they rebel against. Sternhell stresses just this point when he repeats, in each of his studies of fascist ideology, that no one responded to fascism so enthusiastically as the intellectuals—and they did so, moreover, not so much because of the threat of revolutionary materialism as because of its failure. See in this connection Eugen Weber's fascinating study "Men of the Archangel," *International Fascism*, pp. 317–43.

For the record, one ought to cite from a letter that Bataille wrote to Alexandre Kojève in December 1937: "I grant (as a likely supposition) that from now on history is ended (except for the denouement). However, I picture things differently (I don't attribute much importance to the difference between fascism and communism; on the other hand, it certainly doesn't seem impossible that, in some very distant time, everything will begin again)." "Letter to X, Lecturer on Hegel," *The College of Sociology*, 1937–39, ed. Denis Hollier, trans. Betsy Wing (Minneapolis: University of Minnesota Press, 1988), p. 90. The original draft of this letter was lost. Hollier indicates that he has "reconstituted" the original from fragments scattered throughout the *œuvre*. See Bataille (OC5:369–71/G123–25).

34. *La crise est dans l'homme* (Paris: Librairie de *La revue française*, 1932), p. 183.

35. Recall Yeats's picture of Byzantium in *A Vision* (London: Macmillan, 1937):

I think that in early Byzantium, maybe never before or since in recorded history, religious, aesthetic and practical life were one, that architect and artificers—though not, it may be, poets, for language had been the instrument of controversy and must have grown abstract—spoke to the multitude and the few alike. The painter, the mosaic worker, the worker in gold and silver, the illuminator of sacred books, were almost impersonal, almost perhaps without the consciousness of individual design, absorbed in their subject-matter and that the vision of a whole people. They could copy out of old Gospel books those pictures that seemed as sacred as the text, and yet weave all into a vast design, the work of many that seemed the work of one, that made building, picture, pattern, metalwork of rail and lamp, seem but a single image; and this vision, this proclamation of their invisible master, had the Greek nobility, Satan always the still half-divine Serpent, never the horned scarecrow of the didactic Middle Ages. (pp. 279–80)

Compare David Carroll's account of Maulnier's "poetical" political theory in *French Literary Fascism*, esp. p. 234:

> What ultimately defines a poem as authentically *poetic* is its ability to act poetically without exterior restraints, to transform the totality of its parts, no matter how apoetic or antipoetic, into integral parts of the poem. What defines a people is exactly the same capacity for the people to act as itself and transform the totality of its history, experiences, and even the foreign elements within it into what could be called a cultural or political poem.

Carroll's argument is that Maulnier's rejection of mass politics and the myth of the leader who wields absolute power from above is a criticism of Italian fascism and German Nazism, but is not for all of that anti-fascist; on the contrary, Maulnier was critical of Italian fascism and German racism for not being fascist enough. See *French Literary Fascism*, pp. 236–38.

36. Quoted by Sternhell, "Fascist Ideology," *Fascism: A Reader*, p. 356. "Totalitarianism," Sternhell wrote in this 1976 essay, "is the very essence of fascism, and fascism is without question the purest example of a totalitarian ideology" (p. 356). But in *Neither Right nor Left* Sternhell makes the argument that, precisely because it never came to power and so was never required to adapt its ideas to the workings of a party or the management of a regime, French fascism—the fascism of the spirit—gives us the clearest picture we can have of fascism as an ideological system.

37. See Eugen Weber, "France," *The European Right*, pp. 108–10. The question of the anti-Semitism of the *Combat* group is vexed. Both Mehlman and Sternhell emphasize Maulnier's and Blanchot's anti-Semitic slurs against Léon Blum. See *Legacies of Anti-Semitism*, esp. pp. 107–9; and *Neither Right nor Left*, p. xxi: "What was not said about Blum in *Combat*, the journal edited by Thierry Maulnier, at the time of the Popular Front? What injury, what insult, what base insinuation, what vulgar accusation was he spared by Maulnier's friends and collaborators, by the journals and reviews to which Maulnier contributed? Did not Maulnier himself, in an article written in the purest tradition of Drumont anti-Semitism, advocate the practice of a 'reasonable anti-Semitism' toward the Jews, who had 'become our masters.'" He then quotes Maulnier to devastating effect as follows:

> Anti-Semitism can be approached either from the humanistic point of view—the point of view of historical and moral justification—or from the point of view of political effectiveness or "revolutionary" effectiveness, if you will. These two approaches are not necessarily connected. Anti-Semitism can have a philosophical validity (if the Jews are really a force of corruption and enslavement of the people) and yet have no practical application in France (if it is impossible or very difficult to mobilize the French people against the Jews). Or, on the other hand, anti-Semitism can be devoid of philosophical validity (if the Jews are innocent of all the crimes of which they are accused) and yet have a usable practical effectiveness (if anti-Semitism is a good means of crystallizing revolutionary tendencies. (pp. xxi–xxi)

In *What's Left?*, Diane Rubenstein writes that Maulnier was "less Germanophile or sympathetic to Italian fascism (than Robert Brasillach). Maulnier preferred that France find its own unique solutions, and he sided with his friend Maurice Blanchot of *Combat* against Brasillach's militant anti-Semitism" (p. 125). In support of this view Rubenstein quotes Blanchot's letter to her, dated 20 August 1983: "I remember little about *Combat*. I do recall however that, as I was utterly opposed to Brasillach, who was completely committed to Fascism and anti-Semitism, I made it a condition of my participation in the journal that there was no possibility that he would also be a contributor. Moreover, things were reciprocal. Brasillach detested *Combat*, because I had been involved with it. Opposition to Brasillach and what he represented was a constant for me at that time" (p. 187, n. 72; the English translation is given by Michael Holland [BR15]). See the section of chapter 9 below entitled "The Metaphysics of Being Jewish."

38. In *The Cult of Violence: Sorel and the Sorelians* (Berkeley: University of California Press, 1980), esp. pp. 246–47, Jack J. Roth places Maulnier and the *Combat* group in the tradition of Georges Sorel, arguably the ideological father of fascism and author of *Réflexions sur la violence* (1906), for whom violence was indeed the transcendental foundation as well as strategic method of revolution. The principal point is that violence is creative as well as destructive. See Sternhell, *The Birth of Fascist Ideology*, pp. 38–91.

Sorel's influence was pervasive across the ideological spectrum and appears most dramatically in Walter Benjamin's essay "Zur Kritik der Gewalt" (1920): "Every conceivable solution to human problems, not to speak of deliverance from the confines of all the world-historical conditions of existence obtaining hitherto, remains impossible if violence is excluded in principle" (*Gesammelte Schriften* [Frankfurt: Suhrkamp, 1977], vol. 2, bk. 2, p. 196; "Critique of Violence," *Reflections: Essays, Aphorisms, Autobiographical Writings*, trans. Peter Demetz [New York: Schocken Books, 1978], p. 293.) One could also translate *Gewalt* as "power" or "force." So we are very close to the later Foucault here. Compare Jean-Paul Sartre's introduction to Frantz Fanon's *Les damnés de la terre* (1961); *The Wretched of the Earth*, trans. Constance Farrington (New York: Grove Weidenfeld, 1968), pp. 7–34.

Among the Surrealists revolutionary violence was an intoxicating thought. More trenchantly, for Bataille, violence is the condition of existence as such, since existence is fundamentally anarchic ("the movement of existence . . . demands constant distintegration" [OC1:468/VE198]). See Joseph Libertson, "Bataille, and Communication: Savoir, Non-Savoir, Glissement, Rire," *On Bataille: Critical Essays*, ed. Leslie Anne Boldt-Irons (Albany: SUNY Press, 1995), pp. 209–36.

For Maulnier violence may have been transcendental in aesthetic as well as political senses. Carroll gives a good account of the internal link between poetry and violence in Maulnier's poetics. See *French Literary Fascism*, pp. 231–33, esp. p. 232: "In principle, all authentic poetry is violent, for a poetry devoid of cruelty and violence is an abstract, formalist, aestheticist poetry, a nonpoetic poetry. A people and a culture without violence are thus also a people and a culture without poetry."

39. See the reprint of this article in *Gramma*, 5 (1976), 69. The passage is given in English by Mehlman, *Legacies of Anti-Semitism in France*, p. 11. Blanchot, in this essay, seems closer to Brasillach than to Maulnier, as Eugen Weber notes in *Action Française*, p. 513. Weber quotes from an interview that Maulnier gave to a Canadian journalist in 1940: " 'The duty of French youth is, above all, to perpetuate tradition, that is, to reintroduce dignity into the life of France by giving intellectual, moral, and spir-

itual values their true place; it is to believe that cultural values dominate political and economic values which are no more than their application, their tangible reflection.' 'In that case,' the Canadian pursued, 'you do not believe in a *revolution* in France?' 'Yes, yes we do,' Maulnier answered; 'but not in a noisy, blatant revolution, not in a destructive revolution. We believe . . . in the *revolution of the spirit*' " (p. 514). But of course this was in 1940. Weber suggests that by 1937 "Blanchot opposed the undiscriminating violence of Fascism" (p. 513).

    40. Quoted by Roth, *The Cult of Violence: Sorel and the Sorelians*, p. 246. In *Past Imperfect: French Intellectuals, 1944–56* (Berkeley: University of California Press, 1992), Tony Judt (citing, interestingly, Blanchot's "Le Terrorisme méthode de salut public") remarks on the mythology of terror in French intellectual life both during the 1930s and after the Liberation:

> Terror as an ideal, terror as a method, terror as a regrettable necessity, terror as metaphor, terror in every shape and form permeated intellectual consciousness. Terror, too, was integral to the larger picture of social processes that the Revolution had bequeathed to modern French thought, the idea that all *real* change comes and can only come as the result of a single, clean break. Anything short of such a break was inadequate and thus fraudulent. This obsession with the Revolution disfigured French intellectual life in two ways. It introduced a permissive attitude towards extremist positions of all sorts, just because of their extremism, and it gave hostages to the most radical forms of historicism, especially those that absolved individuals of any private moral responsibility for the era in which history had placed them. It is perhaps for this reason that the French were so vulnerable to the charms of *German* thought [!]. . . . The French lacked (and still lack) a theory of their own historicist practices. The general drift of French philosophy since the early eighteenth century has been in directions distinctly at variance with the trajectory of French social thought, not to speak of French history itself. In these circumstances, German thought, from Hegel to Heidegger, has proved extremely serviceable. (p. 255)

    41. The complexity of Blanchot's case is explored with great care by Steven Ungar in *Scandal and Aftereffect*, pp. 102–36. Ungar gives some of the political as well as conceptual background of "Comment la littérature est-elle possible?," and in addition analyzes an important text that Blanchot published in 1937, "De la révolution à la littérature." The upshot is that terror is appropriated rather than replaced by literature (cf. *FP*97/*BR*56). Particularly valuable is Ungar's discussion of Blanchot's contributions to *L'Insurgé*, which Ungar characterizes as "prophetic and chilling. Their invocation of a new order and their dismissal of political moderation came as close as anything Blanchot ever wrote at the time to endorsing the values of a native French fascism" (p. 112). Ungar characterizes the Blanchot of this period as a "dissident reactionary nationalist" (p. 113), but his research and analyses seem to support the view that Blanchot's commitment to dissidence is constant throughout his career, and that it is mediated differently at different times by the language, concepts, and social movements available to it in the immediate political environment. So Blanchot is fascist vis-à-vis Blum's Popular Front, radical vis-à-vis De Gaulle. France changes, but not Blanchot. See Allan Stoekl's very important discussion of this material in *Agonies of the Intellectual: Commitment,*

Subjectivity, and the Performative in the Twentieth-Century French Tradition (Lincoln: University of Nebraska Press, 1992), pp. 145–73, esp. pp. 166–67.

42. See Sternhell, *The Birth of Fascist Ideology*, p. 29.

43. See David Wieck, "The Negativity of Anarchism" (1975), in *Reinventing Anarchy*, ed. Howard Erlich, Carol Erlich, David DeLeon, and Glenda Morris (London: Routledge and Kegan Paul, 1977), p. 139.

44. A propos of 1968: Blanchot is sometimes credited with the authorship of an anonymous article that appeared in a paper published by the Comité d'Action étudiants-écrivains, a group to which Blanchot and Marguerite Duras belonged. The article calls for a "break with the powers that be, hence with the notion of power, hence everywhere that power predominates." It continues:

> To be the bearers of this break is not merely to dislodge, or attempt to dislodge, from their integration within the social order those forces that promise a break, it is to be sure that really, and each time it occurs, refusal, without ceasing to be active refusal, does not remain a *purely negative moment*. That, politically and philosophically, is one of the most powerful characteristics of the movement. In this sense, radical refusal such as that borne by the movement, and such as that which we have to bear, goes way beyond simple negativity, in so far as it is the negation even of what has not yet been advanced and affirmed. To bring to light the singular character of this refusal is one of the theoretical tasks of the new political thinking. This theoretical undertaking obviously does not entail drawing up a programme or a platform, but rather, independent of any programmatic project, indeed of any project, maintaining *a refusal that is an affirmation*, bringing out or maintaining an affirmation that does not come to any arrangements [*s'arranger*], but rather undoes arrangements [*dérange*], including its own, since it is in relation with dis-arrangement [*le désarrangement*] or disarray [*le désarroi*] or else the non-structurable.

"Mots de désordre," *Liberation*, 28–29 (January 1984), 4–5; "Disorderly Words," trans. Michael Holland (BR200–201). This anti-Gaullist "affirmative refusal" may not be easy to distinguish from the "fascist refusal" of the *Combat* group. Perhaps the same can be said of Blanchot's involvement in the protest against the Algerian war during the late 1950s—he is usually credited with the authorship of the "Manifeste des 121," *Vérité-Liberté: Cahiers d'Informations sur la Guerre d'Algerie*, 4 (September–October 1960); reprinted in *L'Autre Journal*, 9 (November 1985), 67–70. See Madeleine Chapsal's interview with Blanchot in *Le droite à l'insoumission* (Paris: Maspero, 1961), pp. 90–93, a translation of which appears in *The Blanchot Reader* (BR196–99). It is worth noticing that in this interview Blanchot uses a traditionally liberal language very different from his own when he speaks of insubordination as a "right": "I say right and not duty, a term that some people, in an ill-considered way, wished the Declaration to use, no doubt because they believe that the formulation of a duty goes further than that of a right. But that is not the case: an obligation depends upon a prior morality, that vouches for it, guarantees and justifies it. . . . A right, on the contrary, depends only on itself, on the exercise of the freedom of which it is the expression. Right is a free power for which each person, for his part and in relation to himself, is responsible, and which binds him completely and freely: nothing is stronger, nothing is more solemn. That is why one must say: the right to insubordination; it is a matter of each person's sovereign decision" (BR196–97).

45. An interesting text to study in this context is Bataille's "The Psychological Structure of Fascism" (1936), which understands fascism as an essentially anarchistic phenomenon whose violence is a reaction against the imperative power of bourgeois culture. Bataille writes that the

> fascist leaders are incontestably part of heterogeneous existence. Opposed to democratic politicians, who represent in different countries the platitude inherent to *homogeneous* society, Mussolini and Hitler immediately stand out as something *other*. Whatever emotions their actual existence as political agents of evolution provokes, it is impossible to ignore the *force* that situates them above men, parties, and even laws: a *force* that disrupts the regular course of things, the peaceful but fastidious homogeneity powerless to maintain itself (the fact that laws are broken is only the most obvious sign of the transcendent, *heterogeneous* nature of fascist action). (OC1:348/VE143)

In "Les intellectuels en question" (1984), Blanchot defends Bataille against the charge of fascism, saying that from late 1940 he saw Bataille on an almost daily basis and can vouch for his "horror of Nazism, as well as of the Pétain regime and its ideology (family, labour, fatherland). He came to regret the pages he wrote on 'The psychological structure of Fascism' . . . and which could have lent themselves to misunderstanding" (IQ20/BR226).

One could look for a symmetry between the psychological structure of fascism," as Bataille understands it, and the structure of Blanchot's poetics, with its commitment to the heterogeneous and the interruption of order. Compare Blanchot on Bataille in *La communauté unavouable*. Blanchot begins the first part of this text, entitled "La communauté négative," with an epigraph from Bataille: *La communauté de ceux qui n'ont pas de communauté* (The community of those who have no community). Blanchot here discusses briefly another group from the 1930s, "Acéphale," a quasi-secret, anarchistic society that formed around Georges Bataille: "'Acéphale' is still bound to its mystery. Those who participated in it are not certain they had a part in it. They have not spoken, or else the inheritors of their words are tied to a still firmly maintained reserve. The texts published under that title do not reveal its scope, except for a few sentences which much later still stun those who wrote them" (CI28/UC13). Blanchot then gives the following description of the group:

> Each member of the community is not only the whole community, but the violent, disparate, exploded, powerless incarnation of the totality of beings who, tending to exist integrally, have as corollary the nothingness they have already, and in advance, fallen into. Each member makes a group only through the absoluteness of the separation that needs to affirm itself in order to break off so as to become relation, a paradoxical, even senseless relation, if it is an absolute relation with other absolutes that exclude all relation. Finally, the "secret"—which signifies this separation—is not to be looked for directly in the forest where the sacrifice of a consenting victim should have occurred, a victim ready to receive death from the one who could *give* it to him only by dying. It is too easy to evoke

The Possessed and the dramatic vicissitudes during which, in order to cement the group of conspirators, the responsibility for a murder committed by one person was destined to enchain one to another all of those who kept their egos in the pursuit of a common revolutionary aim that indeed should have merged them all into one. What we are left with is the mere parody of a sacrifice set up not to destroy a certain oppressive order but to carry destruction into another order of oppression.

The Acéphale community, insofar as each member of the group was no longer only responsible for the group but for the total existence of humanity, could not accomplish itself in only two of its members, given that all had in it an equal and total share and felt obliged, as at Massada, to throw themselves into the nothingness that was no less incarnated by the community. Was it absurd? Yes, but not only absurd, for it meant breaking with the law of the group, the law that constituted it by exposing it to that which transcended it without that transcendence being other than the group's, i.e., to the outside which was the intimacy of the group's singularity. In other words, the community, by organizing and by giving itself as project the execution of a sacrificial death, would have renounced its renunciation of creating a *work*, be it a work of death, or even the simulation of death. The impossibility of death in its most naked possibility (the knife meant to cut the victim's throat and which, with the same movement, would cut off the head of the "executioner"), suspended until the end of time the illicit action in which the exaltation of the most passive passivity have been affirmed. (CI28–29/UC13–14)

See Jean-Michel Besnier, *La politique de l'impossible: L'intellectuel entre révolte et engagement* (Paris: Éditions la découverte, 1988), esp. pp.123–28.

46. Mehlman notes that Blanchot's "final text for *Combat*, 'On demande des dissidents' (December 1937), is a protracted meditation on the transition 'from the same to the same [*du même au même*],' the near impossibility of achieving the measure of heterogeneity termed dissidence" (*Legacies of Anti-Semitism*, p. 21).

47. Compare Bataille on sovereignty: "sovereign art is such only in the renunciation, indeed in the repudiation, of the functions and the power assumed by real sovereignty. From the viewpoint of power, sovereign art is an abdication" (OC8:448/AS2:421). And again: "Whoever speaks on behalf of a sovereign art places himself outside a real domain on which he has no hold, against which he is without any rights. The artist is NOTHING in the world of things, and if he demands a place there, even if this only consisted in the right to speak or in the more modest right to eat, he follows in the wake of those who believed that sovereignty could, without being surrendered, have a hold on the world of things" (OC8:301/AS2:257).

Chapter 2: Poetry after Hegel

1. Blanchot's terms of art—poetry, literature, writing—are not interchangeable, but they are porous and unstable, liable to turn into one another in any given context. Blanchot, for example, makes no effort to reduce these words conceptually; each emphasizes in different ways *la matérialité du langage* (PF316/GO46/WF327). However, in

his later, fragmentary texts Blanchot comes to speak almost exclusively in terms of *l'écriture*.

2. As published in *La part du feu* (1949), "Littérature et la droit à la mort" comprises two essays, "Le règne animal de l'esprit," *Critique*, 18 (1947), 387–405, and "Littérature et la droit à la mort," *Critique*, 20 (1948), 30–47.

3. *Les mots et les choses: une archéologie des sciences humaines* (Paris: Éditions Gallimard, 1966), p. 313; *The Order of Things: An Archeology of the Human Sciences* (New York: Random House, 1970), p. 300.

4. "Politics as Opposed to What," *The Politics of Interpretation*, ed. W. T. J. Mitchell (Chicago: University of Chicago Press, 1987), p. 199.

5. A somewhat different, at all events milder picture of reading appears in *L'espace littéraire* (1955), where reading is given a Heideggerian turn: "Reading does not produce anything, does not add anything. It lets be what is. It is freedom: not the freedom that produces being or grasps it, but freedom that welcomes, consents, says yes, can say only yes, and, in this the space opened by this yes, lets the work's overwhelming decisiveness affirm itself, lets be its affirmation that it is—and nothing more" (*EL*255/*SL*194). What this later text retains is the idea that reading is not subjectivist, not a cognitive assertion that brings what is read under rational control.

6. See Bataille, "La notion de dépense" (*OC*1:318/*VE*127): "In historical agitation, only the word Revolution dominates the customary confusion and carries with it the promise that answers the unlimited demands of the masses." Revolution is not an event that can be produced according to plan; it is the expression of the fundamental anarchy of existence, where existence is like the sun, expending energy without why and without recompense. In "Front populaire dans la rue" (1936), Bataille gives this description:

> Derided humanity has already known surges of power. These chaotic but implacable power surges dominate history and are known as Revolutions. On many occasions entire populations have gone into the street and nothing has been able to resist their force. It is an incontestable fact that if men have found themselves in the streets, armed, in a mass uprising, carrying with them the tumult of the total power of the people, it has never been the consequence of a narrow and speciously defined political alliance.
> What drives the crowds into the street is the emotion directly aroused by striking events in the atmosphere of a storm, it is the contagious emotion that, from house to house, from suburb to suburb, suddenly turns a hesitating man into a frenzied being. (*OC*1:403/*VE*162)

In 1962 Bataille characterized this event as a "politics of the impossible" (*OC*3:520). See Jean-Michel Besnier, *Politiques de l'impossible—Système et communication chez Georges Bataille* (Paris: La Découverte, 1988); cf. Besnier, "Georges Bataille in the 1930s: A Politics of the Impossible," trans. Amy Reid, *On Bataille*, ed. Allan Stoekl, *Yale French Studies*, 78 (1990), pp. 177–78.

7. Cf. Hegel, *Phänomenologie*, 6.B.3, "Die absolute Freiheit und der Schrecken": "Universal freedom . . . can produce neither a positive work nor a deed; there is left for it only *negative* action; it is merely the *fury* of destruction [*die Furie des Verschwindens*]" (§589). Whence the famous line that interests Blanchot: "The sole work and

deed of freedom is therefore *death*, a death too which has no inner significance or fill-ing, for what is negated is the empty point of the absolutely free self. It is thus the cold-est and meanest of deaths, with no more significance than cutting off a head of cab-bage or swallowing a mouthful of water" (§590). *Hegel's Phenomenology of Spirit*, trans. A. V. Miller (Oxford: Clarendon Press, 1977), pp. 359–60. On "Littérature et la droit à la mort" as a reading of Hegel's *Phenomenologie*, see Simon Critchley, "*Il y a*—A Dy-ing Stronger than Death (Blanchot with Levinas)," *Oxford Literary Review*, 15 (1994), 104–9.

8. Bataille writes:

> To know is always to strive, to work; it is always a servile operation, indefinitely resumed, indefinitely repeated. Knowledge is never sovereign: to be *sovereign* it would have to occur in a moment. But the moment remains outside, short of or beyond, all knowledge. We know regular sequences in time, constants; we know nothing, absolutely, of what is not in the image of an operation, a servile modal-ity of being, subordinate to the future, to its concatenation in time. We know nothing absolutely of the moment. In short, we know nothing about what ulti-mately concerns us, what *is supremely* [*souverainement*] *important to us*. The operation leaves off as soon as sovereignty is its object.
>
> Yet we are in fact conscious of the moment. (Indeed, we are conscious of nothing but the moment.) But this consciousness is at the same time a slipping-away of the moment, insofar as it might be clear and distinct, insofar as it is not a vague knowledge of oneself but knowledge of an object: knowledge of an ob-ject needs to apprehend that object caught up in duration, beyond the present moment. Consciousness of the moment is not truly such, is not sovereign, ex-cept as *unknowing*. Only by canceling, or at least neutralizing, every operation of knowledge within ourselves are we in the moment, without fleeing it. This is possible in the grip of strong emotions that shut off, interrupt or override the flow of thought. (OC8:253–54/AS2:202–3)

See also Bataille's "Deux fragments sur rire," *Le coupable* (OC5:388–92/G143).

9. In 1965 Blanchot speaks of this moment as an interval, a between-time, like an interruption of speech (*l'entre-dire*) "when everything ceases, everything is arrested," in-cluding, since nothing is forbidden, the desire to speak, as if speech were never any-thing but a response to what prohibits it. "Always pending, this instant of silent frenzy is also the instant at which man, by a cessation wherein he affirms himself, attains his true sovereignty; he is no longer only himself, not only nature (natural man), but that which nature never is: consciousness of the infinite power of destruction—that is, of negation—through which consciousness ceaselessly makes and undoes itself" (EI336–37/IC226). The phrase *le droit à la mort* derives from Hölderlin ("For what I want is to die, and it is for man a right" [cited by Blanchot, EI64/IC45]), perhaps by way of Alexandre Kojève, "L'idée de la mort dans la philosophie de Hegel," *Introduction à la lecture de Hegel* (Paris: Gallimard, 1947), p. 558 ("C'est donc bien dans et par la Ter-reur que cette liberté se propage dans la société, et elle ne peut pas être atteinte dans un État 'tolerant', qui ne prend pas ses citoyens suffisamment au sérieux pour leur as-surer leur droit politique à la mort").

10. Compare Blanchot's "De la revolution à la littérature," *Insurge* (January 1937),

and see Steven Ungar's discussion of this article and its connection with "Littérature et la droit à la mort" in *Scandal and Aftereffect*, pp. 113–23.

11. Cf. Bataille, *L'Érotisme* (1957) (OC10:164–75: "L'homme souverain de Sade").

12. See Kojève, *Introduction à la lecture de Hegel*, pp. 474–75; *Introduction to the Reading of Hegel: Lectures on The Phenomenology of Spirit*, ed. Allan Bloom, trans. James H. Nichols (Ithaca: Cornell University Press, 1969), pp. 200–201: "The being which negates the given real dialectically also preserves it as negated—that is, as unreal [*irréel*] or 'ideal': it preserves what is negated as the 'meaning' ['*sens*'] of the discourse by which it reveals it. Hence it is 'conscious' of what it negates." The "being which negates the given real dialectically" is man, that is, the "*human*, essentially negating reality." Cf. Blanchot, "Le mythe de Mallarmé" (originally "Mallarmé et langage," 1946): "The word has meaning only if it rids us of the object it names [*s'il nous débarrasse de l'objet qu'il nomme*]: it must spare us its presence or 'concrete reminder' ['*le concret rappel*']. In authentic language, speech has a function that is not only representative but also destructive. It causes to vanish, it renders the object absent, it annihilates it" (PF37/WF30).

Recent readings of Hegel, particularly among North American scholars, are inclined to regard Hegel as less of a hyperrationalist than did Kojève. See, for example, Robert Pippin, *Hegel's Idealism: The Satisfactions of Self-Consciousness* (Cambridge: Cambridge University Press, 1988) and *Modernism as a Philosophical Problem: The Dissatisfactions of European High Culture* (Cambridge: Basil Blackwell, 1991); Terry Pinkard, *Hegel's Phenomenology: The Sociality of Reason* (Cambridge: Cambridge University Press, 1994); and Paul Redding, *Hegel's Hermeneutics* (Ithaca: Cornell University Press, 1996), esp. pp. 119–83.

Still, Kojève captures something. Hegel, in his early Jena lectures, calls language "the name-giving power," where the giving of a name is an appropriation or taking-possession of what is named, in which I am able to address all things *as mine*, that is, as names.

> [We might ask, for example,] What *is* this? We answer, It *is* a lion, a donkey, etc.—it *is*. Thus it is not merely something yellow, having feet, etc., something on its own [existing] independently. Rather, it is a *name*, a sound made by my voice, something entirely different from what it is in being looked at—and this [as named] is its true *being*. [We might say:] This is only its *name*, the thing itself is something different; but then we fall back onto the sensory representation. Or: It is *only* a name, in a higher sense, since to begin with, the name is itself only the very superficial *spiritual being*. By means of the name, however, the object has been born out of the I *as being*. This is the primal creativity exercised by the Spirit. Adam gave a name to all things. This is the sovereign right [of Spirit], its primal taking-possession of all nature—or the creation of nature out of Spirit.

By naming, in other words, I assert ownership and mastery over the world as a conceptual order (likewise, as Blanchot says, "We cannot do anything with an object that has no name" [PF312/GO41/WF322]). Thus Hegel: "The I is first of all in *possession* of names; it must preserve them in its Night—as serviceable, obedient to the I. Not only must it regard names in general, it must also look at them in its space as a *fixed* order— for this is their interrelation and necessity, the intrinsic relation of many different names." See *Hegel and the Human Spirit: A Translation of the Jena Lectures on the Philosophy of Spirit (1805–6)*, trans. Leo Rauch (Detroit: Wayne State university Press, 1983), pp. 89–91.

Contrast Heidegger: "Words have become instruments for hunting down and hitting, namely in the 'procedure' and 'labor' of representing everything [as surely as] precision-firing. The machine-gun, the camera, the 'word,' the poster—all have this same fundamental function of putting objects in retainment" (GA55:70).

I cannot help citing here, as a last turn of the screw, my favorite passage from Horkeimer and Adorno's "Odysseus or Myth and Enlightenment," on the internal link between laughter and naming (both are divine prerogatives):

> Even though laughter is still the sign of force, of the breaking out of blind and obdurate nature, it also contains the opposite element—the fact that through laughter blind nature becomes aware of itself as it is, and thereby surrenders itself to the power of destruction. This duality of laughter is akin to that of the name, and perhaps names are no more than frozen laughter, as is evident nowadays in nicknames—the only ones that retain something of the original action of namegiving. Laughter is marked by the guilt of subjectivity, but in the suspension of law which it indicates it also points beyond thralldom. It is a promise of the way home. (*Dialectic of Enlightenment*, p. 78)

There is, in other words, something anarchic in naming as in laughter. Blanchot inquires into the one but not the other—laughter is not a possibility for Blanchot. This is the only feature he shares with Jürgen Habermas, who cites the passage from Horkheimer and Adorno just quoted only to stare at it in dumb horror. See *The Theory of Communicative Action*, 1:383.

13. In other words, to the question "Comment la littérature est-elle possible?," the answer is: death. See Steven Ungar's commentary on this line in *Scandal and Aftereffect*, pp. 114–23, esp. p. 121. The quotation from Hegel, however, is crucial. See Simon Critchley's gloss on this line in *"Il y a—A Dying Stronger than Death,"* 107–8: "Dialectical thought, which is also the active dynamic of *Erfahrung* [experience] and the movement of the *Begriff* [concept] for Hegel, consists in the emergence of new, true objects for consciousness through the labor of negation. What Hegel calls the Life of the Spirit is this 'magical power' to live through the negative, to produce experience out of a labour of negation. This work of negation whereby the in-itself becomes for-itself and the immediate mediated is then likened, by Hegel, to *death*: '. . . Of all things the most dreadful, and to hold fast to what is dead requires the greatest strength.' Thus, the Subject produces itself through tarrying with death and looking it in the face; the Life of the Spirit endures death and maintains itself in death." Cf. Bataille's discussion of this matter (which takes its inspiration from "Littérature et la droit à la mort"), "Hegel, Death, and Sacrifice," trans. Jonathan Strauss, *Yale French Studies*, 78 (1990), 9–28, esp. 13–16.

There is a good account of "the importance of death" in Hegel (as Kojève imagines him) by Barry Cooper, *The End of History: An Essay on Modern Hegelianism* (Toronto: University of Toronto Press, 1984), pp. 90–94.

14. However, as Kojève explains, death can only be predicated of man, or man of death: "La réalité *humaine* est donc en dernière analyse 'la réalité-objective de la *mort*':

l'Homme n'est pas seulement *mortel*; il est la *mort* incarnée; il *est* sa propre mort" (*Introduction à la lecture de Hegel*, p. 569).

15. Blanchot writes: "In a text dating from before *The Phenomenology*, Hegel, here the friend and kindred spirit of Hölderlin, writes: 'Adam's first act, which made him master of the animals, was to give them names, that is, he annihilated them in their existence (as existing creatures).'" In a note Blanchot cites Kojève's thought that "for Hegel comprehension was equivalent to murder" (*PF*312/GO42/WF323). See *Introduction à la lecture de Hegel*, pp. 553–54. Cf. Emmanuel Levinas, *Totalité et infini*: "The relation with Being that is enacted as ontology consists in neutralizing the existent in order to comprehend or grasp it. It is hence not a relation with the other as such but a reduction of the other to the same. Such is the definition of freedom: to maintain oneself against the other, despite every relation with the other to ensure the autarchy of an I. Thematization and conceptualization . . . are not at peace with the other but suppression and possession of the other. For possession affirms the other, but within a negation of its independence" (*TeI*36–37/*TI*46).

16. Compare *Being and Time*: "Truth (uncoveredness [*Entdecktheit*]) is something that must always first be wrested from entities. Entities get snatched out of their hiddenness [*Das Seiende wird der Verborgenheit entrissen*]. The factical uncoveredness of anything is always, as it were, a kind of robbery [*ein Raub*]" (*SZ*222/*BT*265); and Foucault, *L' ordre du discours* (Paris: Éditions Gallimard, 1971), p. 55, where discourse is "a violence that we do to things."

17. Nothing? Or everything? This is the question—the contradiction—that these pages of "Littérature et la droit à la mort" are trying to resolve. In the early essay on Char, for example, Blanchot speaks of the "poetic contradiction" between presence and absence, possibility and impossibility, everything and nothing:

> It is, in a way, because the poem exists that the future is possible. The poem is this movement toward what is not and, even more, the enjoyment of what has not been granted, the appropriation, in the most substantial presence of This is not yet there [*Ceci n'est pas encore là*], This will be there only if I myself have disappeared. . . . One feels that the horizon of absence and unreality that surrounds the poem, and the indulgence of the imaginary and the marvelous, signify only one of the terms of fundamental poetic contradiction: the poem goes toward absence, but it is to reconstruct the total reality with it; it is striving toward the imaginary, but it aims for "the productive knowledge of Reality." The search for totality, in all its forms, is the poetic claim par excellence, a claim in which the impossibility of being accomplished is included as its condition, so that if it ever happens to be accomplished, it is only as something not possible, because the poem claims to include its impossibility and its non-realization in its very existence. (*PF*108/WF103–4)

18. In a preface Bataille mentions that the first edition of *L'impossible* was entitled "Hatred of Poetry" (evidently in the sense of poetry's hatred): "It seemed to me that true poetry was reached only by hatred. Poetry had no powerful meaning except in the violence of revolt. But poetry attains this violence only by evoking the *impossible*. Almost no one understood the meaning of the first title, which is why I prefer finally to speak of *The Impossible*" (*OC*3:102/*I*10).

19. See Besnier, *La politique de l'impossible: L'intellectuel entre révolte et engagement* (Paris: Éditions la découverte, 1988), esp. 131–61. The phrase "politics of the impossible" is from Georges Bataille in a letter to Jérôme Linden, 9 January 1962 (OC3: 521), and refers basically to the idea of revolution as a species of nonproductive expenditure. The desire that revolution satisfies is not utopian, that is, its aims are fulfilled not in what it makes possible but in what it evacuates.

20. *Heidegger on Being and Acting: From Principles to Anarchy*, pp. 275–81.

21. See "Affirmer le rupture" (1968), where the refusal of integration into the social order is "not a purely negative moment":

> To bring to light the singular character of this refusal is one of the theoretical tasks of the new political thinking. This theoretical undertaking obviously does not entail drawing up a programme or a platform, but rather, independent of any programmatic project, indeed of any project, maintaining *a refusal that is an affirmation*, bringing out or maintaining an affirmation that does not come to any arrangements, but rather undoes arrangements, including its own, since it is in relation with dis-arrangement or disarray or else the non-structurable. (BR200–201)

22. Contrast this with Blanchot's earlier description of poetic language in "La poésie de Mallarmé est-elle obscure?" in *Faux pas*: "En d'autres termes, le langage n'est seule un moyen accidentel de l'expression, une ombre qui laisse le corps invisible, il est aussi ce qui existe en soi-même comme ensemble de sons, de cadences, de nombres, et, à ce titre, par l'enchaînement des forces qu'il figure, il se révèle comme fondement des choses et de la réalite humaine" (FP129). Cf. "Poésie et langage" (FP160–61).

23. To avoid misunderstanding: materiality as Blanchot figures it is outside the alternatives of idealism and materialism. The dialectic of negation that produces a world is a dialectic of labor as well as of discourse, in which case Blanchot's critique of the dialectic would include materialist accounts of production as well as idealist theories of meaning. Language for Blanchot is, in a sense, more than linguistic; it is the whole productive system of work and speech that constructs human history and culture.

24. Likewise there are moments when the sheer descriptiveness of plain prose invades its own lucidity: "what slip in are vague recollections rising from deep down in the earth, expressions that are in the process of metamorphosing, words in which a thick fluidity of vegetable growth insinuates itself under the clear meaning. Doesn't everyone think he understands these descriptions, written in perfectly meaningful prose? Doesn't everyone think they belong to the clear and human side of literature? And yet they do not belong to the world but to the underworld; they do not attest to form but to lack of form" (PF322–23/GO53/WF335). Blanchot suggests that Francis Ponge with his poetry of objects is perhaps on the threshold of world and underworld — or, in Heidegger's idiom, of world and earth (PF323/GO53).

25. On "the impossibility of dying," see chapter 3, below, and John Gregg, "Blanchot's Suicidal Artist: Writing and the (Im)possibility of Dying," *Sub-Stance* 55, 17, no. 1 (1988), 47–58; rpt. in *Maurice Blanchot and the Literature of Transgression*, pp. 35–45.

26. In a footnote Blanchot suggests a symmetry between this interminable, incessant "resifting of words" and the "anonymous and impersonal flow of being" that Emmanuel Levinas characterizes with the idiomatic expression *il y a*: there is (PF320/

GO51/WF332). See Levinas, *De l'existence à l'existant* (DEE93–95/EE57–58, 65–66). See chapter 3 below, where the *il y a* is examined in greater detail. With respect to the *il y a* Levinas and Blanchot seem to be thinking one another's thoughts—Levinas, for example, cites the opening pages of *Thomas l'obscur* as "a description of the *il y a*"—which is what Thomas experiences in chapter 4, discussed at the outset of this chapter. See Joseph Libertson's "Negativity and *il y a* in Proximity," *Proximity: Levinas, Blanchot, Bataille, and Communication*, pp. 201–11, esp. pp. 206–7 on "the fundamental inextrication of the thought of Blanchot and Levinas."

27. See "La valeur d'usage de D. A. F. Sade": "The work of philosophy as well as of science or common sense . . . has always had as its goal the establishment of the homogeneity of the world" (OC2:60/VE96). Against this project Bataille proposes the valuation of whatever cannot be appropriated within such a world, that is, whatever is heterogeneous to "political, juridical, and economic institutions":

> Sexual activity, whether perverted or not; the behavior of one sex before the other; defecation; urination; death and the cult of cadavers . . . ; the different taboos; ritual cannibalism; the sacrifice of animal gods; omophagia; the laughter of exclusion; sobbing (which in general has death as its object); religious ecstasy; the identical attitude toward shit, gods, and cadavers; the terror that so often accompanies involuntary defecation; the custom of exchanging brilliant, lubricious, painted and jeweled women; gambling; heedless expenditure and certain fanciful uses of money, etc. . . . together present a common character in that the object of the activity (excrement, shameful parts, cadavers, etc. . . .) is found each time treated as a foreign body (*das ganz Anderes*); in other words, it can just as well be expelled following a brutal rupture as reabsorbed through the desire to put one's body and mind entirely in a more or less violent state of expulsion (or projection). The notion of the (heterogeneous) *foreign body* permits one to see the elementary *subjective* identity between types of excrement (sperm, menstrual blood, urine, fecal matter) and everything that can be seen as sacred, divine, or marvelous; a half-decomposed cadaver fleeing through the night in a luminous shroud can be seen as characteristic of this unity. (OC2:57/VE94)

Chapter 3: *Il y a, il meurt*

1. See Françoise Collin, *Maurice Blanchot et la question de l'écriture*, pp. 36–38.

2. Compare Heidegger, "Der Ursprung des Kunstwerkes": "In a work . . . this fact, that it *is* as a work, is just what is unusual. The event of its being created does not simply reverberate through the work; rather, the work casts before itself the eventful fact that the work is as this work, and it has constantly this fact about itself. The more essentially the work opens itself, the more luminous becomes the uniqueness of the fact that it is rather than is not. The more essentially this thrust comes into the Open, the stranger and more solitary [*befremdlicher und einsamer*] the work becomes" (GA5:52–53/PLT65–66).

3. See Joseph Libertson's discussion of the "essential solitude" in *Proximity*, pp. 42–55. Libertson clarifies Blanchot's concepts by translating them into his own (sometimes technical) vocabulary, one which embraces Bataille and Levinas as well as Blan-

chot. So his account is not always easy to follow, but nonetheless it captures a good deal of what is important in Blanchot's thinking. For example: "Essential solitude or separation is, for Blanchot as well as Levinas, a moment indefinable by the classical ontology of identity and noncontradiction. It is in fact the defection and contamination of such identity" (pp. 47–48). So to enter into the essential solitude is to experience something like an evacuation of one's subjectivity: one is no longer oneself purely and simply but rather one is always traversed by an alterity that cannot be captured by any category. "Essential solitude in Blanchot," therefore, "is a solitude belonging to No one. By comparison with the notion of a personal or identical self, this solitude may be thought quite literally as an anonymity or impersonality. It is a time and place without person" (p. 55).

4. See *De l'existence à l'existant* (DEE103/EE63), and "Littérature et la droit à la mort" (PF320/GO51/WF332). Death, that is, the movement of negation, is what allows a world (that is, a world of concepts and meanings in which everything is subject to human consciousness) to come into being for man. But existence is not exhausted by the work of negation. On the contrary, existence is an-archic: a resistance to death. So on the one side, "death is man's possibility, his chance, it is through death that the future of a finished world is still there for us; death is man's greatest hope, his only hope of being man. This is why existence is his own real dread, as Emmanuel Levinas has clearly shown, existence frightens him, not because of death which could put an end to it, but because it excludes death, because it is still there underneath death, a presence in the depths of absence, an inexorable day in which all days rise and set." Then in a footnote Blanchot quotes Levinas: " 'Isn't dread in the face of being—horror of being—just as primordial as dread in the face of death? Isn't fear of being just as primordial as fear for one's being? Even more primordial, because one could account for the latter by means of the former' " (PF325/GO55/WF336–37).

In one of Blanchot's stories from the 1930s, *Le dernier mot*, the howling of dogs is said to resound "like the echo of the words *il y a*" (AC66/VC45).

5. Simon Critchley gives a good account of the *il y a* in a valuable and important essay, "*Il y a*—A Dying Stronger than Death (Blanchot with Levinas)," *Oxford Literary Review*, 15, nos. 1–2 (1993), esp. 110–16. See also Paul Davies, "A Linear Narrative? Blanchot with Heidegger in the Work of Levinas," *Philosophers' Poets*, ed. David Wood (London: Routledge, 1990), pp. 37–69, and esp. pp. 42–58; and "A Fine Risk: Reading Blanchot Reading Levinas," *Re-Reading Levinas*, ed. Robert Bernasconi and Simon Critchley (Bloomington: Indiana University Press, 1991), pp. 201–26, esp. 214. Critchley seems right when he says that "the *il y a* is a kind of primal or primitive scene in Blanchot's work, something to which it keeps returning as an unstable point of origin, as the origin of the artwork." This is an origin in which nothing is originated. The return of the artwork to the *il y a* is a movement to which Blanchot gives the name *désœuvrement*, which is not a destructive (or deconstructive) movement aimed at something already in place. In a sense that remains to be explained, *désœuvrement* is outside the alternatives of construction and destruction; as Derrida might phrase it, it is, like the *il y a*, older than deconstruction. Imagine an event in which nothing happens, as in the case of the interruption. See also Joseph Libertson, *Proximity*, pp. 204–208, and esp. p. 206. Libertson is right when he says that the themes associated with the *il y a* are rather more characteristic of Blanchot than of Levinas.

6. See *Unterwegs zur Sprache* (US258/OWL127). Cf. Levinas, *Ethics and Infinity: Conversations with Philippe Nemo* (Pittsburgh: Duquesne University Press, 1985), pp. 47–48, where Levinas distinguishes the *il y a* from Heidegger's "joyful" and "abundant" *es gibt*.

7. *Sur la poésie* (Paris: GLM, 1974), p. 26.

8. The phrase "impossibility of death" is for Blanchot a term of art, which (as we shall see) he derives from Kafka's obsession with the interminability of existence. In "La lecture de Kafka" (1945), Blanchot recalls the character in Kafka's "The Hunter Gracchus" who suffers a fatal injury but does not die: "He had joyously accepted life and joyously accepted the end of his life—once killed, he awaited his death in joy: he lay stretched out, and he lay in wait. 'Then,' he said, 'the disaster happened.' This disaster is the impossibility of death, it is the mockery thrown on all humankind's great subterfuges, night, nothingness, silence. There is no end, there is no possibility of being done with the day, with the meaning of things, with hope: such is the truth that Western man has made a symbol of felicity, and has tried to make bearable by focusing on its positive side, that of immortality, of an afterlife [*survivance*] that would compensate for life. But this afterlife is our actual life" (PF15/WF7–8).

The nothingness celebrated by romantic nihilists or existentialists, in other words, is an illusion. The anguish or dread that accompanies existence is not a fear of annihilation; on the contrary, "it comes from the fear that this refuge might be taken from us, that nothingness might not be there, that nothingness might just be more existence. Since we cannot depart from existence, this existence is unfinished" (PF16/WF8–9). Existence is excessive, anarchic, without beginning or end.

9. Stanley Cavell asks: "What is the object of horror?" (*The Claim of Reason* [New York: Oxford University Press, 1971], p. 418). "Fear," he says, "is of danger; terror is of violence, of the violence I might do or that might be done me. I can be terrified of thunder, but not horrified by it." Horror is of the human as it approaches and exceeds its limits, as it becomes excessive, no longer human: inhuman or monstrous. "Horror is the title I am giving to the perception of the precariousness of human identity, to the perception that it may be lost or invaded, that we may be, or may become, something other than we are, or take ourselves for" (pp. 418–19). Cavell imagines "a mode of tragedy in which what we witness is the subjection of the human being to states of violation, a perception that not merely human law but human nature itself can be abrogated. The outcast is a figure of pity and horror; different from ourselves and not different. The particular mysteriousness in Hamlet's motivation may be our persisting in looking through his events for an object of horror. We should try looking at him as a figure of horror to himself" (pp. 419–20).

10. Writing is a movement into this space. "To write," Blanchot says, "is to let fascination rule language [*Écrire, c'est disposer le langage sous la fascination*]" (EL31/SL33). Compare attention, and its relation to affliction:

What is attention? Affliction has a relation to time. Through affliction we endure "pure" time, time without event, without project and without possibility; a kind of empty perpetuity that must be borne infinitely, and at every instant (just as fatigue and hunger must be borne in the extreme destitution of need). Let it be over. But it is without end. Deprived of ourselves, deprived of the I upon which we naturally lean, deprived of a world that in normal times exists in our place and disburdens us of ourselves, we are time, indefinitely endured. Attention is this same relation to time. Attention is waiting [*L'attention est l'attente*]: not the effort, the tension, or mobilization of knowledge around something with which one might concern oneself. Attention waits. It waits without precipitation, leaving empty what is empty and keeping our haste, our impatient desire, and, even more, our horror of emptiness from prematurely filling in. Attention is the emptiness of thought oriented by a gentle force and maintained in an accord with the empty intimacy of time.

Attention is impersonal. It is not the self that is attentive in attention; rather, with an extreme delicacy and through insensible, constant contacts, attention has always already detached me from myself, freeing me for the attention that I for an instant become. (EI176/IC121)

See Libertson's discussion of fascination in *Proximity: Levinas, Blanchot, Bataille, and Communication*, pp. 242–53.

11. Levinas summarizes his plan of the escape from the *il y a* in *Ethics and Infinity*, pp. 51–52:

My first idea was that perhaps a "being," a "something" one could point at with a finger, corresponds to a mastery over the "there is" which dreads in being. I spoke thus of the determinate being or existent as a dawn of clarity in the horror of the "there is," a moment where the sun rises, where things appear for themselves, where they are not borne by the "there is" but dominate it. Does one not say that the table is, that things are? Then one refastens being to the existent, and already the ego there dominates the existents it possesses. I spoke thus of the "hypostasis" of existents, that is, the passage going from *being* to a *something*, from the state of verb to the state of thing. Being which is posited, I thought, is "saved." In fact this idea was only a first stage. For the ego that exists is encumbered by all these existents it dominates. For me the famous Heideggerian "Care" took the form of the cumbersomeness of existence.

From whence an entirely different movement: to escape the "there is" one must not be posed but deposed; to make an act of deposition, in the sense one speaks of deposed kings. This deposition of sovereignty by the *ego* is the social relationship with the Other, the dis-inter-ested relation. I write it in three words to underline the escape from being it signifies. I distrust the compromised word "love," but the responsibility for the Other, being-for-the-other, seemed to me, as early as that time, to stop the anonymous and senseless rumbling of being. It is in the form of such a relation that the deliverance from the "there is" appeared to me. Since that compelled my recognition and was clarified in my mind, I have hardly spoken again in my books of the "there is" for itself. But the shadow of the "there is," and of non-sense, still appeared to me necessary as the very test of dis-inter-estedness.

Cf. Levinas, *Autrement qu'être*, where signification as one-for-the-other delivers us from the anonymity and non-sense (the rumbling and buzzing) of the *il y a* (AE255–56/OTB164–65).

12. Compare the insomniac's habitation of the night in which consciousness is de-

prived of its place of refuge. In *De l'existence à l'existant* Levinas says that sleep entails a fundamental relationship between consciousness and *place*. Waking means traversing a surface, going from place to place. "Sleep reestablishes a relationship with a place qua base. In lying down, in curling up in a corner to sleep, we abandon ourselves to a place; qua base it becomes our refuge. . . . Sleep is like entering into contact with the protective forces of a place; to seek after sleep is to gropingly seek after that contact. When one wakes up one finds oneself shut up in one's immobility like an egg in its shell" (*DEE*97/*EE*69–70). So insomnia is linked internally to the condition of exile.

13. *Diaries*, trans. Joseph Kresh, Martin Greenberg, Hannah Arendt (New York: Schocken Books, 1964), pp. 393, 407.

14. See Jill Robbins, *Prodigal Son/Elder Brother: Interpretation and Alterity in Augustine, Petrarch, Kafka, and Levinas* (Chicago: University of Chicago Press, 1991), p. 73. Robbins shows how Kafka's and Levinas's reading of the Abraham story dovetail (as they do in Blanchot's text). She writes:

> Kafka's Abraham (who is also to a certain extent, in my reading, Blanchot's Abraham) is a nomad. He errs. But his exile is distinctive. For unlike Augustine's place of exile—the *regio egestatis*, the "region of lack"—and unlike the prodigal son's *regio longinqua*—the "distant country" which he inhabits before he "returns to himself"—Abraham's exile is not a region or place at all. *This* Abraham, Kafka's Abraham (who is also, in my reading, Kafka "himself"), is in exile. But this exile is not a place he inhabits; it is not an exile where he could *find himself* exiled. His is a radical exile; he is exiled even *from* his exile, as Blanchot argues. Thus excluded from himself, his is a peripety without anagnorisis. . . .
>
> [Likewise] For Levinas . . . Abraham's peripety must be . . . a peripety of *essence* and ontology, that is, an inversion or reversing of the dominant tendencies of thought in the West. . . . Levinas poses Abraham paradigmatically for an ethics that is specifically Hebraic. "To the myth of Odysseus returning from Ithaca, we would like to oppose the story of Abraham leaving forever his homeland for a land yet unknown and forbidding his servant to bring even his son to this point of departure."
>
> In Levinas's reading, Abraham's departure *without* return figures the very departure from self and from self-reference that is the movement of ethics and responsibility. For ethics, the imperative to be responsible to the other, requires such a departure from self-reference. Responsibility to the other is not something that is first filtered through the self; it is not an imperative that I deliver to myself. Rather, it is a being delivered over to the other. (pp. 77–78)

For both Kafka and Blanchot, however, the other to which I am delivered over is not an ethical alterity but an "elsewhere": the no-man's-land of writing.

15. See "Kafka et la littérature":

> It is as if the possibility that my writing represents essentially exists to express its own impossibility—the impossibility of writing that constitutes my sadness. Not only can it not put it in parentheses, or accommodate it without destroying it or being destroyed by it, but it really is possible only because of its impossibility. If language and, in particular, literary language did not constantly hurl itself ea-

gerly at its death, it would not be possible, since it is this movement toward its impossibility that is its nature and its foundation; it is this movement that, by anticipating its nothingness, determines its potential to be this nothingness without actualizing it. In other words, language is real because it can project itself toward non-language, which it is and does not actualize. (PF27–28/WF20)

16. See 3 May 1915:

Completely indifferent and apathetic. A well gone dry, water at an unattainable depth and no certainty it is there. Nothing, nothing. Don't understand the life in Strindberg's *Separated;* what he calls beautiful, when I relate it to myself, disgusts me. A letter to F., all wrong, impossible to mail it. What is there to tie me to a past or a future? The present is a phantom state for me; I don't sit at the table but hover round it. Nothing, nothing. Emptiness, boredom, no, not boredom, merely emptiness, meaninglessness, weakness. Yesterday in Dobrichovice. (*Diaries*, p. 339)

17. Horkeimer and Adorno, *Dialectic of Enlightenment*, trans. John Cumming (New York: Seabury Press, 1972), p. 183.

18. See Critchley on "the impossibility of death," "*Il y a*—A Dying Stronger than Death," 120–28, and esp. 127: "There would seem to be a two-fold claim being made by Blanchot's work: firstly, writing has its unattainable source in an experience of worklessness [*désœuvrement*] and a movement of infinite dying. . . . And yet, secondly, the extremity of this experience cannot be faced, it would be intolerable to the human organism, and the writer is therefore necessarily blind to the guiding insights of his or her work, requiring the metaphysical comfort of the Apollonian to save them from the tragic truth of the Dionysian. The writer necessarily experiences bad faith with regard to writing, and is therefore maintained in an ambiguous relation, divided between two slopes, and drawn by two opposing temptations." Or, alternatively, and in ways that still need to be explained, poetry or writing is for Blanchot a limit-experience—like suffering, for example, or rather like affliction (*malheur*). In an essay on Simone Weil, Blanchot writes:

The thought of affliction is precisely the thought of that which cannot let itself be thought. Affliction is an "enigma." It is of the same nature as physical suffering, from which it is inseparable. Physical suffering [*la souffrance*], when it is such that one can neither suffer it nor cease suffering it, thereby stopping time, makes time a present without future and yet impossible as present (one cannot reach the following instant, it being separated from the present instant by an impassable infinite, the infinite of suffering; but the present of suffering is impossible, it being the abyss of the present.) Affliction makes us lose time and makes us lose the world. The individual who is afflicted falls beneath every class. The afflicted are neither pathetic nor pitiable; they are ridiculous, inspiring distaste and scorn. They are for others the horror they are for themselves. Affliction is anonymous, impersonal, indifferent. It is life become alien and death become inaccessible. It is the horror of being where being is without end. (EI174–75/IC120)

For Blanchot, writing is not a performance but an affliction. It is a limit-experience in the sense that it cannot be experienced by an "I," or rather the one who experiences it no longer occupies the logical position of the subject but has been reduced to a pure passivity, that is, a passivity which is no longer a term in a relation, no longer the negative of action. So writing is not a pursuit or a choice. Think of it as an affliction of language. Imagine words invading one's body like a deadly disease.

19. See Françoise Collin, *Maurice Blanchot et la question de l'écriture*, pp. 120–59.

20. See John Gregg's useful study, "Blanchot's Suicidal Artist: Writing and the (Im)Possibility of Death," *Sub-stance*, 55, no. 1 (1988), esp. 57: "Suicide and writing both have something in common; on the surface each of these activities purport to accomplish something, and yet each must ultimately be considered as failing to do so. Each activity represents an extreme situation, an experience of limits, the crossing of which implies entering a domain where power is not of prime importance. . . . Each of these experiences exceeds an ontology based on power and therefore is considered by Blanchot to be a transgressive act. He defines transgression as 'the inevitable accomplishment of what is impossible to accomplish, and it would be dying [*le mourir*] itself.'"

21. Walter Benjamin, "Das Paris des Second Empire bei Baudelaire," *Gesammelte Schriften*, vol. 1, bk. 2 (Frankfurt: Suhrkamp, 1974), p. 578; *Charles Baudelaire: A Lyric Poet in the Era of High Capitalism*, trans. Harry Zohn (London: Verso, 1974), p. 75.

22. *L'irréalité* is a concept Blanchot has made his own. Irreality is neither real nor unreal; it is outside all metaphysical distinctions between true and untrue, outside all categories pertaining to knowledge. Essential death (essential solitude, essential art) belongs to this *irreal*, deterritorialized space. Contra Sartre (*La nausée*):

> The greatest difficulty does not come from the pressure of beings, from what we call their reality, their persistent affirmation, whose action can never be altogether suspended. It is in irreality [*irréalité*] itself that the poet encounters the resistance of a muffled presence. It is irreality from which he cannot free himself; it is irreality that, disengaged from beings, he meets with the mystery of "those very words: *it is* [*c'est*]." And this is not because in the irreal something subsists — not because the rejection of real things was insufficient and the work of negation brought to a halt too soon — but because when there is nothing, it is this nothing itself which can no longer be negated. It affirms, keeps on affirming, and it states nothingness as being, the inertia of being [*dit le néant comme être, le désœuvrement de l'être*]. (EL138/SL110)

Désœuvrement: the uneventfulness of being, where the uneventful is something like an interruption of being, that is, a pure event in which nothing occurs, the interval or *entre-temps* that divides a state of affairs infinitely into the still-future and already-past. Dying, writing are in this respect pure events. In Blanchot's later texts *désœuvrement* becomes the principal concept for the clarification of the fragmentary and the neutral (cf. ED30/WD14).

23. Herman Rapaport correctly emphasizes the importance of Blanchot's essay on Heidegger, "La parole 'sacrée' de Hölderlin" (1946), as a text that clarifies the double temporality of the *pas*. See Rapaport, *Heidegger and Derrida: Reflections on Time and Language* (Lincoln: University of Nebraska Press, 1989), pp. 115–23.

24. Sartre reads Mallarmé's life as the Igitur-experience of an endlessly deferred suicide, where the deferment is Mallarmé's gift to himself, his endless self-renewal or self-creation: he is no longer dependent on his progenitors for his existence; he is, dialectically, now a product of his own hand insofar as he has stayed his hand against himself. *Mallarmé: la lucidité et sa face d'ombre*, pp. 142–43.

Chapter 4: Blanchot/Celan: *Unterwegssein*

1. "Poetryworld" is a take-off on Arthur Danto's "The Artworld," *Journal of Philosophy*, 61, no. 19 (1964), 571–84. This famous essay is an attempt to clarify the question of what counts as a work of art when the work of art just is the real object it purports to represent. Danto's example is Andy Warhol's Brillo Box. "What in the end makes the difference between a Brillo box and a work of art consisting of a Brillo box is a certain theory of art. It is the theory that takes it up into the world of art, and keeps it from collapsing into the real object which it is (in a sense of *is* other than that of artistic identification). Of course, without the theory one is unlikely to see it as art, and in order to see it as part of the artworld, one must have mastered a good deal of artistic theory as well as a considerable amount of the history of recent New York painting" (581). Danto develops this so-called "institutional" theory of art further in *The Transfigurations of the Commonplace* (Cambridge: Harvard University Press, 1981).

For Danto (as, in a somewhat different way, for Blanchot) it is important to situate the work of art not only against its own (local) historical and theoretical background but also within the larger history of philosophical aesthetics dominated by Hegel's thesis that art, for us, is a thing of the past. Much of Blanchot's poetics is a rejection of this thesis.

2. GW3:167/CP15: "German poetry is going in a very different direction from French poetry. No matter how alive its traditions, with most sinister events in its memory, most questionable developments around it, it can no longer speak the language which many willing ears seem to expect. Its language has become more sober, more factual. It distrusts 'beauty.' It tries to be truthful. If I may search for a visual analogy while keeping in mind the polychrome of apparent actuality: it is a 'greyer' language, a language which wants to locate even its 'musicality' in such a way that it has nothing in common with the 'euphony' which more or less blithely continued to sound alongside the greatest horrors."

3. For Adorno, works of art are social facts like any other, and insofar as they "help reinforce the existence of a separate domain of the spirit and culture whose practical impotence and complicity with the principle of unmitigated disaster are painfully evident," they are politically and morally culpable objects (AT348/AeT333). At the same time, however, works of art are external to society in critical and even subversive ways; they "assist the non-identical in its struggle against the repressive identification that rules the outside world [*das der Identitätszwang in der Realität unterdrückt*]" (AT14/AeT6).

What Deleuze and Guattari say of Kafka's relation to German, cited earlier, has application to Celan. Perhaps writing poetry is always a process of "deterritorialization" (K29–31/KFM26).

4. In "L'absence de livre," Blanchot distinguishes between the empirical book (that

one might actually take up and read) and the book as *either* the transcendental form of absolute consciousness *or* language:

The book admits of three distinct investigations. There is the empirical book. The book acts as a vehicle of knowledge; a given, determinate book receives and gathers a given, determinate form of knowledge. But the book as book is never simply empirical. The book is the *a priori* of knowledge. We would know nothing if there did not always exist in advance the impersonal memory of the book and, more essentially, the prior disposition to write and to read contained in every book and affirming itself only in the book. The absolute of the book, then, is the isolation of a possibility that claims to have originated in no anteriority. An absolute that will later tend to be affirmed with the romantics (Novalis), then more rigorously with Hegel, then still more radically (though in a different way) with Mallarmé as the totality of relations (absolute knowledge, or the Work) in which would be accomplished either consciousness, which knows itself and comes back to itself after having exteriorized itself in all its dialectically linked figures, or language, closing upon its own affirmation and already dispersed. (*EI*621/*IC*423)

For Blanchot, consciousness and language are asymmetrical. The one moves dialectically toward totality, the other disperses in fragments.

5. And where Heidegger thinks of the work as structured as a rift (*Riß*) of earth and world, Blanchot speaks of "*une telle intimité déchirée*": "The work is this torn intimacy inasmuch as it is the 'unfurling' of that which nevertheless hides and remains closed— a light shining on the dark, a light bright from the clarity of this darkness, which abducts and ravishes the dark in the first light of the unfurling, but also disappears into the absolutely obscure whose essence is to close in upon whatever would reveal it, to attract this disclosure to itself and swallow it up" (*EL*300/*SL*226).

6. Heidegger speaks of poetry as an *Anfang*—"a peculiar leap out of the unmediable [*des Anfangs, das Eigentümliche des Sprunges aus them Unvermittelbaren her*]," which "always contains the undisclosed abundance of the uncanny [*die unerschlossene Fülle des Ungeheuren*], which means that it also contains strife with the familiar and the ordinary" (*GA*5:64/*PLT*76).

"Whenever art happens," Heidegger says, "—that is, whenever there is a beginning—a thrust [*Stoss*] enters history, history either begins or starts over again" (*GA*5:65/*PLT*77). The work, in effect, maintains the world in fragments, beginnings without endings.

7. See Andrei Codrescu, *The Disappearance of the Outside: A Manifesto of Escape* (Reading, Mass.: Addison Wesley, 1990), esp. pp. 37–56 ("Exile, a Place").

8. Blanchot says of aesthetics, for example, that "it talks about art, makes of it an object of reflection and of knowledge. Aesthetics explains art by reducing it or then again exalts it by elucidating it, but in all events art for the aesthetician is a present reality around which he constructs plausible thoughts at no risk" (*EL*313/*SL*234). So far as aesthetics is possible you wouldn't want it.

9. See Martine Broda's discussion of Lucile and Lenz, "Dialogisme et destination: à propos du 'Méridien,'" *Dans la main de personne: Essai sur Paul Celan* (Paris: Éditions du Cerf, 1986), pp. 119–26.

10. Celan makes the following comment:

Please note, ladies and gentlemen: "One would like to be a Medusa's head" to . . . seize the natural as the natural by means of art! One would like to, by the way, not: I would [Man *möchte heißt es hier freilich, nicht*: ich *möchte*]. (GW3:192/CP42)

As if the "I" could not be used by an artist, which is an old story, but not Celan's. For Celan the "I" cannot be used hypothetically or interchangeably; it is not a universal. It is untranslatable. So he makes a point of distinguishing Lenz, the hero of Büchner's *Lenz* (a fragment), and the historical Lenz, "the Lenz who 'on the 20th of January was walking through the mountains,' he—not the artist thinking about art—he as an 'I'" (GW3:194/CP46). See Jacques Derrida, *Schibboleth* (S18–28).

11. See Krzysztof Ziarek, *Inflected Language* (Albany: SUNY Press, 1994), pp. 138–80. See also Gerhard Buhr, *Celans Poetik* (Göttingen: Vandenhoeck and Ruprecht, 1976), pp. 64–77; Holger Pausch, *Paul Celan* (Berlin: Otto Bess, 1981), pp. 49–51; David Brierly, *"Der Meridian": Ein Versuch zur Poetik und Dichtung Paul Celans* (Frankfurt: Peter Lang, 1984), pp. 156–83.

12. See Olson, "Projective Verse," *Selected Writings*, ed. Robert Creeley (New York: New Directions, 1966), esp. pp. 16–22.

13. See Thomas Sparr, "Celans Poetik des Raums," *Celans Poetik des hermetischen Gedichts* (Heidelberg: Carl Winter, 1989), pp. 137–53, on Celan's poetics of *Ortlosigkeit* (p. 149).

14. See Véronique M. Fóti's account of "Der Meridian" in *Heidegger and the Poets: Poiesis, Sophia, Techne* (Atlantic Highlands, N.J.: Humanities Press, 1992), esp. pp. 99–114. Fóti is finally critical of Celan for falling short or despairing of "an ethics of alterity" (pp. 113–14). Cf. the "post-ethical" interlinear reading of Celan's "Todesfuge" by John D. Caputo (a.k.a. Rebecca Morgenstern), with commentary, in *Against Ethics: Contributions to a Poetics of Obligation with Constant Reference to Deconstruction* (Bloomington: Indiana University Press, 1993), pp. 176–86. Here the poem is (always) a cry of suffering, a moment of irrepressible expressiveness, the chorus of a history that never comes to an end, the sound that Auschwitz or the disaster makes again and again every time it occurs. "The notion that the poem is a cry seems to derive from Lyotard, from the notion that the silence of the differend seeks an idiom and from the idea that the silence of the victim is an 'alarm' that sounds, that calls us [philosophers] to the scene of a disaster, like the disaster's *glas*" (p. 184). Postethical as it may be, this is a familiar picture of the philosopher—as ever the observer called to inspect a scene. As if the philosopher were by definition one who has never lived through anything (one recalls that tragedy for Aristotle, as for philosophy generally, is not something one lives through but something one watches). For a different view of the relation of poetry and the ethical in Celan, see Krzysztof Ziarek, *Inflected Language*, esp. pp. 137–60.

15. Levinas appropriates Celan to his conception of alterity, explicitly *contra* Heidegger's ontology, in "Paul Celan: De l'être à l'autre," *Noms propres* (Paris: Fata Morgana, 1976), pp. 49–56. Lacoue-Labarthe argues to the contrary that Celan cannot be separated out from Heidegger so easily. There is, he says, no other that is "otherwise than being." See *La poésie comme expérience* (Paris: Christian Bourgois, 1986), pp. 97–98, and also Mark Anderson's critique of Lacoue-Labarthe's Heideggerian reading

of Celan, " 'The Impossibility of Poetry': Celan and Heidegger," *New German Critique*, no. 53 (Spring/Summer 1991), 3–18, esp. 14: "Lacoue-Labarthe privileges the Heideggerian question of the *Riß* of Being over that of ethics and history." The question of who or what the poem addresses is relevant here, and so is Ossip Mandelstam's essay, "The Interlocutor," which was translated into French for the first time in 1959 on Celan's instigation. Mandelstam stresses the dialogical character of poetry, which is always in the vocative case, but it is a dialogue structured, as Blanchot would be the first to point out, by the unbreachable distance that separates me from the other. Mandelstam says: "poetry as a whole is always directed toward a more or less distant, unknown addressee." Trans. Jane Gary Harris and Constance Link, *Mandelstam: Critical Prose and Letters*, ed. Jane Gary Harris (Ann Arbor: Ardis, 1979), p. 73. There are good discussions of this matter by Martine Broda in *Dans la main de personne*, pp. 61–94.

16. In *Schibboleth* Derrida takes *Sache* in the sense of *res* or subject of concern (S24). But the effect of the term is to extend the question of alterity beyond the limits of ethical theory.

17. Here again Lacoue-Labarthe reads Celan against Levinas and in favor of Heidegger: "Mais cet autre espace ou cet espace autrement éclairé n'est en aucune façon 'au-delà' de l'être. L'expérience du toi, la recontre, n'ouvre à rien d'autre qu'à l'expérience de l'être: du rien étant—que Celan désigne, dans les termes de Hölderlin précisément (et non de Rilke) comme l''ouvert', le 'vide', le 'libre' " (*La poésie comme expérience*, p. 98). So *Toposforschung* reduces to "topology of being." But this seems to rush past the reserved, guarded, questioning character of Celan's address, which is almost without assertion.

18. See *Le dernier à parler* (Paris: Fata Morgana, 1984), pp. 22–23; "The Last One to Speak," trans. Joseph Simas, *Translating Tradition: Paul Celan in France*, ed. Benjamin Hollander (San Francisco: ACTS, A Journal of New Writing, 1988), pp. 231–32.

19. In the "Brief über den Humanismus" Heidegger explicates "dwelling-place" as the abode of strangeness, namely the house of Heraclitus the Obscure, who is, however, utterly ordinary—although, as a final turn of the screw, Heidegger has him harboring the "unfamiliar ones," namely the gods.

20. In Lacoue-Labarthe's reading of "Der Meridian," the poetic act is "catastrophique: rapport renversant à ce qui est en renversement, dans l'étant, verse le néant (l'abîme)" (*Poésie comme expérience*, p. 99).

Chapter 5: Blanchot/Levinas

1. See Jacques Derrida, *De l'esprit* (DE141–42/OS90–91).

2. More accurately, for Blanchot revelation is of the outside, which is neither nothing nor something, neither being nor nonbeing (ED178/WD115). Prophecy is a limit-experience—an experience of the "inaccessible" and the "unknown" in which consciousness is deprived of subjectivity (EI305/IC205). With respect to the future prophecy is a *pas au-delà*, interminable waiting, patience in the face of "the non-arrival of what comes about" (PD132/SNB95).

3. The concept of the Fourfold or the proximity of earth and sky, gods and mortals, should not be collapsed into a totality or even a unity. The idea that nothing is excluded does not mean that everything is the same. One wants to say that *das Vier* is a

space in which nothing is the same but everything alien is *Gegen-einander-über*: open to one another. See my discussion of *das Vier* in *Heidegger's Estrangements: Language, Truth, and Poetry in the Later Writings* (New Haven: Yale University Press, 1989), pp. 74–85. In Heidegger's later vocabulary, the Fourfold is the Open, a region of responsibility or *Gelassenheit*. It is important to understand that Being is no longer a word in this vocabulary.

4. Here one should consult Paul Davies, "A Linear Narrative? Blanchot with Heidegger in the Work of Levinas," in *Philosophers' Poets*, ed. David Wood (London: Routledge, 1990), pp. 37–69, esp. pp. 44–48; and "A Fine Risk: Reading Blanchot Reading Levinas," in *Re-Reading Levinas*, ed. Robert Bernasconi and Simon Critchley (Bloomington: Indiana University Press, 1991), pp. 201–26, esp. pp. 210–12, where Davies takes up the difference between the language and philosophy and "a 'wholly other language' (the language of the 'fragment')" (p. 210). And also, in particular, Simon Critchley, "*Il y a*—A Dying Stronger than Death (Blanchot with Levinas)," *Oxford Literary Review*, 15, nos. 1–2 (1993), esp. 110–16. My purpose here is not so much to adjudicate the issue between Levinas and Heidegger as to clarify the disagreement between Levinas and Blanchot as to what counts as otherness. On the question of Levinas and Heidegger, see Krzysztof Ziarek, *Inflected Language*, pp. 181–205.

5. Recall the question in Heidegger's case of whether language is otherwise than human. See Heidegger, "Die Sprache," where language is said to speak in "the peal of stillness": "The peal of stillness is not anything human [*Das Geläut der Stille ist nichts Menschliches*]" (*US*30/*PLT*207). See *Heidegger's Estrangements*, pp. 95–97.

6. What Levinas calls *discours* is routinely translated as "conversation" (*TeI*43/*TI*50), but it is clear that the concept of dialogue in the sense of give-and-take is not applicable here. *Discours* is a nonreciprocal relation, a relation to infinity or transcendence, that is, to an exteriority that has no interiority. Compare *Autrement qu'être*: "Those who wish to found on dialogue and on an original *we* the upsurge of egos, refer to an original communication behind the *de facto* communication (but without giving this original communication any sense other than the empirical sense of a dialogue or a *manifestation* of one to the other—which is to presuppose that *we* that is to be founded), and reduce the problem of communication to the problem of its certainty [i.e., the certainty that the *truth* is being told]. In opposition to that, we suppose that there is in the transcendence involved in language a relationship that is not empirical speech, but responsibility" (*AE*190/*OTB*119–20).

7. The text in which Blanchot most clearly inscribes his difference from Levinas is perhaps "Le rapport du troisième genre (homme sans horizon)," where "man without horizon" means something like man at the limit of being: "Man without horizon, and not affirming himself on the basis of horizon—in this sense a being without being, a presence without a present, thus foreign to everything visible and to everything invisible—he is what comes to me as speech when to speak is not to see. The Other speaks to me and is only this exigency of speech. And when the Other speaks to me, speech is the relation of that which remains radically separate, the relation of the third kind affirming a relation without unity, without equality" (*EI*98/*IC*69). A relation of the third kind is a relation of neither/nor in which we, myself and the other, are neither one nor the other: ours is a neutral relation, outside the alternatives of, among other things, the human and the nonhuman. Cf. "L'interruption (comme sur une surface de Riemann)" (*EI*109/*IC*77).

8. Recall "Littérature et la droit à la mort": "Literature is a concern for the reality of things, for their unknown, free, and silent existence; literature is their innocence and their forbidden presence, it is the being which protests against revelation, it is the defiance of what does not want to take place outside. In this way, it sympathizes with darkness, with aimless passion, with lawless violence, with everything in the world that seems to perpetuate the refusal to come into the world" (PF319/WF330).

9. See Derrida, "Violence et métaphysique" (EeD219/WaD147). Derrida notes that for Levinas a "nonviolent language would be a language which would do without the verb *to be*." This would, in effect, be a language without language (a language outside of language?). It would be a language without propositions (without *la phrase*). However, "if one remains within Levinas's intentions, what would a language without phrase, a language which would say nothing, offer to the other? Language must give the world to the other, *Totality and Infinity* tells us." Of course, Derrida has things turned around slightly: it is the other who speaks, not me. I have nothing to give the other by way of speaking. But Derrida is clearly pulling on a thread in a crucial seam in Levinas's thought.

10. For clarity's sake it should be pointed out that poetry for Levinas is not what it is for Blanchot. Levinas still thinks of poetry in terms of versification. He is closer to Valéry's formalism than to Blanchot's conception of poetry as a refusal of philosophy.

11. See Derrida, "Violence et métaphysique" (EeD163/WaD110): "The least one might say is that Levinas does not do so [i.e., break with phenomenology and ontology], and cannot do so, without renouncing philosophical discourse. And, if you will, the attempt to achieve an opening toward the beyond of philosophical discourse, by means of philosophical discourse, which can never be shaken off completely, cannot possibly succeed *within language*."

12. "Le dieu des suppliants" (1962): "The suppliant is not weaker or the weakest, he is so low he is utterly beyond reach: separate, sacred. His moves are religious because in himself he belongs to a region of separation. . . . What then, finally, gives him a chance? It is the fact that he speaks. The suppliant is, par excellence, the one who speaks. Through speech, he, very low, is in relation to the very high and, without breaking down the distance, makes his powerful interlocutor enter into a space they do not yet have in common but that is between them" (EI135/IC95). The suppliant, in other words, occupies the site of the poet (perhaps the poet vis-à-vis the philosopher).

13. See Françoise Collin's discussion of Blanchot's conception of alterity, *Maurice Blanchot et la question de l'écriture*, pp. 99–119. See also Gilles Deleuze, "Michel Tournier et le monde sans autrui" (LdS350–72/LS301–21).

14. See Bataille's preface to the second edition of *L'impossible* (1962):

Humanity is faced with a double perspective: in one direction, violent pleasure, horror, and death—precisely the perspective of poetry—and in the opposite direction, that of science or the real world of utility. Only the useful, the real, have a serious character. We are never within our rights in preferring seduction: truth has rights over us. Indeed, it has every right. And yet we can, and indeed we must, respond to something which, not being God, is stronger than every right, that *impossible* to which we accede only by forgetting the truth of all these rights, only by accepting disappearance. (OC3:102/I10)

15. Bataille's list—"madmen, leaders, poets"—should not go unremarked. The quotation is from "La structure psychologique du fascisme" (1936), and the fact that his list of heterogeneous types includes leaders as well as misfits is prelude to his idea that "the fascist leaders are incontestably part of heterogeneous existence." Bataille's theory of fascism emphasizes its excessive, anarchic, revolutionary character: "Opposed to democratic politicians, who represent . . . homogeneous society, Mussolini and Hitler immediately stand out as something *other*. Whatever emotions their actual existence as political agents of evolution evokes, it is impossible to ignore the *force* that situates them above men, parties, and even laws: a *force* that disrupts the regular course of things, the peaceful but fastidious homogeneity powerless to maintain itself (the fact that laws are broken is only the most obvious sign of the transcendent, *heterogeneous* nature of fascist action" (OC1:348/VE143). Possibly this captures something of the nature of Blanchot's attraction to fascism as well. For Bataille, the heterogeneous is itself heterogeneous insofar as it breaks up into transcendental and debased regions, with the Duce and the Führer asserting a sovereignty different from the sovereignty of the untouchable who is irreducible to any social function—different, but symmetrical, since both are external or, indeed, irrational and incommensurable with respect to the social order that they either dominate or from which they are expelled. Blanchot seems interested only in the sovereignty, which is to say the exteriority, of the outcast—the madman, poet, or untouchable. That is, in contrast to Levinas *and* Bataille, Blanchot's conception of alterity is without horizons, dimensions, or other topographical features; it is the Outside—the open-ended surface traversed by the exile. Rodolphe Gasché gives an excellent account of Bataille's "heterology" in "The Heterological Almanac," *On Bataille: Critical Essays*, ed. Leslie Anne Boldt-Irons (Albany: SUNY Press, 1995), pp. 157–208.

Chapter 6: Blanchot/Bataille

1. There is a very interesting volume of essays that explores this "optical imperative"—called in this case "ocularcentrism." See *Modernity and the Hegemony of Vision*, ed. David Michael Levin (Berkeley: University of California Press, 1993). See especially David Levin's "Decline and Fall: Ocularcentrism in Heidegger's Reading of the History of Metaphysics," pp. 186–217.

2. See the end of "Tenir parole," where Blanchot speaks of "two centers of gravity of language" (EI92/IC65), corresponding to the speech of the "I" and the speech that is addressed to me by the other: "The one is a speech of power, of confrontation, of opposition and of negation in order to reduce everything opposed, and in order that the truth be affirmed in its entirety as silent equality." Meanwhile: "The other is a speech beyond opposition, beyond negation, and does nothing but affirm; but it is also outside affirmation, because it says nothing but the infinite distance of the Other and the infinite exigency that is *autrui* in its presence; that which eludes all power to negate and to affirm" (EI92/IC64–65).

3. The phrase *le grand refus* is actually Yves Bonnefoy's, from "L'acte et le lieu de la poèsie" (1959), in *L'improbable: suive de un rêve fait à mantoue* (Paris: Mercure de France, [1959] 1980), p. 105. Bonnefoy, like Blanchot, thinks of poetry as a discourse that preserves the singularity of things against their conceptual reduction. Blanchot

thinks, however, that "when Bonnefoy rises up against the clarity of the concept, decisively taking the part of the sensible, he well knows that by entering into the play of oppositions and determinations that are elaborated precisely by the rational order, he is still thinking and speaking within, and in favor of, this conceptual order whose value he seeks to challenge, or at least delimit" (*EI*56–57/*IC*40). Bonnefoy still thinks of poetry as desiring a cognitive relation with things, trying to grasp them in their immediate presence, and failing because, once more, language is inadequate to intuition: there is always a gap between perception and expression. Poetry is perhaps a longing or hope for a place where language and reality are present to one another without interruption. But Blanchot's idea is that this is incoherent; that is, poetry's relation to things is outside this whole system of presence and absence, neither one nor the other. It is, in ways Blanchot tries to explain in "Le grand refus," a nonrelation.

4. Recall "Littérature et la droit à la mort": "In speech what dies is what gives life to speech; speech is the life of that death, it is 'the life that endures death and maintains itself in it.' But something was there and is no longer there. Something has disappeared. How can I recover it, how can I turn around and look at what exists *before*, if all my power consists of making it into what exists *after*?" (*PF*316/*GO*46/*WF*327).

5. In a digression Blanchot says: "Even death is a power. It is not a simple event that will happen to me, an objective and observable fact; here my power to be will cease, here I will no longer be able to be here. But death, insofar as it belongs to me and belongs to me alone, since no one can die my death in my stead or in my place, makes of this non-possibility, this impending future of mine, this relation to myself always open until my end, yet another power [*pouvoir*]. Dying, I can still die, this is our sign as man. Retaining a relation to death, I appropriate it as a power; this is the utmost limit of my solitary resolution. And we have seen that death seized as a power, as the beginning of the mind, is at the center of the universe where truth is the labor of truth" (*EI*59/*IC*42).

6. Blanchot sometimes seems to regard psychoanalysis as a camouflaged version of torture in which the speech is extracted under the guise of liberating a subject from mental bondage. See "La parole analytique" (*EI*347–48/*IC*233–34). This text is discussed in chapter 10 below.

7. Later, a propos of Simone Weil, Blanchot will distinguish between physical suffering (*la souffrance*) and affliction (*le maleur*):

Physical suffering, when it is such that one can neither suffer it nor cease suffering it, thereby stopping time, makes time a present without a future and yet impossible as present (one cannot reach the following instant, it being separated from the present by an impassable infinite, the infinite of suffering; but the present of suffering is impossible, it being the abyss of the present). Affliction makes us lose time and makes us lose the world. The individual who is afflicted falls beneath every class. The afflicted are neither pathetic nor pitiable; they are ridiculous, inspiring distaste and scorn. They are for others the horror they are for themselves. Affliction is anonymous, impersonal, indifferent. It is life become alien and death become inaccessible. It is the horror of being where being is without end. (*EI*174–75/*IC*120)

Compare various texts on waiting (*l'attente*), including "L'attente," in *Martin Heidegger zum Siebsigten Geburtstag* (Pfulligen: Neske, 1959), pp. 217–24, later incorporated into *L'attente, l'oubli* (1962). See esp. AO56: "At each step one is here and yet beyond [*A chaque pas, on est ici, et pourtant au delà*]." Waiting belongs to the same anarchic temporality as suffering—anarchic because it is without beginning or end, that is, it contains no internal necessity driving it backward and forward. So forgetting is as much a part of this temporality as the endless vigil in behalf of the messiah (or death, or the end of history) that never arrives.

8. The term *Grenzsituation* derives from Karl Jaspers, *Psychologie der Weltanschauungen* (Berlin: Julius Springer, 1919), p. 229: "These situations, which are felt, experienced, conceived, everywhere at the limits of our existence, we call 'limit-situations' [*Grenzsituationen*]. What they have in common is that—within the objective world as dichotomized into subject and object—there is nothing firm or stable, no indubitable absolute, no enduring support for experience or thought. Everything is in flux, in restless movement of question and answer; everything is relative, finite, split into opposites—nothing is whole, absolute, essential." Cf. section 53 of Heidegger's *Sein und Zeit*, where the endless looming imminence of death is a condition which is "nonrelational" (*unbezügliche*) and "not to be outstripped" (*unüberholbare*) (SZ263–64/ BT308).

Blanchot met Bataille in 1940. For a discussion of their relationship, see Michel Surya, *Georges Bataille: La mort à l'œuvre* (Paris: Librairie Séguier, 1986), esp. pp. 314–23.

9. Cf. "Le mythe de Sisyphe" in *Faux pas* (FP70–71).

10. See the *Introduction to the Reading of Hegel*, pp. 31–70, esp. 34–35, 68–70; and Lutz Niethammer, *Posthistoire: Has History Come to an End?*, trans. Patrick Camiller (London: Verso, 1992), pp. 62–68. The most interesting discussion of Kojève that I've seen is Michael Roth's *Knowing and History: Appropriations of Hegel in Twentieth-Century France* (Ithaca: Cornell University Press, 1988), pp. 81–95. Roth has found lists of those attending Kojève's lectures—Bataille is among them, of course, and Lacan, but not Blanchot, who probably didn't pick up on Kojève until after he met Bataille in 1940. See also Barry Cooper, *The End of History: An Essay on Modern Hegelianism* (Toronto: University of Toronto Press, 1984), esp. pp. 78–122 ("How History Ended"). Shadia Drury gives a thoroughly unsympathetic but still interesting account of Kojève's "last man" in her *Alexandre Kojève: The Roots of Postmodern Politics* (New York: St. Martin's Press, 1994), pp. 79–87. Kojève, on Drury's view, is the chief source of the "dark romanticism" of postmodernism, a reactionary melancholy experienced by those who see themselves at the end of history, which "spells the absolute and unmitigated victory of being as opposed to nothingness, of truth as opposed to ideology, of reason as opposed to madness, of the feminine as opposed to the masculine, and of slavery as opposed to mastery. Banished from the world are any hint of negativity, mastery, inequality, ideology, madness, or virility. The result is a profound disenchantment with the world born of the belief that everything great and glorious, strong and masterful, delirious and delightful, has been irretrievably lost" (pp. 86–87). Drury doesn't mention Blanchot, but she has an interesting chapter on Bataille, whom she sees as "the father of postmodernism," who bequeathed to us, among other things, "a Dionysian madness rooted in the abhorrence of reason," and "an appetite for endless negation and 'ceaseless overturning'" (p. 123). Almost right: Bataille, like Blanchot, is more of an anarchist than nihilist—someone who believes in endlessness rather than in negation.

11. See John Gregg's excellent account of the theory of the endlessness of history in the opening chapters of *Maurice Blanchot and the Literature of Transgression*, esp. pp. 10–34.

12. See Bataille's review of *Le dernier homme*, "Ce monde où nous mourons," *Critique*, nos. 123–24 (1957), 675–84.

13. The narrator repeats this point obsessively: "How was he present, with that simply, evident presence, near us, but in some sense without us, without our world, maybe without any world?" (*DH*57/*LM*30).

14. See Blanchot's essay on Bataille, "L'expérience intérieure," in *Faux pas*: "Le non-savoir . . . il n'est plus un mode de compréhension, mais le mode d'exister de l'homme en tant qu'exister est impossible" (*FP*48). See Libertson's discussion of experience in Bataille and Blanchot in *Proximity: Levinas, Blanchot, Bataille, and Communication*, pp. 253–68.

15. In "La notion de dépense," poetry is "synonymous with expenditure; it in fact signifies, in the most precise way, creation by means of loss. Its meaning is therefore close to that of sacrifice" (*OC*1:307/*VE*120). Poetry is a nonproductive expenditure of language or language in excess of the production of meaning. Bataille clarifies this in terms of the poet as a reprobate who squanders language.

16. In connection with Simone Weil Blanchot writes: "There is in us something that must be called divine, something by which we already dwell close to God: it is the movement by which we efface ourselves, it is abandon—the abandonment of what we believe to be, a retreat outside ourselves and outside everything, a seeking of emptiness through the desire that is like the tension of this emptiness and that, when it is the desire for desire (then a surnatural desire), is the desire of emptiness itself, emptiness desiring" (*EI*167/*IC*115).

17. In "Sur un changement d'époque: L'exigence du retour" (1970), Blanchot imagines a language "in which the categories that up until now have seemed to support it would lose their validity: unity, identity, the primacy of the Same, the Self-subject": in other words, a moment of logical catastrophe. However, Blanchot continues, instead of catastrophe "let us suppose that, supposing the end of history, we were to suppose all these categories not abolished, certainly, but realized, comprehended and included, affirmed in the coherence of a discourse from now on absolute. The book now closed again, all questions answered and all answers organized in the whole of a sufficient or founding speech—now, writing, there would no longer be any reason or place for writing, except to endure the worklessness [*désœuvrement*] of this *now*, the mark of an interruption or break there where discourse falters, in order, perhaps, to receive the affirmation of the Eternal Return" (*EI*406/*IC*272).

18. Of course, poetry is among the "forms of expenditure" by which Bataille characterizes "inner experience," and what is expended is language, which is no longer a medium of communication; rather this medium is turned inside out and, so to speak, wasted. See "Digression sur la poésie et Marcel Proust": "Of poetry, I will now say that it is, I believe, the sacrifice in which words are victims. Words—we use them, we make of them the instrument of useful acts. We would in no way have anything of the human about us if language had to be entirely servile within us. Neither can we do without the efficacious relations which words introduce between men and things. But [in poetry] we tear words from these links in a delirium" (*OC*5:156/*ExI*209–10/*IE*135–36).

19. Compare the conversations in *Celui qui ne m'accompagnait pas*: "A dialogue which I felt was so disappointing, so uselessly closed only through my own fault and also through the fact that my words—and the same was true of his—could only return to their point of departure; why? if I had known that, a great burden would have been lifted from me. I imagined it had to do with time. After all, we were talking, but perhaps everything had been said" (*CAP20/OW13*).

20. In an essay on Beckett's *Comment c'est*, Blanchot says that this text is one to be heard rather than read, since it is characterized by "the disappearance of every sign that would merely be a sign for the eye. Here the force of seeing is no longer what is required; one must renounce the domain of the visible and of the invisible, renounce what is represented, albeit in negative fashion. Hear, simply hear" (*EI481/IC329*). Hear what? "A voice that is old, older than any past. . . . Not something to hear, perhaps the last written cry, what is inscribed in the future outside books, outside language" (*EI483,486/IC330,331*).

Chapter 7: Blanchot/Celan: Désœuvrement

1. Blanchot might disagree: "Silence is impossible," he says in *L'écriture du désastre*. "That is why we desire it" (*ED23/WD11*). Blanchot is thinking of Wittgenstein's motto from the *Tractatus* ("That whereof we cannot speak . . ."), in contrast perhaps to Heidegger's idea from *Sein und Zeit* that "*keeping silent* is another possibility of discourse" (*SZ164/BT164*). If there is anything outside the history of discourse, it is not silence but writing, which exposes us to an incessant, unsilenceable murmur.

2. See Foucault, "La folie, l'absence d'œuvre," *Dits et écrits*, Vol. 1 (Paris: Gallimard, 1994), pp. 412–20; and David Carroll's interesting discussion of Foucault, "Literature and Madness," in *Paraesthetics* (New York: Methuen, 1987), pp. 107–18.

3. Blanchot says that the *Histoire de la folie* is "not so much a history of madness as a sketching out of what might be [quoting Foucault] 'a history of *limits*—of those obscure gestures, necessarily forgotten as soon as they are accomplished, by which a culture rejects something that, for it, would be the Exterior [*l'Extérieur*].' It is on this basis—in the space between madness and unreason—that we have to ask ourselves it if is true that literature and art might be able to entertain these limit-experiences and thus, beyond culture, pave the way for a relation with what culture rejects: a speech of borders, outside of writing" (*EI292/IC196*).

4. *Critique*, 45 (February 1941), 101; see "Madness *par excellence*" (*BR111*).

5. Derrida discusses *La folie du jour* in "La loi du genre" (*P265–87*). What interests Derrida is not so much the madness of the day as the madness of Blanchot's text, its irreducibility or exteriority with respect to the law of genre—but note: "La loi est folie. La loi est folie, la folie, mais la folie n'est pas le prédicat de la loi. Il n'y a pas de folie sans la loi, on ne peut penser la folie que depuis son rapport à la loi. C'est la loi, c'est une folie, la loi" (*P286*). See also Levinas, "Exercices sur 'La folie du jour,'" *Sur Maurice Blanchot* (*SMB53–73*). See esp. p. 62 on the self-contradictory character of Blanchot's *récits*. Writing earlier on Blanchot's *L'attente l'oubli*, Levinas remarked, "Cette parole de la poésie devient pour Blanchot parole qui se contredit. . . . L'affirmation est suivie, souvent dans la même proposition, de sa négation. Le dire lâche ce dont il se saisir. . . . La poésie transformerait les mots, indices d'un ensemble, moments d'une to-

talité, en signes délivrés perçant les murs de l'immanence, dérangeant l'ordre" (*SMB*38–39).

For Blanchot, the "madness of writing" is to be found, among other places, in the texts of the Marquis de Sade. The madness is not just in the depiction of horrible scenes of cruelty. "Something more violent comes to light in this frenzy of writing, a violence that cannot be either exhausted or appeased by the excesses of a superb and ferocious imagination, but that is nonetheless always inferior to the transports of a language that will not tolerate stopping any more than it conceive of a term." Sade's texts belong to the temporality of the *il y a*, that is, of the incessant and interminable: "Sade's major impropriety resides in the simply repetitive force of a narration that encounters no interdict (the whole of this limit-work recounting the interdict by way of the monotony of its terrifying murmur) because there is no other time than that of the interval of speaking [*l'entre-dire*]: the pure arrest that can be reached only by never stopping speaking" (*EI*328/*IC*221).

Désœuvrement is an-archic: without beginning and without end. It is not discourse that violates "the idea of order, of regularity guaranteed by law" (*ED*122/*WD*75); it is speech on the hither side of whatever world order and regularity hold in place.

6. Compare *L'écriture du désastre*, where Blanchot says that, at first, the "fragmentary exigency" was "obeyed lazily, as though it were a matter of stopping at fragments, sketches, studies: preparations or rejected versions of what is not yet a work. That this demand traverses, overturns, ruins the work because the work (totality, perfection, achievement) is the unity which is satisfied with itself—this is what F. Schlegel sensed, but it is also what finally escaped him, though in such a way that one cannot reproach him with this misunderstanding which he helped and still helps us to discern in the very movement whereby we share it with him" (*ED*98–99/*WD*60). The idea is that *désœuvrement* is not the failure of anything. The fragmentary is not a failure of unity—one could just as well say that unity is a failure to respond to the claim of what lies outside the dialectic, that is, outside the production of the work.

7. In *L'écriture du désastre* Blanchot takes special care to make this point. The fragmentary is not dialectically opposed to totality or systematicity but outside it, as if in a different temporality:

> The correct criticism of the System does not consist (as is most often, complacently, supposed) in finding fault with it, or in interpreting it insufficiently (which even Heidegger sometimes does), but rather in rendering it invincible, invulnerable to criticism or, as they say, inevitable. Then, since nothing escapes it because of its omnipresent unity and the perfect cohesion of everything, there remains no place for fragmentary writing unless it come into focus as the impossible necessary: as that which is written in the time outside time, in the sheer suspense which without restraint breaks the seal of unity by, precisely, not breaking it, but by leaving it aside without this abandon's ever being able to be known. It is thus, inasmuch as it separates itself from the manifest, that fragmentary writing does not belong to the One. (*ED*100/*WD*61)

8. *Arrière-histoire du Poème pulvérisée* (Paris: Jean Hughes, 1972), p. 7.

9. In *Le pas au-delà* Blanchot speaks of a line that, although neither a barrier nor a form of mediation or distinction, separates past from future (that is, is structured as the

eternal return): "Let there be a past, let there be a future, with nothing that would allow the passage from one to the other, such that the line of demarcation would unmark
them the more, the more it remained invisible: hope of a past, completed of a future.
All that would remain of time, then, would be this line to cross, always already crossed,
although not crossable, and, in relation to 'me,' unsituatable [*non situable*: the English
translation reads, "unsuitable"]. Perhaps what we would call this 'present' is only the
impossibility of situating this line" (PD22/SNB12).

10. In "Le dernier mot" (1935) the last word is the *il y a*, which is incessant and interminable, that is, its temporality, as Blanchot says in *Apres coup*, is that of *not yet* and
no longer. The last word means: "everything has been said, there is nothing more that
can be written"; the last word can be neither interpreted nor supplemented, neither
contested nor revised; but then again neither does it begin or end. In *Apres coup* Blanchot has this anecdote:

> I remember the story, *Madame Edwarda*. I was surely one of the first to read
> it and to be convinced (overwhelmed to the point of silence) of what was unique
> about this work (only several pages long) and what set it above all literature, and
> in such a way that there could never be any word of commentary attached to it.
> I exchanged a few emotional words with Georges Bataille, not in the way you
> talk to an author about a book of his you admire, but in order to make him un-
> derstand that such an encounter was enough for my entire life, just as the fact of
> having written the book should have been enough for his. All this happened
> during the worst days of the Occupation. This small book—the most minimal of
> books, published under a pseudonym and read by just a few people—was des-
> tined to sink clandestinely into the probable ruin of each of us (author,
> reader)—with no traces left of this remarkable event. As we know, things turned
> out differently.
>
> Even so, without overstepping the bounds of tact, I would like to add some-
> thing. Later, when the war was over and George Bataille's life had also changed,
> he was asked to republish the book—or, more accurately, to allow it to be given
> a real publication. To my great horror, he told me one day that he wanted to
> write a sequel to *Madame Edwarda* and asked my advice. I felt as though some-
> one had just punched me; I blurted out: "It's impossible. I beg of you, don't
> touch it." The matter was then dropped, at least between the two of us. It will be
> remembered that he could not prevent himself from writing a preface under his
> own name, chiefly to introduce his name, so that he could take responsibility
> (indirectly) for a piece of writing that was still scandalous. But this preface, no
> matter how important it was, did not in the least undermine the absolute nature
> of *Madame Edwarda*—nor have the full-scale commentaries it has inspired. . . .
> All that can be said, all that I can say myself, is that the reading of the book has
> probably changed. Admiration, reflection, comparison with other works—the
> things that perpetuate a book are the very things that flatten or equalize it; if the
> book raises up literature, literature reduces it to its own level, no matter what im-
> portance we might give it. What remains is the nakedness of the word "writing,"
> a word no less powerful than the feverish revelation of what for one night, and
> forever after that, was "Madame Edwarda." (AC89–91/VC62–63)

11. The "fear of language" is ambiguous with respect to who or what is afraid. See, for example, the long fragment in *Le pas au-delà*:

This fear of language, it was incumbent upon him not to see in it anything but the possibility, always open, that any word, belonging to the order of words that are only such by their belonging to language, could turn on this language in order to detach itself from it and to raise itself above it in mastering it, perhaps in shattering it, at least in pretending to assign it a limit. Fear does not signify that language would be afraid, even metaphysically, but that fear is a piece of language, something that it would have lost and that would make it entirely dependent on this dead piece: entirely, that is, precisely in reconstituting itself without unity, piece by piece, as something other than a collection of significations. Certainly, metaphor intervenes finally to hold in suspense, making it inoffensive, the possibility of language's being other than a process of meaning. Through metaphor, the fear of language becomes a fear of speaking or the fear which, being the essence of any speech, would make any use of speech, as any silence, frightening. The fear of language: the fear that strikes language when it loses a word that is then *a surplus word, a word too many*: fear, God, madness. Or the "he/it" [*il*] displaced from its rank and role as subject. (*PD*84–85/*SNB*59)

12. See Mary Ann Caws, *The Presence of René Char* (Princeton, N.J.: Princeton University Press, 1976), p. 208, where Valéry is cited: "BREATHING. Freedom is a sensation. It is to be breathed."

13. See Adorno, *Prisms*, trans. Samuel and Shierry Weber (Cambridge: MIT Press, 1967), p. 34: "To write poetry after Auschwitz is barbaric. And this corrodes even the knowledge of why it has become impossible to write poetry." One can think of Blanchot and Celan of giving different interpretations of "the impossibility of poetry." In *Negative Dialectics* Adorno seems less willing to interpret the Holocaust as the end of poetry (p. 362).

14. See Hans-Georg Gadamer's afterword to *Wer bin Ich und wer bist Du? Ein Kommentar zu Paul Celans "Atemkristall"* (Frankfurt: Suhrkamp, 1973), pp. 110–34, in which he responds to Peter Szondi's biographical reading of "Du liegst im grossen Gelausche," in "Eden," *Celan-Studien* (Frankfurt: Suhrkamp, 1972), pp. 113–25, esp. pp. 117–19. The question here has to do with the nature of the difficulty that Celan's poetry poses to interpretation. Is the poem in some sense a private document that one might contextualize in a way that would make its meanings public? See Szondi, pp. 119–21. What Gadamer objects to is just the reduction of the poem to the propositional style of referential discourse. Derrida splits the difference between Szondi and Gadamer. In an admirable phrase, he says that "the poem speaks from beyond knowledge [*le poème parle au-delà du savoir*]" (*S*63). This doesn't mean that we give up all efforts to understand the poem. It means, as both Gadamer and Derrida show, learning to read one poem in terms of another rather than taking the poem to be made of cryptic language that one could get inside of. Shibboleths are finally not passwords.

15. "La loi est césure," says Derrida (*S*16).

16. See "Morning of Acmeism," *Critical Prose and Letters*, p. 64.

17. See Dietland Meinecke, *Wort und Name bei Paul Celan* (Bad Homburg: Gehlen, 1970). See also Jean Bollack, "Paul Celan sur sa langue," *Argumentum e Silen-*

tio: International Celan Symposium, ed. Amy Colin (Berlin: Walter de Gruyter, 1987), pp. 113–29, and Derrida, *Schibboleth* (S97–112), on "Einem, der vor der Tür stand" (GW1:242), in which a proper Jewish name is uttered (with gnashing teeth) in the context of the circumcised (and, on Derrida's reading, unspeakable) word: the shibboleth.

18. Stéphane Mosès has shown that the narrative voice (no-one's voice) that opens "Gespräch im Gebirg" is actually a play or concert of voices, in which literary German and an idiomatic Jewish-German are laced with both anti-Semitic and Yiddish expressions. The text moves from this concert of voices to a dialogue to a monologue or confession that one can read as Celan's acknowledgment of his Judaism. See "Quand le langage se fait voix (*Paul Celan*: Entretien dans la montagne)," *Contre-Jour: Études sur Paul Celan*, ed. Martine Broda (Paris: Éditions du Cerf, 1986), pp. 117–31. John Felstiner has also discussed the multilayered character of this text, with its abundant echoes of Büchner, Nietzsche, Kafka, Buber, and Mandelstam. Felstiner also gives us the biographical context: "In July 1959, Celan with his wife Gisèle de Lestrange, a Parisian artist, and his five-year-old son Eric, went to Sils-Maria in the Engadine region of the Swiss alps. There he was to have met the sociologist T. W. Adorno. But Celan returned early to Paris, and so—'not accidentally,' he once said—missed meeting Adorno then. In August, out of this failed encounter Celan wrote *Gespräch im Gebirg*, 'Conversation in the Mountains,' a sort of folk-tale where Jew Little meets Jew Big, and they schmoose for a while." "Goodbye Silence: Paul Celan's *Conversation in the Mountains*," *Stanford Humanities Review*, 1, no. 1 (1989), 33. This issue also contains Felstiner's translation of "Gespräch im Gebirg," 41–43, which captures the disconnectedness of Celan's prose. See also Georg-Michael Schulz, "Individuation und Austauschbarkeit: Zu Paul Celans *Gespräch im Gebirg*," *Deutsche Vierteljahrsschrift für Literaturwissenschaft und Geistesgeschichte*, 53 (1979), 463–77. The most detailed and valuable reading of "Gespräch im Gebirg" is by Renate Böschenstein-Schäfer, ""Anmerkungen zu Paul Celans "Gespräch im Gebirg," *Neue Zürcher Zeitung* (October 1968), reprinted in *Über Paul Celan*, ed. Dietland Meinecke (Frankfurt: Suhrkamp, 1970), 226–38.

19. Cf. "Mit allen Gedanken," from *Niemandsrose*:

stieg ein Hauch in den Äther,	a breath rose up to the aether
und was sich wölkte, wars nicht,	and that which made clouds, was it
wars nicht Gestalt und von uns her,	not,
wars nicht	was it not a shape come from us,
so gut wie ein Name?	was it not
(GW1:221)	as good as a name?
	(PPC167).

and "Hüttenfenster":

Das Aug, dunkel:	The eye, dark:
als Hüttenfenster. Es sammelt,	as tabernacle window. It gathers
was Welt war, Welt bleibt: den	what was world, remains world: the
Wander-	migrant
-Osten, die	East, the
Schwebenden, die	hovering ones, the

Menschen-und-Juden,	human beings-and-Jews,
das Volk-vom-Gewölk, magnetisch	the people of clouds, magnetically
ziehts, mit Herzfingern, an	with heart-fingers, you
dir, Erde:	it attracts, Earth:
du kommst, du kommst	you are coming, coming,
wohnen werden wir, wohnen, etwas	we shall dwell at last, dwell, some-
—ein Atem? ein Name?—	thing
(GW1:278)	—a breath? a Name?—
	(CPP213)

Recall "Der Meridian," where Celan says: "I believe I have met poetry in the figure of Lucile, and Lucile perceives language as shape, direction, breath [*nimmt Sprache als Gestalt und Richtung und Atem wahr*]. I am looking for the same thing here, in Büchner's work. I am looking for Lenz himself, as a person, I am looking for his shape: for the sake of the place of poetry, for the sake of liberation [*Freisetzung*], for the sake of the step" (GW3:194/CP45).

20. Celan's conclusion to "Der Meridian"—"I had encountered myself" (GW3:201/CP53)—serves as a kind of warrant to the idea of self-dialogue. See Jerry Glenn, *Paul Celan* (New York: Twayne, 1973), p. 43. Self-encounter here should perhaps be taken in the complicated sense of encountering the other in oneself rather than as the working out of a logic of self-identity. See Derrida, *Schibboleth*. Being Jewish, says Derrida, is being nonidentical as such. Being himself Jewish, Derrida says, makes him free to say that the essence of the Jew is to have no essence (S91). Cf. Blanchot on "Being Jewish" (EI185–86/IC126–28), and chapter 9 below.

21. Compare the following:

Es ist ein Land Verloren,	There is a country Lost,
da wächst ein Mond im Ried,	a moon grows in its reeds,
und das mit uns erfroren	where all that froze to death
es glüht umher und sieht.	with us, glows and sees.
Es sieht, denn des hat Augen,	It sees, for it has eyes,
die helle Erden sind.	each eye an earth, and bright.
Die Nacht, die Nacht, die Laugen.	The night, the night, the eyes.
Es sieht, das Augenkind.	The eye-child's gift is sight.
Es sieht, est sieht, wir sehen,	It sees, it sees, we see,
ich sehe dich, du siehst.	I see you, you see.
Das Eis wird auferstehen,	Before this hour is ended
eh sich die Stunde schließt.	ice will rise from the dead.
(GW1:224)	(PPC173)

22. In "Der Meridian" Celan distinguishes between the Lenz of Büchner's fragment (*der Büchnersche Lenz*) and the "other" Lenz: "I am looking for Lenz himself, as a person, I am looking for his shape: for the sake of the place of poetry, for the sake of liberation, for the sake of a step." And shortly he adds:

"Death," we read in a work on Jakob Michael Reinhold Lenz published in Leipzig, in 1909, from the pen of a Moscow professor, M. N. Rosanow, "death was now slow to deliver him. In the night from the 23rd to the 24th of May, 1792, Lenz was found dead in a street in Moscow. A nobleman paid for his funeral. His grave has remained unknown."

Thus *he* had lived *on*.

He: the real Lenz, Büchner's figure [i.e., model], the person whom we encountered on the first page of the story, the Lenz who "on the 20th of January was walking through the mountains,"—he—not the artist thinking about art—he is an "I." (GW3:194/CP45)

23. The distinction between speaking and talking is perhaps as old as the difference between grammar and rhetoric, but it is developed anew by Heidegger in section 34 of *Sein und Zeit*, where talk (*reden*) is the "existential-ontological" (as against logical) foundation of discourse or language. For Heidegger as for Celan, *reden* is older than *sprechen*, which is to say that naming, designation and assertion, are not foundational for human *Dasein*. *Reden* opens the space of *mitsein* in which we are with one another, and where Dasein therefore comes into being for the first time. Talking here is not monological. For example, listening (*Hören*) belongs to talking as an "existential possibility": "Listening to . . . is Dasein's existential way of Being-open as Being-with for Others. Indeed, listening constitutes the primary and authentic way in which Dasein is open for its ownmost potentiality-for-Being—as in hearing the voice of the friend whom every Dasein carries with it" (SZ163/BT206). Likewise keeping silent belongs to talking: "To be able to keep silent, Dasein must have something to say" (SZ165/BT208).

With respect to Celan's text, if the sticks and stones speak, but do not talk, it is perhaps because they are not in the existential mode of listening that talking presupposes. Perhaps one could say that the sticks and stones are in a syncopated relation, that is, they constitute a duet rather than a conversation.

24. In an essay on the Surrealists, "Le demain joueur," Blanchot allegorizes André Breton's Nadja as an anonymous figure of pure encounter: "The encounter with Nadja is the encounter with encounter, a double encounter. Naturally, Nadja is real [*vraie*] or, more precisely, she is not real [*vraie*]; she remains apart from every interpretable truth, signifying only the unsignifying particularity of her presence; and this presence is that of encounter—brought forth by chance, taken back again by chance, as dangerous and fascinating as it is, and finally vanishing in and of itself, in the frightening *between-two* opened by the aleatory between reason and unreason [*dans l'effrayant entre-deux ouvert par l'aléa entre raison et déraison*]. But this encounter that necessarily takes place in the continuity of the world is given precisely in such a way that it breaks this continuity and affirms itself as interruption, interval, arrest, and opening" (EI607 /IC413).

25. Obviously this question already presupposes Blanchot's Greek interpretation of "being Jewish," or rather his interpretation of the relationship between God and the Jews. Blanchot says, "what we owe to Jewish monotheism is not the revelation of the one God, but the revelation of a speech as the place where men hold themselves in relation with what excludes all relation: the infinitely Distant, the absolutely foreign. God speaks, man speaks to him" (EI187/IC127). But this speech is an infinite conversation where the distance between the interlocutors is not diminished; "on the contrary, it is maintained, preserved in its purity by the rigor of the speech that upholds absoluteness of difference. . . . Jewish thought does not know, or refuses, mediation and speech as mediating. . . . To speak to someone is to accept not introducing him into the

system of things or of beings to be known; it is to recognize him as unknown and to receive him as foreign without obliging him to break with this difference" (EI187/IC128).

Possibly one should say that Blanchot's personne is "jewgreek" in the manner of Levinas's le qui or l'un—the who or (as Lingis translates) the me. See Levinas's analysis of the neutral soi (oneself) in Autrement qu'être. The soi is not a subject. It is a "term in recurrence . . . on the hither side of consciousness and its play, beyond or on the hither side [par-delà ou en deçà] of being which it thematizes, outside of being, and thus in itself as in exile" (AE163/OTB103). The soi is that which is called out or exposed in the hypostatic relation that Levinas explicates as "responsibility for others" (AE167/OTB105). In this event, "the hypostasis is exposed as oneself in the accusative form, before appearing in the said proper to knowing as the bearer of a name" AE167/OTB106). Its anonymity is, one might say, its essence. The soi, Levinas says, is like "a sound that [is] audible only in its echo" (AE167/OTB106), that is, without being and without identity. "Prior to the play of being, before the present, older than the time of consciousness that is accessible in memory . . . , the oneself is exposed as a hypostasis, of which the being it is as an entity is but a mask. It bears its name as a borrowed name, a pseudonym, a pro-noun" (AE168/OTB106). The oneself is not a reflexive term but a term in a recurrence in which the relation between the one and the self is a relation of the third kind, a nonrelation in the sense that Levinas explains as follows: "Neither a vision of oneself by oneself, nor a manifestation of oneself to oneself, the oneself does not coincide with the identifying of truth, is not statable in terms of consciousness, discourse, or intentionality." Prior to reflection, "it is first a non-quiddity—no one [personne]—clothed with purely borrowed being, which masks its nameless singularity by conferring on it a role"—a role that Levinas figures as a "comic mask" (AE168/OTB106–7).

26. Lacoue-Labarthe has an interesting discussion of the (neither positive nor negative) "theology" of "Psalm" in La poésie comme expérience, pp. 104–22. Compare Martine Broda, Dans la main de personne, pp. 30–40. A detailed analysis of the poem is given by Gerhard Buhr, Celans Poetik (Göttingen: Vandenhoeck and Ruprecht, 1976), pp. 156–80.

27. Ann Smock, translating le désœuvrement du neutre (in L'écriture du désastre) as "the uneventfulness of the neutral" (ED30/WD14), brings out precisely this sense of a relation that works like an interval or interruption where something does not take place. See her footnote in explanation of désœuvrement as "uneventfulness" (WD148).

28. Recall "Der Meridian": "Only the space of conversation can establish what is addressed, can gather it into a 'you' around the naming and speaking I. But this 'you,' come about by dint of being named and addressed, brings its otherness [Anderssein] into the present. Even in the here and now of the poem—and the poem has only this one, unique, momentary present—even in this immediacy and nearness [Unmittelbarkeit und Nähe], the otherness [dem Anderen] gives voice to what is most its own: its time" (GW3:198–99/CP50).

Chapter 8: Infinite Discretion

1. See Foucault, "Maurice Blanchot: The Thought from the Outside," pp. 53–58. Elsewhere Foucault writes:

Beginning with *Igitur*, Mallarmé's experience (he was Nietzsche's contempo-rary) demonstrates that the game of autonomous language itself came into being in precisely the place where man had just disappeared. We may say that, since then, literature has been the place where man has never stopped disappearing in favor of language. Where *"ça parle,"* man no longer exists. Works as different as Robbe-Grillet's and Malcolm Lowry's, Borges's and Blanchot's, testify to this disappearance of man in favor of language.

Quoted by Luc Ferry and Alain Renaut, *French Philosophy of the Sixties: An Essay on Antihumanism*, trans. Mary Schnackenberg Cattani (Amherst: University of Massa-chusetts Press, 1990), p. 98.

2. Actually this is an honor Blanchot conferred on the surrealists. See "Quelques réflexions sur le surréalisme" (1945):

> The surrealists became well aware—and they made use of it admirably—of the strange nature [*le caractére bizarre*] of words: they saw that words have their own proper spontaneity. For a long time, language had laid claim to a kind of partic-ular existence: it refused simple transparency, it was not just a gaze, an empty means of seeing; it existed, it was a concrete thing and even a colored thing. The surrealists understand, moreover, that language is not an inert thing: it has a life of its own, and a latent power that escapes us. Alain wrote that one must always verify where ideas are—they do not stay in place, that is why they cannot be on their guard. It is the same for words: they move, they have their demand [*exi-gence*], they dominate us. (*PF*93/*WF*88–89)

3. This "pure dissipation" becomes, nearly thirty years later, pure *passivité*: "dying, silent intensity; that which cannot be welcomed, which is inscribed wordlessly; the body in the past, the body of no one, of the interval: being's suspense, a seizure like a cut in time, which we cannot evoke except as wild, unnarratable history having no meaning in the present" (*ED*49/*WD*28). The increasing fragmentation of Blanchot's *œuvre* hardly diminishes the obsessiveness of his thinking. Herman Rapaport has some indispensable pages on temporality in Blanchot in the context of Derrida's reading of Heidegger, in which Blanchot proves to be Derrida's major conceptual resource. See *Heidegger and Derrida: Reflections on Time and Language*, pp. 104–48. Rapaport reads Blanchot as a go-between who clarifies the complex and unstable relations between Derrida and Heidegger. In the bargain his book is perhaps the best account that we have of Blanchot's philosophical importance. Rapaport has said to me on many occa-sions that he does not regard Blanchot as much of a thinker ("neither original nor pro-found"), but his own book shows how far the facts are otherwise. In any case Rapaport is the first to take up the question of temporality in Blanchot's *Le pas au-delà* (is the first to take up this difficult text). The puns in Blanchot's title, including Derrida's vari-ations on them, are unpacked in several directions.

4. These words are vague without being in any sense deficient: vague in the sense of vagabond; words which are neither exact nor inexact but *anexact*. In *Mille plateaux*, Gilles Deleuze and Félix Guattari, following Husserl, give the example of the circle, which is exact, in contrast to roundness, which is vague or nomadic (*MP*454–55/ *TP*367). Blanchot is absolutely rigorous in his anexactitude.

5. At (evidently) a crucial moment in *Celui qui ne m'accompagnait pas*, the narrator's companion says something "brusquely in a tone of incredible scorn that seemed to me to come from a different mouth—oh, from an infinite past." What was said exactly seems hardly to matter (the companion repeats, in an incredulous tone, the words just spoken by the narrator, which is how their conversation frequently proceeds). The effect on the narrator is that "something quite different had come to light through this remark, had sought a way out, something older, dreadfully old [*quelque chose de plus ancien, d'effroyablement ancien*], which had perhaps taken place at all times, and at all times I was tied to the spot" (CAP47–48/OW23–24). If I understand, the narrator hears in his companion's voice the voice of "the anonymous, the nameless" (CAP90/OW47), namely the voice of the neuter: "*Voice of no one, once more* [Voix de personne, à nouveau]" (ED121/WD75). The sound detaches the narrator from himself in a decisive fashion: at once he begins speaking of himself in the third person. See Roger Laporte, *Maurice Blanchot: L'ancien, l'effroyablement ancien* (Paris: Fata Morgana, 1987), esp. pp. 22–25.

6. See Gilles Deleuze, "He Stuttered," *Gilles Deleuze and the Theater of Philosophy*, ed. Constantin V. Boundas and Dorothea Olkowski (London: Routledge, 1994), pp. 23–29. The stutter is to be thought of as an invention of language rather than a defect of speech. Deleuze thinks of it as the production of a minor language within a major, that is, a foreign space within one's native tongue. His most emphatic example is that of Kleist:

And Kleist? What kind of language was he awakening in the depths of German by means of grins, slips of tongue, grinding of teeth, inarticulate sounds, elongated connections, brutal speeding up and slowing down, risking always to provoke Goethe's horror—Goethe, the most important representative of the major language—and reaching for strange goals, petrified visions, and vertiginous melodies? (p. 25)

7. Here it would be helpful to consult *Celui que ne m'accompagnait pas* once more, since the nature of the relation (or nonrelation) between the narrator and his companion is very much what *Le pas au-delà* is trying to clarify: it is a space that the narrator tries to fill with a logical relation—designation, predication, description, narration—which the companion meanwhile tries to keep open:

"Wouldn't it be more convenient if I could name you?"
"You would like to give me a name?"
"Yes, at this moment I would like to." And when he did not answer: "Wouldn't that make thing easier? Don't we have to come to that?"
But he still seemed to be dwelling on his question.
"Give me a name? But why?"
"I don't know exactly: maybe to lose my own."
Which, strangely enough, caused him to recover his good humor:
"Oh, you won't get out of it that way!"
A reply which, I understood very well, summoned my own, awaited my own:
"But I don't want to get out of it."

And to avoid that expectation which sought to beguile in me words that had already been spoken, I had to make an effort that resulted in this question.

"Aren't there already many words between us?"

"Yes, certainly, many writings."

Then I remarked with some incoherence:

"You mean there shouldn't be any name between us?"

"Yes, that's it," but he added, with a lack of connection that showed that my own [incoherence] had not escaped him:

"You know, words should not frighten us." (CAP42–43/OW21)

In *Le pas au-delà* Blanchot speaks of the "vain struggle for the anonymous. Impersonality is not enough to guarantee the anonymous. The work, even if it is without author and always becoming in relation to itself, delimits a space that attracts names" (PD53/SNB36). The task of writing, in ways that will always remain difficult to explain, is to keep this space (as Celan might say) "open, empty, and free."

8. Cf. Deleuze, *Logique du sens*, where being young is an example of the modality of the event whose presence is divided into past and future *ad infinitum:* "It is neither at the same time, nor in relation to the same thing, that I am younger or older, but it is at the same time and by the same relation that I become so" (LdS46/LS33). Cf. Blanchot on the near and the distant: "The distant calls to the near, repelling it, not to define itself in it by opposition, nor to form a couple with it by resemblance and difference, but in such a way that the separation between the two still belongs to the distant. The near, repelling it, calls to the immediate that consumes it. The near is always only near. The proximity of the present does not make itself present, because presence is never near, it has always already affirmed the absolute of presence which is there one time and for all without relation or progression, nor dawn nor dusk" (PD98/SNB69–70). We recognize this as the modality of conversation in *Celui qui ne m'accompagnait pas:*

"You're tall, aren't you?"

But I didn't realize where these words were coming from, nor why they enveloped me once again with the impression of naturalness that had always marked our relations. I didn't realize it because I seemed to hear him in the tranquil simplicity of the past, but when I answered him: "Fairly tall," and he added: "Couldn't you describe to me what you're like?" I had such a strong feeling—probably at finding myself once again in the truth of his reserve, at the very moment when I feared I was left out of it—that I could only think of answering:

"Yes, that's easy." As I said this, I thought, in fact, that there was a mirror on the wall on the other side of the table, though I didn't intend to look at myself in it, but the memory of that mirror helped me to say to him:

"I believe I look rather young."

"Young? Why?"

I thought for a moment:

"It's because I'm thin."

A remark that didn't seem to reach him, he seemed so occupied with allowing the word "young" to come to him, profoundly, in a disturbing way, repeating it as though he wanted henceforth to confine himself to it, to the point that, understanding that he wouldn't let go of it again of his own accord, I made haste in order to deflect him from it, to find another reason. . . . (CAP162–64/OW86–87)

Cf. *Le pas au-delà:* "*And he knew, thanks to the too ancient knowledge, effaced by the ages, that the young names, naming twice, an infinity of times, one in the past, the other in the future, that which is found only on this side, that which is found only beyond, named hope, deception. Hand in hand, from threshold to threshold, like immortals, one of whom was dying, the other saying: 'would I be with whom I die?'* " (PD186–87/ SNB137).

9. *Discipline and Punish: The Birth of the Prison,* trans. Alan Sheridan (New York: Vintage Books, 1979), p. 191.

10. *Points of Departure,* trans. Stephen Mitchell (Philadelphia: Jewish Publication Society of America, 5742/1981), p. 25.

11. *The Political Philosophy of Poststructuralist Anarchism,* p. 47.

12. In *Logique du sens,* Gilles Deleuze develops an extended commentary on Lewis Carroll's narratives of "pure becoming," a condition that entails "the paradox of infinite identity." Language tries to set limits to becoming in the form of naming, predication, cognition, etc., but language itself supersedes its own function. This comes out in *Alice in Wonderland* and *Through the Looking-Glass,* where episodes resolve themselves into a single plot:

The contesting of Alice's personal identity and the loss of her proper name. The loss of the proper name is the adventure which is repeated throughout all Alice's adventures. For the proper or singular name is guaranteed by the permanence of *savoir.* The latter is embodied in general names designating pauses and rests, in substantives and adjectives, with which the proper name maintains a constant connection. Thus the personal self requires God and the world in general. But when substantives and adjectives begin to dissolve, when the names of pause and rest are carried away by the verbs of pure becoming and slide into the language of events, all identity disappears from the self, the world, and God. This is the test of *savoir* and recitation which strips Alice of her identity. In it words may go awry, being obliquely swept away by the verbs. It is as if events enjoyed an irreality which is communicated through the language to the *savoir* and to persons. (LdS11/LS3)

Cf. Heidegger's worlding of the world and Levinas's verbalization of the verb.

13. In *L'écriture du désastre* Blanchot gives the example of the "mythical or hyperbolic 'cancer'":

Why does it frighten us with its name, as if thereby the unnamable were designated? It claims to defeat the coded system under whose auspices, living and accepting to live, we abide in the security of a purely formal existence, obeying a model signal according to a program whose process is apparently perfectly normative. "Cancer" would seem to symbolize (and "realize") the refusal to respond: here is a cell that doesn't hear the command, that develops lawlessly, in a way that could be called anarchic. It does still more: it destroys the very idea of a program, blurring the exchange and the message: it wrecks the possibility of reducing everything to the equivalent of signs. Cancer, from this perspective, is a political phenomenon, one of the rare ways to dislocate the system, to disarticulate, through proliferation and disorder, the universal programming and signifying power. (*ED*137/*WD*86–87)

14. In *Logique du sens* Deleuze distinguishes two rival and incompatible notions of temporality: "on the one hand, the always limited present, which measures the action of bodies as causes and the state of their mixtures in depth (Chronos); on the other, the essentially unlimited past and future, which gather incorporeal events, at the surface, as effects (Aion) (*LdS*77/*LS*61). The distinction between Aion and Chronos was developed further by Deleuze and Guattari in *Mille plateaux*:

Aeon: the indefinite time of the event, the floating line that knows only speeds and continually divides that which transpires into an already-there that is at the same time not-yet-here, a simultaneous too-late and too-early, a something that is both going to happen and has just happened. *Chronos:* the time of measure that situates things and persons, develops a form, and determines a subject. Boulez distinguishes tempo and nontempo in music: the "pulsed time" of a formal and functional music based on values versus the "nonpulsed time" of a floating music, both floating and machinic, which has nothing but speeds or differences in dynamic. In short, the difference is not at all between the ephemeral and the durable, nor even between the regular and the irregular, but between two modes of individuation, two modes of temporality (*MP*320/*TP*262).

Cf. Deleuze and Guattari, *What Is Philosophy?*:

This is what we call the Event, or the part that eludes its own actualization in everything that happens. The event is not the state of affairs. It is actualized in a state of affairs, in a body, in a lived [state], but it has a shadowy and secret part that is continually subtracted from or added to its actualization: in contrast with the state of affairs, it neither begins nor ends but has gained or kept the infinite movement to which it gives consistency. . . . The event is immaterial, incorporeal, unlivable: pure *reserve*. (*WP*156)

They add: "Two thinkers have gone the farthest into the event—Péguy and Blanchot."
15. See *Celui qui ne m'accompagnait pas*:

I see them all, never one in particular, never one single one in the familiarity of an undivided gaze, and if, even so, I try to stare at one of them separately, what I'm looking at then is a terrible, impersonal presence, the frightening affirmation of something I don't understand, don't penetrate, that isn't here and that nevertheless conceals itself in the ignorance and emptiness of my own gaze. (*CAP*142–43/*OW*75–76)

Should we count the narrator as a philosopher?
16. See *Faux pas* (1943), where dread is already a condition of fragmentation or *désœuvrement*:

His [the writer's] will, as the practical power to order what is possible, itself becomes full of dread. His clear reason, still capable of establishing a dialogue with itself, becomes, because it is clear and discursive, the equal of the impenetrable madness that reduces him to silence. Logic identifies with the unhappiness and fright of consciousness [*au malheur et à l'effroy de la conscience*]. However, this substitution can only be temporary . . . active reason quickly imposes the stability that is its law; full of dread a moment before, it now turns dread into a reason; it turns anxious seeking into a chance for forgetfulness and repose. Once this usurpation has taken place, and even before it happens, just in the threat of it that is glimpsed even in the most carefully distrustful use of the creative mind, all work becomes impossible. Dread requires the abandonment of what threatens to make it weaker; it requires it, and this abandonment . . . increases dread enormously; it . . . moves toward a strange satisfaction; as it reduces itself, it no longer sees more than itself, it is contemplation that veils itself and perception that fragments itself; a sort of sufficiency comes into being along with its insufficiency; the devastating movement that it is draws it toward a definitive splitting apart. (*FP*15/*GO*10)

17. See *Différence et répétition*, where Deleuze speaks of a "categorical reversal" that predicates being of becoming, the one of the multiple, identity of difference. "That identity not be first, that it exist as a principle but as a second principle, as a principle *become*; that it revolve around the Different: such would be the nature of a Copernican revolution which opens up the possibility of difference having its own concept, rather than being maintained under the domination of a concept already understood as identical. Nietzsche meant nothing more than this by eternal return" (*DeR*58/*DR*40–41). Eternal return presupposes a world without identity, that is, "a complete reversal of the world of representation, and of the sense that 'identical' and 'similar' had in that world" (*DeR*384/*DR*301). This we should now be able to recognize (from *L'espace littéraire*) as Blanchot's upside-down world of poetic insubordination.

18. In fact this fragment is a rewriting of the text placed after the prefatory note to *L'entretien infini* in which two elderly friends meet to continue their longstanding conversation. Curiously, in this earlier text one of the friends—the one who receives the visit of the other—although in deep fatigue, is still "robust." After a while the visitor "*becomes aware that this conversation will be the last*" (*EI*ix/*IC*xiii). The two talk a good deal about their fatigue. At one point one of them, evidently the visitor, asks, "*How will we manage to disappear*" (*EI*xi/*IC*xiv). This is obviously a question of some delicacy, or perhaps urgency. It is not so much left unanswered as that the two friends interrupt one another with unfinished sentences—"*Well, it would suffice for us . . .*"—"*No, it would not suffice . . .*" The word "suffice" seems an omen: "*From the instant that this word—a word, a phrase—slipped between them, something changed, a history ended*" (*EI*xi–xii/*IC*xiv). A fragment that follows seems to offer an explanation:

There is a moment in the life of a man—consequently, in the life of men—when everything is completed, the books written, the universe silent, beings at rest. There is left only the task of announcing it: this is easy. But as this supplementary word threatens to upset the equilibrium—and where to find the force to say it? where to find another place for it?—it is not pronounced and the task remains unfinished. One writes only what I have just written, finally that is not written either. (EIxii/ICxv)

In *Le pas au-delà* the task of announcing the end is taken up once more, and perhaps fulfilled. It takes the form of an answer to the question *"But tell me, what has happened?"* [qu'est-il arrivé]" *(EIxiv/ICxvi)*. And of course what has happened is *"An event: what nevertheless does not arrive . . ." (EIxix/ICxviii)*.

19. Cf. *L'entretien infini*, where the moment is perhaps somewhat more embellished:

And softly too he asks: "But tell me what has happened?" and in the same way receives the response: "What had to happen, something that doesn't concern me." At once he is struck by the manner in which this statement remains at a distance; it is not solemn, it hardly makes any call on him; it does not change the morning light. He knows that it is, after all, only a sentence, and that it would be better not to translate it into this other that he nevertheless cannot refrain from offering: "Do you want me to understand that this might concern me?"—"It concerns one of us." The silence has a character to which he does not attend, given up entirely to the impression that a threshold has been crossed, a force of affirmation broken, a refusal thrust aside, but also a challenge issued—not to him, the benevolent interlocutor, but impersonally, or—yes, it is strange—to someone else, to the event in which precisely neither one is involved. (EIxiv–xv/ICxvi)

20. In *Logique du sens*, apropos of Blanchot, Deleuze writes:

Why is every event a kind of plague, war, wound, or death? Is this simply to say that there are more unfortunate than fortunate events? No, this is not the case since the question here is about the double structure of every event. With every event, there is indeed the present moment of actualization, the moment in which the event is embodied in a state of affairs, an individual, or a person, the moment we designate by saying *"here,* the moment has come." The future and the past of the event are evaluated only with respect to this definitive present, and from the point of view of that which embodies it. But on the other hand, there is the future and the past of the event considered in itself, sidestepping each present, being free of the limitations of a state of affairs, impersonal and pre-individual, neutral, neither general nor particular, *eventum tantum. . . .* It has no other present than that of the mobile instant which represents it, always divided into past-future, and forming what must be called the counter-actualization. In one case, it is my life, which seems too weak for me and slips away at a point which, in a determined relation to me, has become present. In the other case, it is I who am too weak for life, it is life which overwhelms me, scattering its singularities all about, in no relation to me, nor to a moment determinable as the present, except an impersonal instant which is divided into still-future and already past. No one has shown better than Maurice Blanchot that this ambiguity is essentially that of the wound and of death, of the mortal wound. Death has an extreme and definite relation to me and my body and is grounded in me, but it also has no relation to me at all—it is incorporeal and infinitive, impersonal, grounded only in itself. On the one side, there is part of the event which is realized and accomplished; on the other, there is that "part of the event which cannot realize its accomplishment." There are thus two accomplishments, which are like actualization and counter-actualization. (LdS177/LS151–52)

21. *Le pas au-delà* contains a number of fragments on dying, the most lucid of which really gives the whole theory of the event:

But dying, no more than it *cannot* finish or accomplish itself, even in death, does not let itself be situated or affirmed in a relation of life, even as a declining relation, a declining of life. Dying does not localize itself in an event, nor does it last in the way of a temporal becoming; dying does not last, does not end, and, prolonging itself in death, tears this away from the state of a thing in which it would like to retreat peacefully. It is dying, the error of dying without completion, that makes the dead one suspect and death unverifiable, withdrawing from it in advance the benefit of an *event*. And life knows nothing of dying, says nothing about it, without, however, confining itself to silence; there is, suddenly and always, a murmur among words, the rumor of absence that passes in and to the outside of discourse, a non-silent arrest that intervenes, there where the noise of writing, order of the somber curator, maintains an interval for dying, while dying, the interval itself perhaps, cannot take place in it. (PD129/SNB93–94)

Chapter 9: Blanchot's "holocaust"

1. Regarding the "new": "The new [*Le neuf, le nouveau*], because it cannot take its place in history, is also that which is most ancient: an unhistorical occurrence to which we are called upon to answer as if it were the impossible, the invisible—that which has always long since disappeared beneath ruins" (ED63/WD37). The new is a name for the present, but like the present it withdraws into the no longer and the not yet.

2. Earlier, in "L'oubli, la déraison" (1961), Blanchot had characterized forgetting in Nietzschean terms as a condition of possibility—for example, "the capacity to forget is essential to speech" (EI289/IC194), or again: "We are able to forget and, thanks to this, able to live, to act, to work, and to remember—to be present: we are thus able to speak usefully" (EI290/IC195). So it is something like the power to exclude. But "this ability-to-forget does not belong solely to the realm of possibility" (EI290/IC195). Obscurely, Blanchot speaks of forgetting "getting away. It escapes. . . . At the same time as we make use of forgetting as a power, the capacity to forget turns us over to a forgetting without power, to the movement of that which slips and steals away: detour itself" (EI290/IC195). This is the movement of dispersal or disarrangement that "reduces to insignificance every power already organized, suspending any possibility of reorganization and yet giving itself, outside every organizing organ, as the space between: the future of the whole where the whole withholds itself" (EI30/IC22). So forgetting is as much a figure of anarchy as it is of possibility. One might think of it as the anarchic realm out of which everything returns, without why. What if history-writing were the attempt of totality to secure itself against this realm?

3. The word "intensity" is a Bataille-word, a figure of anarchy, impossibility, or ex-teriority: "Intensity is an excess, an absolute disruption which admits of no regimen, regulation, direction, erection, insur-rection, nor does it admit of their simple con-traries; thus it wrecks what it makes known, burning the thought which thinks it and yet requiring this thought in the conflagration where transcendence, immanence are no longer anything but flamboyant, extinguished figures—reference points of writing which writing has always lost in advance" (ED93/WD56). Intensity is outside the neg-ative, outside language; it is the inspiration of the fragmentary—"Intensity: the attrac-tiveness in this name lies not only in its generally escaping conceptualization, but also in its way of coming apart in a plurality of names, de-nominations which dismiss the power that can be exerted as well as the intentionality that orients and also sign and sense, and the space that unfolds and the time that expatiates" (ED93/WD56).

4. Paul Davies, writing from the side of Levinas, gives an excellent account of the Levinas-Blanchot dialogue on responsibility, and helps to clarify some very difficult fragments in L'écriture du désastre, in "A Fine Risk: Reading Blanchot Reading Lev-inas," Re-Reading Levinas, esp. pp. 214–18.

5. Quoted by Michel Surya, Georges Bataille: La mort à l'oeuvre, p. 319.

6. See Sarah Kofman, Paroles suffoquées (Paris: Galilée, 1987); Kevin Newmark, "Resisting Responding," Responses: On Paul de Man's Wartime Journalism, ed. Werner Hamacher, Neil Hertz, and Thomas Keenan (Lincoln: University of Nebraska Press, 1989), pp. 343–49; Lawrence Langer, Holocaust Testimonies: The Ruins of Memory (New Haven: Yale University Press, 1991), pp. 39–40, 69, 75–76, 121; Allan Stoekl, "Blanchot, Violence, and the Disaster," Auschwitz and After: Race, Culture, and 'the Jewish Question' in France, ed. Lawrence D. Kritzman (New York: Routledge, 1995), pp. 133–48.

7. See Henry Rousso, The Vichy Syndrome: History and Memory in France since 1944, trans. Arthur Goldhammer (Cambridge, Mass.: Harvard University Press, 1991). On Rousso's account the crucial event in the awakening of France to the realities of the Vichy years and in particular to the Holocaust was the showing in 1971—after two years' suppression—of Marcel Ophuls's Le chagrin et la pitié, a documentary of every-day life in Clermont-Ferrand, "a city allegedly typical of France under the Occupa-tion" (p. 101). It is interesting that the most important historical study of the Vichy years is by an American historian, Robert O. Paxton, Vichy France: Old Guard and New Or-der (New York: Columbia University Press, 1972; 2nd ed., 1982). See Steven Ungar, "Vichy as Paradigm of Contested Memory," Scandal and Aftereffect, pp. 1–33.

8. On the fate of the Jews in France during the Occupation, see Michael R. Mar-rus and Robert O. Paxton, Vichy France and the Jews (New York: Basic Books, 1981), esp. pp. 177–214.

9. See Pierre Vidal-Naquet, "The Holocaust's Challenge to History," trans. Roger Butler-Borruat, in Auschwitz and After, ed. Lawrence D. Kritzman, p. 28: "I would say that the only great French historical work on the massacre . . . is not a book but a film, Shoah, by Claude Lanzmann." But one should not forget Alain Resnais's documen-tary, Nuit et brouillard (1956). Henry Rousso comments that, "Unlike Shoah . . . Resnais focused more on the deportation of resistance fighters and political prisoners than on deportation for racial reasons" (The Vichy Syndrome, p. 229).

10. See The Vichy Syndrome, pp. 132–67, "Obsession (After 1974): Jewish Memory."

11. See Richard I. Cohen, "The Fate of French Jewry in World War II in Historical Writing (1944–1983)," *The Historiography of the Holocaust Period: Proceedings of the Fifth Yad Vashem International Historical Conference, Jerusalem 1983*, ed. Yisrael Gutman and Gideon Greif (Jerusalem: Yad Vashem, 1988), pp. 155–86. See Michael Marrus and Robert Paxton, *Vichy France and the Jews*, and Serge Klarsfeld, *Vichy-Auschwitz: Le role le Vichy dans la solution finale de la question juive en France* (Paris: Fayard, 1983). For a comprehensive summary and an extensive bibliography, see Sanford Gutman, "The Holocaust in France," *Holocaust Literature: A Handbook of Critical, Historical, and Literary Writings*, ed. Saul S. Friedman (Westport, Conn.: Greenwood, 1993), pp. 321–63. Jeffrey Mehlman's *Legacies of Anti-Semitism in France* (1982), cited earlier, which brings to light the anti-Semitic themes in Blanchot's writings from the 1930s, is part of this systematic reappraisal.

12. "Blanchot, Violence, and the Disaster," in *After Auschwitz*, p. 145. Actually, Blanchot does not refer to the Holocaust as an "emblem." He writes: "Concentration camps, annihilation camps, emblems wherein the invisible has made itself visible forever. All the distinctive features of a civilization are laid bare" (*ED129/WD81*). The camps are part of the technology of negation that show the internal coherence between work and death in a culture structured according to the dialectic. See the next section of this chapter.

13. In "L'absence de livre" (1969), Blanchot distinguishes between the Book, which is Hegelian, and the Work, which is Mallarméan: "The book is the whole, whatever form this totality might take, and whether the structure of the totality is or is not wholly different from what a belated reading assigns to Hegel. The Work is not the whole, is already outside the whole, but in its resignation it still designates itself as absolute. The Work is not bound up with success (with completion) as the book is, but with disaster: although disaster is yet another affirmation of the absolute" (*EI629/IC429*). The absolute here is another figure of exteriority: "The Work, the absolute of voice and of writing, unworks itself [*se désœuvre*] even before it is accomplished" (*EI627–28/IC428*). Blanchot contrasts the work of writing with the edifice of Law, "understood as prohibition and limit" (*EI631/IC430–31*) but also as the categorical imperative: "One must [*il faut*]" (*EI635/IC433*). Writing is not so much a transgression of the Law as the outside of it, the side on which the law is itself written, as if the law were always somewhat beside itself, outside its own reach, without why. See Marc-Alain Ouaknin, *The Burnt Book: Reading the Talmud*, trans. Llewellyn Brown (Princeton: Princeton University Press, 1995).

14. Recall the sentence from the essay on Simone Weil: "It may be (and are we not continually having this experience?) that the further thought goes toward expressing itself, the more it must maintain somewhere within itself, something like a place that would be a kind of uninhabited, uninhabitable thought, *a thought that would not allow itself to be thought*" (*EI173/IC119*).

15. *Shoah: An Oral History of the Holocaust* (New York: Pantheon Books, 1986), p. 200.

16. The cry is the language of the Holocaust—"the voiceless cry [*cri*: scream would be a better translation], which breaks with all utterances, which is addressed to no one and which no one receives, the cry that lapses and decries. Like writing . . . , the cry tends to exceed all language, even if it lends itself to recuperation as language

effect. . . . The patience of the cry: it does not simply come to a halt, reduced to non-sense, yet it does remain outside of sense—a meaning infinitely suspended, decried, decipherable-indecipherable" (*ED86/WD51*).

Contrast the cry and the yell, which is also part of the sonority of the Holocaust: "The howling voice of Fascist orators and camp commandants shows the other side of the same social condition. The yell is as cold as business. They both expropriate the sounds of natural complaint and make them elements of their technique. Their bellow has the same significance for the pogrom as the noise generator in the German flying bomb: the terrible cry which announces terror is simply turned on." See Horkeimer and Adorno, *Dialectic of Enlightenment*, p. 183.

17. See Blanchot, "N'oubliez pas," *L'Arche* (May 1988), 68–71 (*BR245–49*). This is a letter to Salomon Malka, who had written to Blanchot for his opinion of the Heidegger affair. Blanchot begins by remarking how important Judaism has become to him, and by recalling his long friendship with Levinas. Blanchot deplores Heidegger's "unforgivable silence" with respect to the Holocaust, and refers to the exigency of Auschwitz, "an event that makes a ceaseless appeal to us, imposes, through testimony, the indefeasible duty not to forget: remember, beware of forgetfulness and yet, in that faithful memory, *never will you know*. I stress that, because what it says refers us to that which there can be no memory of, to the unrepresentable, to unspeakable horror, which however, one way or another and always in anguish, is what is immemorial" (*BR247–48*). Blanchot then cites the passage from *L'écriture du désastre* just quoted. Blanchot has forgotten (as, perhaps, no one else can) his attacks during the 1930s on Léon Blum. Here one must acknowledge Zeev Sternhell's scathing account of those French intellectuals whose unrestrained anti-Semitism in the thirties was mysteriously replaced by an equally unrestrained philo-Semitism in the sixties. Sternhell is thinking in particular of Thierry Maulnier, whose *L'honneur d'être juif* (Paris: Laffront, 1971) is quite a somersault from his "Notes sur l'antisémitisme," *Combat* (June 1938). Sternhell could just as well have cited Blanchot as an example. Recall that Jeffrey Mehlman sent Blanchot a copy of his essay "Blanchot at *Combat*: Of Literature and Terror," in which Mehlman cites some of Blanchot's anti-Semitic remarks and speaks of Blanchot's later efforts to "liquidate" his anti-Semitic past. Mehlman indicates that Blanchot replied, disagreeing with much of what Mehlman had to say, but not denying his early anti-Semitism. See *Legacies of Anti-Semitism in France*, pp. 107–9, and p. 117.

18. Cf. *Probing the Limits of Representation: Nazism and the "Final Solution."* Friedlander in his introduction raises the question of how Holocaust studies can negotiate postmodern critiques of representation—he is thinking of Hayden White's structuralist approach to historiography, which holds that "when it comes to apprehending the historical record, there are no grounds to be found in the historical record itself for preferring one way of construing its meaning over another" (cited by Friedlander, p. 7). Blanchot's critique of dialectical thinking is pre-postmodern, that is, it is not so much deconstructive in Hayden White's sense as it is pre-constructive, since Blanchot's idea would be to preserve the singularity of "historical record," say the testimony of a survivor of the Holocaust, and this means resisting its assimilation into any historical narrative. The testimony must be allowed to speak in its own fragmentary voice as memory rather than as history. The point is not to transform it into a meaning or to make it part of a conceptual totality. (One of Blanchot's fragments reads: *"The danger that the*

disaster acquire meaning instead of body" [ED71/WD41].) Quite possibly Blanchot might question the term Holocaust itself as a category that would tend to efface the historicity of the survivor's fragment, which is perhaps why the word holocaust appears in his text only as a word, not as a proper name.

19. See Dominick LaCapra's contribution to *Probing the Limits of Representation*, "Representing the Holocaust: Reflections on the Historian's Debate," pp. 108–27.

20. For a different reading of "Être juif," see Allan Stoekl's valuable essay, "Blanchot, Violence, and the Disaster," *Auschwitz and After*, pp. 133–48. Stoekl reads Blanchot as more of a poststructuralist than an anarchist, and so he characterizes the negative in Blanchot's thinking as more of a diacritical than a dialectical relation. "In this sense Blanchot is . . . merely reversing commonly accepted poles, and in so doing he affirms a quite traditional positive/negative structure of values" (p. 37). Whereas Blanchot thinks of exteriority as neutral, neither positive nor negative. Being Jewish is, in this respect, neutral with respect to traditional alterities—being and non-being, presence and absence, inside and outside, and so on. Stoekl is right to question whether this interpretation doesn't negate the "specificity" of being Jewish all the same. The question is a nice one. Blanchot might respond by saying that singularity is different from specificity; that is, singularity is a condition that can only be clarified outside the alternatives of general and specific, universal and particular, and so on. These alternatives can only be what they are within a logical operation that organizes everything into a conceptual harmony. So being Jewish is not a negativity in reverse but an affirmation outside the alternatives of affirming or denying. This matter is discussed further below.

21. In a late text, "Grâce (soit rendu) à Jacques Derrida," *Revue philosophique*, 2 (1990), 167–73 (BR317–23), Blanchot reflects on Moses' prophetic stammer, which he takes to be symbolic of what is finally Moses' nonmediation (his nonrelation) between God and the Hebrew people.

22. See Levinas, *Nine Talmudic Readings*, trans. Annette Aronowicz (Bloomington: Indiana University Press, 1990), p. 35:

> Philosophy . . . can be defined as the subordination of any act to the knowledge that one may have of that act, knowledge being precisely this merciless demand to bypass nothing, to surmount the congenital narrowness of the pure act, making up in this manner for its dangerous generosity. The priority of knowledge is the temptation of temptation. The act, in its naiveté, is made to lose its innocence. Now it will arise only after calculation, after a careful weighing of pros and cons. It will no longer be either free or generous or dangerous. It will no longer leave the other in its otherness but will always include it in the whole, approaching it, as they say today, in a historical perspective, at the horizon of the All. From this stems the inability to recognize the other person as other person, as outside all calculation, as neighbor, as first come. (p. 35)

23. In *Heidegger and "the jews,"* trans. Andreas Michel and Mark Roberts (Minneapolis: University of Minnesota Press, 1990), Jean-François Lyotard borrows freely from Blanchot—and pretty much flattens him out. Lyotard's "jews" are not to be confused with "real Jews" (p. 3). "The jews" are a category of exclusion, namely whatever resists "foundational thinking" in Western thought—whatever remains unfinished and unfinishable within the "accomplishments, projects, and projects" of our culture:

They are what cannot be domesticated in the obsession to dominate, in the compulsion to control domain, in the passion for empire, recurrent ever since Hellenistic Greece and Christian Rome. "The jews," never at home wherever they are, cannot be integrated, converted, or expelled. They are also always away from home when they are at home, in their so-called own tradition, because it includes exodus as its beginning, excision, impropriety, and respect for the forgotten. They are required more than guided by the cloud of free energy that they desperately try to understand, even to see, storm cloud in the Sinai. They can only assimilate, said Hannah Arendt, if they also assimilate anti-Semitism. (p. 22)

With anti-Semitism, however, the distinction between "the jews" and the Jews of history grows indeterminate: "The anti-Semitism of the Occident should not be confused with its xenophobia; rather, anti-Semitism is one of the means of the apparatus of its culture to bind and represent as much as possible—to protect against—the originary terror, actively to forget it. It is the defensive side of its attack mechanisms—Greek science, Roman law and politics, Christian spirituality, and the Enlightenment, the 'underside' of knowledge, of having, of wanting, of hope. One converts the Jews in the Middle Ages, they resist by mental restriction. One expels them during the classical age, they return. One integrates them in the modern era, they persist in their difference. One exterminates them in the twentieth century" (p. 23).

24. This sounds very much like an Adorno-statement, a mystification of silence as the only possible response to the Holocaust. In *L'écriture du désastre* Blanchot says: "There is a limit at which the practice of any art becomes an affront [*une insulte*] to affliction" [*ED*132/*WD*83]), but it remains to be seen whether affliction is a name for the Holocaust, and in any case Blanchot thinks of silence differently: "Keep silence [*Garde le silence*]. Silence cannot be kept; it is indifferent with respect to the work of art which would claim to respect it—it demands a wait which has nothing to await, a language which, presupposing itself as the totality of discourse, would spend itself all at once, disjoin and fragment endlessly" (*ED*51/*WD*29).

It may be that Blanchot means no more than that the Holocaust is on the hither side of language and history, that it can only be articulated by a "history from below" that possesses neither a before nor an after. ("We are not above but beneath time," Blanchot writes: "this is eternity"—that is, the interminable [*EI*174/*IC*120].) Perhaps we can think of Blanchot's poetics as a poetics from below, where speech or writing becomes a turning or detour away from the negative toward the space-between, the fragmentary space ("the place of dispersion, disarranging and disarranging itself, dispersing and dispersing itself beyond all measure" [*EI*30/*IC*23]). Perhaps we can say that the disaster marks the temporality of this between (the *entre-temps*), which would help to account for the link that Blanchot sees between the disaster and the fragmentary. But what sort of link? In "The Book of Destruction," Geoffrey Hartman describes the fragmentary character of survivor testimonies as follows:

For the survivors of the Holocaust, simply to tell their story is a restitution, however inadequate. Ordering one's life retrospectively brings some mastery, and so relief, to the unmastered portion. Yet that factor is less crucial than something that goes back to the special nature of their agony. In the camps they were systematically deprived of foresight: though they saw all too forcefully what was before their eyes, their ability to discern a normal pattern that could eventually be expressed in the form of a story was disrupted or disabled. Few could hope to makes sense of the events, could hope to hope, could link what they had learned in the past to what now befell them. The promise of extending experience from past to future via the coherence of the stories we tell each other, stories that gather as a tradition—that promise was shattered.

See *Probing the Limits of Representation: Nazism and the "Final Solution,"* pp. 324–25.

25. Affliction is a limit-experience: "The self has never been the subject of this experience. The 'I' will never arrive at it, nor will the individual, this particle of dust that I am, nor even the self of us all that is supposed to represent absolute self-consciousness. Only the ignorance of the I-who-dies would incarnate by acceding to the space where in dying it never dies in the first person as an 'I' will reach it. Thus it is necessary to indicate one last time the strangest and most waiting trait of this situation. We speak of it as though this were an experience, and yet we can never say we have undergone it. An experience that is not lived [*qui n'est pas un événement vécu*], even less a state of our self; at most a *limit-experience* at which, perhaps, the limits fall but that reaches us only at the limit" [*EI*311/*IC*210]).

26. Robert Antelme, *The Human Race,* trans. Jeffrey Haight and Annie Mahler (Marlboro, Vt.: Marlboro Press, 1992), p. 76. *The Buchenwald Report,* trans. David A. Hackett (Boulder, Colo.: Westview Press, 1995), a remarkable document composed immediately following the liberation of Buchenwald in 1945 by an intelligence unit of the Psychological Warfare Division, reports that at the time of liberation there were approximately four thousand Jews in the camp (p. 8). It's possible that Antelme might not have known there were any at all because of the practice of "submerging" Jews among the political prisoners as a way of protecting them. See the account, "The History of the Jews in Buchenwald," *The Buchenwald Report,* pp. 161–68.

Antelme in any case is evidently being metaphorical. The notion of substitution here shouldn't be taken in Levinas's sense of responsibility. It is rather that "being Jewish" is the condition of absolute abjection, and that anyone who suffers *in extremis* is, by transference, Jewish. An extended quotation might give some sense of how the expression should be taken:

One group of prisoners is to extract the stones, another to push the cart. But there aren't enough picks, and most of those who aren't pushing the cart are standing around in the cold. We have nothing to do, but the important thing is that we stay outside. We have to stay here, agglutinated in small groups, our shoulders hunched, shivering. The wind goes through the zebra suits, our jaws become paralyzed. This bag of bones is thin, there's almost no flesh left on it. Will alone remains at the core, a disconsolate will, but only through it can we hold on. We have to have the will to wait. To wait until the cold goes away, the cold that attacks hands and ears and any part of your body that can be killed without killing you. Cold in the SS manner. The will to keep on your feet; you don't die standing up. The cold will pass. You mustn't scream, rebel, try to run somewhere. You have to go inwardly to sleep, and just let the cold take its course, like torture; afterwards you'll be let go. Until tomorrow; until soup: patience, patience. . . . In reality, after the soup, hunger will take over from the cold; then the cold will start up again and will envelop hunger. Later, lice will envelop cold and hunger; then the unending war will envelop rage, lice, cold, and hunger. And the day will come when your face will reappear in the mirror, yelling, "*I'm still here.*" And all the moments spent with their incessant language will enfold lice, death, hunger, your face. And forever impassable space will hem everything within the circle of hills: the church where we sleep, the factory, the latrines, the place occupied by our feet, the place occupied by this heavy, frozen stone here that we have to unstick with our swollen, unfeeling hands and lift up and walk with and throw into the cart.

We are becoming very ugly to behold. For this the fault lies with us. It's because we are a human pestilence. Around here the SS don't have any Jews to hand. We take their place. They are too used to dealing with people guilty through birth. If we weren't pestilential we wouldn't be violet and gray [the colors of the prisoner's zebra-uniforms]; we'd be clean and neat; we'd stand up straight; we'd hoist the stones properly; we wouldn't be red from the cold. Finally, we'd dare look people straight in the face, we'd dare look straight at the SS, that model of force and honor, upholders of that virile discipline which only evil seeks to elude. (pp. 75–76)

Antelme (1912–90) was married to Marguerite Duras during the war. Alain Vircondelet's biography of Duras has this interesting paragraph:

This was the period (1945–47) in which Duras and her friends began to undergo a "Judaization complex." Well before the famous slogan of 1968, "We are all German Jews," they were making this identification which, in their eyes, became inevitable. Yes, she, Duras, was a Jew, following the example of all those who were destroyed in the Shoah plan, a Jew like her future character Aurélia Steiner, a Jew like all of those who were gassed—"there are words so difficult to utter"—a Jew so that she could tell about it, the extermination of the Jewish people, thought out, planned, and beyond that, a Jew in telling of exclusion, rejection by others, a Jew for those who are poor, exiled, exploited, mad, those who write, those who are damned.

See *Duras: A Biography*, trans. Thomas Buckley (Normal, Ill.: Dalkey Archive, 1994), p. 110.

27. *The Destruction of the European Jews* (New York: Harper, 1961), pp. 595–96.

28. Recall that for Blanchot suicide is an act of self-affirmation ("personal representation" [PD135/SNB97]), not so much in defiance of as by means of death. Blanchot thinks of it as an instance of self-naming, attributing the anonymous to oneself (PD135/SNB98), an act of indiscretion provoked or inspired by impatience—"all this in exaltation, fatigue, unhappiness [*le malheur*], fear, uncertainty, all movements that end up covering up the *indiscretion* of such an act, however obviously and essentially committed: ambiguous refusal to submit oneself to the requirement [*l'exigence*] of dying silently and discreetly. Respecting silence in the act of being quiet. The *impossibility* of suicide is alone able to attenuate the frightful indiscretion: as if one had pretended to pretend, there in broad daylight, but in a light such that, despite its ostentation, nobody sees anything, nobody knows anything of what happens (PD135/SNB98).

29. *Survival in Auschwitz* (New York: Orion Press, 1960), p. 90.

30. Testimony of G. Stroka, *Témoignages strasbourgeois* (Paris: Les Belles-Lettres, 1947), p. 89; quoted by Léon Pliakov, *Harvest of Hate: The Nazi Program for the Destruction of the Jews* (New York: Holocaust Library, 1979), pp. 222–23. This is the revised and expanded version of *Bréviare de la haine* (Paris: Calmann-Lévy, 1951).

31. *Probing the Limits of the Holocaust*, p. 326. The Holocaust, Hartman says, demystifies once for all the pastoral ideology that our culture maps onto history as well as experience. The pastoral is "the healing mode of representation" (p. 334), but the Holocaust is a wound that remains, perhaps must remain, open.

32. Vircondelet, *Duras: A Biography*, p. 108.

33. Blanchot is sometimes thought of as a philosopher *malgre lui*—the following from *L'écriture du désastre* is frequently quoted: "To write in ignorance of the philosophical horizon—or refusing to acknowledge the punctuation, the groupings and separations that mark this horizon—is necessarily to write with a facile complacency (the literature of elegance and good taste). Hölderlin, Mallarmé, so many others, do not permit this" (*ED*160/*WD*103). But what counts as the "philosophical horizon" for Blanchot? The answer is: death—that is, the limit of mastery that defines both Plato's cave and the philosopher's fate (the philosopher: he who lives for death, the "truth" of philosophy):

> In Plato's cave, there is no word to designate death, and no dream or image to intimate its unspeakableness. Death is there, in the cave, as excess, and forgetfully; it arrives from outside into the words of the philosopher as that which reduces him in advance to silence; or, it enters him the better to set him adrift in the futility of a semblance of immortality, making of him a mere shade, the perpetuation of shadow. Death is named solely as the necessity to kill those who, having freed themselves—having had access to the light—come back and reveal, thereby troubling order, disturbing the tranquility of the shelter, and thus desheltering. Death is the act of killing. And the philosopher is he who undergoes the supreme violence. But he also calls upon it, for the truth which he bears and which he tells by his return is a form of violence. (*ED*60/*WD*35)

Chapter 10: The Anarchist's Last Word

1. It is no wonder Hélène Cixous reads these pages of *L'écriture du désastre* with unconcealed hostility. See *Readings: The Poetics of Blanchot, Joyce, Kafka, Kleist, Lispector, and Tsvetayeva*, trans. Verena Conley (Minneapolis: University of Minnesota Press, 1991), pp. 19–26.

2. *Jacques Lacan & Co.: A History of Psychoanalysis in France, 1925–85*, trans. Jeffrey Mehlman (Chicago: University of Chicago Press, 1990), pp. 295–96.

3. But perhaps Blanchot's obsession starts with Kafka. See "La lecture de Kafka" (1945), on the ambiguity of death in "The Hunter Gracchus": "He had joyously accepted life and joyously accepted the end of his life—once killed, he awaited his death in joy: he lay stretched out, and he lay in wait. 'Then,' he said, 'the disaster happened.' This disaster is the impossibility of death, it is mockery thrown on all humankind's greatest subterfuges, night, nothingness, silence. There is no end, there is no possibility of being done with the day, with the meaning of things, with hope: such is the truth

that Western man has made a symbol of felicity, and has tried to make bearable by fo-cusing on its positive side, that of immortality, of an afterlife [*survivance*] that would compensate for life. But this afterlife is our actual life" (*PF*15/*WF*7–8).

4. See *Introduction à la lecture de Hegel*, pp. 174–75; *Introduction to the Reading of Hegel*, pp. 46–47, on the "existential impasse" of mastery.

5. "A Fine Risk," *Re-reading Levinas*, p. 216.

6. Compare the following fragment: "The disaster: break with the star, break with every totality, never denying, however, the dialectical necessity of fulfillment; the dis-aster: prophecy which announces nothing but the refusal of the prophetic as simply an event to come, but which nonetheless opens, nonetheless discovers the patience of vig-ilant language" (*ED*121/*WD*75). Vigilant language might well be poetry, responding to the impossible. Paul Davies has a paragraph that speaks to this point—and also sheds some light on the temporality of survival:

> For Blanchot, we might say, what speaks in the work [of art] is *no longer* gods nor men, *no longer* their presence or their absence. It is the movement of the sur-vival of the work itself, living on after every theme has been forgotten and after the forgetting itself has been forgotten. When we name the work as *this* surviv-ing, we name it as the interminable *not yet*. This is why we can speak of there being a poetic grasp of the future, but a powerless one, for it is a grasping from a time that is never in time, a time *en deça de* time. ("A Linear Narrative?" *Philoso-phers' Poets*, p. 48)

7. Blanchot goes on to assimilates the child to the myth of Narcissus, who experi-ences something like a revelation of the outside when he looks at his reflection in the pool. Blanchot allegorizes as follows: "the aspect of the myth which Ovid finally forgets is that Narcissus, bending over the spring, does not recognize himself in the fluid im-age that the water sends back to him. It is thus not himself, not his perhaps nonexistent 'I' that he loves or—even in his mystification—desires" (*ED*192/*WD*125). The image that Narcissus sees is like the starless sky that the child encounters ("the image charac-teristically resembles nothing . . . the image exerts the attraction of the void, and of death in its falsity" [*ED*192–93/*WD*125]); that is, like the original Blanchovian image of the cadaver, it is figure of exteriority, a magic looking-glass onto the other of all worlds. Blanchot adds that Narcissus never made it into language ("if there is one thing to be retained from the classical commentators, who are always quick to rationalize, it is that Narcissus never began to live" [*ED*193/*WD*126]): he never speaks, he only echoes—"he has no language save the repetitive sound of a voice which always says to him the self-same thing, and this is a self-sameness which he cannot attribute to himself" because he never acquires a self of which anything can be predicated (*ED*194/*WD*127). Blan-chot adds: "Such is the fate of the child one thinks is repeating the last words spoken, when in fact he belongs to the rustling murmur which is not language, but enchant-ment" (*ED*195/*WD*127).

8. See Arthur Redding, "The Dream Life of Political Violence: Georges Sorel, Emma Goldman, and the Modern Imagination," *Modernism/Modernity*, 2, no. 2 (1995), 4–5, 8.

9. Blanchot has already distinguished between "warlike" critique where "political impatience has won out over the patience proper to the 'poetic,'" and *l'écriture* that

"persists in a relation of irregularity with itself—and thus with the utterly other—[and which therefore] does not know what will become of it politically" (*ED*125–26/*WD*78).

10. It is interesting that Blanchot should appeal to the dead demonstrators as "constitutive" of this community. In *La communauté désœuvrée* Jean-Luc Nancy writes that "it is through death that the community reveals itself. . . . Community does not weave a superior, immortal, or transmortal life between its subjects . . . , but is constitutively, to the extent that it is a matter of a 'constitution' here, calibrated on the death of those whom we call, perhaps wrongly, its 'members' (inasmuch as it is not a question of an organism" (*CD*41/*IC*14). (The English text includes two essays not in the French edition, "L'amour en éclats" ["Shattered Love"] and "Des lieux divins" ["Of Divine Places"].) In *La communauté inavouable* Blanchot takes up Bataille's idea that "'the basis of communication' is not necessarily speech, or even the silence that is its foundation and punctuation, but the exposure to death, no longer my own exposure, but someone else's, whose living and closest presence is already the eternal and unbearable absence, an absence that the travail of the deepest mourning does not diminish" (*CI*46/*UC*25).

11. On the complicated relationships between Nancy's *La communauté désœuvrée* and Blanchot's *La communauté unavouable*, see Robert Bernasconi, "On Deconstructing Nostalgia for Community within the West: The Debate between Nancy and Blanchot," *Research in Phenomenology*, 18 (1993), 3–21, esp. 6–12. At issue here is the possibility of a community without immanence, that is, without sacrifice of singularity in behalf a totality. Singularity here is either an anarchic concept of alterity (of nonrelation), as it is for Blanchot, or of shared as against common identity, as it is for Nancy, for whom sharing (*partage*) is a complex, antitotalist concept entailing division as well as relation. Nancy writes:

> A like-being [*semblable*] resembles me in that I myself "resemble" him: we "resemble" together, if you will. That is to say, there is no original or origin of identity. What holds the place of an "origin" is the sharing [*partage*] of singularities. This means that this "origin"—the origin of community or the originary community—is nothing other than the limit: the origin is the tracing of the borders upon which or along which singular beings are exposed [to death]. We are alike because each of us is exposed to the outside that *we* are *for ourselves*. The like is not the same [*le semblable n'est pas le pareil*]. I do not rediscover *myself* in the other: I experience the other's alterity, or I experience alterity in the other together with the alteration that "in me" sets my singularity outside me and infinitely delimits it. Community is that singular ontological order in which the other and the same are alike [*sont le semblable*]: that is to say, in the sharing [*partage*] of identity. (*CD*83–84/*IC*33–34)

Simon Critchley has several valuable pages on the political (*le politique*: v. politics [*la politique*]) in Nancy and Lacoue-Labarthe in *The Ethics of Deconstruction*, pp. 200–19, esp. pp. 217–19. See also Christopher Fynsk's very helpful forword to the English translation of *La communauté désœuvrée* (*IC*vii–xxxv); and Anne-Lise Schulte Nordholt, *Maurice Blanchot: L'écriture comme expérience du dehors* (Geneva: Librairie Droz, 1995), pp. 229–304.

12. See Nancy's *Le partage des voix* (Paris: Éditions Galilée, 1982), translated by Gayle Ormiston as "Sharing Voices," *Transforming the Hermeneutic Context: From Ni-*

etzsche to Nancy, ed. Gayle L. Ormiston and Alan D. Schrift (Albany: SUNY Press, 1990), pp. 211–49. The concept of sharing voices bears a close resemblance to Blanchot's notion of plural speech (*EI*133–16/*IC*80–82).

13. See Larysa Ann Mykyta, *Vanishing Point: The Question of Woman in the Works of Maurice Blanchot* (Ph.D. thesis, SUNY-Buffalo, 1980).

14. "His solitude no longer seemed so complete . . . something real had knocked against him and was trying to slip inside . . . something extreme and violent was happening, for from all evidence a foreign body had lodged itself in his pupil and was attempting to go further. . . . Around his body, he knew that his thought, mingled with the night, kept watch. He knew with terrible certainty that it, too, was looking for a way to enter him. Against his lips, in his mouth, it was forcing its way toward a monstrous union" (*TO*18–20/*TTO*15–16).

15. See Bataille's letter to Kojève, *The College of Sociology*, 1937–39, p. 90: "If action ('doing') is—as Hegel says—negativity, the question arises as to whether the negativity of one who has 'nothing more to do' disappears or remains in a state of 'unemployed negativity.'"

16. See also, more recently, Philippe Mesnard, "Maurice Blanchot, le sujet et l'engagement," *L'infini*, 48 (1994), 103–28.

17. The example of Heidegger's support of Hitler is obviously relevant here, as Blanchot had perhaps suggested in an earlier footnote:

> The more important Heidegger's thought is taken to be, the more it is necessary to try and clarify the sense of his political adhesion in 1933–34. At a push, it is possible to argue that it was in order to serve the University that Heidegger agreed to become its Rector. One can even go further and play down the importance of his adhesion to Hitler's party, seeing it as a pure formality intended to ease the administrative duties of his new post. But there remains the inexplicable and indefensible fact of Heidegger's political declarations, in which he expresses his agreement with Hitler, either in order to extol National Socialism and its myths by hailing the 'hero' Schlageter; or by recommending a vote for the Führer and his referendum (on withdrawal from the League of Nations); or by encouraging his students to respond positively to the Labour Service—and all of that in the language of his own philosophy, which he placed without a qualm in the service of the worst of causes, and hence discredited it by the use to which it was put. That, for me, is the gravest responsibility: what took place was a falsification of writing, an abuse, a travesty and a misappropriation of language. Over the latter, from then on, there will hang a suspicion. (*IQ*5/*BR*226)

In *Scandal and Aftereffect* Steve Ungar notes that this was written before the Heidegger case became a scandal in France in the wake of Victor Farias's book, *Heidegger et Nazism* (1987) (pp. xxi–xxii). Ungar gives an excellent account of *l'affair Heidegger*, pp. 34–59.

18. Fear here is perhaps not a subjective state but a communication in Bataille's sense of something that spreads like a contagion or like laughter and tears. It is something that appropriates me, grips me and deprives me of my self-possession and, of course, my dignity and my good name. The worse thing would be for someone to see how frightened I am. Fear is the way bad conscience impinges on the good.

Index of Names

Adorno, Theodor, xvi, xxi–xxiii, 82, 158, 267, 286, 294, 296, 309, 310, 324
Anderson, Mark, 298–99
Antelme, Robert, 222–23, 228–31, 244, 327–28
Arendt, Hannah, xviii
Aron, Raymond, 27
Artaud, Antonin, 32, 145, 149–50, 155
Austin, Roger, 267

Bakunin, Michael, 242, 267
Bartleby the Scrivener, 32–33, 146, 148, 211–12, 228–29, 237, 242
Bataille, Georges, xii, 31, 45, 46, 94, 118, 192, 212, 240, 255, 271, 276, 285, 304, 305, 308, 331; on fascism, xvii–xviii, 274, 276, 281, 302; on heterogeneity, xvii–xviii, 281, 289, 302; on revolution, 41–42, 283, 288; on poetry, 45, 287, 301, 306; on ecstasy, 52–53; on "unemployed negativity," 130–31, 332; on interior experience, 136–41; on sovereignty, 282, 284
Bayle, Jean-Louis Loubet de, 23–24
Beckett, Samuel, 20–21, 50, 67, 107–8, 152, 271
Benjamin, René, 27, 258
Benjamin, Walter, xv, 278, 295
Bernasconi, Robert, xxv, 331
Besnier, Jean-Michel, 47, 282, 283, 288
Blanchot, Maurice: "L'absence du livre," 97, 270, 296–97, 323; "L'affirmation (le desir, le malheur)," 291–92, 294–95, 303, 305, 326; "L'affirmer le rupture," 288; "L'amitié," 120–21; "De angoisse au langage," 20–21, 32, 318–19; Apres coup, 308; L'arrêt de mor, xi; "Ars nova," 5–6; "L'art, la littérature, et la expérience originelle," 82–87; "L'atheisme et l'écriture: L'humanisme et le cri," 65, 142–43, 232; "L'Athenaeum," 148–49; "L'attente," 303; L'attente, l'oubli, 68, 306; Au moment voulu, xi, 176; Celui qui ne m'accompagnait pas, xi, 71–77, 151, 154, 176, 178, 306, 315–16, 318; "Comment découvrir l'obscur?" 22; "Comment littérature est-elle

possible?" 5, 28–29, 279, 286; La communauté inavouable, xii, 30–31, 157–58, 234, 244–47, 282–83, 331; "Connaissance de inconnu," 118–19, 133, 135, 138–39, 195; "La cruelle raison poétique," 149–50; "Le demain joueur," 312; Le dernier homme, xi, 131–35, 197; "Le dernier mot," 152, 177, 181–82, 290, 308; Le dernier à parler, 299; "Le dieu des supplicants," 301; "Le douleur du dialogue," 204; L'écriture du désastre, xii, 3, 4, 30–32, 32–33, 45, 52, 65, 119, 139–40, 150, 175, 176, 178, 180, 186, 188–89, 194, 199, 202, 205, 207–44, 295, 299, 306, 307, 315, 317, 321–22, 323–24, 325–26, 329–31; "L'effet d'etrangeté," 133–34; L'entretien infini (introduction), 200–201, 319–20; "L'espece humaine," 216–17, 222–23, 228, 231, 243–44; L'espace littéraire, 56–70, 82–87, 202, 225, 291, 295, 297; "Être juif," 100, 216–21, 312–13, 326; "L'expérience interieur," 305; "L'expérience-limite," 130–31, 138–39, 192, 204–5, 217, 227, 249–51, 299, 327; "L'expérience de Simone Weil," 221–22; La folie du jour, 148; "La folie par excellence," 147–48; "Grâce (soit rendu) à Jacques Derrida," 305; "Le grand refus," 20, 30, 44, 125–29, 132, 139, 234, 239, 270, 302–3; "L'indestructible," 170, 216–17; "L'insurrection, la folie d'écriture," 141, 284; "Les intellectuels en question," xii, 254–65, 281; "L'interruption," 116, 168, 300; "Le jeu de la pensée," 141–42; "Kafka et la littérature," 293–94; "La lecture de Kafka," 52, 69, 329–30; "La littérature encore une fois," xv–xvi; "Littérature et la droit à la mort," xi, 34–35, 38–55, 58, 84, 88, 126, 128–29, 143, 155, 175, 184, 200, 217, 222, 250, 282–83, 285–86, 287, 290, 301, 303; "Le livre à venir," 269; "Manifeste des 121," xi; "Mots de désordre," 280; "Le mythe de Mallarmé," 8, 285; "Nietzsche et l'écriture fragmentaire," 144; "N'oubliez pas," 324; "On demand des dissidents," 26; "L'oubli,

Index of Names

Index of Names

Index of Names

Nordholt, Anne-Lise Schulte, 331
Novalis, 148

Olson, Charles, 92, 298
Ophuls, Marcel, 322
Orpheus (and Eurydice), 47, 62–71, 72, 121, 125, 189–90, 246, 150, 250, 262–63; gaze of, 70–73, 176, 195, 234
Ory, Pascall, 273
Ouaknin, Marc-Alain, 323

Pagis, Dan, 185
Pascal, Blaise, 242
Pausch, Holger, 298
Paxton, Robert, 322–23
Péguy, Charles, 256–57, 318
Perloff, Marjorie, xiii
Pinkard, Terry, 285
Pippin, Robert, 285
Poe, Edgar Allan, 69
Poliakov, Leon, 213
Ponge, Francis, 288
Proudhon, Pierre-Joseph, 267

Rapaport, Herman, xxiv, 268, 296, 314
Redding, Arthur, 242, 330
Redding, Paul 285
Renaut, Alain, 314
Resnais, Alain, 322
Ricoeur, Paul, 15, 271
Rilke, Rainer Maria, 62–66, 83
Robbins, Jill, 293
Roth, Michael, 304
Roudinesco, Elisabeth, 283
Rousso, Henry, 213
Rubenstein, Diane, 273, 275, 277

Sade, Marquis de, 33, 42–44, 141, 307
Sartre, Jean-Paul, xii, 17, 20, 38, 39, 64, 242, 260, 270, 271, 278, 296
Schalk, Robert, 273

Schlegel, Friedrich, 83, 148–49, 307
Schulz, Georg-Michael, 310
Schürmann, Reiner, 48, 268, 288
Shapiro, Ian, 268
Sirinelli, Jean-François, 273
Smock, Ann, 313
Sorel, Georges, 242, 258, 278
Soucy, Robert, 267, 274
Souveraine, Boris, 255
Stein, Gertrude, 194
Sternhell, Zeev, xviii–xx, 24–28, 254, 267, 273–74, 275–76, 277, 280, 324
Stoekl, Allan, xii, 27, 213–14, 272, 276, 279–80, 323, 325
Strauss, Leo, 23, 272
Surya, Michel, 304, 322
Szondi, Peter, 309

Trakl, Georg, 103

Ungar, Steven, xii, xviii, xx, 274, 279, 285, 322

Valéry, Paul, 255–57, 301, 309
Vattimo, Gianni, 270, 271
Vidal-Naquet, Pierre, 322
Vircondelet, Alain, 328–29

Waldrop, Rosemarie, 95
Weber, Eugen, 274, 275, 276, 277, 278–79
Weber, Max, 267
Webern, Anton, 6
Weil, Simone, 177, 259–60, 294, 323
Wieck, David, 280
Wittgenstein, Ludwig, 149, 194, 243
Wohl, Robert, 267

Yeats, William Butler, 276

Ziarek, Krzysztof, 298, 300
Zola, Émile, 260

Index of Topics

affliction (*le malheur*), 31, 66, 177, 221–22; v. attention, 291–92; v. suffering, 294, 303; and writing, 295

anarchism, xxi–xxiii, 9–10, 267; fascist, xvii–xviii; Blanchot's, xxi, 28–33, 242–43, 259–61, 268

anarchy, 6, 22, 32, 48, 53, 150–52, 188–89, 231; of the work of art, 11–16, 18–20, 84–86; and poetry, 12–16, 46–48, 50–55, 84–87, 122–24, 152–53, 165; revolutionary, 41–42; of existence, 49–55, 58–61, 69–70, 93–95, 136–39, 191–92, 290; Levinas on, 124–25; of the fragmentary, 192–94; of the rhizome, 201; of lovers, 246–47; of the everyday, 253–54; of existence, 290–91

anti-Semitism, xx, 217, 220–21, 255–57, 277–78, 324, 325–26

book, the, 7–8, 21, 39, 49, 83, 269, 297; v. the work, 323

community, 31, 117–21, 157–58, 244–47, 281–82, 330–31

conversation, 71, 95–96, 134, 141–42, 151–53, 165, 204, 236–38, 300, 306, 313

cry, the, 65, 143, 158, 167, 171, 187, 216, 232, 298, 306, 323–24

death, 42; speech of, 44–47; v. dying, 51–52, 54–55, 66–70, 203–4, 291; power of the negative, 51–52, 55, 125–27, 197, 239, 284, 286, 290, 303; double, 66–67, 202, 227–28; and work, 131, 222–24, 286, 288, 327–28; and philosophy, 329

désoeuvrement: as fragmentary writing, xxiii, 13, 32, 88, 97–98, 144, 147–48, 290, 307; as uneventfulness, 5, 170, 172, 198, 295, 313, 295; experience of, 152, 154, 294; and community, 244–42

dying, 51–52, 64, 66–70, 131–35, 202–6, 221, 225, 239, 288, 291, 294, 321

ecstasy, 18–19, 52–53, 118

end of history, xv–xvi, 22, 55, 130–31, 138–41, 175, 208–9, 242–43, 305

Eternal Return, the, 130, 190–92, 211–12, 305, 319

exile, 19–20, 52–53, 86–87, 99–101, 123, 217–18, 293

experience: as *Erfahrung*, 14–15, 137; of words, 36, 38, 75–77, 134–35, 176–77, 188; of strangeness, 36–38, 116–19, 128–29; original, 62, 66, 82, 86–87, 143; interior, 52–53, 136–41, 251; limit-, 84–87, 125–31, 133–34, 138, 142–44, 204–5, 208–9, 217, 240–42; with (of) language, 103–5, 129, 193; as seeing, 123–24

exteriority, xvi–xvii, 11–16, 17–20, 49–51, 56–65, 76, 86–87, 95–101, 107, 110–12, 136, 139–40, 150–51, 226–27

fascination, 58–61, 118, 176–77, 209–10, 291

fascism, xi, xvii–xx, 23–33, 213, 246, 258–59, 267, 274–77, 279, 301

fragmentary, the, 13, 148–54, 156, 178, 186, 192–98, 204, 145, 307

freedom, 9–11; negative, 41–42, 51, 88–89, 92, 283–84, 287; ontological, 47–48, 88–95, 98–101, 158, 161; as anarchy, 93, 161, 167

friendship, 31, 119–21, 198–206, 212

gaze, the, 59–60, 72–73, 318; of Orpheus, 70–73, 195, 235

horror, 59–60, 291

il y a, the, 37, 52–61, 93, 110–11, 117, 128, 131, 133, 142, 181, 187, 195, 208–9, 219, 288–90, 308

image, the, 18–19, 59–60, 66–67, 134, 139–40

insomnia, 50–51, 59, 64, 123, 209, 292–93

insubordination, 26, 29–33, 41–43, 47–48, 84, 123, 143, 261, 280–81

337

Index of Topics

Index of Topics

The Library of Congress has cataloged the hardcover edition
of this book as follows:

Bruns, Gerald L.
  Maurice Blanchot : the refusal of philosophy / Gerald L. Bruns.
    p.   cm.
  Includes bibliographical references and index.
  ISBN 0-8018-5471-7 (alk. paper)
  1. Blanchot, Maurice—Philosophy.   I. Title.
PQ2603.L3343Z57   1997
843'.912—DC20   96-34860
                    CIP